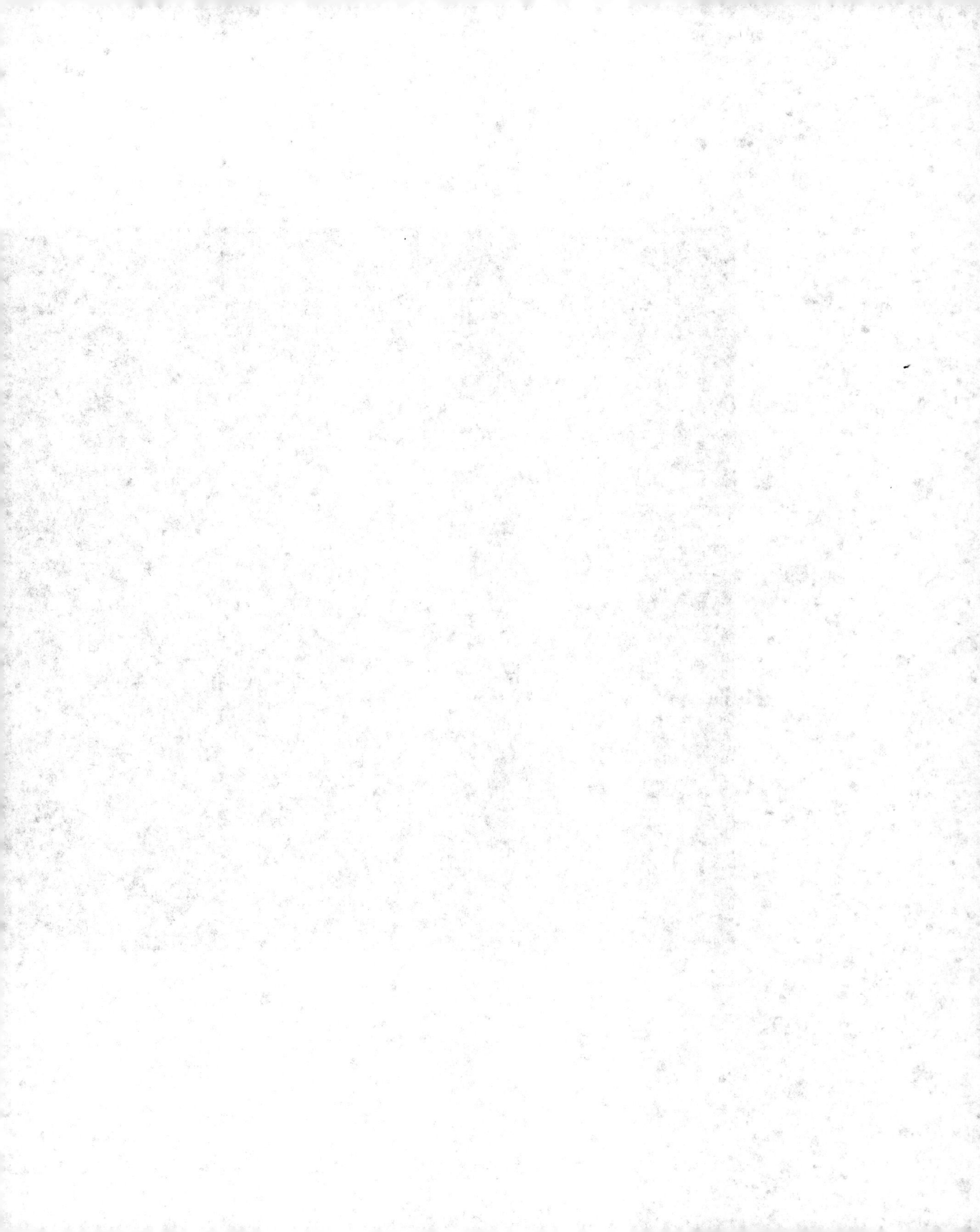

Go by Example

PROGRAMMER'S GUIDE TO
IDIOMATIC AND TESTABLE CODE

INANC GUMUS

MANNING
SHELTER ISLAND

For online information and ordering of this and other Manning books, please visit www.manning.com.
The publisher offers discounts on this book when ordered in quantity.

For more information, please contact

 Special Sales Department
 Manning Publications Co.
 20 Baldwin Road
 PO Box 761
 Shelter Island, NY 11964
 Email: orders@manning.com

Manning Publications Co.
20 Baldwin Road
PO Box 761
Shelter Island, NY 11964

Development editor:	Katie Sposato
Technical development editor:	Marion Newlevant
Review editor:	Dunja Nikitović
Production editor:	Kathy Rossland
Copy editor:	Keir Simpson
Proofreader:	Melody Dolab
Technical proofreader:	Tim van Deurzen
Typesetter:	Tamara Švelić Sabljić
Cover designer:	Marija Tudor

ISBN 9781617299896
Printed in the United States of America

To my parents, who bought me my first computer. Rest among the stars, Dad.

brief contents

contents

The following appendixes aimed to help Go beginners meet the prerequisites for the book are available in the ePDF, ePUB, and liveBook versions of the book, as well as via download on the book product page at https://www.manning.com/books/go-by-example.

preface

Simplicity is the ultimate sophistication.

—Leonardo da Vinci

I thought Go was easy, but the story was different. Go was simple. Back in 2012, I needed to design a distributed network program. This program had to pull and interpret various kinds of data from thousands of external sources and send the results to other services in real time. It needed to run fast because I was working with constantly updating data sources, and other services depended on timely and accurate results.

I had heard good things about Go, such as its ease of use, strong type safety, and great support for concurrency, so my team and I started writing our program in Go. My team consisted of veteran programmers, but this was our first experience with Go. We came up with a prototype within a month. Initially, everyone in the company was satisfied with the efficiency of the program, but after a short while, things started to fall apart.

We were coding in Go as though it was an object-oriented language we already knew. Instead of finishing the task at hand, we spent a lot of time trying to design our program with unending abstractions. Circular dependency issues were everywhere, and our code became challenging to read and work with. In the end, we had to rewrite most of it.

Instead of spending more time on premature abstractions, we decided to unlearn habits from other languages and focus on finishing the task at hand. The results were promising. Adding new features became straightforward, and the code was understandable without explanation.

When we decided to give our program another shot, we weren't just adopting a new language but also embracing a philosophy that values simplicity, explicitness, and clarity. Go's limited, purposeful feature set guided us naturally toward simple solutions and away from overly engineered and speculative designs. Our success wasn't an overnight miracle; it came from using Go's features as they were designed to be used.

Go is pragmatic. It nudges us toward solving today's problems in the simplest way possible. This approach allows us to produce code that can reliably evolve and adapt to changing requirements without becoming overly complicated or difficult to maintain.

With more than a decade of experience in Go, I've distilled much of this wisdom into this book. It took me three years and many rewrites until I was truly happy. You're reading the latest distilled, perfected version. I hope this book guides you in adopting Go's philosophy and helps you develop the right mindset for thinking in idiomatic Go.

acknowledgments

Writing a book is a long journey that requires sacrifice. I couldn't have done it without my amazing wife, Ebru, who patiently covered for me on countless weekends while I wrote. I also missed a lot of precious playtime with my kids, Aren and Lina, and our golden retriever, Rosie. Yes, I missed playing videogames, too.

A heartfelt thank-you goes to my mom and dad, who bought me my first computer when I was little. I wouldn't have become proficient with computers without their support and encouragement. I'm also thankful to my brother, Kivanc, with whom I built amazing software as a kid. Special thanks go to the kind guy at the computer hardware store who gave me my first programming book and patiently answered all my silly questions back in the day.

I'm grateful to Manning for believing in me and having the courage to support this book from start to finish.

To all the reviewers: Aaron Barton, Andy Robinson, Barnaby Norman, Brent Honadel, Christopher Haupt, Clifford Thurber, Francisco Rivas, Frans Oilinki, James Bishop, Jim Amrhein, Joel Holmes, Jonathan Reeves, Katia Patkin, Martin Dehnert, Michael Bang, Ori Pomerantz, Paolo Antinori, Paul Snow, Peter Sellars, Ramanan Natarajan, Rich Yonts, Ronald Haring, Ryan Burrows, Steven Edwards, and Walter Alexander Mata Lopez. Your thoughtful suggestions greatly improved this book.

I want to give special thanks to my technical development editor, Marion Newlevant, and my development editor, Katie Sposato, for their deep patience. A heartfelt thank you to Tim van Deurzen, whose contributions elevated this book beyond anything I imagined.

Finally, thank you for reading this book. Your support means everything.

about this book

A language that doesn't affect the way you think about programming is not worth knowing.

—Alan Perlis, *Epigrams on Programming*

Many programmers initially find Go straightforward only to discover that grasping its unique philosophy—its emphasis on simplicity and pragmatism—is a deeper journey. *Go by Example* is your practical, hands-on guide not just to writing Go but also to thinking in Go. This book isn't a collection of trivial, out-of-context code snippets. It immerses you in realistic projects, from command-line tools and concurrent clients to services. With these examples, you not only learn to write Go but also understand its idiomatic philosophies and principles:

- Move beyond syntax to embrace the Go mindset. We'll focus on writing code that is simple, straightforward, pragmatic, and easy for fellow Go developers to understand.
- Discover how Go's principles and tooling help us write code that is robust and easy to test from the ground up, leading to more reliable and maintainable software.
- Structure packages effectively, handle errors robustly, structure for concurrency, and compose types from well-defined simple building blocks for adaptability.
- See how much you can accomplish with Go's rich set of built-in packages, fostering a preference for standard solutions before reaching for external dependencies.

Each chapter encourages active, hands-on practice, guiding you through building functional programs while offering practical insights, best practices, and common pitfalls to avoid. This book aims to equip you with the Go mindset, valuing simplicity, explicitness, composition, and testability so that you can build high-quality Go programs with confidence and skill.

Who should read this book

Humans are allergic to change. They love to say, "We've always done it this way." I try to fight that. That's why I have a clock on my wall that runs counterclockwise.
— Grace Hopper, *The OCLC Newsletter*, March/April, 1987, No. 167

This book is for experienced programmers who are ready to master the principles of writing idiomatic, maintainable, efficient, and testable code by learning to think differently about programming. If you're ready to move beyond syntax and grasp Go's unique philosophy, this book is for you. It is particularly well suited for

- *Experienced developers*—If you have a solid programming background in languages like Java, C++, Python, and JavaScript, this book will help you transition effectively. It focuses on unlearning habits that don't align with Go's design and quickly gets you productive in writing Go the Go way, avoiding common frustrations.
- *Existing Go developers seeking deeper insights*—If you know the basics of Go but want to elevate your skills, this book offers more profound insights into advanced patterns for concurrency, API design, package structuring, and idiomatic testing, empowering you to build more sophisticated, robust, and maintainable systems.

A firm grasp of programming fundamentals, including object-oriented concepts (even if to appreciate Go's compositional alternatives), functional programming, and concurrency principles, will allow you to get the most out of this book. You'll find practical guidance here for developing the right mindset to write Go code that is idiomatic, robust, and testable.

How this book is organized: A road map

For the things we have to learn before we can do them, we learn by doing them.
— Aristotle

This book is meant to be read from cover to cover. Don't just skim; ideally, sit in front of your computer, actively following along with each listing to get the most out of this book. Each chapter has exercises to help solidify your knowledge, so make sure you do them.

The appendices are slightly different; read them based on your Go knowledge. If you're new to Go, start with appendix A, where you'll learn how to initialize your Go modules, and continue from appendix B to appendix E. The appendices cover the language's fundamentals to get you started quickly or serve as a refresher. Besides fundamentals, they explain idiomatic practices using core language constructs.

Go by Example: consists of 10 chapters:

- Chapter 1, "Getting started," explains why idiomatic and testable code matters and briefly introduces Go's philosophies, principles, and distinctive features.
- Chapter 2, "Idioms and testing," explains some conventions and dives into idiomatic testing techniques, establishing the necessary mindset for the chapters ahead.
- Chapter 3, "Test coverage and optimization," challenges us to think beyond mere test coverage and shows how benchmarks and profiling uncover inefficiencies.
- Chapter 4, "Command-line interfaces," discusses building testable and maintainable CLI tools, covering argument parsing, flag handling, and input validation.
- Chapter 5, "Dependency injection," introduces techniques for decoupling code from external dependencies to simplify testing and enhance maintainability.
- Chapter 6, "Synchronous APIs for concurrency," introduces push iterators and concurrent pipelines and demonstrates how to structure concurrent code.
- Chapter 7, "Responsive and efficient programs," explores making concurrent programs reliable through cancellation propagation and efficient I/O handling.
- Chapter 8, "Structuring packages and services," explores how to organize packages to eliminate complexity and import cycles and introduces building an HTTP service.
- Chapter 9, "Composition patterns," shows how composition patterns create modular functionality, covering middleware, interface wrapping, context value propagation, type assertions to extract optional features, and so on.
- Chapter 10, "Polymorphic storage," covers working with SQL databases and dives into interfaces to simplify programs, making them easier to test and extend. It also covers the driver pattern, which uses concrete types as an API for polymorphism.

This book has a Go crash course in the appendices (available in the ePDF, ePUB, and liveBook versions of the book, as well as via download on the book product page at https://www.manning.com/books/go-by-example):

- Appendix A, "Modules and packages," explains initializing Go modules, declaring importable and nonimportable packages, and running executable programs.
- Appendix B, "Variables and pointers," introduces variables, zero values, pointers, and Go's pass-by-value mechanics.
- Appendix C, "Arrays, slices, and maps," covers essential collection types in Go.
- Appendix D, "Object-oriented programming," explains structs, methods, method receivers, interfaces, and idiomatic ways to use these features.
- Appendix E, "Concurrent programming," explains fundamental concurrency concepts, including goroutines, channels, multiplexing, and semaphores.
- Appendix F, "Self-referential functions," presents an alternative options API.

- Appendix G, "Cross-compiling Go programs," explains how to cross-compile Go code for different platforms and architectures.

About the code

Every chapter contains many source code examples. There are listings with numbers (e.g., listing 2.1) and code snippets without numbers. If you follow along, *apply only the listings* to your local project. Code snippets are only for demonstrating concepts and techniques.

Code annotations accompany many listings and snippets to highlight key points. Sometimes, I use `bold` formatting within the code to emphasize lines or sections that have changed from previous examples or highlight important details. All code in the text appears in a fixed-width font `like this` to clearly distinguish it from regular text. An ellipsis (. . .) means that the code is unchanged from previous examples or is not important.

I occasionally reformat code examples by adjusting indentation or adding line breaks to better fit the space. They may appear on a single line in the book's repository, but that won't change their meaning. Occasionally, when a line is too long, I wrap it using a line-continuation marker (➡).

You can find all the source code for this book in the GitHub repository at https://github.com/inancgumus/gobyexample. Alternatively, you can see each listing in the book with syntax highlighting at https://mng.bz/26gd.

You can get executable snippets of code from the liveBook (online) version of this book at https://livebook.manning.com/book/go-by-example. The complete code for the examples in the book is also available for download from the Manning website at https://www.manning.com/books/go-by-example.

This repository won't mirror your local structure directly as you follow along. Still, each section in the book has a corresponding folder matching the book's explanation. The code for section 2.3, for example, is located in the `02-idioms-and-testing/03-testing` folder. This approach allows you to see the code's evolution throughout chapters and sections. All code examples are guaranteed to work with Go version 1.24.2.

liveBook discussion forum

Purchase of *Go by Example* includes free access to liveBook, Manning's online reading platform. Using liveBook's exclusive discussion features, you can attach comments to the book globally or to specific sections or paragraphs. It's a snap to make notes for yourself, ask and answer technical questions, and receive help from the author and other users. To access the forum, go to https://livebook.manning.com/book/go-by-example/discussion.

Manning's commitment to our readers is to provide a venue where meaningful dialogue between individual readers and between readers and the author can take place. It is not a commitment to any specific amount of participation on the part of the author, whose contribution to the forum remains voluntary (and unpaid). We suggest that you try asking the author some challenging questions lest his interest stray! The forum and the archives of previous discussions will be accessible on the publisher's website as long as the book is in print.

Other online resources

Here are a few online resources you might find helpful as you read this book:

- https://go.dev—Check out the Go home page.
- https://go.dev/play—Run small Go code snippets.
- https://x.com/inancgumus—Follow this account for Go tips, tricks, and news.
- https://github.com/inancgumus/learngo—Learn Go by fixing more than 1,000 programs.

about the author

INANC GUMUS is a programmer and passionate educator with decades of experience in software engineering. He began programming at an early age, developing expertise in C. He designed large-scale distributed systems and led engineering teams. Specializing in Go since 2012, he has educated more than 100,000 developers through his social media presence, GitHub repositories, online courses, and blog.

about the cover illustration

The figure on the cover of *Go by Example* is "Habitant du Tyrol," or "Resident of Tyrol," taken from a collection by Jacques Grasset de Saint-Sauveur, published in 1788. Each illustration is finely drawn and colored by hand.

In those days, it was easy to identify where people lived and what their trade or station in life was by their dress alone. Manning celebrates the inventiveness and initiative of the computer business with book covers based on the rich diversity of regional culture centuries ago, brought back to life by pictures from collections such as this one.

Getting started

This chapter covers

- Why you should read this book
- The importance of writing idiomatic and testable code
- Go's prominent features

Go is a simple, modern programming language that makes it convenient for individuals and distributed teams to work together to develop efficient, adaptable, maintainable, and scalable software that harnesses the full power of today's multicore CPU systems. This chapter explores the book's goals, introduces Go, and showcases Go's key features without delving fully into its mechanics and idioms. I'll leave the details to other chapters.

1.1 Why should you read this book?

Getting up to speed with Go is so straightforward that in 2020, I tweeted "Go is easy to learn. Hard to master." Experienced programmers can learn the basics of Go in a week. Yet using Go to its full potential requires a deep understanding of its idioms and mechanics. So this book has three practical goals:

- Learning by example
- Crafting idiomatic, readable code
- Crafting testable, maintainable code

The following sections dive into these goals.

1.1.1 Learning by example

Rather than presenting boring examples such as foo, bar, baz, Person, and Animal, this book demonstrates how to craft idiomatic, testable Go code from scratch, using practical and realistic examples. This approach will show you why and when to use Go's features and how to avoid common mistakes, so this book doesn't provide trivial examples.

Together, we'll build command-line tools, design concurrent programs, and structure HTTP clients and servers. The projects are close to real-world scenarios but simplified to fit into a book and stay understandable. Every project aims to introduce some part of Go's standard library and language mechanics. Some projects take an unconventional approach, such as simulating parts of a program before implementing them fully. This approach focuses on Go techniques and concepts and avoids heavy refactoring.

Each chapter encourages you to code along and tackle exercises to solidify your learning. You'll need to work through the listings and examples to fully grasp what this book offers. From my 30 years of programming experience, I can say that this hands-on approach is the best way to master a new programming language—or anything else.

I'm writing this book for experienced programmers who are learning Go. Even those who are already familiar with Go will find valuable insights here. To get the most out of the book, you should have a solid understanding of programming fundamentals and general computer-science concepts, such as how CPUs, memory, networks, and object-oriented and concurrent programming work. By the end of this book, you'll be knowledgeable enough to use Go effectively in real-world projects.

1.1.2 Crafting idiomatic code

> *Programs are meant to be read by humans and only incidentally for computers to execute.*
>
> —Harold Abelson and Gerard J. Sussman
> *Structure and Interpretation of Computer Programs* (MIT Press, 1996)

Every programming language has idioms, and Go is no different. Idiomatic Go is a set of well-established conventions that have matured over the years and are shared by the majority of the Go community. These values and conventions closely align with the language's core design principles and are the conventional way of writing Go code.

Some idioms have valid reasons for use; others are accepted without any clear justification. Some are only conventions. Therefore, when you're learning idiomatic Go, expecting to find a reason behind every idiom is fruitless. Nevertheless, idioms play essential roles in establishing a consistent tone across Go projects.

When you write idiomatic Go code, you ensure that your programs are clear, effective, efficient, and maintainable, which makes it easier for other Go developers to read and understand your code. Adhering to Go's conventions helps you avoid common pitfalls and use the language's strengths to produce robust, reliable software. Here's what idiomatic Go code looks like:

- *Simple*—Code is straightforward to read and understand.
- *Pragmatic*—Code solves today's problems rather than speculating about tomorrow's. It lacks unnecessary abstractions that make the code harder to understand.
- *Explicit*—You can read the code without making many guesses about how it works.
- *Testable*—Code is straightforward to test.

Achieving these qualities is not easy. The journey from learning Go to mastering it can be quite a ride. To craft idiomatic Go code, you must deeply understand Go philosophies and language mechanics. Otherwise, you'll fight with the language and bring your knowledge from other programming languages to Go, which will eventually bite and frustrate you.

NOTE Writing complex code is easy. Achieving simplicity is not.

This book aims to show how to craft idiomatic code that is straightforward to understand and maintain. Throughout this book, you'll discover insights and techniques that help you write high-quality idiomatic code in Go. What this book discusses will give you the proper mindset and set you on the right path to achieving your goals faster and reliably with Go.

Still, there are no absolute truths, only guidelines. This book's goal is not to create perfect code because there is no such thing. Different people can look at the same code, and some think, "Oh, this is terrible!" while others think, "This is awesome!" Ultimately, our goal is to create code that is good enough to survive by adapting quickly to changing needs.

1.1.3 Crafting testable code

> *Nothing endures but change.*
>
> —Heraclitus

Automated tests help you write code that works as expected, even after modifications. But even with tests, developing an entirely bug-free program is challenging. Your tests might touch every line of the program but most likely don't test every possible path. As chapter 3 shows, 100% test coverage doesn't mean that programs are bug-free.

Luckily, finding bugs is only one side of the testing story. Equally important is crafting inherently testable code—an art form in its own right. Testable code has superpowers; it's a shape-shifter, capable of adapting to new requirements and standing the test of time.

When you write tests, you put your code through its paces from the perspective of those tests. This approach allows you to experience firsthand how easy or challenging it is to interact with your code, leading you to forge resilient, adaptable, well-designed, and testable code.

Most chapters in the book are crafted to provide insights into the world of testable code. You may notice variations in the number of tests presented in each chapter. In chapters 2 and 3, for example, the emphasis is on testing itself to explain the fundamentals. As you progress through the book, discussions shift toward writing idiomatic, inherently testable code. Although later chapters contain fewer tests, they still demonstrate writing testable code.

NOTE   I won't necessarily follow the test-driven development (TDD) methodology. Depending on the goals of each chapter, testing may precede, accompany, or follow the coding process, which allows flexibility while ensuring that the final code remains testable and maintainable. Fans of TDD are free to apply it to the exercises.

1.2   Why Go?

> *Fools ignore complexity. Pragmatists suffer it. Some can avoid it. Geniuses remove it.*
> —Alan J. Perlis, *Epigrams on Programming* (*SIGPLAN*, 1982)

Now that I've presented the book's goals, the rest of the chapter focuses on Go itself. To explain why Go exists, I'll start with a short history of Go and then briefly introduce Go's flagship features.

In 2007, three seasoned programmers came together to create Go: Ken Thompson (instrumental in the creation of the C language and UTF-8), Rob Pike (co-inventor of UTF-8), and Robert Griesemer. They aimed to address the problems they faced with other languages: slow compilation times and complex, cumbersome features in resource-efficient languages like C and Java, as well as the lack of resource efficiency in developer-friendly languages like Python and JavaScript.

After five years of development, Go was released. It offered a solution that balanced simplicity, reliability, and efficiency in software development. This balance is a key reason for Go's success. It appeals to developers and companies worldwide, including tech giants Amazon, Apple, and Google, which rely on Go to build modern software.

NOTE   Go 1's backward compatibility ensures that code written 15 years ago still runs with the latest release. See https://go.dev/doc/go1compat for details.

Go is great for crafting all kinds of programs, especially the following:

- *Command-line tools*—Go's simplicity and its powerful standard library make it an excellent choice for developing cross-platform, efficient, easy-to-deploy command-line tools.
- *Clients and servers*—Go's standard library provides comprehensive networking support, including HTTP and TCP protocols, which simplifies the development of client-server programs such as microservices.

- *Distributed network programs*—Go's concurrency model, centered on goroutines and channels, is a game changer for writing distributed systems. It lets you manage multiple concurrent tasks without the overhead of traditional threading, making Go a perfect fit for implementing distributed systems.

Although Go is a general-purpose language, its most extensive user base consists of backend developers. Companies such as Google, Dropbox, and Uber use Go for their web services, using its performance and simplicity to handle high-traffic APIs and services. Go's concurrency features make it a popular choice for companies such as Netflix and Cloudflare that must efficiently manage millions of concurrent network connections.

TIP Check out https://go.dev/solutions/use-cases for more information.

Trivia: Go vs. golang?

Rob Pike proposed the language's name in an email he sent on September 25, 2007:

> Subject: Re: prog lang discussion
> From: Rob 'Commander' Pike
> Date: Tue, Sep 25, 2007 at 3:12 PM
> To: Robert Griesemer, Ken Thompson
>
> I had a couple of thoughts on the drive home.
>
> 1. name
> 'go'. you can invent reasons for this name but it has nice properties.
> it's short, easy to type. tools: goc, gol, goa. if there's an
> interactive debugger/interpreter it could just be called 'go'.
> the suffix is .go
>
> . . .

Disney had already registered the domain go.com. So the Go team registered the domain golang.com instead, and the word *golang* became part of the language. To this day, most people call the language golang. The actual name, of course, is Go.

In a practical sense, however, the golang keyword makes it easier to find something related to Go on the web. You can read more about the history of Go at https://mng .bz/Z9EO.

1.3 *Hello, gophers!*

Let's write a simple program to taste Go before exploring Go's prominent features. This trivial executable program's goal is to say hello to gophers. Like all Go code, it's written in a package. Suppose that you have a directory called `gobyexample` with a `hello.go` file in it:

```
// gobyexample/hello.go                    package main can be compiled
package main                               into an executable program.

import "fmt"                        Imports the fmt (formatting) package
                                    from the Go standard library
func main() {
    message := "Hello Gophers 👋!"          Go code is UTF-8 encoded
    fmt.Println(message)                   and hence supports emojis.
}
```

> **NOTE** Go programmers are conventionally called *gophers*. See https://go.dev/ blog/gopher.

Running this program is straightforward. You can use the go tool to compile, link, and run the program. This tool is central to Go and comes with a compiler, linker, tester, and so on. Type the following commands to run the program:

```
$ go mod init github.com/username/repository         Initializes a new Go module
$ go run .                                            to run the example
Hello Gophers 👋!          Runs the executable program
                          in the current directory
```

Instead of getting bogged down in how this program works, let's continue the tour. Later chapters go deeper into the processes of structuring, designing, and writing Go programs.

> **TIP** Go is a simple language, and its mechanics are outlined in a short document called the Go spec. Anyone can build a Go compiler, such as TinyGo, by following the spec. Visit https://go.dev/ref/spec for more information.

1.3.1 *Statically and strongly typed language*

Go is a statically typed language—that is, the type of every variable is known at compile time. This enables the compiler to ensure type consistency and reduces the likelihood of trivial bugs. Because the memory layout of the types is known at compile time, the compiler can generate optimized machine code. Also, code editors can do a better job of analyzing the code and helping you while you edit. More important, types become the documentation.

Static typing also has some potential drawbacks. Code is typically more verbose than in languages that are dynamically typed, for example. Luckily, Go is in a sweet spot between dynamically typed languages like Python and statically typed languages like C. It combines the best of both worlds, fusing the ease of use of dynamic languages with a statically typed language. In the preceding example program, Go guesses the type of the message variable without requiring you to specify it as a string variable.

> **TIP** Appendix B introduces variables and pointers in Go.

1.3.2   *Compilation and static binary*

Go doesn't require an intermediary execution environment like an interpreter or a virtual machine. As figure 1.1 shows, Go compiles code into efficient (fast) native machine code targeted for major operating systems (such as Linux) and architectures (such as AMD-64). Go compiles so fast that it feels like you're working with an interpreted language like Python.

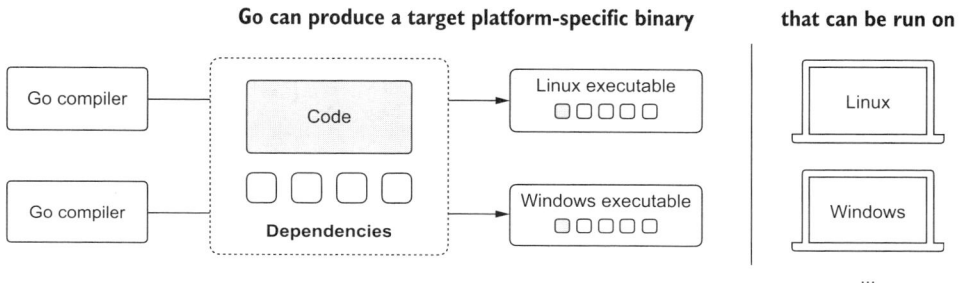

Go can produce a target platform-specific binary   **that can be run on**

Go compiler → Code → Linux executable → Linux

Go compiler → Dependencies → Windows executable → Windows

Figure 1.1   The Go compiler compiles code with all necessary dependencies into a single executable binary targeted for a specific operating system and architecture.

Go's approach differs from that of interpreted languages. Python, for example, requires a Python interpreter, whereas Java requires a virtual machine. By contrast, a Go binary requires only an operating system to run, making it straightforward to distribute Go programs.

Imagine managing a fleet of 1,000 servers. All you need to do is compile the program once, copy it to the target machines, and run it without any concerns about dependencies.

> **NOTE** You still need to compile the code separately for each target platform and architecture. See appendix G for information on cross-compiling Go programs.

Deep dive: How does Go compile so fast?

Unlike Python and Java, Go compiles directly to efficient native machine code, bypassing an intermediary interpreter. Compiling a Go program is often quicker than in most languages despite this compilation step. Go's fast compiler helps you develop rapidly, and its speed is due to its design. For more information, visit https://go.dev/talks/2012/splash.article.

1.3.3   *Go runtime*

Let's explore how Go enables running executable programs independently. In Go, every executable binary includes the Go runtime, which is compiled for the target operating system. Figure 1.2 illustrates what's inside an executable Go program.

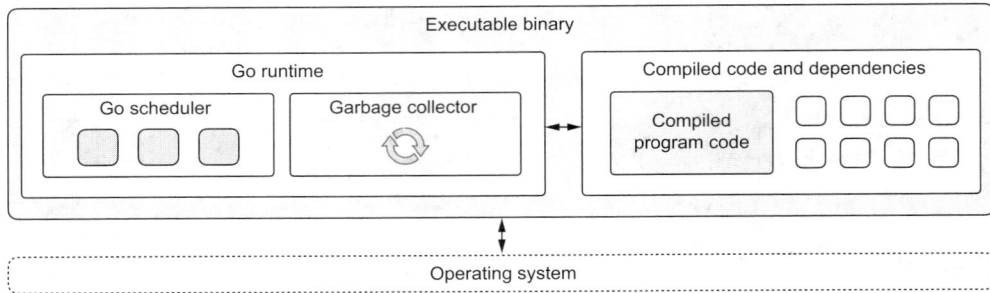

Figure 1.2   A statically linked binary that includes everything it needs to run

The Go runtime provides essential services for executable Go programs. These services include concurrency support, automatic memory management, and other low-level operations that are necessary for the efficient and correct running of executable programs:

- *Go scheduler*—Orchestrates concurrent functions called *goroutines*.
- *Garbage collector*—Runs in the background and automatically reclaims memory that is guaranteed to no longer be in use, allowing you to write code without worrying about freeing memory. Go's garbage collector is also concurrent and scheduled by the Go scheduler.

The next two sections explore two of Go's most significant features: concurrency and the type system. These features make Go a powerful choice for developers who want an efficient yet simple programming language.

NOTE   If you're curious about the garbage collector's internals, visit https://golang.org/doc/gc-guide.

1.4   *Concurrency*

Go was born out of necessity while the language's creators worked with highly concurrent servers at Google. Go's basic idea of concurrent programming is that concurrent functions communicate by sending and receiving messages. This model draws inspiration from Tony Hoare's 1978 article "Communicating Sequential Processes." In Go terminology

- Sequential processes are concurrent routines (i.e., goroutines).
- Channels enable communication between goroutines.

Go abstracts classical concurrent programming constructs like threads and synchronization with goroutines and channels, making concurrent programming more straightforward. The following sections give you a general sense of Go's approach to concurrency.

> **NOTE** For details on communicating sequential processes, see https://doi.org/10.1145/359576.359585. Appendix E and chapter 6 dive into concurrent programming in Go.

1.4.1 Goroutines

Goroutines are independently running concurrent functions. Figure 1.3 is a simplified illustration of two goroutines that run a sequential function concurrently.

Concurrency is not an afterthought in Go; it's a fundamental part of the language and the Go runtime. The beauty of Go is that it doesn't differentiate between concurrent and sequential code in terms of syntax. Writing concurrent code is as straightforward as writing sequential code. Suppose that you have a function that crawls a web page's content:

```
func crawl(url string) {
. . .          ◄——————┐
}                     | Sequential code
```

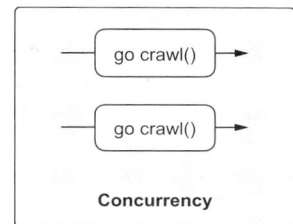

Figure 1.3 The go statement before a function spawns a new goroutine that runs the given function concurrently. This figure illustrates running the crawl function concurrently in two separate goroutines.

You can run this function concurrently like this:

```
go crawl(". . .")
go crawl(". . .")
```

The `go` keyword schedules the sequential `crawl` function to run concurrently. This code runs the `crawl` function in the background concurrently, using two separate goroutines.

In traditional programming languages, thread pools are often used to manage the high execution cost of running multiple threads. In Go, the story is different. Goroutines are incredibly lightweight, eliminating the need for a thread pool. This efficiency allows you to run millions of goroutines on a regular machine, opening a world of possibilities.

> **NOTE** Using a pool of goroutine workers can be beneficial in specific scenarios. Goroutines are lightweight, but if your tasks are small and frequent, creating new goroutines repeatedly may introduce unnecessary overhead.

1.4.2 Go scheduler

An operating system runs executable programs in separate processes. Every process comprises smaller units called *threads* that run code on one of the CPU cores.

Switching between threads (known as *context switching*) is typically expensive: the operating system pauses and saves the state of the running thread, loads the state of the next thread, and then runs it. This thread-switching overhead can significantly degrade performance in programs with many threads competing for processor time. Go's solutions to this problem are

- Abstracting operating system threads with goroutines
- Abstracting the operating system's scheduler with a goroutine scheduler

As figure 1.4 shows, the scheduler distributes goroutines to threads. Context switching between goroutines is tremendously more efficient than thread context switching because Go's scheduler doesn't have to involve the operating system kernel. Kernel-space calls are an order of magnitude slower than user-space calls.

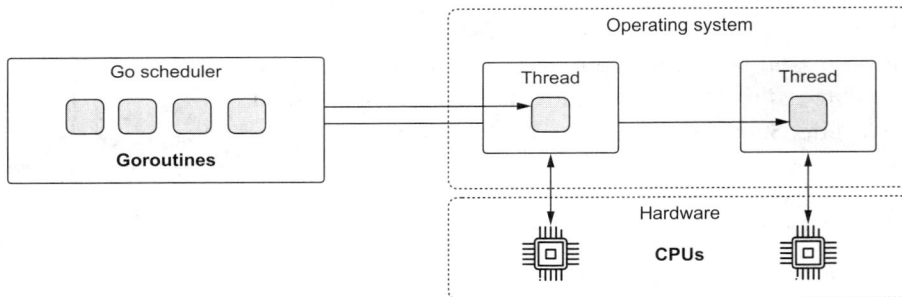

Figure 1.4   The scheduler multiplexes goroutines onto threads for efficiency. Parallelism occurs at runtime when multiple CPU cores can run multiple threads in parallel.

If a goroutine blocks, perhaps due to channel or I/O operations, the scheduler parks it, and the thread runs another ready goroutine. Goroutines are cheap and start with 2 KB of stack memory, which can grow or shrink as needed, significantly reducing memory resource costs compared with traditional operating system threads.

For I/O-bound work (waiting for input/output operations to be completed), Go uses nonblocking I/O to avoid blocking underlying operating system threads. Numerous goroutines can send thousands of HTTP requests with a single thread, for example.

Go's approach minimizes the overhead of thread context switching, enabling Go to integrate concurrency into the language and lead to more efficient concurrent processing. Because goroutines are efficient, millions of them can be scheduled to run on a small set of threads.

NOTE Go scheduler's inner mechanics are more complicated than explained here. Visit https://youtu.be/watch?v=YHRO5WQGh0k if you're curious.

1.4.3 Channels

Don't communicate by sharing memory. Share memory by communicating.

—Rob Pike

Channels are a key part of Go's concurrency model, setting it apart from other languages. Think of channels as network cables or UNIX pipes between goroutines. They allow goroutines to communicate and synchronize safely. Figure 1.5 illustrates a few goroutines that communicate through channels by passing messages.

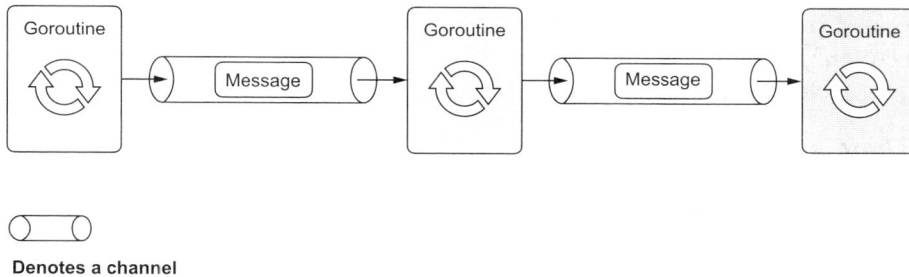

Denotes a channel

Figure 1.5 Goroutines that are running concurrently communicate over channels. These goroutines forward the message to the next goroutine. Each goroutine performs some computation on the received message before sending it to the next one.

Channels promote a clearer view of code as sequential stages and simplify data flow. What you see in the figure is the *pipeline pattern*, in which goroutines send messages through channels to transfer data to the next goroutine. While goroutines execute, sending and receiving a message pauses them for a while so they can synchronize.

Although classical concurrency primitives such as mutexes (which Go supports) are useful for serializing and protecting concurrent access to a shared resource, such as a counter or cache, the idiomatic way is to use channels when you want goroutines to communicate and synchronize while performing tasks like passing a piece of data, distributing tasks, or communicating results.

Unlike languages that use a global shared state for thread communication, which can complicate data flow, Go makes concurrency easy to reason about. When structured correctly, this message-passing approach of channels simplifies concurrent programming by making the data flow between goroutines explicit and reducing the likelihood of concurrency-related bugs. Channels are at the heart of Go, but classical synchronization primitives can still be useful when sharing state directly is simpler.

> **Deep dive: Goroutines, channels, and ownership**
>
> Go does not have a strict ownership model. Goroutines share the same memory space, and there is no memory isolation between them. Passing messages between channels won't protect you; you're responsible for the correct use of shared memory.

If the only tool you have is a hammer, you tend to see every problem as a nail.

—Abraham Maslow's law of the instrument

Many newcomers to the Go programming language fall into the trap of applying Go's concurrency features to every problem they encounter, mainly because Go makes it relatively easy to turn sequential programs into concurrent ones. This approach is rarely the best one, however. Although Go's concurrency model makes working with concurrent code easier, humans are naturally better at understanding sequential execution. Therefore, it's important to resist the temptation to use concurrency unless it's necessary to solve the problem at hand.

1.5   *Type system*

The next standout feature of Go is its simple, effective type system. Unlike popular programming languages that rely heavily on classes and inheritance, Go implements a lean version of object-oriented programming. Go's type system is *flat*, meaning that there are no type hierarchies, classes, or inheritance. Go favors composition over inheritance. Runtime polymorphism is possible only through interface types. Although it is possible to imitate similar flat types in other languages by avoiding inheritance and using only interfaces to achieve polymorphism, Go requires this approach, which prevents unintentional complexity caused by overusing type hierarchies.

NOTE   Appendix D covers object-oriented programming in Go.

1.5.1   *Composition instead of inheritance*

This section presents a high-level overview of composition and polymorphism in Go. Later chapters delve into these concepts and explain them in detail. Having a rough understanding is sufficient for now.

Inheritance is a fundamental concept in most object-oriented programming languages. In this concept, a new class, known as a *child class,* derives its attributes and behaviors, including methods, from an existing class, known as a *parent class.* This relationship allows the child class to inherit reusable code from the parent, facilitating code reuse. Inheritance also enables *polymorphism,* in which a child class instance can be treated as an *instance* of its parent class, simplifying code management and promoting flexibility in object use.

Go's type system eschews this type of classical inheritance in favor of a flat-type structure. Instead of inheritance, Go prefers composition via struct embedding, allowing one struct type to include another's methods and fields. Unlike inheritance, however, embedding doesn't establish a parent–child relationship; the types remain distinct and aren't interchangeable.

TIP Think of struct types as similar to lightweight classes.

Figure 1.6 roughly illustrates the differences between inheritance and embedding. The distinction is crucial: when a struct embeds another, it doesn't inherit from it. This concept maintains clear boundaries between types and prevents some common pitfalls of inheritance, such as tight coupling and difficulty in understanding code hierarchies. It's part of what gives Go its characteristic simplicity and power in design.

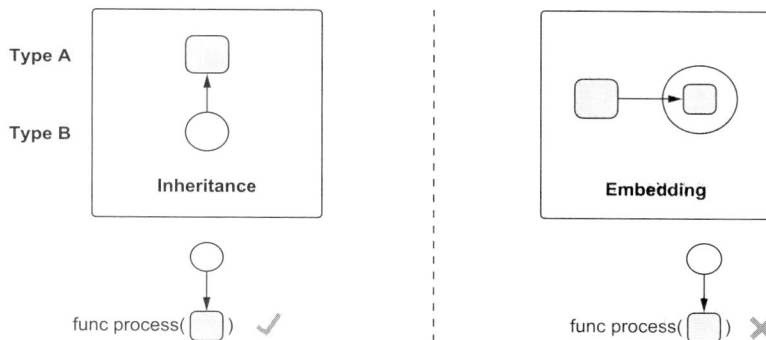

Figure 1.6   Inheritance creates a type hierarchy; embedding does not. In inheritance, you can pass parent (square) and child (circle) types interchangeably to a function that expects only the parent type. With embedding, the function can work only with the specified type. Embedding does not form a type hierarchy; it simply makes one type's methods and data part of another type.

Programmers who are new to Go are often surprised to learn that they can't use a struct type that embeds another in place of the embedding struct type. They are surprised because they mistakenly think that embedding is inheritance, which Go does not support.

As later chapters discuss, embedding offers a convenient syntax for composition but does not support polymorphism. For runtime polymorphism, Go provides interfaces, which I explore in the next section.

NOTE Chapter 9 dives into field embedding.

1.5.2   *Implicit interfaces*

Go interfaces blend the flexibility of dynamically and statically typed languages. You can pass types to functions based solely on their methods (*duck typing*: if it quacks like a duck and walks like a duck, it should be a duck). At the same time, Go offers the benefits of static typing. Like Java, Go checks at compile time whether the types match the interface's methods. Thus, Go's approach provides both flexibility and reliability in your code.

Go can achieve this flexibility because interfaces are implicitly satisfied. Types do not have to mention that they implement an interface explicitly. If a type implements all the methods of an interface, you can use the type wherever that interface is expected.

> **NOTE** Go's implicit interfaces empower you to craft code that's easy to maintain.

Figure 1.7 illustrates how to use Go's implicit interfaces. Suppose that you have an interface called `runner` with a `run` method and two concrete types, each with its own `run` method (behavior). You also have a function that expects the `runner` interface.

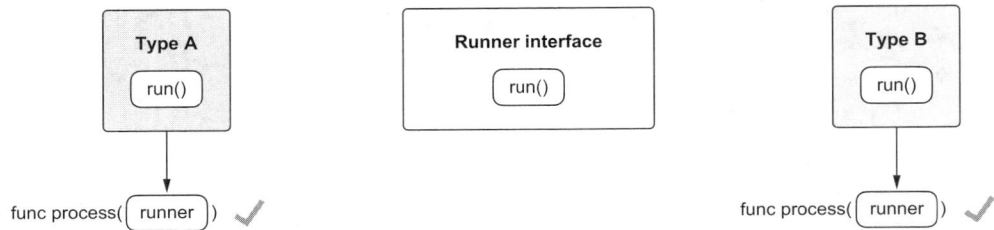

Figure 1.7   The function expects a type that implements the `runner` interface—any type with a `run()` method. You can pass either of these types to the function interchangeably because each has a `run()` method and implicitly satisfies `runner`.

Notice that these types say nothing about the `runner` interface. Each implements only the `run` method, which allows you to pass any of them to the `process` function. If you pass a type without the `run` method to the function, the code won't compile.

In practice, Go's implicit interfaces offer tremendous simplicity, flexibility, and reliability in program design. By decoupling the concrete implementations from their behaviors, Go encourages a more modular, scalable code structure.

You don't have to design interfaces up front. Go's approach empowers you to write code that is easy to maintain and adaptable to future changes without requiring extensive refactoring.

> **NOTE** Chapter 10 and appendix D discuss how to use interfaces idiomatically.

1.5.3   *Testing with implicit interfaces*

This section briefly explores how Go's implicit interfaces boost the testability of code. Mithril is an imaginary payment processor, and you want to test code that uses Mithril's

API. As figure 1.8 shows, when you run the test, the code charges users for money. How can you test this code without sending requests to Mithril's live servers?

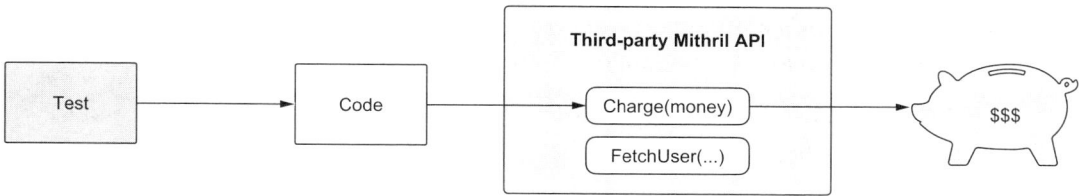

Figure 1.8 This expensive test runs code that invokes the `Charge` method of Mithril's API and contacts live servers. It's not the best way of testing.

The problem is that Mithril's API doesn't offer interfaces, which poses a challenge for testing. This is where Go's implicit interfaces shine. Instead of running costly tests against Mithril's servers, you can decouple your code by declaring a tiny interface with a subset of Mithril's API methods. Here's the recipe (see figure 1.9 for an illustration):

1 Declare an interface (`Charger`) with a single `Charge` method.
2 Declare a test-only concrete type (`FakeCharger`) with a `Charge` method.
3 Change your code to accept the `Charger` interface.
4 Pass your fake concrete type to the code while testing.

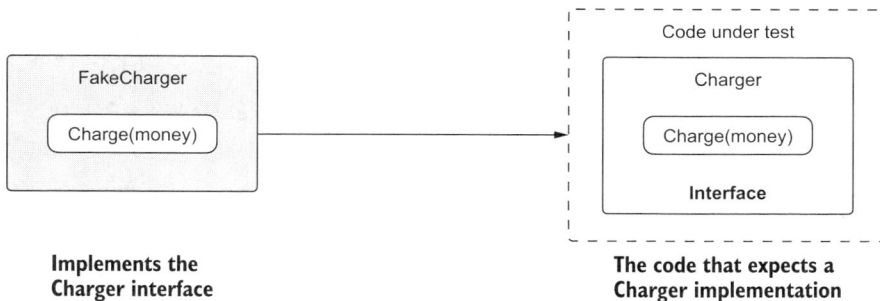

Figure 1.9 Testing the code with a fake payment provider

The code no longer depends on Mithril's API; instead, it accepts the `Charger` interface. This approach enables you to pass any type with a `Charge` method to the code (including the fake payment processor while testing or the actual Mithril API). Mithril's lack of an interface was never a barrier to testing. In Go, you can always defer declaring an interface until needed, making your code straightforward to evolve and also testable. This scenario is a prime example of Go's practicality.

Go allows you to craft testable code without designing interfaces up front, effectively enabling you to evolve your code confidently even when third-party interfaces are unavailable. This technique and others you'll learn in this book showcase the fact that Go is engineered for building solid software.

NOTE   Go has limited support for generics. For details, check out https:// go.dev/doc/faq#Type_Parameters.

1.6   *Standard library*

Go comes with a rich set of packages called the *standard library*. These packages include functionality ranging from simple tasks such as string manipulation to running HTTP servers. By reusing the functionality offered by the standard library, you can develop your programs rapidly. Here is an example of running an HTTP server using the standard library:

Imports Go's standard library's http package to
use its functionalities in this source-code file

Declares a function variable.
(Functions are first-class citizens in Go.)

The first input is an interface
(http package's ResponseWriter).

The second input is a pointer to
the http package's Request type.

Writes "hello, gophers!" as a
series of bytes to the client

```
package main

import "net/http"

func main() {
    handler := func(
        w http.ResponseWriter,
        r *http.Request,
    ) {
        w.Write([]byte("hello, gophers!"))
    }
    http.ListenAndServe("localhost:8080", http.HandlerFunc(handler))
}
```

This program listens on `localhost`'s port 8080. When it receives an HTTP request, the server sends the client a `"hello, gophers!"` message. Thanks to concurrently serving requests with goroutines, even this basic server can handle hundreds of thousands of requests per second.

NOTE   Chapter 8 explains in detail how to structure and write HTTP services.

Although Go's standard library is extensive and provides a solid foundation for many everyday programming tasks, it does not cover all specific needs or the most advanced use cases. Luckily, Go has a vibrant, mature ecosystem of third-party packages. It's straightforward to download and use these packages using Go's built-in module system. But using the standard library is wise if it offers the packages you need.

The standard library is a tribute to reliability, having undergone rigorous testing and tight integration with the Go runtime, often leading to more robust and efficient code. Moreover, most Go developers are familiar with standard-library code, so it's easier for everyone to understand everyone else's code and work together effectively.

This book uses the standard library for all examples. Chapter 2 introduces the `testing` package for automated testing, chapter 4 uses the `flag` package for command-line flags, chapter 7 uses the `http` package for sending requests, and so on.

> **TIP** You can see the standard library's packages at https://pkg.go.dev/std. Besides Go's standard library, you can find useful experimental packages, some of which soon became part of Go's standard library. See https://pkg.go.dev/golang.org/x.

1.7 Tooling

Another reason why Go is so successful and popular is its great built-in tooling support. Go tools play a critical role in a gopher's workflow, from automatically managing dependencies and formatting code to compiling. You can use all the tools with a single `go` command such as this:

```
$ go test .
PASS
```

Go prioritizes tests as first-class citizens. With the `go test` tool, you can effortlessly run tests, benchmark, and profile your code to identify the areas where it's spending the most time. You can also use the `go fmt` tool to format your code automatically from this

```
package main;import "fmt"; func main() {
fmt.Println("hello, gophers!") }
```

to this:

```
package main

import "fmt"

func main() {
    fmt.Println("hello, gophers!")
}
```

The formatting tool is tremendously helpful for keeping code consistent across every Go project—no more tabs-versus-space wars. Thanks to Go's tooling, you can focus on coding. Here are a few more tools:

- `go build` compiles Go code.
- `go run` compiles and runs Go code.

- go get downloads third-party packages and adds them to your project's Go module so you can import them into your program.
- go vet finds potential problems in Go code to improve code quality.
- go doc displays documentation for packages.
- go generate generates Go code for repetitive tasks.

Visit https://pkg.go.dev/cmd/go for more information on other Go tools.

1.8   Outro

This chapter dissects why Go exists and the problems it's crafted to solve, cutting through the trivia and diving into the heart of what makes Go stand out—its simplicity, pragmatism, and efficiency. With an introduction to Go's strengths, you've begun the journey toward understanding how Go makes constructing reliable, performant software easier.

As the first chapter concludes, I hope you're beginning to recognize the reasons to delve further into the world of Go and continue reading. This book is structured to help you develop the right mindset for using the Go language's idioms and mechanics effectively. It will guide you in crafting maintainable and testable code in Go.

Before reading chapter 2, check out appendices A to E if you're new to Go programming or if you're experienced but want to refresh your idiomatic Go knowledge. Then proceed to chapter 2. The appendices provide a fast-paced primer designed to get you up to speed on the advanced topics discussed in this book.

1.9   Source code and Go module

The source code for this book is available in the GitHub repository at https://github .com/inancgumus/gobyexample. You can find each listing in the book by visiting https://mng.bz/RwZ0.

You can visit listings to see the changes or navigate each section's final code. Every listing in this book corresponds to a unique Git commit. This approach makes it easy to follow how the code evolves within a chapter and across chapters. By comparing changes, you can see how features are added, logic is refined, and structure improves step by step.

Before getting started, you may want to install the latest version of Go at https:// go.dev/doc/install. I use Go version 1.24.2 for all examples in the book.

When you finish, create a new directory, and initialize a Go module, replacing the username and repository parts to suit your taste (such as github.com/inancgumus/ gobyexample):

```
$ go mod init github.com/username/repository
```

For each project discussed in the book, create a new directory under this root directory, but you can continue using the same Go module. You'll be all set. These steps for initializing a Go module are also detailed in appendix A; check it out before you start.

WARNING Make sure to initialize a Go module so that the examples in the book will work.

Summary

- Idiomatic Go is a set of shared values and the conventional way to write Go code.
- Go is a simple language that blends dynamically and statically typed languages.
- Go compiles code into efficient native machine code, producing a single static binary with an embedded runtime, scheduler, and garbage collector for easy deployment.
- Concurrency is built into Go. Lightweight goroutines run code concurrently. Channels simplify communication and synchronization between goroutines.
- Go's flat type system favors composition over inheritance, which Go lacks. Interfaces are implicitly satisfied and provide runtime polymorphism.
- Go offers a comprehensive standard library and extensive tooling support for a broad range of programming tasks, facilitating rapid development.

Idioms and testing

2

This chapter covers

- Exploring idiomatic principles with packages
- Satisfying the standard library interfaces
- Writing and running tests using the tools provided by Go
- Using table-driven testing and subtests to improve maintainability
- Writing example tests to generate runnable documentation

Automated tests ensure that code works today and will continue to work in the future. Focusing on testing right away builds a solid mindset for the remainder of the book. This chapter covers testing fundamentals; the following chapters explore this topic in greater depth.

We'll explore how to write and test a simple URL parser package called `url`, a replica of the standard library's `url` package with the same name. Although simple, it shows the proper way to name packages and their items, handle errors, and implement interfaces from the standard library. When we have its basic version in place, we'll test the package.

After learning the fundamentals of testing in Go, we'll explore table-driven tests to reduce duplication. Although table-driven testing is helpful, it has some pitfalls, which we'll address using subtests. Last, we'll learn how to generate documentation using example tests. Chapter 3 dives into measuring test coverage, benchmarking, and optimization.

> **NOTE** Read appendix A to see how to initialize a Go module before getting started. Also check out appendices B, C, and D for information on variables, pointers, and object-oriented programming concepts in Go, such as methods and interfaces. Otherwise, progressing in this chapter may be challenging if you're new to Go.

2.1 Groundwork

We'll start with the `url` package by exploring its overview and seeing what it offers other packages. Then we'll move on to implementation and the idiomatic decisions we make in our package.

> **NOTE** Each section has a designated directory in the book's repository for its final code. This section's code is at https://mng.bz/26Kd.

2.1.1 Overview

Figure 2.1 shows an overview of the `url` package. We have a `Parse` function that can parse a URL string and return a URL pointer and an error. The returned `*URL` points

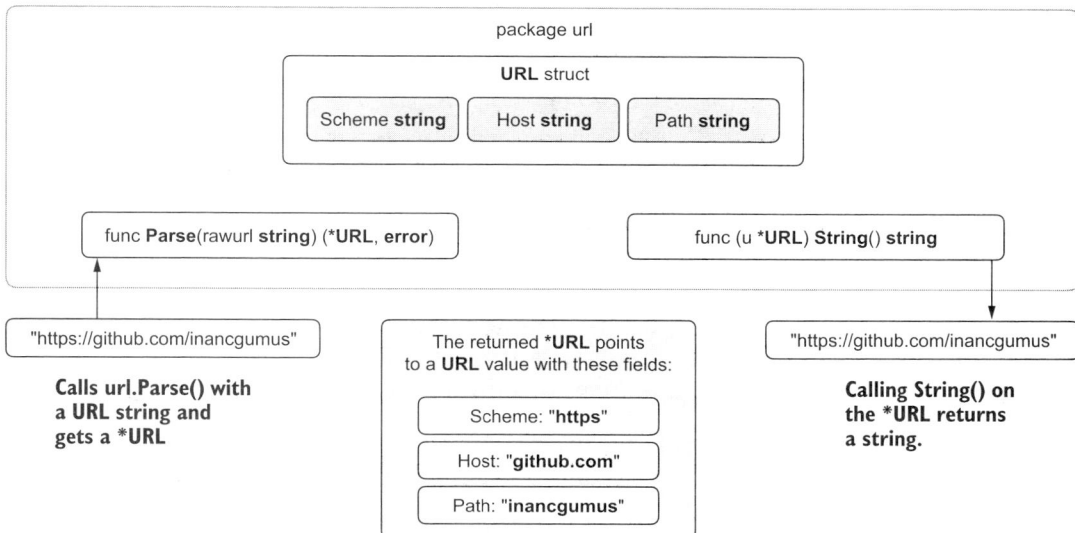

Figure 2.1 The `url` package's overview. `Parse` returns a pointer to a URL value that contains the parsed URL's parts. `String` reassembles the URL value as a string.

to a URL value in memory. (The pointer is not shown in the figure for brevity.) A URL value's fields include the parsed URL string's parts, such as Scheme, Host, and Path. We also have a String method to reassemble a URL string for easy logging.

Now that we've seen our package's overall structure, let's look at its implementation. As shown in the next listing, for now, Parse returns hardcoded values and always succeeds. String, on the other hand, works as expected in most cases. (We'll see where it fails later.)

Listing 2.1   Implementing the url package (url/url.go)

```go
package url

import "fmt"

// A URL represents a parsed URL.
type URL struct {
    Scheme string
    Host   string
    Path   string
}

// Parse parses a URL string into a URL structure.
func Parse(rawURL string) (*URL, error) {          // Creates a pointer
    return &URL{                                   // to a URL value
        Scheme: "https",
        Host:   "github.com",                      // Sets the URL value's fields
        Path:   "inancgumus",
    }, nil                                         // Returns a *URL (a pointer to the URL
}                                                  // value) and a nil error (success)

// String reassembles the URL into a URL string.
func (u *URL) String() string {
    return fmt.Sprintf("%s://%s/%s", u.Scheme, u.Host, u.Path)
}
                                                   // Reassembles a URL string from the URL
                                                   // value's fields that the *URL points to
```

We declared the URL struct type and the Parse function in the url package. URL has three string fields where we can store the parts of a URL string after parsing it with Parse, which returns a nil error, meaning that it parses the URL string successfully. String gets a *URL receiver, combines the fields in a string using Sprintf, and returns the string.

Last, commenting package items, as in the listing, enables Go to generate documentation from the code automatically. Read more at https://go.dev/doc/comment.

NOTE   Each listing is in the book's repository. Listing 2.1, for example, is at https://mng.bz/15GV.

2.1.2 Implementation

Now that we have implemented the url package, let's look at its use. As the next listing shows, we parse a URL string, handle the error, and print the URL parts.

Listing 2.2 Using the `url` package (`url/cmd/url.go`)

```
package main                          ◄──┐  Declares a
                                         └  nonimportable package
import (
    "fmt"
    "log"
    "github.com/inancgumus/gobyexample/url"   ◄──┘  Imports our url package
)
                                      ┌  Designates main as the
                                      │  program's entry point
func main() {                    ◄────┘
    uri, err := url.Parse("https://github.com/inancgumus")
    if err != nil {
        log.Fatal(err)           ◄──┐  Terminates the program
    }                               └  with an error message
    fmt.Println("Scheme:", uri.Scheme)   ◄──────┐  Prints https
    fmt.Println("Host   :", uri.Host)    ◄──────┘
    fmt.Println("Path   :", uri.Path)    ◄──────┐  Prints github.com
    fmt.Println(uri)                 ◄──────────┘
}                                                │  Prints inancgumus
        ┌  Prints https://github.com/
        │           inancgumus
```

Running this code prints the following:

```
$ go run ./url/cmd          ◄──┐  Compiles the program and
Scheme: https                  └  runs the func main()
Host   : github.com
Path   : inancgumus
https://github.com/inancgumus
```

> **WARNING** You'll see the `go: cannot find main module` error message if you haven't initialized your Go module. Make sure to review appendix A.

Because we call the `Parse` function from another package (in this case, `main`), we prepend the function name `Parse` with its package name `url` (`url.Parse`). We can call `Parse` from another package because we export `Parse` (with a capital `P`) from the `url` package.

If the `Parse` function returns a non-nil error, something went wrong, and we should handle the problem. In this case, we terminate the program with an error message using the `Fatal` function from the `log` package. On the other hand, if no error occurs (the error is `nil`), we continue to print the URL details because we're sure that the returned URL is valid. As discussed in the chapter intro, we keep our package simple to focus on testing.

> **TIP** A `nil` error value indicates a successful operation. We often avoid using any other returned values (such as `*URL`) if a function returns a non-nil error, which means a failure.

2.2   *Idioms*

Our package may look simple, but it includes idiomatic decisions that we follow carefully. This section discusses naming conventions and error handling, as well as when to export struct fields and the importance of satisfying standard library interfaces. This section is a starting point; we'll keep exploring idioms throughout the rest of the book.

2.2.1   *Names*

A package's name should concisely communicate what it offers, not what it does. The `url` package, for example, provides a way to work with URLs, so we name it `url` instead of something like `urlparser` (even though it parses only URLs for now). Our package can include everything related to working with URLs, so we chose a generic name for it.

For readability and clarity, a package's name should be meaningful when used in combination with its exported items. The name should make clear what each item does:

```
uri, err := url.Parse("https://github.com/inancgumus")
```

The package name, along with `Parse`, makes it easy to grasp what `Parse` does. `url.Parse` parses a URL, for example. Without the package name, it wouldn't be easy to see what `Parse` does.

Last, for clarity, it's idiomatic to avoid stuttering when naming package items. If `Parse` were named `ParseURL`, it would stutter: `url.ParseURL`. A concise package name like `url` also prevents excessive repetition: `urlparser.Parse`.

> **TIP** Conventions are nice until they meet the real world. The standard library's `url.URL` type stutters, for example. Initially, this type belonged to the `http` package. Due to circular import problems, it was moved to the `url` package. `url.Value` could be an alternative, but within the `url` package, a `Value` type may be confusing and too generic. In this case, the stuttering can be accepted as idiomatic.

Now let's turn our attention to variable names. Conventionally, variables get shorter names in a smaller scope, making them faster to read and type; in a broader scope, they get longer names. This is fine as long as the context in which those variables are used makes their purpose clear. Instead of declaring a `parsedURLString` variable, for example, we use `uri`. A method receiver is also a variable and is often named with one or two letters (as in `u`). This convention keeps method signatures easy to read and type without verboseness.

Go enforces and suggests a uniform style through conventions, as is evident from tools like `gofmt`. These conventions minimize debates about individual styles and ensure consistency across projects, making Go code easier to type, read, and grasp regardless of the project. Just as tabs versus spaces is not a problem in Go, neither is the use of concise names.

2.2.2 Errors

Returning to `Parse`, we see that it returns an `error` because it can fail to parse a URL string:

```
func Parse(rawURL string) (*URL, error)
func (u *URL) String() string
```

Returns an error as the last result value

Does not return an error

If an error occurred during parsing, the returned `error` would explain what went wrong. By contrast, the `String` method does not need to return an `error` because in our case, reassembling a URL into a string is never expected to fail. Unlike errors in other languages, errors in Go are not exceptional conditions, and Go does not have exceptions. Instead, we handle errors explicitly in the normal flow of our program code:

```
uri, err := url.Parse("https://github.com/inancgumus")
if err != nil { . . . }
```

Handles the error in the normal flow of the code

This approach clarifies error handling, leading to more robust programs when used correctly. Because errors are ordinary values, we can return them from functions or methods and pass them around. This approach is no different from processing other values. Currently, `Parse` succeeds by returning a `nil` error, but we'll soon improve it to return non-nil errors.

> **NOTE** Return an `error` result if a function is expected to fail. It is idiomatic to specify the `error` type as the last result value of a function. Instead of `func() (error, T)`, for example, `func() (T, error)` is a widely used convention.

We'll explore many error-handling techniques throughout the book. In the meantime, you may want to read Rob Pike's article on errors at https://go.dev/blog/errors-are-values.

2.2.3 Fields

Conventionally, we don't add unnecessary indirection to fields with methods. In Go, You Aren't Gonna Need It (YAGNI) is an essential philosophy because it prevents us from overengineering based on speculation rather than actual needs.

The URL type exposes its fields directly to other packages—`Scheme`, `Host`, and `Path`—because we don't require immutability or implement special business logic. We don't necessarily need to use getter and setter methods to make the fields available. By contrast, `URL.String` is a method because it reassembles URL strings.

Whether to export fields depends on the specific problem we're trying to solve, such as immutability. Suppose that the URL type had an unexported `scheme` field. We could have a `SetScheme` method to prevent other package codes from mutating `URL` values directly:

```
func (u *URL) SetScheme(s string) *URL {        Copies the URL value by the
    nu := *u                                    assignment after finding the
    nu.scheme = s                               original value through the pointer
    return &nu           Sets the scheme field of
}                        the copied URL value

                         Returns a new pointer
                         to the copied URL value
```

Mutability can be useful because it prevents concurrency problems with shared variables across goroutines. We should avoid adding unnecessary indirection to fields with methods, however, if we don't need encapsulation, immutability, or performance.

> **TIP**   I mention performance because `URL` may have methods that return existing `URL`s from a memory pool rather than create new ones each time. Managing `URL`s internally and preventing direct field access could reduce allocations.

2.2.4   *Standard interfaces*

It's idiomatic and practical to implement the standard library's interfaces whenever possible so we can better integrate our code with the existing functionality of the standard library and other third-party packages. Take the standard library's `fmt.Stringer` as an example:

```
type Stringer interface {        The Stringer interface is
    String() string              declared in the fmt package.
}
                     Stringer has a single String
                     method that returns a string.
```

Our `*URL` type satisfies the `Stringer` with the pointer receiver `String` method:

```
func (u *URL) String() string { . . . }     A pointer receiver method named String
                                             receives a *URL when called on a *URL.
```

`Println` can automatically detect and call the `*URL.String` method:

```
uri, err := url.Parse(            The uri variable's type is *URL.
  "https://github.com/inancgumus",
)
. . .                      Prints https://github
fmt.Println(uri)           .com/inancgumus
```

We'll build on our idiomatic knowledge throughout the book.

NOTE Passing a *URL to Println automatically calls String, but passing a URL value to Println does not because Println wraps each provided argument in an empty interface (the any type) value. We can't call methods with pointer receivers using an interface value that wraps a nonpointer value of that type. See appendix D.

2.3 *Testing*

Go comes with built-in testing support, and we don't have to install third-party tools. We can use the following components to write and automatically run our tests and verify our code:

- go test *tool*—A command-line utility that runs tests and shows their results
- testing *package*—A set of functions and types for writing tests

Testing in Go isn't much different from writing Go code. Tests are written inside regular functions in the usual Go source files with specific conventions:

- Test file names end with _test.go.
- Test function names begin with Test.
- Test functions take a *testing.T input, idiomatically named t.

NOTE For brevity, I'll say *T when referring to *testing.T from now on.

Figure 2.2 shows a test setup for the Parse function. Because we want to test the url package's Parse function, we name the test file url_test.go and the test function TestParse (takes a *T input).

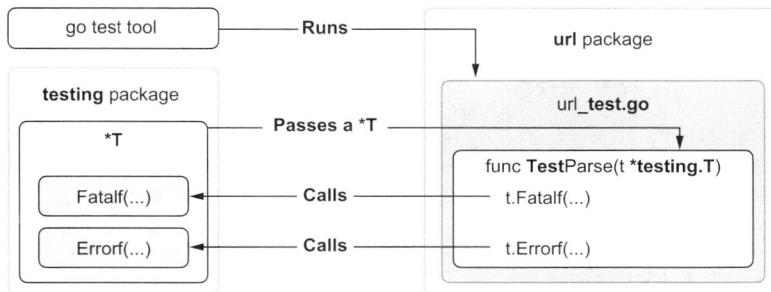

Figure 2.2 The go test tool and the testing package collaborate on running tests. Tests get a *T, which has methods for tests to call, log, report failures, and so on.

NOTE We can create multiple test files, and each file can have various tests.

The *T is a pointer to a T struct type with test-related methods attached. We can use *T's methods from our test functions to report results, print logs, and so on. Fatalf, for example, marks a test function as failed and stops its execution immediately, which is ideal when a failure is so critical that no further testing makes sense. `Errorf`, on the other hand, logs a failure but lets the test continue. We'll see these functions in action in section 2.3.1.

> **TIP** Although both `Fatalf` and `Errorf` mark a test as failed, `Fatalf` stops the current test's execution, preventing any further code in that specific test from running. Other tests (in the same package or other packages) continue to run. Note that each test runs in isolation (in a separate goroutine), so a `Fatalf` stops only the test function that called it.

2.3.1   *Writing tests*

Now that we know the theory, let's practice our knowledge. As the next listing shows, the test function `TestParse` receives `t` of type `*T` and reports failures with `t.Fatalf` or `t.Errorf`.

Listing 2.3   Testing the `Parse` function (`url/url_test.go`)

```go
package url

import "testing"                         // Imports the testing package
                                          // to use its functionality

func TestParse(t *testing.T) {
    const uri = "https://github.com/inancgumus"

    got, err := Parse(uri)                // Assigns the result values of Parse
                                          // to the variables got and err
    if err != nil {                       // Stops the test run with a failure message
        t.Fatalf(
            "Parse(%q) err = %q, want <nil>",
            uri, err,
        )
    }
    want := &URL{                         // Declares a pointer variable
                                          // that points to the URL value
        Scheme: "https", Host: "github.com", Path: "inancgumus",
    }
    if *got != *want {                    // Dereferences the pointers
        t.Errorf(                         // to compare the URL
            "Parse(%q)\ngot  %#v\nwant %#v",   // values they point to
            uri, got, want,               // Reports a test failure
        )
    }
}
```

Uses \n (newline) for readability in test results

Returning to our test, we first declare a constant `uri`, the target URL string we want to parse. Then we call `Parse`, which returns a `*URL` and an `error`. If `Parse` fails, we report a failure and halt the test with `Fatalf` because there's no point in proceeding with an invalid URL.

TIP Dereferencing a `nil` `*URL` would cause a panic (runtime crash), so we call `Fatalf` to stop the test after we get a `nil` URL and a non-nil error value.

When we confirm that the parsing is successful, we compare the actual result (`got`) with the expected result (`want`). Then we use `Errorf` to report a failure if the results don't match. Even if `Parse` gives us something unexpected, the test can carry on.

Let's look at another example. The following listing demonstrates writing a test function `TestURLString` to test the `url` package's `String` method. We verify whether `String` can reassemble a `*URL` into a string.

Listing 2.4 Testing the `URL.String` method (`url/url_test.go`)

```
func TestURLString(t *testing.T) {
    u  := &URL{
        Scheme: "https",
        Host:    "github.com",
        Path:    "inancgumus",
    }

    got  := u.String()
    want := "https://github.com/inancgumus"
    if got != want {
        t.Errorf("String() = %q, want %q", got, want)
    }
}
```

This test verifies that the `String` method can reassemble the original URL string. In this case, we don't use `Fatalf` because there's no reason to stop the test early.

Understanding when to use `Fatalf` versus `Errorf` is crucial for effective test results. `Fatalf` is best for errors that invalidate the rest of the test because it stops execution. In less severe cases, use `Errorf`. This way, the test yields more information even after a failure, and we have a complete picture of problems without having to rerun tests.

TIP Name tests according to what they test. Using `TestParse` for `Parse` and `TestURLString` for the URL type's `String` method, for example, prevents conflicts with tests of other types that may contain a `String` method.

2.3.2 Running tests

Now that we have tests, we can run them using the `go test` tool. The tool is versatile and lets us run tests in many ways. We'll start by looking at the simplest way to run tests. Run this command in the Go module directory:

```
$ go test ./url
PASS
ok      github.com/inancgumus/gobyexample/url        0.15s
```

The `go test` tool compiles the tests, instructs the `testing` package to run them, displays the results, and discards the compiled test binary. Here, our tests pass and run in about 0.15 second. Rerunning the test takes less time because the test tool caches the results:

```
$ go test ./url
PASS
ok      github.com/inancgumus/gobyexample/url       (cached)
```

> **TIP** We can use the `-count=1` flag to force Go to rerun our tests, skipping the cache.

We know that our tests pass, but we don't know which ones run. Let's turn on the verbose flag (`-v`) to ensure that all the tests run. Tests can also output logs (such as with `T.Log`) when this flag is set:

```
$ go test ./url -v
--- PASS: TestParse
--- PASS: TestURLString
```

Moreover, we can shuffle the tests to ensure that each one is isolated. Tests that depend on the success or failure of other tests make it difficult to find the cause of potential problems:

```
$ go test ./url -v -shuffle=on
-test.shuffle 1746390063096132000      ◀──┐  Shuffling seed
--- PASS: TestURLString
--- PASS: TestParse
```

If we compare the tests with the preceding run, we see that they are shuffled. We also got a *shuffling seed* number, which we can use to run the tests in the same order. This approach is useful when we find a bug and want to reproduce it until we fix the issue:

```
$ go test ./url -v -shuffle=1746390063096132000
-test.shuffle 1746390063096132000
--- PASS: TestURLString
--- PASS: TestParse
```

We'll look at other interesting ways of using the `go test` tool in this chapter and throughout the book.

> **TIP** Tests files are processed only by the `go test` tool. Go's compiler ignores tests during regular builds (such as `go build`), keeping the final binary size small.

2.3.3   *Writing a failing test*

We've verified that our code can parse a URL. Now we want to test `Parse` with different URLs to ensure that it can parse various URLs. The following listing shows adding another test to verify that `Parse` can parse a different URL. We know from listing 2.1 that it cannot.

Listing 2.5   Testing `Parse` function 2 (`url/url_test.go`)

```go
func TestParseWithoutPath(t *testing.T) {
    const uri = "https://github.com"

    got, err := Parse(uri)
    if err != nil {
        t.Fatalf("Parse(%q) err = %q, want <nil>", uri, err)
    }

    want := &URL{
        Scheme: "https", Host: "github.com", Path: "",
    }
    if *got != *want {
        t.Errorf("Parse(%q)\ngot  %#v\nwant %#v", uri, got, want)
    }
}
```

Compares the struct values after dereferencing the pointers ◀

TIP   Go has specific rules for comparing types. We can compare structs directly if all their fields are comparable types, such as strings, integers, or bools. We can't compare then directly if they include fields such as slices, maps, or functions.

Running the tests reports a failure. I show the following failure message with added newlines and spaces to make it more readable. (Check out the sidebar "Comparing complex values and printing diffs" in section 2.3.4 for an alternative method.)

```
$ go test ./url
--- PASS: TestParse
--- PASS: TestURLString
--- FAIL: TestParseWithoutPath
    url_test.go: Parse("https://github.com")
        got  &url.URL{Scheme: "https",
                      Host:   "github.com",
                      Path:   "inancgumus"},
        want &url.URL{Scheme: "https",
                      Host:   "github.com",
                      Path:   ""}
```

◀ **Shows the function that we're testing and its input**

Shows the value we got after calling the function

Shows the values we wanted to see after calling the function

We're starting to duplicate the test logic in our parsing tests, which are identical except that they use different inputs and outputs. Section 2.4 addresses this problem.

2.3.4   *Writing descriptive test failure messages*

First, let's discuss what this message says about the test's failure and its usefulness. The failure message showed us that `Parse` was given a URL but parsed it incorrectly. The bright side is that we got a descriptive message to diagnose the problem, which is crucial for effective debugging. Here's the failure message format we use to see what's wrong instantly:

```
t.Errorf(
    "Parse(%q)\ngot  %#v\nwant %#v",      ◀────┐  The %#v verb prints the Go
    uri, got, want,                            │  syntax of a given value.
)
```

This formatting approach shows us how the test failed. We format the failure message by calling `t.Errorf` and use `\n` for newlines and `%#v` for values, making the output easy to read when we compare the expected and received values from a test.

The `got, want` convention provides a clear snapshot of what we get versus what we want. It helps us identify which part of the code failed without looking at the tested code—a real time-saver when we're working with large codebases or a large number of tests.

TIP `Errorf` calls the `URL` type's `String` method automatically if we use the `%s` verb (meaning string) instead of the `%#v` verb (meaning Go syntax). That result would not be what we want, however, because it would be like testing the `String` method's output. Because we want to see the values of the fields, we use the `%#v` verb.

Comparing complex values and printing diffs

Comparing struct values can be tricky. If we have a complex type with many nested fields and pointers to follow, we can use the `reflect` package's `DeepEqual` method. A much better approach, however, is to use `go-cmp`. We can get the package as follows:

```
$ go get github.com/google/go-cmp/cmp
```

Then we can import the `cmp` package in the test file and compare values like this:

```
if diff := cmp.Diff(want, got); diff != "" {
    t.Errorf("Parse(%q) mismatch (-want +got):\n%s", uri, diff)
}
```

The failure message looks like this after the test runs (and is customizable):

```
Parse("https://github.com/inancgumus") mismatch (-want +got):
      &url.URL{
            Scheme: "https",
            Host:   "github.com",
    -       Path:   "",
    +       Path:   "inancgumus",
      }
```

Check out the documentation at https://pkg.go.dev/github.com/google/go-cmp/cmp to learn more.

2.3.5 Fixing the code

We'll finish this section by fixing `Parse`, using the `strings` package's `Cut` function to parse a URL. Figure 2.3 shows how `Cut` works. This function splits a string using a separator, yielding the portions `before` and `after`. It also tells us whether the separator is `found` within the string and returns the entire string value in the `before` variable if the separator is not found.

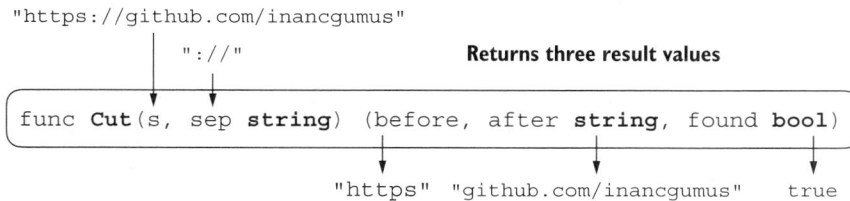

Figure 2.3 The `Cut` function cuts a string, returning segments `before` and `after` the separator. The `found` result value indicates that the separator was detected.

Let's use `Cut` within `Parse` to parse a URL, as shown in listing 2.6. We start by parsing the scheme. If the URL lacks a scheme, parsing stops, and an error is returned. Otherwise, we continue and parse the host and path. In this case, we ignore the third return value from `Cut` with an underscore (also known as the *blank identifier*) because not all URLs require a path part. (https://github.com, for example, does not have a path.) If necessary, we could handle missing paths separately, but in this case, it doesn't prevent us from parsing the URL successfully. Last, we inject what we parse into a new URL value, returning a pointer to this URL value and a `nil` error (success).

Listing 2.6 Fixing the `Parse` function (`url/url.go`)

```go
package url

import (
    "errors"
    "fmt"
    "strings"
)

. . .

func Parse(rawURL string) (*URL, error) {
    scheme, rest, ok := strings.Cut(rawURL, "://")    // Cuts the URL by "://" and saves the URL's scheme in the scheme variable and the rest into the rest variable
    if !ok {
        return nil, errors.New("missing scheme")      // Returns an error value that contains the missing scheme message
    }

    host, path, _ := strings.Cut(rest, "/")           // Ignores the third return value
```

```
    return &URL{
        Scheme:  scheme,
        Host:    host,
        Path:    path,
    }, nil
}
```

We've implemented `Parse` to parse various URLs instead of using a hardcoded one.

TIP   The book's repository contains every code change throughout the book. See https://mng.bz/PwZ9.

Also, we use the `errors` package's `New` function to return an `error` value containing the `missing scheme` message. Callers of `Parse` can see this error message if they want to print the error. In upcoming chapters, we'll explore alternative ways to handle errors.

This fix was straightforward. Let's rerun our tests to see whether they pass or fail:

```
$ go test ./url -v
--- PASS: TestParse
--- PASS: TestURLString
--- PASS: TestParseWithoutPath
```

The tests pass. We could also write a test function that verifies whether `Parse` returns an error when it gets a URL string that lacks a scheme. I'll leave this exercise to you. With this introductory knowledge, we're ready to dive deep into testing in Go.

Deep dive: Using named return values for clarity

The following `Cut` function takes two strings and returns two `string`s and a `bool`:

```
func Cut(s, sep string) (string, string, bool) {
    . . .
}
```

Deciphering this function's purpose is challenging because it's hard to see what each returned `string` or `bool` value represents. Instead, we can name each return value, making it easier to understand what each return value represents, especially when dealing with multiple return values of primitive types such as `string`, `int`, or `bool`:

```
func Cut(s, sep string) (before string, after string, found bool) {
    . . .
}
```
← before, after, and found are available here as variables.

We should be cautious when naming return values, however, because they become variables within a function. In this function, `before`, `after`, and `found` are variables:

```
func Cut(s, sep string) (before string, after string, found bool) {
    if i := strings.Index(s, sep); i >= 0 {
```

```
        before, after = s[:i], s[i+len(sep):]
    }
    return before, after, found
}
```

◄———— **Forgot to set the found variable**

◄———— **Returns found as false even after finding the separator**

We forgot to set `found` to `true` after we found the separator in the string. The compiler allows us to assign values to `before` and `after` because we declared them as named result values. If we hadn't used named results, this assignment would have triggered a compile-time error. Use named results only if they clarify intent; otherwise, avoid them.

2.4 Table-driven tests

Earlier, we crafted two tests to test `Parse`. Looking at them in listings 2.3 and 2.5 may be helpful before proceeding. These tests have identical testing logic. Instead of duplicating this logic for each URL we want to test, the idiomatic approach uses table-driven testing, which separates the test data from logic and reuses that logic to run separate test cases. Table-driven tests make it easy to add new test cases, reduce duplication through reuse, and improve maintainability.

Figure 2.4 shows how to reuse the test logic shared by our earlier tests. In the table-driven testing approach, we run and test each test case (data) using the same test logic. Here, the `uri` field is the URL string we pass to `Parse`, and `want` is what we expect `Parse` to return.

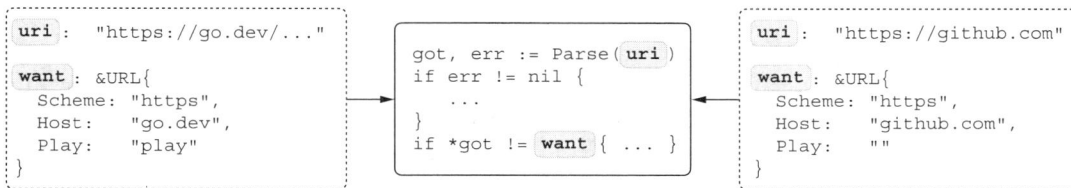

```
uri :    "https://go.dev/..."

want : &URL{
  Scheme: "https",
  Host:   "go.dev",
  Play:   "play"
}
```

```
got, err := Parse( uri )
if err != nil {
    ...
}
if *got != want { ... }
```

```
uri :    "https://github.com"

want : &URL{
  Scheme: "https",
  Host:   "github.com",
  Play:   ""
}
```

Figure 2.4 **Using the same test logic for testing with various data**

Figure 2.5 shows how to represent the test cases (the data). We have a table for our test cases and the corresponding Go code: a slice of anonymous struct values that map test cases. The same test logic can use these slice elements to test `Parse` from various angles.

We put the data in an anonymous struct slice and use the test logic once in a single test. Although we currently have two test cases, adding more is straightforward. We can use the same test logic to reduce duplication and increase test coverage, which we'll do in chapter 3. For now, we omit some edge cases to keep them short.

Columns to struct fields

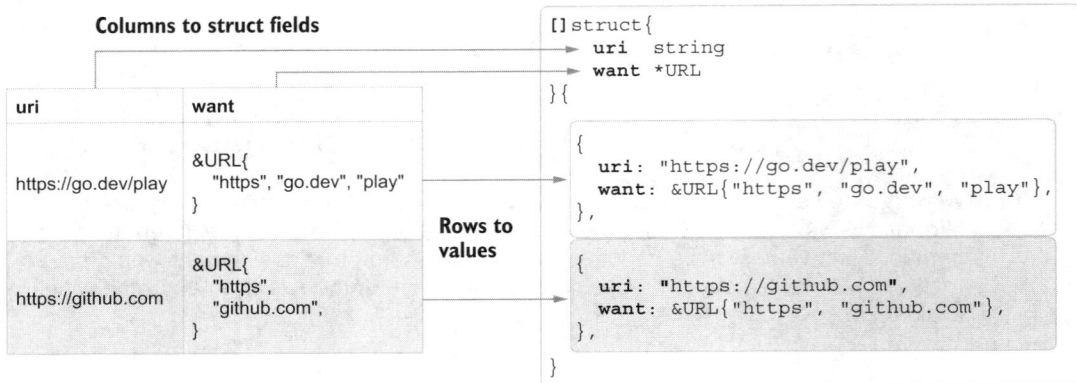

Figure 2.5   **Mapping a table of test cases to a slice of struct values**

> **NOTE**   Check out appendix C for more information about slices and appendix D for details about anonymous structs.

2.4.1   Creating a table of test cases

Now that we've learned about table-driven tests, let's create a table of test cases. Listing 2.7 shows the declaration of a package-level anonymous struct variable named `parseTests`.

> **TIP**   Although package variables stay alive for the entire program execution and are never garbage-collected, the ones defined by tests are alive only during testing.

First, we define the struct slice type with the `name`, `uri`, and `want` fields. Because we'll run each test case under the same test function, the `name` field will log the currently running test case. The `uri` field is the URL string, and `want` is the expected result. We'll pass `uri` to `Parse` and test whether it returns the expected URL.

After declaring the type, we fill out the slice with the test cases. We're adding the data that `TestParse` and `TestParseWithoutPath` used previously.

Listing 2.7   A table-driven test case (`url/url_test.go`)

```go
var parseTests = []struct {        Declares an anonymous struct slice
    name string                    with name, uri, and want fields
    uri  string
    want *URL
}{
    {
        name: "full",
        uri:  "https://github.com/inancgumus",     The first element
        want: &URL{                                in the struct slice
            Scheme: "https",
```

```
            Host:    "github.com",
            Path:    "inancgumus",
        },
    },
    {
        name: "without_path",
        uri:  "https://github.com",
        want: &URL{
            Scheme: "https",
            Host:    "github.com",
            Path:    "",
        },
    },
    /* many more test cases can be easily added */
}
```

The second element in the struct slice

We declared a package variable (think global) that the test functions in the `url` package can use. Sharing the test cases lets us use them from different tests when needed. We'll use these test cases to upgrade our test function to subtests, for example.

Another bright side is that this `parseTests` variable is available only to tests; nontest code cannot reach it because test code is considered only while running tests. We can add useful test-specific code without worrying that it will be included in production builds.

> **NOTE** Table-driven tests simplify adding new test cases. When we find a bug, we can easily add a new test case without modifying the existing test logic.

2.4.2 Writing a table-driven test

Now that we have a slice of test cases, let's implement our test logic in listing 2.8. We use the `TestParseTable` name for illustration purposes. In practice, we would call it `TestParse`. Picking distinct names for tests makes it easy to refer to them in the book; it also prevents constant refactoring and distracting repetition.

Listing 2.8   A table-driven test (`url/url_test.go`)

Iterates over the test cases

Logf emits a log below a test's run output that we can see by turning on the verbose flag (-v).

```
func TestParseTable(t *testing.T) {
    for _, tt := range parseTests {
        t.Logf("run %s", tt.name)

        got, err := Parse(tt.uri)
        if err != nil {
            t.Fatalf(
                "Parse(%q) err = %v, want <nil>",
                tt.uri, err,
            )
        }
        if *got != *tt.want {
            t.Errorf(
                "Parse(%q)\ngot  %#v\nwant %#v",
```

Fetches the data from a test case

```
            tt.uri, got, tt.want,          ◀ Fetches the data
        )                                     from a test case
    }
  }
}
```

We loop through test cases and run the same test logic for each one. The `tt` loop variable contains the data for the next test case. `Logf` makes it easy to see which test case we're running. This test is similar to the preceding parsing tests; the most significant difference is that the test logic fetches data from a slice of anonymous structs.

> **TIP** Repeating letters (`tt`) is a convention that differentiates variables or refers to multiples of something, making it easy to read and type as long as the surrounding context clarifies the use. We use `tt` for each test case to differentiate from the `t` variable, for example.

2.4.3   *Running a specific test*

In this section, we'll run the table test. We can use the `run` flag to execute only `Test-ParseTable` to focus on this specific test. `$` denotes the end of a line/text, enabling us to run only `TestParseTable` instead of other tests with the same test name prefix.

```
$ go test ./url -v -run=TestParseTable$          The same test logic
=== RUN    TestParseTable                        runs the first test case.
    run full
    run without_path            ◀───────  The same test logic runs
--- PASS: TestParseTable                          the second test case.
```

The test succeeded. But unlike in previous tests, which ran each case independently, `TestParseTable` handles multiple test cases together (the same test function runs them). This consolidates our tests and reduces duplication, but at the expense of the *isolation* we had before. We need to assess the implications of this tradeoff.

> **TIP** The `run` flag runs only the specified tests and supports regular expressions using the RE2 syntax. Visit https://github.com/google/re2/wiki/Syntax for more information.

2.4.4   *Identifying problems with table-driven tests*

Our table-driven test setup has two outstanding shortcomings. Figure 2.6 shows the first problem: a fatal failure (`Fatalf`) causes the test to skip running the remaining test cases. When each test case was independent, a failure in one didn't

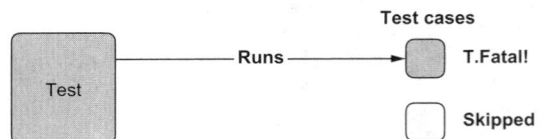

Figure 2.6   Skips the other case because of a fatal failure while running the first

affect the others. But we now run all test cases in a single test, and a fatal failure stops all of them.

Let's reveal the problem with an example. Listing 2.9 adds another test case at the start of our table: a valid URL with a data scheme containing a Base64-encoded text. Although the scheme exists, our parser can't parse this URL and returns a `missing scheme` error.

Listing 2.9 Inserting a data scheme test case (`url/url_test.go`)

```go
var parseTests = []struct {
    name string
    uri  string
    want *URL
}{
    {
        name: "with_data_scheme",
        uri:  "data:text/plain;base64,R28gYnkgRXhhbXBsZQ==",
        want: &URL{Scheme: "data"},
    },
    {
        name: "full",
        . . .
    },
    {
        name: "without_path",
        . . .
    },
}
```

This test case should cause our test to call `Fatalf` and skip the remaining test cases:

```
$ go test ./url -v -run=TestParseTable$
=== RUN   TestParseTable
    run with_data_scheme
    Parse("data:. . .") err = missing scheme, want <nil>
--- FAIL: TestParseTable
```

Our test calls `Fatalf` during the data test case step, causing the remaining test cases to be skipped. Another problem—perhaps a less significant one in our case—is that we can't selectively run a specific test case using the `run` flag because we have a single test function. In section 2.5, we solve these problems using subtests.

NOTE In a table-driven test, if one test case encounters a fatal failure (`Fatalf`), it stops the entire test function, preventing the remaining test cases from running.

We're familiar with table-driven testing:

- Test cases are scenarios with the input and output data we want to test.
- Table-driven tests reuse the same test logic, reducing duplication and improving maintainability and test coverage.

Table-driven testing also has downsides:

- We can't run test cases individually because they run within the same test function.
- A fatal test failure causes the remaining test cases to be skipped.

2.5 Subtests

Earlier, we created a table-driven test and learned that fatal failures while running test cases can cause the remaining ones to be skipped. Fortunately, subtests solve this problem. As with regular test functions, we can run subtests independently by name.

> **TIP** Subtests can fail without stopping others. Like regular test functions, subtests run independently, so a failure in one does not stop the others from running.

2.5.1 Understanding subtests

Compare the table-driven and subtest approaches in figure 2.7. The left side shows our early approach: the same test function runs all the test cases. On the right, we use subtests within a test function, with each subtest function running a separate test case.

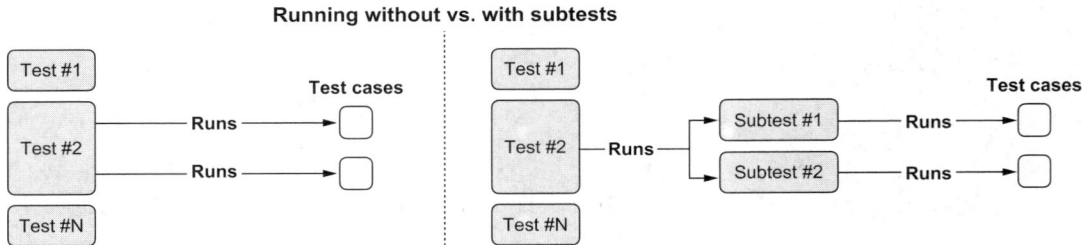

Figure 2.7   **Running test cases within the same test and in separate subtests**

We can run a subtest using the *T type's Run method. Figure 2.8 shows a test that calls Run to launch two subtests. Each subtest runs a test case in a separate goroutine. As stated in chapter 1, goroutines run a function concurrently. For the Run method to run a test case in a separate goroutine, we must pass it a function to execute. This function contains test logic and runs a test case from our test cases table in a new goroutine.

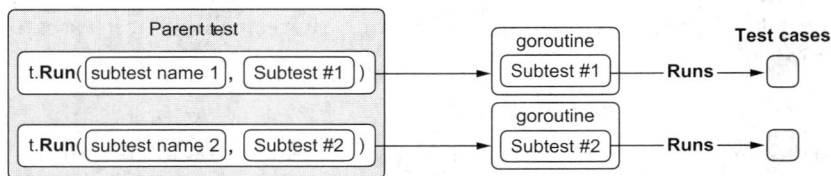

Figure 2.8   **Test runs two subtests, each running a test case in a new goroutine**

To wrap up, subtests are test functions run separately and are impervious to the fatal failings of other tests. Like ordinary test functions, subtests have names and run in separate goroutines, which isolates subtests and allows us to run them optionally in parallel.

2.5.2 *Writing a table-driven test with subtests*

Now that we're familiar with subtests, let's dive into using them. We'll iterate over our table-driven tests, running each test case in a subtest to bolster test resiliency. Listing 2.10 puts subtests into practice. As in our previous test, we loop over our test cases. On each iteration, we call the Run method to run a subtest. Each subtest gets a unique name and a closure that wraps the test logic that runs a test case. Because closures can access their surroundings, we can continue using tt.uri and tt.want.

> **DEFINITION** *Closures* are functions that retain access to their surrounding scope, such as variables, even after their outer function returns.

Listing 2.10 Table-driven subtests (`url/url_test.go`)

```
var parseTests = []struct {
    . . .
}{
    {
        name: "with_data_scheme",
        . . .
    },
    {
        name: "full",
        . . .
    },
    {
        name: "without_path",
        . . .
    },
}

func TestParseSubtests(t *testing.T) {
    // We can put common test setup and teardown logic here.

    for _, tt := range parseTests {
        t.Run(tt.name, func(t *testing.T) {        ◄──   Runs a subtest. t is a new
            got, err := Parse(tt.uri)                     separate variable from
            if err != nil {                               the parent test's t.
                t.Fatalf(
                    "Parse(%q) err = %v, want <nil>",
                    tt.uri, err,
                )
            }
            if *got != *tt.want {
                t.Errorf(
```

```
                    "Parse(%q)\ngot  %#v\nwant %#v",
                    tt.uri, got, tt.want,
                )
            }
        })
    }
}
```

Our test has become more robust. Although the code inside each subtest's closure remains logically the same as our previous table-driven test, subtests run independently. We can run and examine more test results even in the presence of fatal failures, allowing us to get a complete picture of the test run instead of rerunning the tests after each failure.

NOTE   Similar to a test function, each subtest function runs in a new goroutine.

In the listing, we see a comment at the beginning about shared test setup and teardown logic. Because the same test function runs subtests, we can add common setup and teardown logic for the subtests to share, such as opening and closing a database connection.

2.5.3 *Understanding the role of specific T pointers*

Let's take a closer look at our test to discuss the role of *T before wrapping up. Each *T represents a single test function, providing granular control of that specific test's execution and failure handling. Each test function (or subtest) can call `Fatalf` without failing others because the *T is unique per test (or subtest) function.

The `testing` package's Run function delivers a new *T to each closure so that each subtest can call `Fatalf` and `Errorf` only to report failure for itself. That's why even if one subtest fails with `Fatalf`, other tests continue.

WARNING   Each *T is specific to a test function, making the test function independent. Never share a test function's *T with another test function (including subtests). Doing so could lead to unpredictable behavior and compromise the validity of overall test results.

Deep dive: Closures and memory management

Closures are functions that can capture and hold pointers to variables from their surrounding scope even after their outer function returns. This means they can extend the lifetime of these variables beyond the function that created them. The garbage collector cannot reclaim memory for variables still referenced by actively referenced closures. If we keep closures around too long or share them improperly, we risk memory leaks, so we should be extra careful when sharing closures with other parts of our programs.

2.5.4   *Running subtests*

Recall from section 2.4.4 that our table-driven test didn't run the rest of the test cases when a previous one failed. Now that we're using subtests, let's see the difference. The parent test `TestParseSubtests` will run the subtests sequentially and wait for them to complete:

```
$ go test ./url -v -run=TestParseSubtests$
--- FAIL: TestParseSubtests
    --- FAIL: TestParseSubtests/with_data_scheme
    --- PASS: TestParseSubtests/full
    --- PASS: TestParseSubtests/without_path
```

Thanks to our new subtest approach, the rest of the test cases run even if one of them fails. Here, the first subtest fails, leading to the parent test's failure. Still, the parent test continues to run the rest of the subtests because each subtest function is run independently.

Moreover, because subtests have names, we see them in the test report, which enhances readability and maintainability, allowing us to understand the test's purpose at a glance. As with regular tests, we can use their names to run individual subtests selectively:

```
$ go test ./url -v -run=TestParseSubtests/full$
--- PASS: TestParseSubtests
    --- PASS: TestParseSubtests/full
```

This time, the parent test passed because the subtest also passed. Although the parent test calls `Run` for all our subtests to run them, the `testing` package intentionally skips them because of our filter and runs only the `TestParseSubtests/full` subtest.

2.5.5   *Fixing the code*

Sometimes, stopping tests at the first sign of trouble can streamline debugging. For this purpose, I've contributed the `failfast` flag, released in Go 1.10. This flag halts further testing on the first reported test failure, letting us focus our attention where it's needed most. We can use the `failfast` flag to see the first failing test:

```
$ go test ./url -run=TestParseSubtests -failfast
--- FAIL: TestParseSubtests (0.00s)
  --- FAIL: TestParseSubtests/with_data_scheme (0.00s)
      Parse("data:text/plain;. . .") err = missing scheme, want <nil>
FAIL    github.com/inancgumus/gobyexample/url   0.177s
$
```

> **TIP**   The choice between halting immediately or after all failures depends on whether we're isolating a specific problem or assessing the overall health of the code.

To fix this problem, as the next listing shows, we improve `Parse` to interpret both opaque (e.g., `data:...`) and regular URLs (e.g., `https://...`). We use string slicing to detect URL types.

Listing 2.11 Fixing the `Parse` function for the data scheme (`url/url.go`)

```go
func Parse(rawURL string) (*URL, error) {
    scheme, rest, ok := strings.Cut(rawURL, ":")      ◄── Cuts the raw URL with ":",
    if !ok {                                               unlike the previous code's "://"
        return nil, errors.New("missing scheme")
    }
    if !strings.HasPrefix(rest, "//") {               ◄── Checks whether the rest
        return &URL{Scheme: scheme}, nil                   of the URL starts with "//"
    }

    host, path, _ := strings.Cut(rest[2:], "/")       ◄── Slices the rest of the URL to get
                                                           a string after the initial 2 bytes
    return &URL{
        Scheme: scheme,
        Host:   host,
        Path:   path,
    }, nil
}
```

Instead of cutting URLs at `"//"`, we do it at `":"` to be compatible with opaque and regular URLs. Let's see what our variables would look like for both URL schemes:

- *Opaque*—rawURL=`"data:text/plain"`, scheme=`"data"`, rest=`"text/plain"`
- *Regular*—rawURL=`"https://github.com/inancgumus"`, scheme=`"https"`, rest=`"//github.com/inancgumus"`

NOTE A URL is considered opaque if the part after the scheme doesn't have a slash.

When the scheme is parsed, `Parse` stops if it encounters an opaque URL, returning a URL with only the scheme; otherwise, it proceeds to parse the host and path from `rest[2:]`. This *string slicing* omits the first 2 bytes. `"//github.com"` becomes `"github.com"`, for example.

As appendix C explains, a *slice* is a view of a fixed array. Slicing returns a slice that sees all or some part of its underlying array. Similarly, slicing a string returns a string without copying the underlying byte data from its array. Also, `rest[2:]` is a shortcut for typing `rest[2:len(rest)]`. Similarly, `rest[:2]` is a shortcut for typing `rest[0:2]`.

Strings can be sliced because they are inherently byte slices. Be careful when slicing strings, however, because the underlying bytes might be used for Unicode encoding (multibyte code points). Slicing such strings might be dangerous because a single character can span multiple bytes. Read more about strings at https://go.dev/blog/strings. After adjusting `Parse`, we should rerun our tests to verify the fix:

```
$ go test ./url -v -run=TestParseSubtests$
--- PASS: TestParseSubtests
    --- PASS: TestParseSubtests/with_data_scheme
    --- PASS: TestParseSubtests/full
    --- PASS: TestParseSubtests/without_path
```

With these changes, `Parse` can interpret newer and traditional URL formats correctly. Although this example is good progress toward a robust parser, our focus will remain on testing rather than creating a full-fledged parser that can handle any URL format.

To prevent confusion and distraction, I didn't explain that tests are also subtests. Internally, the `testing` package runs top-level tests (tests whose names start with `Test`) using the `Run` method in a new goroutine. Subtests are hierarchical, and one subtest can run another.

2.6   *Example tests*

It's time to add documentation showing how to use our package. We want to do this so that our documentation never goes out of date. Whenever we change our code, our documentation should update itself automatically.

Go has built-in support for what we want: example tests. Figure 2.9 shows the interactive documentation for the `Parse` function as an example. This documentation autoupdates whenever we update `Parse` or the example test.

```
func Parse

func Parse(rawURL string) (*URL, error)

Parse parses a raw URL into a URL structure.

▼ Example

func main() {
    uri, err := url.Parse("https://github.com/inancgumus")
    if err != nil {
        log.Fatal(err)
    }
    fmt.Println(uri)
}

Output:
https://github.com/inancgumus

                                    [ Share ]  [ Format ]  [ Run ]
```

Figure 2.9   The `Parse` function's documentation provides an interactive example.

An example test provides the example code below the Example heading, and users can click the Run button to interact with it. Example tests not only generate runnable examples for users to try our code interactively inside the documentation, like test functions, but also verify our code.

2.6.1 *Writing an example test*

Listing 2.12 shows how to write an example test for the `url` package's `Parse` function, which will be displayed similarly to figure 2.9. Example tests are like test functions, but they have an `Example` prefix and don't take a `*T` type. Instead of reporting their result using `*T`, they print it directly to standard output (e.g., using `fmt.Println`).

Listing 2.12 Writing an example test (`url/example_test.go`)

```go
package url_test                                    ◄── Declares a test-only package

import (
    "fmt"
    "log"
    "testing"
                                                    Imports the url package
    "github.com/inancgumus/gobyexample/url"    ◄──  to call Parse in the code
)
                                                    Declares an example test
func ExampleParse() {                          ◄──  for the Parse function
    uri, err := url.Parse(
        "https://github.com/inancgumus",
    )                                               The example that will be
    if err != nil {                                 displayed in the documentation
        log.Fatal(err)
    }
    fmt.Println(uri)
    // Output:                                  ◄──
    // https://github.com/inancgumus           ◄──  The lines below this comment are
}                                                   the expected output of the example.
```
            The testing package compares this
            expected output with the actual
            output of the example.

First, we create a new file, `example_test.go`, in the `url` package's directory. Naming the files that house example tests this way is a convention but not required. Then we put our example test in a new package, `url_test`, so that the interactive example works.

Go usually doesn't allow multiple packages in the same directory, but it makes an exception for test packages, such as `url_test`. (The `url` and `url_test` packages can coexist in the same directory, for example.) The naming pattern `packagename_test` denotes a package available only while running tests; we cannot import it from other packages.

After declaring the `url_test` package, we declare the `ExampleParse` function to demonstrate the `Parse` function. This setup allows us to display the interactive example alongside the `Parse` function in the documentation (as in the figure), showcasing how to use it as though the `url` package were imported and used from another package.

> **NOTE** Test packages are named after the packages they test. The `url_test` package tests the `url` package, for example. This is called *black-box testing* because `url_test` can access only the exported items of the `url` package. I don't use this approach in this book because in my experience, they add unnecessary ceremony to testing.

As we'll see in section 2.6.2, we can also run example tests along with ordinary tests. If the `Parse` function fails (returns a non-nil error), we call `Fatal` to cause the test run to end immediately with an exit status of code 1. Because example tests write their results to standard output, the test tool can catch this exit status code and report the failure in the summary.

Another way to check whether the example is successful is to use a special comment. Here, below the `Output` comment, we specify the expected outcome. The example will fail if the output from `Println` does not match the expected output. We must use this comment if we want to have a high-level test for `Parse` and also provide documentation to users.

2.6.2 *Running example tests*

Now that we have an example test for the `Parse` function, we can run it like any other test:

```
$ go test ./url -v -run=ExampleParse$
--- PASS: ExampleParse
```

The `testing` package runs our example test, collects its output, and compares it with the text we wrote under the `Output` comment. Although we don't see its output here, our example test should have the output `https://github.com/inancgumus` because it passed.

Suppose that in the example test, we mistakenly added something like `https://google.com` below the `Output` comment while passing `https://github.com/inancgumus` to `Parse`. In that case, the test would fail, and we would get the following failure message:

```
$ go test ./url -v -run=ExampleParse$
--- FAIL: ExampleParse (0.00s)
got:
https://github.com/inancgumus
want:
https://google.com
```

When we upload our module to a public repository, we can see interactive documentation on the Go package server (https://pkg.go.dev). This website periodically scans information about public modules and packages.

TIP Visit https://pkg.go.dev/about for more details on the package server, and learn more about example tests at https://blog.golang.org/examples.

2.7 *Other testing tools*

Go's built-in testing support via the `go test` tool and the `testing` package provides most of what we need to write, run, and manage tests. In some situations, however, we may benefit from third-party tools that extend or enhance the testing experience. You can find some of these tools at https://github.com/inancgumus/awesome-go#testing.

Although third-party tools can offer additional features and flexibility, Go's built-in testing support is often sufficient for most use cases. The `go test` tool is tightly integrated with Go, providing a lightweight, straightforward solution for writing and running tests. Unless we require specific features, the built-in tools are more than enough for our needs in general.

Summary

- Pick concise package names, and avoid repetitive naming (*stuttering*). A package's name should concisely communicate what it provides and be meaningful when combined with its exported items. Comment on package items for documentation.

- Errors are regular values, not exceptions. Return the error as the last result value.

- Export struct fields generously for direct access. Unexport them only when you need immutability or other business logic. Avoid unnecessary indirection.

- Implement standard library interfaces to improve interaction between your code and the standard library, making your code easier to integrate, reuse, and maintain across different packages without extra work.

- Go's built-in testing uses the `go test` tool and the `testing` package. Tests live in _test.go files and start with the `Test` prefix, taking a `*testing.T` parameter. Nontest builds exclude test code, keeping the final binary smaller.

- Use `T.Errorf` for nonfatal issues that don't stop the test run. Use `T.Fatalf` when the test should stop immediately. Write descriptive failure messages, and use formatting verbs like `%#v` and the `go-cmp` package for complex value comparisons. Use the `got`, `want` convention to quickly identify the reasons for the failure and what was expected.

- Table-driven tests separate test data from logic, reducing duplication. Combine them with subtests to isolate tests, preventing fatal failures from stopping other cases.

- Example tests document your code and also verify its correctness. They start with `Example`, validate expected outputs via comments, and use separate test packages.

Test coverage and optimization

3

This chapter covers

- Measuring test coverage to see what percentage of code is tested
- Optimizing for performance using benchmarks and profiling
- Parallel testing to reduce test runtime and detect data race issues

Chapter 2 introduced idioms and testing, and we implemented and tested a package called `url` using the `testing` package and the `go test` tool. In this chapter, we'll measure our package's test coverage to identify what we still need to test. Then we'll improve our code's performance by benchmarking and profiling, (Idiomatic code is efficient and eliminates unnecessary inefficiencies.) Last, we'll look at running parallel tests and detecting possible data race issues.

3.1 Test coverage

As radar scans for objects within a radius, test coverage examines our code to identify which parts are tested and which are not. Test coverage is a way of cross-checking which sections of code our tests are exercising and verifying—in other words, *covering*. This section discusses test coverage. We'll measure the test coverage of our url package and see what it means to reach 100% test coverage. Then we'll start fixing bugs in our code.

3.1.1 *Measuring test coverage*

We can measure the test coverage of the url package by using the coverprofile flag:

```
$ go test ./url -coverprofile cover.out
. . .coverage: 87.5% of statements
```

◄──── **Measures the test coverage of the url package and outputs the result to cover.out**

The tool analyzes the url package's code and saves the resulting test coverage profile to the cover.out file in the same directory. Our tests have a high coverage rate: 87.5%. Let's find out what parts of our code the tests cover by feeding this profile into the coverage tool:

```
$ go tool cover -html=cover.out
```

Running this command opens a browser window and displays the coverage report, which may be similar to figure 3.1. This figure is best viewed in color, so it may be a good idea to run the command on a local machine.

```
          func Parse(rawURL string) (*URL, error) {
Covered       scheme, rest, ok := strings.Cut(rawURL, ":")
              if !ok {
                  return nil, errors.New("missing scheme")       Not covered
              }
              if !strings.HasPrefix(rest, "//") {
                  return &URL{Scheme: scheme}, nil
              }

              host, path, _ := strings.Cut(rest[2:], "/")
Covered
              return &URL{
                  Scheme: scheme,
                  Host:   host,
                  Path:   path,
              }, nil
          }
```

Figure 3.1   Tests cover every line except the part that returns the missing scheme error. Remember that this output normally appears in color.

The green lines are the areas in the code that tests cover (Covered); the red lines are the areas that tests don't cover (Not Covered). The rest are gray and not crucial for the test coverage (the first and last lines in the source code). Looking at the report, we see that our tests exercise every line of code in Parse except the missing scheme error.

Avoiding the browser

If we want to avoid the browser and see the function-by-function coverage report from the command line, we can use the `func` flag as follows (methods are functions too):

```
$ go tool cover -func=cover.out
url/url.go:17:   Parse        87.5%
url/url.go:36:   String       100.0%
total:           (statements) 87.5%
```

3.1.2 Perfecting test coverage

Now that we've discovered that we haven't covered all the behaviors of our `Parse` function, we'll increase test coverage by adding tests. Although our current tests cover only the happy path, the following one verifies some edge cases in which `Parse` must return an error.

Listing 3.1   Testing for edge cases (`url/url_test.go`)

```
func TestParseError(t *testing.T) {
    tests := []struct {
        name string
        uri  string
    }{
        {name: "without_scheme", uri: "github.com"},

        /* we'll add more tests soon */
    }
    for _, tt := range tests {
        t.Run(tt.name, func(t *testing.T) {         Fails if Parse succeeds
            _, err := Parse(tt.uri)                  (returns nil)
            if err == nil {
                t.Errorf("Parse(%q) err=nil; want an error", tt.uri)
            }
        })
    }
}
```

This test will fail if `Parse` doesn't return an error. We have only one test case, but we'll soon add more. Now let's check the coverage percentage without a profile file:

```
$ go test ./url -cover
coverage: 100.0% of statements
```

Our tests cover every line of code in the `url` package. We could stop here and celebrate because we have 100% coverage. But does total test coverage mean bug-free code? Should we optimize for test coverage or correctness or both? There's more to the story.

3.1.3   *100% test coverage != bug-free code*

Having 100% test coverage does not mean having bug-free code. Test coverage shows us only which parts of the code the tests run, but it cannot unearth bugs for us or guarantee that our tests verify every possible behavior of our code. Let's write some tests to see whether our code has bugs despite the full test coverage.

THE EMPTY SCHEME BUG

The `Parse` function may have a bug. Can it handle URLs with an empty scheme name (such as `"://github.com"`)? Let's add a test case in the next listing to see whether this bug is hiding in the code.

Listing 3.2   Adding an `empty_scheme` **test case** (`url/url_test.go`)

```go
func TestParseError(t *testing.T) {
    tests := []struct { /* omitted */ }
        {name: "without_scheme", uri: "github.com"},
        {name: "empty_scheme", uri: "://github.com"},
    }
    for _, tt := range tests {
        t.Run(tt.name, func(t *testing.T) {
            _, err := Parse(tt.uri)
            if err == nil {
                t.Errorf("Parse(%q) err=nil; want an error", tt.uri)
            }
        })
    }
}
```

Now that we have an `empty_scheme` test case, we can run the test:

```
$ go test ./url -cover
--- FAIL: TestParseError/empty_scheme
    Parse("://github.com")=nil; want an error
coverage: 100.0% of statements
```

Although the test coverage is 100%, the bug was lurking in the code. Let's fix it as shown in listing 3.3. The previous version of `Parse` correctly showed an error if the scheme separator (`":"`) was missing in the URL, but it didn't return an error if the separator was present but the scheme was empty. The fix ensures that `Parse` also returns an error when the scheme is missing.

Listing 3.3   Fix for empty schemes (`url/url.go`)

```go
func Parse(rawURL string) (*URL, error) {
    scheme, rest, ok := strings.Cut(rawURL, ":")
    if !ok || scheme == "" {                          ◄─── Also checks whether the
        return nil, errors.New("missing scheme")           parsed scheme is empty
    }

    if !strings.HasPrefix(rest, "//") {
```

```
        return &URL{Scheme: scheme}, nil
    }
    host, path, _ := strings.Cut(rest[2:], "/")

    return &URL{
        Scheme: scheme,
        Host:   host,
        Path:   path,
    }, nil
}
```

Rerunning the test with this fix results in success:

```
$ go test ./url -cover
PASS
coverage: 100.0% of statements
```

This bug hunt was straightforward. Let's focus on another part of our code.

THE NIL RECEIVER BUG

You may recall from chapter 2 that `*URL` has a `String` method that reassembles a URL string:

```
func (u *URL) String() string {
    return fmt.Sprintf("%s://%s/%s", u.Scheme, u.Host, u.Path)
}
```

We suspect a bug within `String` when it's called on a `nil *URL` pointer, so we're going to put it to the test. As the following listing shows, we're transitioning `TestURLString` to a table-driven approach for extensibility, calling `String` against a `nil *URL`.

> **Listing 3.4 Testing `String` with a `nil` pointer (`url/url_test.go`)**

```
func TestURLString(t *testing.T) {
    tests := []struct {
        name string
        uri  *URL
        want string
    }{
        {
            name: "nil",
            uri:  nil,          ◀──── Provides a nil *URL
            want: "",                 to the test logic
        },
        /* we'll add more test cases soon */
    }
    for _, tt := range tests {
        t.Run(tt.name, func(t *testing.T) {
            got := tt.uri.String()    ◀──── Forces the subtest call
            if got != tt.want {               String on a nil *URL
                t.Errorf(
                    "\ngot  %q\nwant %q\nfor  %#v",
```

```
                    got, tt.want, tt.uri,
              )
          }
      })
  }
}
```

When we run this test, it triggers a panic due to a `nil` pointer dereference, which halts the test run prematurely. A subtest failure should not stop the entire test, but a panic does exactly that, ceasing the parent test abruptly without running the remaining subtests:

```
$ go test ./url -v
--- PASS: TestParse
--- FAIL: TestURLString
--- FAIL: TestURLString/nil
panic: runtime error: invalid memory address
                      or nil pointer dereference [recovered]
. . .
[signal SIGSEGV: segmentation violation
                  code=0x2 addr=0x0 pc=0x1023ec8d8]
```

NOTE   `addr=0x0` is a `nil` pointer that does not point to a valid memory location.

How does `String` on a nil `*URL` cause such chaos? Calling `String` on a nil `*URL` receiver leads to dereferencing a `nil` pointer when accessing the `URL`'s fields. Because there is no `URL` to which this pointer receiver points, Go panics and passes the ball to us:

```
func (u *URL) String() string {          ◄──── u is nil when String is
    return fmt.Sprintf(                        called on a nil *URL.
        "%s://%s/%s",
        u.Scheme, . . .     ◄──── Tries to get the Scheme
    )                              field from a nil *URL
}
```

To make `String` more robust and idiomatic, we'll follow the principle of making the zero value useful. We'll adjust `String` to handle a `nil` receiver gracefully by returning an empty string, which prevents the crash. See the improved version in the following listing.

> **Listing 3.5   Fix for a `nil` pointer (`url/url.go`)**

```
func (u *URL) String() string {
  if u == nil {                          Returns an empty string if
    return ""                            the receiver is nil
  }
  return fmt.Sprintf("%s://%s/%s", u.Scheme, u.Host, u.Path)
}
```

After this tweak, our test should run smoothly, without panics:

```
$ go test ./url
--- PASS: TestParse
--- PASS: TestURLString
    --- PASS: TestURLString/nil
--- PASS: TestParseWithoutPath
. . .
PASS
```

◄——— **Other tests continue to run because the program doesn't panic.**

We can call a method (such as `String`) on a `nil *URL` because *internally*, a method is a function that takes a receiver argument as its first parameter:

```
func String(u *URL) string {
    . . .
}
```

Suppose that `uri` is a `*URL` variable. Calling `u.String()` is equal to calling

```
(*URL).String(uri)
```

The `(*URL)` part tells the compiler which type's `String` method to call. Here, we call the `*URL` type's `String` method, passing it `uri` as a receiver. Because the receiver name of the `String` method is `u`, `String` *receives* the `uri`'s copy as `u`. Both point to the exact memory location.

THE EMPTY URL BUG

Let's continue our bug hunt by discovering and fixing one more bug. `String` reassembles a URL string without checking whether the URL fields are missing, so we suspect that it produces URL strings incorrectly. Let's verify this behavior with a test.

Listing 3.6 Testing `String` with an empty URL (`url/url_test.go`)

```
func TestURLString(t *testing.T) {
    tests := []struct {
        name string
        uri  *URL
        want string
    }{
        {
            name: "nil",
            uri:  nil,
            want: "",
        },
        {
            name: "empty",
            uri:  new(URL),
            want: "",
        },
    }
```

◄——— **Returns a new pointer to a new URL value**

```
for _, tt := range tests {
    t.Run(tt.name, func(t *testing.T) {
        got := tt.uri.String()
        if got != tt.want {
            t.Errorf(
                "\ngot  %q\nwant %q\nfor  %#v",
                got, tt.want, tt.uri,
            )
        }
    })
}
}
```

Running the test reports the following failure:

```
$ go test ./url -v -run='TestURLString/empty'
=== RUN   TestURLString
=== RUN   TestURLString/empty
    url_test.go:
        got  ":///"
        want ""
        for  &url.URL{Scheme:"", Host:"", Path:""}
--- FAIL: TestURLString/empty
```

We got a string with the scheme and path separators instead of an empty URL string. Listing 3.7 fixes the bug by checking each field and reassembling the string. Note that we use a *short declaration* (annotated in the code). It saves Scheme in the sc variable and then checks whether sc is empty. The sc variable is valid only within that if statement's scope. See appendix B for the short declaration syntax.

Listing 3.7   Reassembling a URL (`url/url.go`)

```
func (u *URL) String() string {
    if u == nil {
        return ""
    }
    var s string
    if sc := u.Scheme; sc != "" {          ◄──  The part before the semicolon
        s += sc                                  is called a short declaration.
        s += "://"                         ◄──  We still don't handle
    }                                            opaque URLs.
    if h := u.Host; h != "" {
        s += h
    }
    if p := u.Path; p != "" {
        s += "/"
        s += p
    }
    return s
}
```

Now that we've fixed the issue, let's rerun the test:

```
$ go test ./url -cover
ok..coverage: 100.0% of statements
```

Our `Parse` function and `String` method are in better shape. We could continue hunting bugs, but doing so would distract us further from the rest of our goals. No doubt you can find more bugs in the `url` package code; I'll leave this exercise to you.

Although we have a fix, `String` may be inefficient, but we can't know that without taking a measurement. Next, we'll dive into benchmarking to improve our code's performance.

> **TIP** Learn more about the coverage tool at https://go.dev/blog/cover. Also check out fuzz testing at https://go.dev/doc/security/fuzz. We can fuzz-test our code against random inputs to identify areas that are not handled, improving stability and security.

3.2 Benchmarking and optimization

In this section, we'll optimize our `String` method using benchmarking and profiling. Without going down the rabbit hole of benchmarking and optimization, remember that it's better to focus on delivering features and fixing bugs than optimizing code unless there's a business need to do so. We should stop if our efforts result in code that is hard to maintain.

Some basic benchmarking is still valuable, however. By capturing current execution times, we can avoid introducing inefficiencies that may go unnoticed after code changes. Benchmarks enable us to monitor the effect of changes over time and help us identify bottlenecks early.

3.2.1 Writing and running benchmarks

Benchmarking is running a piece of code repeatedly to measure its performance. Similar to tests, benchmark functions are written inside test files. Unlike test functions, benchmarks have a `Benchmark` prefix and take a `*testing.B` input. This `*B` struct type supports benchmarking and has nearly every feature of the `*T` type (e.g., `Fatalf`).

Suppose that we want to measure the `String` method's performance. As figure 3.2 shows, the `testing` package passes a `*B` as b when we run the benchmark. Then we run our `String` method in a loop enough times to let the `testing` package measure its performance.

This benchmark calls the `Loop` method as a loop condition. As long as the `Loop` returns `true`, the loop continues and runs the code we want to measure, such as the `String` method. The `Loop` method may return `false` after 1 second (by default). Last, the `go test` tool reports how often the `testing` package calls the measured code during the benchmark.

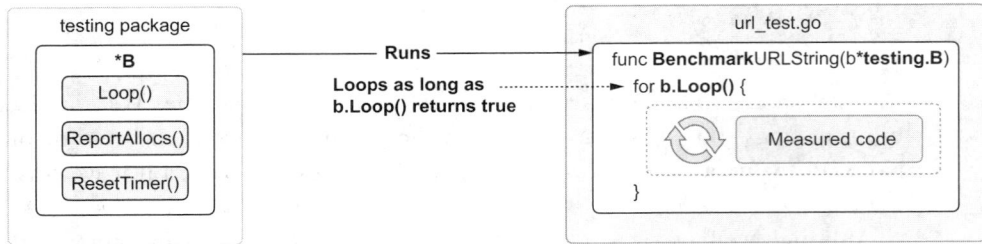

Figure 3.2   Benchmarking the code in a loop to measure performance

Now that we're familiar with benchmarking, let's create one for our `String` method. As listing 3.8 shows, we'll name the benchmark function `BenchmarkURLString` to differentiate it from future benchmark functions. Then we'll declare a `URL` pointer and call `String` in a loop while `b.Loop` is `true`, discarding the result because it's unnecessary.

Listing 3.8   Writing a benchmark for `String` (url/url_test.go)

```go
func BenchmarkURLString(b *testing.B) {
    u := &URL{
        Scheme: "https",
        Host:   "github.com",
        Path:   "inancgumus",
    }
    for b.Loop() {
        _ = u.String()
    }
}
```

We've written a benchmark that calls `String` as long as the `Loop` method returns `true`. We must run benchmarks using the `go test` tool with the `bench` flag, as follows. The dot in `-bench=.` runs all benchmarks. We also pass the optional `benchmem` flag to get the number of memory allocations `String` makes per operation:

```
$ go test ./url -bench=. -benchmem
goos: darwin                                    ← My operating system. (macOS underlyingly uses the Darwin kernel.)
goarch: arm64                                   ← My machine architecture
pkg: github.com/inancgumus/gobyexample/url
cpu: Apple M1 Pro                               ← My machine CPU
BenchmarkURLString-10   12073482   96.07 ns/op   64 B/op   4 allocs/op
```

`op` means *operation* and denotes a single iteration in the benchmark loop. The benchmark terms `ns/op`, `B/op`, and `allocs/op` are standard metrics representing time per operation, bytes allocated per operation, and allocations per operation, respectively.

The `BenchmarkURLString` function ran on 10 CPU cores and returned the following results:

- The benchmark called `String` about 12 million times.
- Each operation took an average of 96.07 nanoseconds.
- Each operation requested 64 bytes of heap memory in total by four calls.

We can also change the default benchmark time using the `benchtime` flag:

```
$ go test ./url -bench=. -benchmem -benchtime=2s
BenchmarkURLString-10  22333120  96.8 ns/op  64 B/op  4 allocs/op
```

The benchmark made about 20 million calls. Other measurements per operation are similar to those of the preceding run because we didn't change anything except the benchmark duration.

The `benchtime` flag controls how long benchmarks run and provides more accurate results by ensuring that performance is measured over a longer period. Also, it may minimize the effect of environmental noise factors (such as machine load).

TIP Tests are run before benchmarks (and we can use the `-v` flag to prove it). We can run benchmarks without running tests using an empty `run` flag: `-bench=. -run=' '`.

Deep dive: Intensive setup and cleanup

In benchmarking, we may set up resource-intensive tasks such as connecting to a database beforehand. Fortunately, the `Loop` method allows us to do that automatically. Suppose we have a function that resizes images from a `[]byte`:

```
func resize(b []byte) { . . . }
```

Now suppose we want to benchmark this function for a large image. We'll pass it 1 million bytes. Allocating a 1-million-byte slice can affect the benchmark results. So we put our setup code before the loop to prevent this, ensuring that only the relevant code is timed:

```
func BenchmarkMemoryFast(b *testing.B) {     Setup part; prepares a large
    image := make([]byte, 1_000_000)    ◄─── slice of bytes before timing
    for b.Loop() {
        resize(image)
    }                    A possible cleanup
    . . .           ◄─── part can be here.
}
```

Next, imagine that the slice allocation is happening inside the loop:

```
func BenchmarkMemorySlow(b *testing.B) {
    for b.Loop() {
```

(continued)
```
        image := make([]byte, 1_000_000)
        resize(image)
    }
}
```

Compare the results:

```
$ go test ./url -bench=BenchmarkMemory -benchmem
BenchmarkMemoryFast-10   496805610   2.138 ns/op        0 B/op  0 allocs/op
BenchmarkMemorySlow-10       28574   41410 ns/op  1007619 B/op  1 allocs/op
```

The second benchmark is about 20,000 times slower than the first, leading to skewed measurements. We should put our intensive setup and cleanup logic outside the loop.

3.2.2 Using sub-benchmarks

As we use subtests, we can use sub-benchmarks to get a richer perspective on String's performance while reassembling URLs of various lengths. Like subtests, the *B type has a Run method that we can use to run a sub-benchmark, as follows.

Listing 3.9 **Writing sub-benchmarks** (`url/url_test.go`)

```
package url

import (
    "fmt"
    "strings"
    "testing"
)

. . .

func BenchmarkURLStringLong(b *testing.B) {
    for _, n := range []int{10, 100, 1_000} {        ◄── Ranges over a slice of integers
        u := &URL{
            Scheme: strings.Repeat("x", n),           Returns a string that repeats the given
            Host:   strings.Repeat("y", n),           string n times. Repeat("x", 10), for
            Path:   strings.Repeat("z", n),           example, returns a string of 10 "x"s.
        }
        b.Run(fmt.Sprintf("%d", n), func(b *testing.B) {
            for b.Loop() {
                _ = u.String()
            }
        })
    }
}
```

We're looping over an `int` slice, creating incrementally larger URLs, and running sub-benchmarks to measure `String`'s performance with these URLs. We use the n variable as a benchmark name after converting n to a `string` using `fmt.Sprintf`.

This setup gives us a clear picture of how the growing size of URLs affects `String`'s performance. Let's use the `bench` flag to run only our new benchmark function:

```
$ go test ./url -bench=BenchmarkURLStringLong -benchmem
BenchmarkURLStringLong/10-10
    13146908   91.10 ns/op  112 B/op   4 allocs/op
BenchmarkURLStringLong/100-10
    8193639 144.60 ns/op  848 B/op   4 allocs/op
BenchmarkURLStringLong/1000-10
    8193639 561.60 ns/op 8192 B/op   4 allocs/op
```

> **Most URLs are about this length.** (points to BenchmarkURLStringLong/**100**-10 line)

These benchmark runs show that `String` takes longer to process as the length of the URLs increases. On the bright side, `String` makes four allocations (`4 allocs/op`) every time. Let's see where it makes these memory allocations so we can understand how to optimize it.

3.2.3 *Profiling: Chasing out memory allocations*

Although benchmarks show us a piece of code's performance, profiling helps us understand why the code behaves that way, revealing where to focus our efforts to optimize it.

Our first step is generating a memory profile, using the `memprofile` flag as follows. This command runs the benchmarks as before and generates a memory profile:

```
$ go test ./url -bench=BenchmarkURLStringLong
                 -benchmem
                 -memprofile=mem.out
. . .
```

Now that we have a memory profile file, we can pass this file to the performance profiling tool (`pprof`) and inspect `String`'s memory allocations using the `list` flag:

```
$ go tool pprof -list String mem.out
. . .
18.83GB     18.83GB (flat, cum)    100% of Total
    .           .          35:func (u *URL) String() string {
    .           .          36:    if u == nil {
    .           .          37:      return ""
    .           .          38:    }
    .           .          39:    var s string
    .           .          40:    if sc := u.Scheme; sc != "" {
    .           .          41:      s += sc
 2.44GB     2.44GB         42:      s += "://"
    .           .          43:    }
    .           .          44:    if h := u.Host; h != "" {
 4.66GB     4.66GB         45:      s += h
    .           .          46:    }
    .           .          47:    if p := u.Path; p != "" {
```

> **Initialization does not allocate because we change only string headers (not the underlying bytes). See appendix c.** (points to line 40–41)

> **Each concatenation allocates new memory because strings are immutable.** (points to lines 42 and 45)

```
4.63GB     4.63GB     48:       s += "/"          Each concatenation allocates new
7.10GB     7.10GB     49:       s += p            memory because strings are immutable.
   .          .       50:     }
   .          .       51:     return s
   .          .       52:}
. . .
```

`String` allocates four times while combining strings, creating new strings. Strings are immutable byte slices that point to a fixed-size underlying byte array. Slicing strings doesn't copy that array, but combining strings copies the underlying array to a new one (*allocates*).

Before optimizing `String`, let's save the current results to a file so we can compare them with the new results later. Because environmental noise (system load, hardware temperature, and so on) may affect the results, we should run benchmarks repeatedly to minimize environmental impact. For that purpose, we can use the `count` flag:

```
$ go test ./url -bench=BenchmarkURLStringLong
                -benchmem
                -count=20 > old.benchmark
```

This command runs the benchmark function 20 times. If we're unsatisfied with the results, we can repeat with a larger number.

TIP See https://go.dev/doc/diagnostics for more about diagnosing Go programs.

3.2.4 Optimizing code

Now let's optimize the `String` method. Instead of producing more work for the garbage collector and slowing `String` by making memory allocation requests from the operating system each time we combine strings, we can use the `strings` package's `Builder` type to combine strings. This type accumulates bytes in its internal buffer without making additional allocations. The new `String` code uses a `Builder` to reassemble a URL string, as follows.

Listing 3.10   Optimizing the `String` method (`url/url.go`)

```
func (u *URL) String() string {
    if u == nil {
        return ""
    }

    const (
        lenSchemeSeparator = len("://")        Calculates the string literal's length
        lenPathSeparator   = len("/")          with the built-in len function
    )
    lenURL := len(u.Scheme) + lenSchemeSeparator +
        len(u.Host) + lenPathSeparator +       Calculates the target
        len(u.Path)                            total string length
```

```
var s strings.Builder                 ◄──
s.Grow(lenURL)                        ◄──────┐
                                             │        Initializes a Builder with
                                             │        an empty internal buffer
if sc := u.Scheme; sc != "" {
    s.WriteString(sc)                 ◄──────┤        Sets the internal buffer size to the total
    s.WriteString("://")              ◄──────┘        length of the URL string we'll produce
}
if h := u.Host; h != "" {
    s.WriteString(h)                  ◄──────┐        Writes the string into the internal
}                                            │        buffer without extra allocation
if p := u.Path; p != "" {
    s.WriteByte('/')                  ◄──────┤
    s.WriteString(p)                  ◄──────┘
}
                                    ┌─── Writes the byte to the internal
return s.String()                 ◄─┤    buffer without extra allocation
}                                   └─── Returns the internal buffer as a string
```

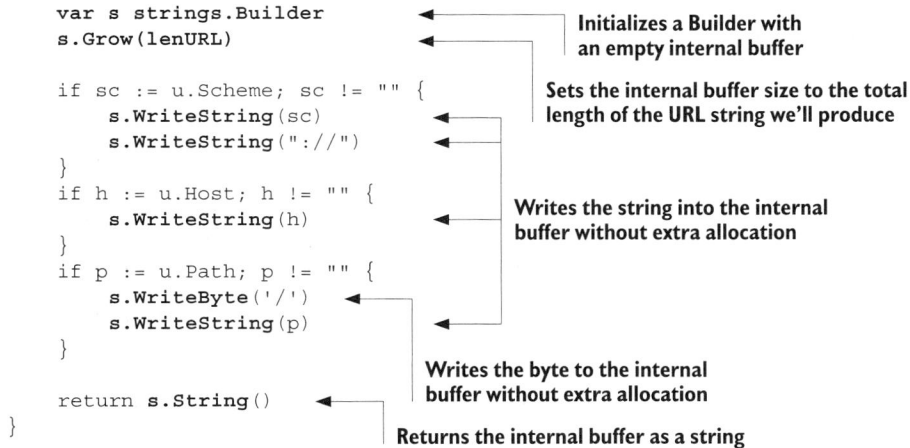

NOTE Byte literals are represented within single quotes (e.g., `'G'`).

When we declare the `Builder` variable `s`, we use `Grow` to set the internal buffer to a large-enough size to hold the final URL string. This allocates a memory block once. Otherwise, `Builder` inefficiently allocates many times when its buffer is full while we add strings.

> **TIP** Calling the built-in `len` function is efficient because it returns the length directly from a string's internal length field without looping over the string to count the bytes.

Next, we write strings to the buffer using `WriteString` and `WriteByte` without making additional memory allocations. Finally, we return the accumulated buffer as a string.

Deep dive: strings.Builder vs. bytes.Buffer and unsafe operations

Besides the `strings.Builder` type, the standard library has the `bytes.Buffer` type. These types have a similar API so that we can switch between them. What is the difference?

We commonly use `Buffer` to capture log messages, assemble HTTP request bodies, and so on. It's handy for accumulating bytes incrementally. When it comes to accumulating bytes (or strings) and then reading them as a string, `Builder` shines because it prevents memory allocations when converting the accumulated bytes to a string using the `String` method, as follows:

```
type Builder struct {
    . . .
    // External users should never get direct access to this buffer,
    // since the slice at some point will be converted to a string
    // using unsafe,. . .
    buf []byte
```

(continued)
```
}

// String returns the accumulated string.
func (b *Builder) String() string {
    return unsafe.String(
        unsafe.SliceData(b.buf),
        len(b.buf),
    )
}
```

Returns the byte slice as a string without copying the bytes

Returns an unsafe pointer to the first byte of a byte slice. The garbage collector does not track unsafe pointers, and they lack type safety: the memory these pointers point to can change unexpectedly, leading to dangling pointers if misused.

`b.buf` is the `Builder`'s internal buffer that holds data written in a byte slice. Converting this buffer to a string with `string(b.buf)` would copy the slice into a new string and make a memory allocation. Instead, the `String` method uses the `unsafe` package to return its buffer as a string without copying, preventing extra memory allocation:

1 `unsafe.SliceData([]T) uintptr` returns a pointer to the first slice element.
2 `unsafe.String(ptr uintptr, len int) string` returns the memory region beginning from the pointer to the length as a string without copying.

Because the returned string shares `b.buf`'s memory, `Builder.String` never allocates memory after conversions. In Go, however, strings are immutable, and modifying their underlying bytes can lead to undefined behavior. Unlike the `Buffer.Bytes` method, which returns its internal buffer, `Builder` doesn't have such a method because it never exposes its internal buffer, which means we can't accidentally change the underlying bytes of the returned strings.

Finally, using `unsafe` in our code should be extremely rare because it is not type-safe and is not covered by the Go 1 compatibility promise. It's more effective to work directly with byte slices to prevent string conversions or to use standard library types like `Builder` to write efficient code that eliminates unnecessary memory allocations. See https://pkg.go.dev/unsafe and https://go.dev/doc/go1compat for more information.

3.2.5   Comparing benchmarks

Now that we have a new implementation, let's benchmark it and find out whether it's efficient. We should consider benchmark results relatively; we can't know whether `String` is inefficient unless we compare it with another `String` implementation. We already have the old results in the `old.benchmark` file. Let's benchmark the new implementation and save:

```
$ go test ./url -bench=BenchmarkURLStringLong
                 -benchmem
                 -count=20 > new.benchmark
```

The next step is using the `benchstat` tool to compare the results. Unlike other Go tools, this one doesn't come with the Go tool chain out of the box, so we must install it ourselves:

```
$ go install golang.org/x/perf/cmd/benchstat@latest
```

Now we can compare the old and new results:

```
$ benchstat old.benchmark new.benchmark
. . .
```

	old.benchmark	new.benchmark	
	sec/op	sec/op	vs base
URLStringLong/10-10	90.54n ± 0%	25.89n ± 0%	-71.40%
URLStringLong/100-10	143.15n ± 0%	50.75n ± 1%	-64.54%
URLStringLong/1000-10	784.0n ± 1%	269.5n ± 2%	-65.62%
geomean	**216.6n**	**70.75n**	**-67.34%**

	old.benchmark	new.benchmark	
	B/op	B/op	vs base
URLStringLong/10-10	112.00 ± 0%	48.00 ± 0%	-57.14%
URLStringLong/100-10	848.0 ± 0%	320.0 ± 0%	-62.26%
URLStringLong/1000-10	8.000Ki ± 0%	3.000Ki ± 0%	-62.50%
geomean	**919.7**	**361.4**	**-60.71%**

	old.benchmark	new.benchmark	
	allocs/op	allocs/op	vs base
URLStringLong/10-10	4.000 ± 0%	1.000 ± 0%	-75.00%
URLStringLong/100-10	4.000 ± 0%	1.000 ± 0%	-75.00%
URLStringLong/1000-10	4.000 ± 0%	1.000 ± 0%	-75.00%
geomean	**4.000**	**1.000**	**-75.00%**

We benchmarked the old and new `String` methods and see 3X improvement compared with the previous version:

- Generating URL strings drops from 216 nanoseconds (ns) to 70 ns.
- Memory per operation drops from 919 bytes to 361 bytes.
- Memory allocations drop from four to one.

NOTE A *nanosecond* is a billionth of a second.

Generating URLs for different URL lengths takes the following times:

- Generating 10-byte URLs drops from 90 ns to 25 ns.
- Generating 100-byte URLs drops from 143 ns to 50 ns.
- Generating 1,000-byte URLs drops from 784 ns to 269 ns.

These improvements result in faster performance and more efficient memory use. The old method rebuilt strings with + on each step, allocating new buffers and scattering data across the heap. The new version reserves one contiguous slice per call, which fits in the CPU's L1 cache. With only one allocation, Go's garbage collector scans far fewer objects.

Suppose that we call `String` in a high-load service. With the new code, even the slowest processing (tail latency) finishes faster, and memory use stays low, leading to more consistent performance under load and fewer garbage-collection pauses. We'll stick with this implementation.

TIP   This output is simplified for clarity. See `benchstat`'s documentation at https://mng.bz/qROw for more information on formatting.

Deep dive: Alternating measurements for accurate results

When we run 20 benchmarks in a row against the old `String` method and 20 against the new one, any drift in machine temperature, CPU frequency, background tasks, or garbage collection can bias one set of results. Currently, we run benchmarks consecutively for each version:

```
// O = old version, N = new version
OOOOOOOOOOOOOOOOOOOO > old.benchmark          ◀── Runs 20 consecutive
NNNNNNNNNNNNNNNNNNNN > new.benchmark                benchmarks against the
                                                    unoptimized String method

                                              ◀── Runs 20 consecutive
                                                    benchmarks against the
                                                    optimized String method
```

For simple methods like `String`, running benchmarks consecutively is fine, but this approach may lead to inaccurate results due to environmental factors between blocks of measurements. We should use the following approach if we want more reliable results:

```
ONONONONONONONONONONONONONONONONONONONON      ◀──┐ Interleaved execution
```

A straightforward way to do this is to compile each version using the `c` and `o` flags. The following commands produce the executables `old.test` and `new.test`. Run the following before optimizing the code:

```
$ go test ./url -c -o old.test
```

Run the following after optimizing the code:

```
$ go test ./url -c -o new.test
```

Now that we have two executable test binaries, we can benchmark them separately:

```
$ ./old.test -test.bench=. -test.benchmem -test.count=1 >> old.benchmark
$ ./new.test -test.bench=. -test.benchmem -test.count=1 >> new.benchmark
```

Repeat these commands 20 times, and then compare the results using `benchstat`. By alternating the benchmark runs between versions this way, we mitigate the effect of environmental noise because we would be measuring both versions under similar conditions.

3.3 Compiler optimizations

Before Go 1.24, a benchmark function looked like this:

```
func BenchmarkPow(b *testing.B) {          Iterates for b.N times
    for range b.N {
        Pow(5, 1)                          Runs this code until getting
    }                                      an accurate measurement
}
```

This benchmark function uses the `testing.B` type's `N` integer variable to loop. The `testing` package may rerun the same benchmark function many times, gradually increasing `N`.

> **WARNING** A function under a benchmark should not use `N` to change its behavior. To get accurate results, avoid using `N` in a function that you benchmark.

Go 1.24 introduced the `testing.B.Loop` method as a safer, more efficient way to write benchmarks, but we commonly see the classical approach in existing code. Understanding the classical approach is important because compiler optimizations can silently strip out the very calls we're trying to benchmark. Recognizing these optimizations helps us write more reliable benchmarks and also deepens our understanding of the Go compiler. Let's start by looking at the classical approach.

3.3.1 Inlining and dead-code elimination

While using the classical benchmarking approach, be careful when benchmarking pure or simple functions that the compiler can optimize away because they might skew benchmark results. Consider the pure function in the following example:

```
func Pow(a, n int) int {
    for range n {
        a *= n
    }
    return a
}
```

This function's code is short, has no side effects, and always returns the same result when called with the same arguments. We can benchmark this function with `b.N` as follows:

```
func BenchmarkPow1(b *testing.B) {
    for range b.N {
        Pow(5, 1)          ◄────  The benchmark does
    }                             not use Pow's result.
}
```

The compiler can remove the Pow call from this benchmark because it can calculate the function's result at compile time or because the benchmark doesn't use the Pow's result. Looking at the measurements, we can prove this. We see a suspiciously fast operation time:

```
BenchmarkPow1-10   1000000000   0.3119 ns/op
```

This result is not correct. We would have received the same result if we removed the Pow call from the benchmark function. This benchmark measures its own loop's performance.

NOTE   Operation time of less than 1 ns is a red flag we should watch out for.

Here's how our benchmark would look after compiler optimizations:

```
func BenchmarkPow(b *testing.B) {
    for range b.N {
        /* empty: no operation */
    }
}
```

The compiler recognizes that Pow's result never affects the benchmark, so it removes the Pow call. First, it inlines Pow's body into the benchmark function (folding Pow's instructions directly into the loop to eliminate call overhead). Next, it sees that those inlined instructions produce a value nobody uses and applies dead-code elimination, stripping them out.

3.3.2 The sink variable

To get an accurate result, we should prevent the compiler from removing the Pow call. One common trick is using an exported package variable named Sink, as follows:

```
var Sink int          ◄────  Declares an exported package
                             variable named Sink
func BenchmarkPow(b *testing.B) {
    var sink int      ◄────  Declares a variable named sink that
    for range b.N {          is local to the benchmark function
        sink = Pow(5, 1)   ◄────  Assigns the Pow's result
    }                             to the local variable
    Sink = sink       ◄────  Assigns the last result to the
}                             package-level variable for once
```

This technique works because it's difficult for the compiler to track cross-package interactions of a package variable like `Sink`, so the compiler can't easily assume that removing `Pow` is safe. The compiler should assume that `Pow`'s result is needed somewhere else in the code.

> **WARNING** A common mistake is using an unexported package-level variable, such as declaring `var sink int` instead of `var Sink int`. We should export the variable to make the compiler's optimization efforts more difficult.

We also use the local variable `sink` to cut CPU memory-access costs associated with a package variable, ensuring a more accurate performance evaluation of `Pow`. We should use this solution only when we're suspicious of our measurements, however, not apply it blindly to every benchmark. Although this method solves the issue, it pollutes the benchmark code. Another drawback is that the compiler is constantly improving, so this solution may not work in a future release.

> **TIP** Avoid complicating benchmarks unless necessary. Clarity matters more.

3.3.3 *A bright new future*

As of Go 1.24, we have a much better way: the `Loop` method. This method helps us benchmark our code safely without dealing with compiler optimizations ourselves:

```
func BenchmarkPow(b *testing.B) {
    for b.Loop() {
        Pow(5, 1)                    ◄─── Automatically safeguards this code
    }                                     against compiler optimizations
}
```

We use `b.Loop` instead of `b.N`, instructing the compiler to turn off optimizations. The compiler recognizes the pattern for `b.Loop() { ... }` and ensures that it doesn't apply optimizations to the code inside the loop. But it can still optimize any functions called by `Pow`, and that's good. We want to see the actual performance of our code to get a complete, accurate picture of how it would perform in real-world scenarios.

Also, `Loop` makes it straightforward to do setup and cleanup work by putting these logics outside the benchmark loop. In the classical approach, we have to call methods, such as `B.ResetTimer` to get accurate measurements, which can be error-prone and tedious.

Moreover, `Loop` is more efficient than the classical approach. One of the downsides of the classical benchmarking approach is that the `testing` package may need to rerun the whole benchmark function to get accurate results. With `Loop`, that's not the case.

Remember, however, that the `Loop` function is still under active development. Some explanations in this chapter may be outdated when new Go versions are released. Always check the documentation and follow new Go releases to keep yourself current.

TIP   Avoid using N and Loop in the same benchmark for more accurate results. Prefer the newer Loop method when writing benchmarks; it's more efficient and simpler, and it's designed specifically to prevent pitfalls in compiler optimizations.

3.4   Parallel testing

Another optimization we can make in our development workflow is running tests in parallel, which reduces the total time it takes to run tests. Running parallel tests is especially useful when dealing with large test suites.

By default, the testing package runs each test function, including subtests, sequentially. Each test runs in a separate goroutine. This doesn't mean that they run in parallel, however. In this section, we'll learn how to run tests in parallel and deal with possible race conditions.

NOTE   Concurrency does not mean parallelism. See appendix E for details.

3.4.1   Running tests in parallel

To finish running tests faster, we can run them in parallel by explicitly marking them with the Parallel method within a test function at the beginning of the test, as follows.

Listing 3.11   Parallel tests (url/parallel_test.go)

```
package url

import (
    "testing"
    "time"
)

func TestParallelOne(t *testing.T) {        Runs the test in
    t.Parallel()                     ◄───┘  parallel to other tests
    time.Sleep(5 * time.Second)      ◄──┐
    . . .
}                                         Simulates a long-running test
func TestParallelTwo(t *testing.T) {
    t.Parallel()
    time.Sleep(5 * time.Second)      ◄──┘
    . . .
}

func TestSequential(t *testing.T) {
    . . .
}
```

We have two parallel tests (TestParallelOne and TestParallelTwo) and one sequential test (TestSequential). Go runs the sequential test first and then the parallel ones:

```
$ go test ./url -run='Parallel|Sequential' -v
=== RUN    TestParallelOne
=== PAUSE TestParallelOne
=== RUN    TestParallelTwo
=== PAUSE TestParallelTwo
=== RUN    TestSequential
--- PASS: TestSequential (0.00s)
=== CONT   TestParallelOne
=== CONT   TestParallelTwo
--- PASS: TestParallelTwo (5.00s)
--- PASS: TestParallelOne (5.00s)
PASS
ok 5.451s
```

Pauses the parallel tests

Runs the sequential test

Resumes the parallel tests

The parallel tests were paused until the sequential test finished running and then resumed. Notice that each parallel test takes 5 seconds to complete. Because some of the tests run in parallel, the total test run took about 6 seconds instead of 10.

We could run tests with reduced parallelism, perhaps because we're running them in a resource-intensive environment. We can control the parallelism using the `-parallel` flag:

```
$ go test ./url -run='Parallel|Sequential' -v -parallel 1
=== RUN    TestParallelOne
=== PAUSE TestParallelOne
=== RUN    TestParallelTwo
=== PAUSE TestParallelTwo
=== RUN    TestSequential
--- PASS: TestSequential (0.00s)
=== CONT   TestParallelOne
=== CONT   TestParallelOne
--- PASS: TestParallelOne (5.00s)
--- PASS: TestParallelTwo (5.00s)
PASS
ok 11.065s
```

Each test ran sequentially, doubling the total run time to 11 seconds. This is the default `testing` package behavior when we don't mark tests with the `Parallel` method. By default, the maximum level of parallelism is set to the number of CPU cores available on the machine or the number allocated to a virtual machine—effectively, the logical CPU count.

> **TIP** We can set the `-parallel` flag to any number, but setting it to a number larger than the CPU cores can backfire and increase the test runtime instead of reducing it. Adjust the level of parallelism depending on the environment or available resources.

3.4.2 *Running subtests in parallel*

Remember that subtests are separate test functions. As listing 3.12 shows, to run them in parallel, we must mark both the subtests and their parent test as parallel. If we don't, the parent test runs sequentially, making any parallel tests wait until the parent test completes.

Listing 3.12   Parallel subtests (`url/parallel_test.go`)

```
func TestQuery(t *testing.T) {
    t.Parallel()

    t.Run("byName", func(t *testing.T) {
        t.Parallel()
        time.Sleep(5 * time.Second)
        . . .
    })

    t.Run("byInventory", func(t *testing.T) {
        t.Parallel()
        time.Sleep(5 * time.Second)
        . . .
    })
}
```

Running this test outputs the following:

```
$ go test ./url -run=Query -v
. . .
--- PASS: TestSequential
--- PASS: TestParallelTwo (5.00s)
--- PASS: TestParallelOne (5.00s)
--- PASS: TestQuery (0.00s)
    --- PASS: TestQuery/byName (5.00s)
    --- PASS: TestQuery/byInventory (5.00s)
PASS
ok      github.com/inancgumus/gobyexample/testing/parallel 5.492s
```

When the sequential test was over, four tests were run in parallel. Having 10 cores on my machine allowed tests to run in parallel; each test took 5 seconds to complete. Because the tests ran in parallel, the test run took about 6 seconds instead of 20 seconds.

3.4.3   Detecting data races

Running tests in parallel helps us detect data race issues within our code or tests early. A *data race* occurs when multiple goroutines access the same variable simultaneously and at least one of them modifies it. The next listing shows an example.

Listing 3.13   Data race (`url/parallel_test.go`)

```
var counter int

func incr() { counter++ }  // line 35 in parallel_test.go

func TestIncr(t *testing.T) {
```

```
    t.Parallel()
    t.Run("once", func(t *testing.T) {
        t.Parallel()
        incr()
        if counter != 1 {
            t.Errorf("counter = %d, want 1", counter)
        }
    })

    t.Run("twice", func(t *testing.T) {
        t.Parallel()
        incr()
        incr()
        if counter != 3 {
            t.Errorf("counter = %d, want 3",
                counter)
        }
    })
}
```

◄——— **This test has a bug because it assumes
that the counter would be 3.**

There are significant issues with these tests and the code:

- Tests depend on one another.
- The counter is not reset between tests.
- The counter is not concurrent-safe.

Recall that different goroutines run different tests. Because incr increments a package-level variable counter, and the tests are running in parallel, this should cause a data race issue. We can catch a potential data race by enabling Go's race detector with the -race flag.

The race detector might not catch every data race, however, so we improve the hit ratio by setting the count flag to an arbitrarily high number:

```
$ go test ./url -run=DataRace -race -count=10
. . .
===================
WARNING: DATA RACE
Read at 0x0001044893e8 by goroutine 1:
  incr()
      parallel_test.go:35 +0x38

Previous write at 0x0001044893e8 by goroutine 2:
  incr()
      parallel_test.go:35 +0x50
===================
. . .
```

◄——— **Goroutine 1 was reading from the
memory address 0x0001044893e8.**

◄——— **Goroutine 2 was writing
to the memory address
0x0001044893e8.**

We see two subtest goroutines: goroutine 1 and goroutine 2. They concurrently read and write to the same counter variable (memory address 0x0001044893e8). While goroutine 1 was reading counter, goroutine 2 was writing the same variable, creating the data race issue:

```
counter++ is the same as counter = counter + 1
                                ^            ^
                              write        read
```

Because the detector adds assembly code to the final binary to monitor memory access, it can significantly slow our programs and use more resources. Therefore, we should use it only in test builds or testing environments, not in production deployments.

> **TIP**   Because the race detector works on the executed code paths, increasing the test coverage may also detect more data races.

3.5   *Exercises*

1 Although we have complete test coverage, the URL.String method still has a bug: it doesn't handle opaque URLs in the form data:text/plain. Add a test case to fix the problem.

2 Add new test cases to test URL.String with a mixture of empty URL fields—a test for a URL without a host, another without a path, and so on.

3 Interpret the benchmark results. Rerun benchmarks with longer strings.

4 Benchmark the difference between growing the buffer up front without using strings.Builder.Grow to observe how it affects the results.

5 Analyze the memory profile of the new String implementation using pprof.

6 Fix the data race in the code that TestIncr tests, and rerun the test. Fix the other issues (the ones in listing 3.13) in the test and the code.

Summary

- Test coverage finds untested parts of the code but doesn't guarantee correctness.
- Benchmarks measure a piece of code's performance by running it repeatedly.
- Profiling helps us understand where our code spends its time and memory.
- Benchmarking trivial functions can produce inaccurate results because of compiler optimizations, such as inlining and dead-code elimination. Using a package-level variable can prevent these optimizations. Prefer using B.Loop, which is immune to most compiler optimizations and more efficient than the traditional B.N approach.
- Running tests in parallel may reduce total test runtime.
- The race detector helps us detect race-condition issues.

Command-line
interfaces

This chapter covers

- Structuring and writing user-friendly command-line tools
- Parsing command-line arguments and flags
- Exploring the standard library's `os` and `flag` packages
- Extending the `flag` package with custom types

Command-line tools are essential for automating tasks, running programs, and improving productivity. Compared with graphical interfaces, command-line tools offer faster, more customizable ways to handle repetitive tasks with greater consistency and fewer errors.

This chapter introduces parsing flags and arguments using the standard library's `os` and `flag` packages. *Arguments* are typically the necessary parameters for the program (i.e., a URL), whereas *flags* are optional settings that modify how the program behaves (e.g., `-n`).

In this chapter and the following three chapters, we'll create a command-line tool named HIT alongside a concurrent HTTP client called HIT client. The HIT tool sends HTTP requests and measures and reports HTTP server performance using the HIT client:

```
$ ./hit -n 1_000_000 -c 20 http://localhost:8082

  /\ \_\ \    /\ \    /\___\
  \ \  __ \   \ \ \   \/_/\ \/
   \ \_\ \_\   \ \_\     \ \_\
    \/_/\/_/    \/_/      \/_/
```

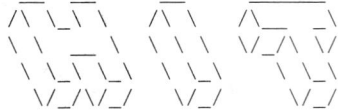

The -n flag is the number of requests to send. The -c flag is the concurrency level.

```
Sending 1000000 requests to "http://localhost:8082" (concurrency: 20)

Summary:
    Success:  100%
    RPS:      97854.73
    Requests: 1000000
    Errors:   0
    Bytes:    12000000
    Duration: 10.22s
    Fastest:  1ms
    Slowest:  5ms
```

> **NOTE** As we've seen, flags customize a program's behavior. The `-v` flag in `go test -v`, for example, instructs the tool to print verbose output.

In the HIT tool's output, we see that the HIT client sends 1 million HTTP requests to an HTTP server. The entire operation finishes in roughly 10 seconds without errors, handling nearly 100,000 HTTP requests per second, with the quickest response taking 1 millisecond.

We'll start by exploring the structure of the HIT tool and client. To understand how flag parsing works under the hood, we'll write a custom parser using the `os` package. Later, we'll switch to the `flag` package and explore its capabilities. Along the way, we'll improve our understanding by adding custom types through `flag` interfaces and input validation. By the chapter's end, you'll have enough knowledge to build your own command-line tools.

> **NOTE** We start by creating the HIT tool itself. In chapter 6, we'll build the HIT client. Beginning with the HIT tool prevents later refactoring that complicates understanding. Instead, we'll focus on specific topics without including unnecessary details. In a real-world project, it might be more effective to follow an opposite approach: start with the client, and then add the tool around it.

4.1   Groundwork

As figure 4.1 shows, our entire program consists of two parts:

- *HIT tool*—Package `main` handles user interactions and prints results.
- *HIT client*—Package `hit` measures and reports the performance of HTTP servers.

We call our command-line interface (CLI) program the HIT tool. The `hit` package is the HIT client. We split the tool logic from the client to improve flexibility. We can modify our CLI program's functionality without touching the client (or vice versa). We can also reuse the client across different programs, such as a web API, and easily test the logic independently of the tool.

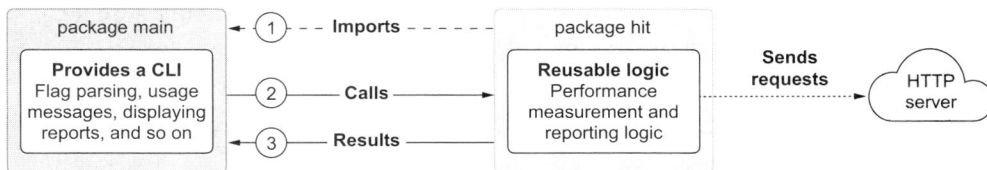

Figure 4.1 **Separating the CLI tool from the `hit` package for reusability. We could add a REST API and reuse the same `hit` package, for example.**

As we see in the following directory structure, we separate executable commands (e.g., the HIT tool) from importable packages (e.g., the HIT client) in different directories to improve the project's reusability, maintainability, and flexibility:

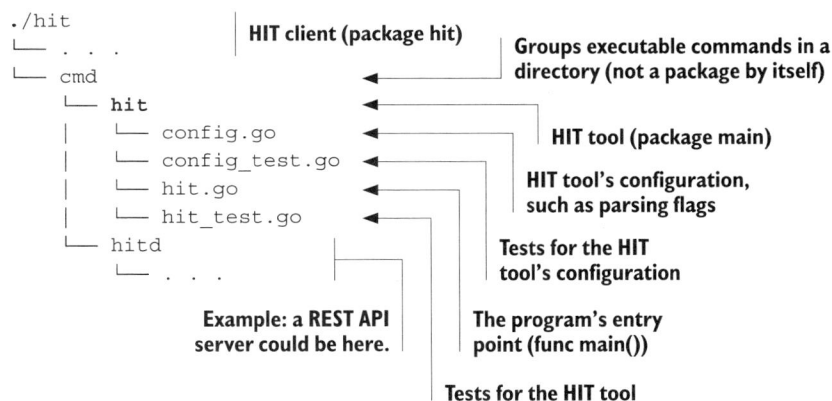

The root directory contains the HIT client for performance measurement and reporting. The files in this directory belong to the `hit` package. Below that directory is a `cmd` directory that contains executable commands, with subdirectories like `hit`, which includes the HIT tool, and `hitd`, which could house a future HTTP server API. Both executables can reuse the same HIT client provided by the `hit` package and print results in the CLI or through the web.

NOTE We will explore writing servers in chapter 8, which includes an exercise on adding a REST API for the HIT client. You can put that API in `cmd/hitd`.

Another advantage of using a `cmd/hit` directory is that `go build` will output an executable with the same name as the directory name. Code built in the `hit` directory, for example, outputs a `hit` executable file (which will be `hit.exe` on a Windows machine).

4.1.1   *Implementing the first version*

Now that we have discussed our project's organization, let's implement the first version. This version prints a logo and a usage message. Usage messages help users understand how to interact with a command-line tool and guide them to use it correctly. The HIT tool's usage message will explain the following flags:

- `-url`—HTTP server URL to send HTTP requests to
- `-n`—Number of requests to send to an HTTP server
- `-c`—Concurrency level while sending HTTP requests
- `-rps`—HTTP requests to send per second

NOTE   We will turn the `-url` flag into a required argument in sections 4.5 and 4.6. For now, we keep it as a flag to focus on understanding how flags work.

These flags will allow users to customize the program's behavior. Because we aim to show the usage, we'll parse the flags later. In the following listing, we declare two package-level constants for the logo and usage message in the `main` package and print them when the tool runs.

> **Listing 4.1   Printing usage** (`hit/cmd/hit/hit.go`)

```go
package main

import "fmt"

const logo = `
 __      __    __     __
/\ \__/\ \   /\ \   /\___  _\
\ \   __ \   \ \ \  \/_/\ \/
 \ \_\ \_\    \ \_\    \ \_\
  \/_/\/_/     \/_/     \/_/`

const usage = `
Usage:
  -url
        HTTP server URL (required)
  -n
        Number of requests
  -c
        Concurrency level
  -rps
        Requests per second`

func main() {
    fmt.Printf("%s\n%s", logo, usage)
}
```

Declares package-level constants, which are accessible throughout the main package

For the values of these constants, we use backticks instead of double quotes. A backtick (`` ` ``) defines a *raw string literal*. The compiler does not interpret escape characters (such as newlines) in raw strings, making it easy to create multiline strings.

> **NOTE** Package-level identifiers such as variables and constants are accessible throughout the package that declares them, even if they are unexported.

4.1.2 Running the first version

Now that we have a simple command-line tool, we can build and run it. The following go build command produces an executable binary named hit in the bin directory:

```
$ go build -o bin/hit ./hit/cmd/hit
```
◀ The -o flag instructs go build to produce a hit (or hit.exe on Windows) executable under the bin directory.

> **TIP** We can change the output binary name using the -o flag.

We can run this binary as follows:

```
$ ./bin/hit
   __   __    __      _____
  /\ \_\ \   /\ \    /\__  _\
  \ \  __ \  \ \ \   \/_/\ \/
   \ \_\ \_\  \ \_\     \ \_\
    \/_/\/_/   \/_/      \/_/

Usage:
  -url
       HTTP server URL (required)
  -n
       Number of requests
  -c
       Concurrency level
  -rps
       Requests per second
```

Although go build is useful before deployment, go run is more practical for rapid development. Instead of rebuilding our program each time we modify its code, we can use

```
$ go run ./hit/cmd/hit
. . .
```
◀ The output is the same as the preceding and omitted for brevity.

Although our program works, it's not easy to maintain. We'll have to change the usage message whenever we modify the flags, which may lead to inconsistent usage messages when the flags change. In section 4.3, we'll look at how to automate this process using the flag package. For now, it's enough to start writing a custom flag parser.

4.2   *Flag parsing*

We have two options for parsing flags:

- Using the os package to parse the flags directly from command-line arguments
- Using the flag package to handle flag parsing automatically

Whether we use os or flag, we always parse flags from command-line arguments because the operating system passes arguments to a program, not flags. Figure 4.2 shows how the HIT tool will use the flag package to parse flags from arguments.

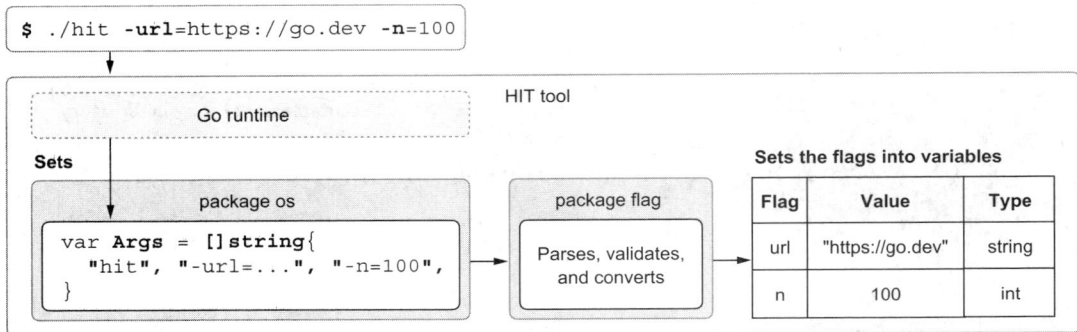

Figure 4.2   The flag package parses and saves the command-line arguments set in os.Args by the Go runtime into type-safe regular Go variables that we provide.

> **NOTE**   n in "-n=100" is the flag's name, and 100 is the flag's value.

The os package's Args variable (a string slice) contains raw command-line arguments. The flag package parses the provided arguments into flags and sets the values of these flags in ordinary and type-safe Go variables. It parses the "-url=https://go.dev" argument and sets "https://go.dev" in a string variable called url, or it assigns 100 to n. We can use these variables in our tool to access the flags and their values.

> **NOTE**   Command-line arguments are string values. The flag package parses each argument into the specified type-safe variable that we can use in our programs.

Instead of starting with the flag package, we'll build a custom flag parser using os. This parser will convert arguments from os.Args into specific variables, setting the stage for adopting the flag package. Although we could jump straight into using the flag package, parsing arguments manually helps us explore Go's language mechanics. Moreover, learning how to parse command-line arguments manually prepares us to handle scenarios in which the flag package alone is insufficient, such as parsing custom argument syntax or supporting flags that aren't supported directly by the flag package.

4.2.1 Overview

Let's take a quick tour to see how the custom flag parser will work. Parsing flags involves reading and then separating command-line arguments into pairs of flag names and values. `"-n=100"`, for example, becomes `"n"` and `"100"`. Then we update the specified integer variable to `100`. Alternatively, `"-url=https://foo.com"` becomes `"url"` and `"https://foo.com"`. In this case, we update a string variable to `"https:/foo.com"`.

As figure 4.3 illustrates, the parser has a flag set map that associates flag names with *flag value parser* functions. The flag parser extracts string flag values from command-line arguments and passes them to the relevant value parsers. An integer value parser, for example, converts `"100"` to `100` and updates the specified integer variable with `100`.

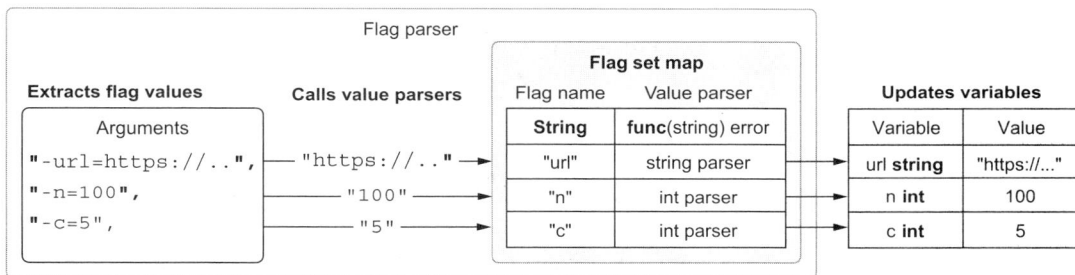

Figure 4.3 Mapping the flags to value parser functions. Value parsers parse the flag values they receive from the flag parser and set the flag values into variables.

Because the flag parser needs to parse string command-line arguments and then set them to variables with various types, we standardize the parsing process through value parsers that have the same signature, allowing us to store and use them uniformly in the map:

```
func(string) error        ◀─────┐ A value parser function's signature
```

Because command-line arguments are always strings, each value parser takes a string input, parses the provided flag string value (e.g., `"100"`), and assigns the parsed flag value to a type-safe and regular Go variable (e.g., `n int`). It also returns an error if it can't parse the flag's value. An integer value parser returns an error if it tries to parse a non-numeric flag value, for example.

4.2.2 Higher-order value parsers

In this section, we'll implement the value parsers and then the flag parser itself. The value parsers take only string input, but the target variable they set is not in their signature. How do they determine which variables to update? The answer is that *higher-order functions* take a pointer to a variable and return a value parser in a closure that updates that variable when the closure is called.

> **TIP** A closure returned by a function can access that function's variables, including its inputs. Functions that return or take other functions are higher-order functions.

Suppose that we want to update an integer variable's value automatically from a parsed flag. As figure 4.4 shows, we call the `intVar` function with that variable's pointer. The function returns a value parser in a closure that wraps around the pointer. Calling the returned closure with a string value (i.e., `"42"`) updates the variable through its pointer to `42`.

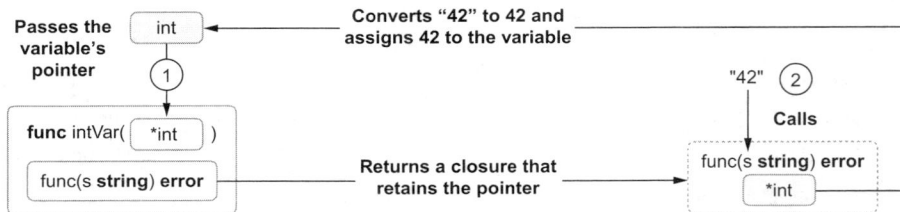

Figure 4.4 Calling `intVar` returns a closure that retains the variable's pointer. Calling the closure updates the original variable's value through the pointer.

Now that we understand how higher-order functions provide value parsers as closures, it's time to implement these functions in code. As listing 4.2 shows, we declare two higher-order functions: `stringVar` and `intVar`. Each function accepts a pointer to the variable it will update and returns a value parser closure that parses and assigns flag values to that variable. We also introduce a function type called `parseFunc` that standardizes the signature for value parsers.

Listing 4.2 Flag value parsers (`hit/cmd/hit/config.go`)

```
package main

import "strconv"

type parseFunc func(string) error

func stringVar(p *string) parseFunc {
    return func(s string) error {
        *p = s
        return nil
    }
}

func intVar(p *int) parseFunc {
```

Declares a function type named parseFunc that takes a string and returns an error

A higher-order function that returns a value parser for parsing string flags

Returns a closure

Modifies the original variable's value through the pointer

A higher-order function that returns a value parser for parsing int flags

```
    return func(s string) error {
        var err error
        *p, err = strconv.Atoi(s)          ◄─────┐ Converts the string to an integer
        return err
    }
}
```

These higher-order functions can work with a specific variable type and return a closure with a consistent function signature. This approach enables us to store value parser functions in a map and use them while parsing flags and their values. Moreover, because higher-order functions are separate, we can easily test them in isolation if needed.

> **NOTE** Atoi is short for *ASCII to integer*. It's a conventional name used since 1971.

4.2.3 Implementing a flag parser

We'll implement the flag parser using the higher-order functions we've developed. As shown in listing 4.3, we'll start by defining a new function called parseArgs. This function takes two parameters: a pointer to a config struct (to save parsed flag values) and a slice of strings (to pass the command-line arguments provided by the operating system). We pass a *config so that parseArgs can update the config fields automatically while parsing.

> **TIP** *Passing a pointer means sharing.* Avoid passing a pointer if you don't want to share the original data with another function. Here, we share the config value with a pointer to allow the parseArgs function to update the original config value's fields.

We declare a flagSet map that binds each flag to a value parser. We bind each value parser to a specific config field. Then we loop over the provided arguments, split each argument into a flag name and its value, and call the value parser to set the corresponding config field. We wrap any parsing errors using Errorf and %w with extra context and return them.

> **Listing 4.3   Flag parser (hit/cmd/hit/config.go)**

```
package main

import (
    "fmt"
    "strings"
    . . .
)

type config struct {
    url string
    n   int
```

```
    c    int
    rps  int
}

func parseArgs(c *config, args []string) error {
    flagSet := map[string]parseFunc{
        "url": stringVar(&c.url),
        "n":   intVar(&c.n),
        "c":   intVar(&c.c),
        "rps": intVar(&c.rps),
    }

    for _, arg := range args {
        name, val, _ := strings.Cut(arg, "=")
        name = strings.TrimPrefix(name, "-")

        setVar, ok := flagSet[name]
        if !ok {
            return fmt.Errorf(
                "flag provided but not defined: -%s",
                name,
            )
        }
        if err := setVar(val); err != nil {
            return fmt.Errorf(
                "invalid value %q for flag -%s: %w",
                val, name, err,
            )
        }
    }

    return nil
}
```

Declares a map of flag names and value parsers

Binds the url flag to a string value parser that will update the config.url field

Binds the flags to integer value parsers that will update the corresponding config fields

Parses an argument into a flag name and value

Removes the leading dash from the flag's name (e.g., -n becomes n)

Fetches the value parser from the map by flag name

setVar parses the flag's value and sets the converted value to a config field.

Passes the %w verb to Errorf to get a new error value that adds context to the error

We implemented a custom flag parser with type-specific value parsers.

The flagSet map binds the flag names to value parsers:

- "url"—stringVar(&c.url)
- "n"—intVar(&c.n)

Each function takes a pointer to a field of the config struct and returns a value parser as a closure. This closure retains the pointer, parses the flag's value, and assigns that value to the provided field. After our flag parser parses the url flag, for example, it passes the flag's value to the closure returned from stringVar(&c.url). Then the closure updates the config.url field.

TIP Naming the struct fields to match the flag names makes it easier to see their relationship. In this case, we use shorter field names for convenience.

Also, passing the %w verb to Errorf returns an error that wraps the original:

```
if err := setVar(val); err != nil {
    return fmt.Errorf(
        ". . .: %w",                    ◄────── %w wraps the error.
        . . ., err,                     ◄──────
    )                                           err is the original error.
}
```

> **TIP** The statement `if err := ...; err != nil` limits the scope of the `err` variable to the `if` statement, preventing potential accidental reuse elsewhere.

`intVar` calls `strconv.Atoi` to parse a flag value. `Atoi` may return a `strconv.ErrSyntax` error if parsing fails. When that happens, our flag parser returns a new error that wraps the `ErrSyntax` error. Then we can detect the wrapped error as follows:

errors.Is(err, strconv.ErrSyntax)

The `errors.Is` function returns `true` if this `err` wraps the `strconv.ErrSyntax` error. This approach enables us to respond precisely by giving users more informative error messages or handling specific errors differently in our program logic. In chapter 8, we'll deep-dive into handling errors using `errors.Is` and see its use in practice.

> **TIP** `errors.Is` detects an underlying error wrapped in an error chain.

Before wrapping up this section, let's discuss some conventions we use in our code. We separate the flags from their parsers to improve maintainability. We can add flags simply by adding new entries in the `flagSet` map. Also, the code is easy to read from top to bottom and maintains left-aligned formatting instead of using deeply nested conditional statements. We can easily see error conditions at a glance, which improves readability and clarity. We favor left-aligned code that returns early, like

```
setVar, ok := flagSet[name]
if !ok {
    return . . .
}
if err := setVar(val); err != nil {
    return . . .
}
```

rather than

```
setVar, ok := flagSet[name]
if ok {
    if err := setVar(val); err != nil {
        return . . .
    }
} else {
    return . . .
}
```

The first version calls `setVar` outside the conditional that checks a flag in the map.

> **TIP** Idiomatic code is left-aligned, which makes exit conditions clear. Avoid deeply right-aligning the code, which makes the code harder to grasp.

Deep dive: Heap allocation and escape analysis

`parseArgs` accepts a `config` pointer instead of returning one. Doing so might prevent a heap allocation because passing pointers to functions usually doesn't cause an allocation on heap, because this operation may use the goroutine's stack. The compiler generates code that automatically manages stacks through simple push and pop operations as functions run and return. By contrast, heap requires additional runtime management, including bookkeeping and garbage collection, making it slower and more expensive.

If the pointer goes out of scope, however, such as when it's returned from a function, it'll likely be allocated on heap. Whether an allocation occurs depends on Go's escape analysis. To analyze whether a variable escapes to heap, we can use the following command:

```
$ go build -gcflags="-m"
```

This command runs the compiler to output escape analysis results, such as which variables will be allocated on heap and which remain on the goroutine's stack. In the following example, the `config` variable escapes to heap:

```
./main.go...: moved to heap: config
```

The line number and whether the config variable escapes to heap are provided for illustrative purposes.

If it stayed on stack, we would see

```
./main.go:...: main config does not escape
```

By analyzing this output, we can make informed decisions about optimizing our code. For a deeper understanding of Go's garbage collection, escape analysis, and allocation strategies, see https://go.dev/doc/gc-guide.

4.2.4   *Integration and setting sensible defaults*

Now that we've built a flag parser, let's integrate it into the HIT tool. In listing 4.4, we skip the first command-line argument (the program's name) and pass the rest to `parseArgs`. We store the parsed flag values in a `config` struct. Then we call `os.Exit` to terminate the program immediately if the parsing fails, returning 1. Status codes help us check success from another program or a script. Usually, code 0 means success, and other codes mean errors.

```go
package main

import (
    "os"
    . . .
)

. . .

func main() {
    var c config
    if err := parseArgs(
        &c, os.Args[1:],
    ); err != nil {
        fmt.Printf("%s\n%s", err, usage)
        os.Exit(1)
    }
    fmt.Printf(
        "%s\n\nSending %d requests to %q (concurrency: %d)\n",
        logo, c.n, c.url, c.c,
    )
}
```

os.Args[1:] skips the program name and returns a slice with the rest of the command-line arguments.

Exits the program and returns the error code 1 to the operating system

Running this program with all flags produces expected results:

```
$ go run ./hit/cmd/hit -url="https://github.com/inancgumus" -n=250 -c=25

 __   __   __      _____
/\ \_\ \  /\ \    /\  __ \
\ \  __ \ \ \ \   \ \/_/\ \/
 \ \_\ \_\ \ \_\   \ \_\
  \/_/\/_/  \/_/    \/_/
Sending 250 requests to "https://github.com/inancgumus" (concurrency: 25)
```

If users skip flags, however, Go falls back to zero values (0 for integers). That leaves the program using and printing zero requests and concurrency:

```
$ go run ./hit/cmd/hit
. . .
Sending 0 requests to "" (concurrency: 0)
```

This isn't helpful. Good command-line tools don't force users to provide every parameter explicitly, especially common ones. Let's improve our tool by setting sensible defaults, which make programs simpler and quicker to use. The next listing shows how to set default values in our program by initializing the config struct fields.

```go
func main() {
    c := config{
        n: 100,
        c: 1,
```

Initializes a config with sensible defaults for n and c fields

```
    }
    if err := parseArgs(&c, os.Args[1:]); err != nil {
        fmt.Printf("%s\n%s", err, usage)
        os.Exit(1)
    }
    fmt.Printf(
        "%s\n\nSending %d requests to %q (concurrency: %d)\n",
        logo, c.n, c.url, c.c,
    )
}
```

Now if users omit some or all flags, the program still behaves sensibly:

```
$ go run ./hit/cmd/hit
. . .
Sending 100 requests to "" (concurrency: 1)
```

Notice that using sensible defaults improves usability. Users aren't forced to provide commonly used values yet can explicitly override these defaults if necessary. The `url` flag is still an empty string, but we'll improve that part when we add validation.

Writing a custom parser from scratch helped us learn about flag handling and other useful Go features. Next, we'll refine our flag handling by exploring the `flag` package, which provides additional functionality that makes parsing more robust and convenient.

4.3   *The flag package*

The `flag` package simplifies many of the manual steps we took earlier, providing built-in support for tasks such as parsing and validating flags and printing usage messages. We'll look at how the `flag` package works and then update our existing `parse-Args` function to use it.

The `flag` package works similarly to our custom flag parser, as figure 4.5 shows. It provides a `FlagSet` type that maintains associations between flag names and individual `Flags`, much like our custom flag parser. Each `Flag` represents a flag, including details such as its name, a usage description, a default value, and a value parser.

We use the `FlagSet` methods, such as `IntVar`, to register a new `Flag` in the `FlagSet` and call its `Parse` method to parse the command-line arguments. `Parse` automatically parses flags and updates the provided variables. Calling `IntVar` with the pointer `&c.n`, for example, registers a flag linked to the `n` field of our `config` value. When we run `Parse` with the argument `"-n=100"`, the `Flag`'s integer value parser updates the `config`'s `n` field to `100`.

Using the `flag` package saves us from manual error handling, parsing, and validation, making our tool easier to maintain.

4.3.1   *Integration*

Now that we've glimpsed how the `FlagSet` type works, let's integrate the `flag` package into our `parseArgs` function, as shown in listing 4.6. After we create a new `FlagSet` with `NewFlagSet`, we register our tool's flags using the `FlagSet` methods

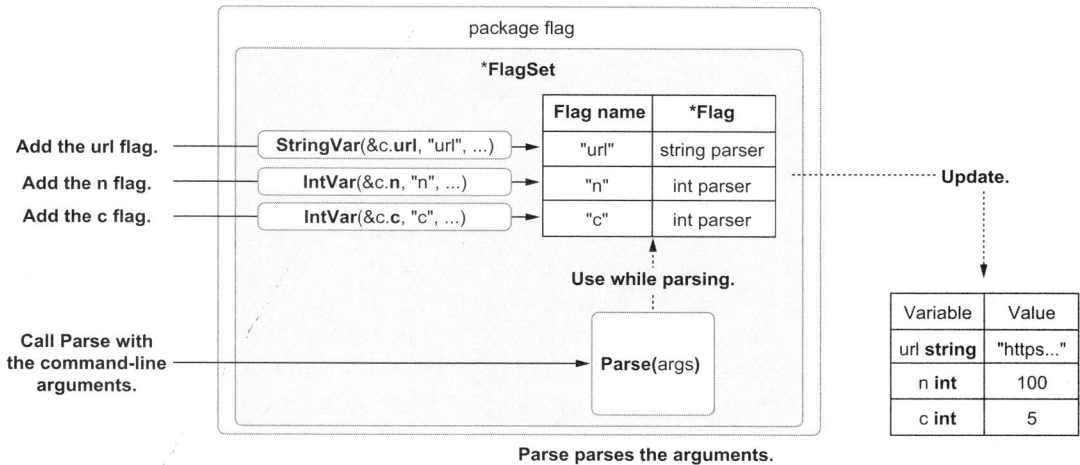

Figure 4.5 `FlagSet` maps flag names to `Flags`. Its `Parse` method parses the flags from command-line arguments, and the value parsers update the variables.

`StringVar` and `IntVar`. Finally, we call the `Parse` method with the command-line arguments to parse the flags and update the `config` fields automatically.

Listing 4.6 Parsing with `FlagSet` (`hit/cmd/hit/config.go`)

```go
package main

import (
    "fmt"
    "os"
    "flag"
)

. . .

func parseArgs(c *config, args []string) error {
    fs := flag.NewFlagSet(
        "hit",
        flag.ContinueOnError,
    )
    fs.StringVar(
        &c.url,
        "url",
        "",
        "HTTP server `URL` (required)",
    )
    fs.IntVar(&c.n, "n", c.n, "Number of requests")
    fs.IntVar(&c.c, "c", c.c, "Concurrency level")
    fs.IntVar(&c.rps, "rps", c.rps, "Requests per second")
```

Sets the FlagSet's name, which is useful in the usage output

Prevents premature exit of the program on errors

Registers a new Flag in the FlagSet that can parse string flag values

Links the url field with the Flag

The name of the command-line flag

The flag's default value (empty string here)

The flag's usage message

```
    return fs.Parse(args)
}
```

The NewFlagSet's first input is the FlagSet's name, usually the program name (such as
"hit"). The second input, ContinueOnError, allows the FlagSet to continue instead
of exiting the program on failures. We want to handle errors and manage status codes
ourselves.

After creating the FlagSet, we register the HIT tool's flags using its StringVar and
IntVar methods. StringVar registers string flags, and IntVar registers integer flags.
StringVar, for example, links the c.url string field to the command-line flag "-url".

Last, we call the Parse method to parse all the flags. Because we set the FlagSet's
behavior to ContinueOnError, if parsing fails, Parse return a non-nil error value. We
can handle this error from our main function to decide what to do, such as exit the
program.

> **TIP** The flag package has a package-level default *FlagSet variable called
> flag.CommandLine and functions such as flag.StringVar and flag.IntVar
> use it to define flags globally. We avoid these functions because the default
> FlagSet can exit the program automatically and write to standard error, mak-
> ing testing harder.

4.3.2 Demonstration

We created a new FlagSet for the HIT tool and set it to continue when an error occurs.
We defined all our flags: url as a string and c, n, and rps as integers. We also set their
default flag values from the config pointer to provide sensible defaults. Now that we can
parse flags using the flag package, let's integrate it into the HIT tool's main function.

Because the FlagSet manages usage messages and prints parsing errors to standard
error on its own, we need to remove the usage constant and avoid printing error messages ourselves if parsing fails. Although I've commented out the lines we'll remove in
the following listing, feel free to remove these lines if you follow along.

Listing 4.7   Removing usage text (hit/cmd/hit/hit.go)

```
package main

. . .

// const usage = . . .

func main() {
    c := config{
        n: 100,
        c: 1,
    }
    if err := parseArgs(&c, os.Args[1:]); err != nil {
        // fmt.Printf("%s\n%s", err, usage)
        os.Exit(1)
```

We can remove
these lines.

```
    }
    fmt.Printf(
        "%s\n\nSending %d requests to %q (concurrency: %d)\n",
        logo, c.n, c.url, c.c,
    )
}
```

We integrated the standard library's `flag` package into our HIT tool. We replaced our custom flag parser with a `FlagSet`, registered each HIT flag (`url`, `n`, `c`, and `rps`) using the `FlagSet` methods (`StringVar` and `IntVar`), and used built-in parsing and error handling. We simplified our code by removing custom error handling and flag parsing.

Let's run the HIT tool and review its output to see the `flag` package in action. First, we'll run our tool with the help flag, `-h`, to see how the `flag` package generates usage messages:

```
$ go run ./hit/cmd/hit -h          ◀──    Boolean flags like -h do
Usage of hit:                              not require a flag value.
  -c int
        Concurrency level (default 1)      ◀──
  -n int                                      Automatically prints the
        Number of requests (default 100)  ◀── flag's sensible defaults
  -rps int
        Requests per second
  -url URL                          ◀──   Prints URL next to the
        HTTP server URL (required)         flag name: -url URL
```

This message lists all registered flags along with their types and sensible defaults. Flags without explicit default values, such as `rps`, don't show a default. The usage also clearly indicates required flags, such as the `url` flag. This output comes directly from the `Flag` definitions we provided when registering flags with methods like `IntVar` and `StringVar`.

> **TIP** Surrounding a text with backticks in a `Flag`'s usage message prints the surrounded text in the final usage message next to the flag's name. The usage message includes `-url URL` because we defined the flag's usage message with `HTTP server `URL` (required)` in listing 4.6.

Next, we run the HIT tool to provide some defined flags explicitly:

```
$ go run ./hit/cmd/hit -c=5 -n=25 -url="https://github.com/inancgumus"

  __  __     __   _____
 /\ \_\ \   /\ \ /\___  _\
 \ \  __ \  \ \ \ \/_/\ \/
  \ \_\ \_\  \ \_\   \ \_\
   \/_/\/_/   \/_/    \/_/

Sending 25 requests to "https://github.com/inancgumus" (concurrency: 5)
```

The tool successfully parses the provided flags and updates the corresponding fields in the `config` struct (c, n, and url). Then it displays a message using the updated fields.

The `flag` package allows flexibility in flag syntax usage. It accepts flags both with and without equal signs, as well as single or double dashes (--), as in this example:

```
$ go run ./hit/cmd/hit -c 5 -n 25 -url "https://github.com/inancgumus"
. . .
$ go run ./hit/cmd/hit --c 5 --n 25 --url "https://github.com/inancgumus"
. . .
```

Observe how the `flag` package handles errors when parsing invalid inputs:

```
$ go run ./hit/cmd/hit -n TWO          ◀──┐   Passes a string to a flag
invalid value "TWO" for flag -n: parse error ◀── that expects an integer
Usage of hit:                          ◀──┐
. . .                                       │   The integer value parser causes the
                                            │   FlagSet to print an error message.

                                      The FlagSet prints the usage
                                      message because of the error.
```

When we provide an invalid value like `"TWO"` for an integer flag, `-n`, the `flag` package automatically prints an error message specifying what went wrong; it also prints the usage again, helping users correct their mistakes without extra instructions.

NOTE POSIX defines single-character options prefixed with one dash (-c). The convention of long, two-dashed flags (--url) comes from GNU. The `flag` package treats `-flag` and `--flag` the same, and a lone `"--"` stops flag parsing. When it sees a standalone --, it treats that as the end of options and stops looking for flags.

Deep dive: Flag definition methods

A `FlagSet` has additional methods for defining flags, including `BoolVar`, `Duration-Var`, `Float64Var`, `Int64Var`, and `TextVar`. The last one is especially useful:

```
func (f *FlagSet) TextVar(
    p       encoding.TextUnmarshaler,
    name    string,
    value   encoding.TextMarshaler,
    usage   string,
)
```

The first parameter requires a type that implements the `TextUnmarshaler` interface, and the third requires one that implements the `TextMarshaler` interface. We can use `TextVar` when one of our types implements those interfaces. Let's look at the `net.IP` type:

```
func (ip IP)  MarshalText() ([]byte, error)   ◄──────┐ Satisfies
func (ip *IP) UnmarshalText(text []byte) error ◄──┐    encoding.TextMarshaler
```
                                                    Satisfies
                                                    encoding.TextUnmarshaler

Because `IP` implements these interfaces, we can parse a flag to an `IP` value as follows:

```
var ip net.IP
fs.TextVar(&ip, "ip", &ip, "`IP` address")
fs.Parse([]string{"-ip", "10.0.0.1"})
fmt.Println(ip)                          ◄─────── Prints 10.0.0.1
```

We can call the `IP` methods on the `ip` variable:

```
fmt.Println(ip.IsPrivate())   ◄─────── Prints true
```

We've parsed the `-ip` flag into the `ip` variable and verified that it's a private IP address.

4.4 Value parsers

The `flag` package's flag value parsers check only whether the provided value can be converted to a specific type; they don't validate whether the resulting value makes sense for the program logic. `IntVar`, for example, checks whether it can convert a flag value to an integer. It accepts nonsensical values, leaving further validation entirely to program logic after parsing. The flags we associate with `IntVar` currently allow negative or zero values, even though using negative requests (`-n`) or zero concurrency (`-c`) doesn't make sense:

```
$ go run ./hit/cmd/hit -n -1
Sending -1 requests to "" (concurrency: 1)
$ go run ./hit/cmd/hit -c 0
Sending 100 requests to "" (concurrency: 0)
```

Currently, we don't send HTTP requests, but when we do, such inputs will be meaningless because we can't send negative or zero requests to an HTTP server. To prevent meaningless inputs like these, we'll delve deeper into the inner workings of the `flag` package in the following sections. We'll explore how a `Flag` can use different value parser types, such as an integer and string flag value parsers. Then we'll create a custom value parser that enforces positive integer values by implementing the `flag.Value` interface. Finally, we'll register this custom value parser with the `FlagSet`'s `Var` method for better validation.

4.4.1   *Value interface*

A `Flag` can work with any flag value parser. As figure 4.6 shows, the `Flag` type's `Value` field can store a type that implements the `flag.Value` interface. This interface represents a value parser that can parse a string flag value and set the result to an associated variable.

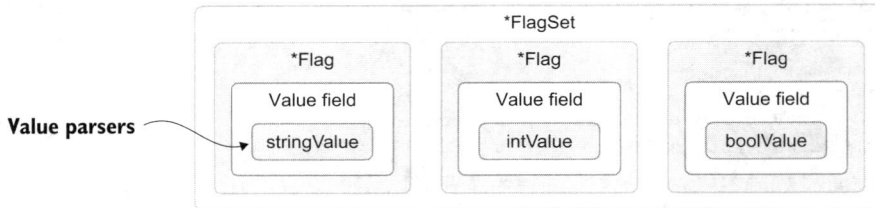

Figure 4.6   A `Flag` has a `Value` field with the type of the `Value` interface. Value parsers, such as `stringValue` and `intValue`, implement the `Value` interface.

A `Flag` can work with any value parser (e.g., `intValue`) depending on how it is defined. The `FlagSet`'s `IntVar` method, for example, can define a new `Flag` in the `FlagSet` with an integer value parser (i.e., `intValue`) that converts the flag string value to an integer. The `flag` package declares the `Flag` type as follows:

```
type Flag struct {
    Name      string          ◀──┐   Flag's name
    Usage     string          ◀──┘   Flag's usage message
    DefValue  string          ◀──┐
    Value     flag.Value      ◀──┤   Flag's default value
}                                 │
                                  └   Flag's flag value parser
```

The `flag` package declares the `Value` interface as follows:

```
type Value interface {
    String() string          ◀──   Queries the associated variable
    Set(string) error        ◀──┐  and returns its value as a string
}                                │
                                 └  Parses a flag's value and sets
                                    it to the associated variable
```

A flag value parser must implement the following methods of the `Value` interface:

- `String` returns the variable's value associated with a `Flag`. A `FlagSet` calls this method once to set the `Flag`'s default value to show it in the usage text later.
- `Set` parses a flag's value and sets it to the variable.

Figure 4.7 illustrates how an `intValue` parser works. Calling `String` returns the associated integer variable's value as a string (`1` becomes `"1"`). Calling `Set` with a string flag value, such as `"42"`, sets that integer variable's value to `42`.

When we define a `Flag`, the `String` method sets its default value. The `Set` method parses and converts the provided string value, updating the corresponding variable.

In summary, `Flag` values have a `Value` field to handle any variable type via a value parser that satisfies the `Value` interface. The `Value` interface has many built-in implementations, including `stringValue`, `intValue`, and `boolValue`. We'll add our custom implementation to validate positive numbers.

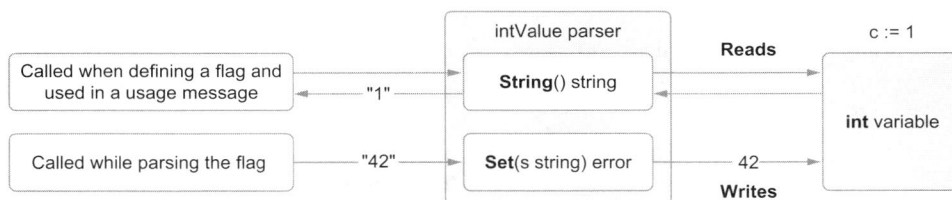

Figure 4.7 The `intValue` is a `Value` implementation that can handle `int` variables. The variable `c` is an integer variable linked to an `intValue` parser.

TIP Idiomatic interfaces like `Value` are lean and focus on shared behavior. In a `FlagSet`, `Flag` instances are concrete types, not interfaces. The `Value` field within a `Flag` is the only interface that reflects its polymorphic behavior. The remaining fields, such as `Name`, remain concrete because they don't require the flexibility of an interface.

4.4.2 Satisfying the Value interface

We've discovered that the `Value` interface allows us to add custom flag value parsing beyond built-in `FlagSet` methods, like `IntVar`. Now we'll implement a custom value parser, `positiveIntValue`, to ensure that the integer flags that our tool uses accept only positive values, which built-in parsers do not enforce.

As listing 4.8 shows, we declare a parser that implements the `Value` interface and add a constructor that can link the parser to an existing integer variable. The parser includes a `String` method to convert the linked variable's value to a string and a `Set` method. `Set` parses and validates a flag value and then updates the linked variable's original value.

Listing 4.8 Satisfying `flag.Value` (hit/cmd/hit/config.go)

```
package main

import (
    "errors"
    "strconv"
    . . .
)

. . .
```

```
type positiveIntValue int

func asPositiveIntValue(p *int) *positiveIntValue {
    return (*positiveIntValue)(p)                          ◄──┐ Returns the *int variable
}                                                              │ as a *positiveIntValue

func (n *positiveIntValue) String() string {
    return strconv.Itoa(int(*n))       ◄──┐ Converts and returns the
}                                          │ variable's integer value as a string

func (n *positiveIntValue) Set(s string) error {
    v, err := strconv.ParseInt(          │ Converts the string input to an integer
        s,
        0,
        strconv.IntSize,       ◄──┐ Tells ParseInt to autodetect
    )                              │ base numerals
    if err != nil {
        return err                 Allows ParseInt to process large numbers,
    }                              such as integers, up to 64 bits
    if v <= 0 {
        return errors.New("should be greater than zero")
    }
    *n = positiveIntValue(v)       ◄──┐ Sets the linked
                                       │ variable's value
    return nil
}
```

We start by declaring a new type, positiveIntValue, based on the built-in int type, and a constructor, asPositiveIntValue, that converts the existing integer pointer to our custom value parser type, linking the original variable to our value parser. Whenever we update the current positiveIntValue's value, we update the original variable's value.

We can convert int pointers to pointers of our value parser because our positive-IntValue type and the built-in int type share an underlying type, int. This lets us link any int variable with our custom value parser without adding complexity.

NOTE   Types that share identical underlying types can be converted to each other. See appendix D for more information on underlying types.

Next, we implement the Value interface with two methods: String and Set. String returns the value of the linked integer variable as a string for use in messages. Set parses the flag value string into an integer using strconv.ParseInt. Then we check whether the integer is positive and return an error if it isn't. If the integer is valid, we update the linked variable's value via the pointer.

NOTE   The Go type system is versatile. We can attach methods to any concrete types in our package, which enables even a simple type like an int to satisfy interfaces.

Our value parser allows us to validate whether integer flags are positive, providing robust validation. Users receive feedback if they enter invalid input, which improves the tool's usability. Next, we'll integrate this value parser into the HIT tool.

> ### strconv.ParseInt vs. strconv.Atoi
>
> Whereas `Atoi` can parse only decimal numbers, `ParseInt` can parse various number formats and bases. It can automatically detect the numbering system:
>
> - A string like `"1000"` is interpreted as decimal (base 10).
> - A string with a leading 0x, such as `"0x50"`, is treated as hexadecimal (base 16).
>
> For details, see https://pkg.go.dev/strconv#ParseInt.

4.4.3 Using Var

Now that we've implemented a value parser, we'll integrate it into our tool by redefining the integer flags, n, c, and rps. Because the FlagSet doesn't support our custom parser directly, we'll use the Var method to link these flags to our parser instead of using IntVar, as shown in the following listing.

Listing 4.9 Using `FlagSet.Var` (`hit/cmd/hit/config.go`)

```go
func parseArgs(c *config, args []string) error {
    fs := flag.NewFlagSet("hit", flag.ContinueOnError)

    fs.StringVar(&c.url, "url", "", "HTTP server `URL` (required)")
    fs.Var(asPositiveIntValue(&c.n), "n", "Number of requests")
    fs.Var(asPositiveIntValue(&c.c), "c", "Concurrency level")
    fs.Var(asPositiveIntValue(&c.rps), "rps", "Requests per second")

    return fs.Parse(args)
}
```

We define each flag using the Var method instead of built-in methods like IntVar. Var expects a Value interface implementation, the flag's name, and its usage message. Because our custom value parser satisfies the Value interface, we can pass it to the Var method.

> **TIP** Var doesn't allow specifying default values. To set a default when using custom parsers, initialize the linked variable to the desired default value before calling Var. See the nearby sidebar for an alternative approach to setting default flag values.

Unlike IntVar and friends, Var doesn't allow us to set a default value for a flag. Instead, Var calls our parser's String method to retrieve the default value from the linked variable. Then it uses that value as the default in the usage message when printing it:

```
$ go run ./hit/cmd/hit -h
Usage of hit:
  -c value
```

```
        Concurrency level (default 1)         ◄─────
-n value                                             These default values are
        Number of requests (default 100)            generated from the result of
-rps value                                           our parser's String method.
        Requests per second
-url URL
        HTTP server URL (required)
. . .
```

Let's verify whether our implementation rejects invalid inputs:

```
$ go run ./hit/cmd/hit -n 0
invalid value "0" for flag -n: should be greater than zero
Usage of hit:
. . .
```

The `FlagSet` automatically calls our parser's `Set` method, which parses and validates the flag's value. If validation fails, `Set` returns an error with an actionable message.

Because `Set` uses `ParseInt`, our tool handles various numeric formats (listing 4.8). Users can use underscores, for example, which make our tool more convenient to use:

```
$ go run ./hit/cmd/hit
        -url https://github.com/inancgumus
        -n 10_000
. . .
Sending 10000 requests to "https://github.com/inancgumus" (concurrency: 100)
```

> **TIP** Using underscores as digit separators improves readability in large numbers. `100_000` is easier to read than `100000` and represents the same value. This approach doesn't affect the number's value; it enhances visual clarity.

Now the HIT tool can validate flags robustly and provide more precise user feedback.

Deep dive: Var

Like `Flag`, `Var` is at the heart of the `FlagSet` type's design. Other `FlagSet` methods also use `Var` internally to define a `Flag` with a specific value parser:

```
func (f *FlagSet) StringVar(
    p *string, name string, value string, usage string,
) {
    f.Var(newStringValue(value, p), name, usage)
}
```

`StringVar` defines a `Flag` with a `stringValue` parser:

```
func newStringValue(val string, p *string) *stringValue {
    *p = val
```

```
    return (*stringValue)(p)
}
```

Other flag definition functions, such as `IntVar`, follow a similar approach.

4.5 Positional arguments

Flags are optional arguments that customize our tool's behavior, but the URL is essential for the tool to function correctly. One way to enforce this is to make the URL a *positional argument*, which ensures that users provide a URL. Because the URL is no longer a flag, we'll retrieve it directly from the command-line arguments. Alternatively, we could make it a required flag, but positional arguments can make specific required inputs more explicit.

> **TIP** Use positional arguments for mandatory parameters that clearly define the tool's primary purpose, such as URLs, and use flags for optional configurations.

4.5.1 Flags vs. positional arguments

Let's start by understanding the differences between flags and positional arguments. Suppose that we have the following `FlagSet`:

```
fs := flag.NewFlagSet("hit", flag.ContinueOnError)
fs.StringVar(&c.url, "url", . . .)
fs.Var(asPositiveIntValue(&c.n), "n", . . .)
```

With this configuration, the `url` flag can be in any position:

```
fs.Parse([]string{
  "-url=https://github.com/inancgumus", "-n=10",
})
fs.Parse([]string{
  "-n=10", "-url=https://github.com/inancgumus",
})
```

This line illustrates the arguments that would be passed to Parse if we ran the program as follows: go run ./hit/cmd/hit -url=https://github.com/inancgumus -n=10.

A positional argument, on the other hand, is sensitive to its position (hence the name):

```
fs.Parse([]string{
  "-n=10", "https://github.com/inancgumus",
})
```

Notice that the last argument isn't a flag. It's `"https://github.com/inancgumus"` without `-url`. We can access this first positional argument using the `FlagSet`'s `Arg` method:

```
fs.Arg(0)
```
◄── **Returns "https://github.com/inancgumus"**

We can retrieve the URL using `Arg(0)` even if there are few or no flags before it:

```
fs.Parse([]string{
  "https://github.com/inancgumus",
})
fmt.Println(fs.Arg(0))          ◄──┘  Prints "https://github.com/
                                      inancgumus"
```

Because flag parsing stops with the first nonflag argument, a positional one should always come after flags. The following example is incorrect, so the flag won't be parsed:

```
fs.Parse([]string{
  "https://github.com/inancgumus", "-n=1",
})                                              Prints "https://github.com/
fmt.Println(fs.Arg(0))          ◄──┘            inancgumus"
fmt.Println(fs.Arg(1))       ◄──┘  Prints "-n=1"
```

Here, both arguments become positional, with the last one no longer treated as a flag. To wrap up, we can call `Arg` to retrieve a positional argument after calling `Parse`.

> **NOTE**   Like flags, positional arguments are available only after calling `Parse`.

4.5.2   *Customizing usage messages*

Because positional arguments are not part of a `FlagSet`, we'll set a custom usage message. Suppose that we have the following `FlagSet`:

```
fs := flag.NewFlagSet("hit", flag.ContinueOnError)
fs.Var(asPositiveIntValue(&c.n), "n", . . .)
```

The usage message no longer includes the `url` flag because we don't define that flag. Fortunately, it's straightforward to generate a custom usage message with the `Usage` field. This field's type is a function that neither takes nor returns anything (such as `func()`):

```
$ go doc -short flag.FlagSet     ◄──┐  Outputs the FlagSet
type FlagSet struct {                  documentation
    . . .
    Usage func()        ◄──┐  An exported field named
    . . .                     Usage with the func() type
}
. . .
```

> **NOTE**   `Usage` is called when an error occurs or help is requested (e.g., with the `"-h"` flag).

We can assign this closure to `Usage` to define a custom usage message:

```
fs.Usage = func() {          ◄──┐   Assigns a new function to Usage,
    fmt.Fprintf(                     overwriting the FlagSet's default
        fs.Output(),                 usage message behavior
        "usage: %s [options] url\n",   Prints a usage header
        fs.Name(),           ◄────    to the FlagSet's output
    )
    fs.PrintDefaults()       ◄──┐   FlagSet's name
}                                   Prints the default flag values
                                    from the defined flags
```

Calling `Usage` would print the following to the standard error (by default):

```
usage: hit [options] url    ◄──┐   Printed by Fprintf
  -n value
       Number of requests (default 100)    Printed by PrintDefaults
```

When printing the usage header, we call `FlagSet.Name()` to get the name instead of using `"hit"` for consistency. This way, we can keep aligned with the `FlagSet`'s name even if we change it later.

Similarly, we write to `FlagSet.Output()` with `Fprintf` for consistency purposes. Otherwise, the behavior of our tool would be confusing for users. Suppose that the `FlagSet` prints to standard error (by default), but we use `Fprintf` to print to standard out. A script running our tool would have to track both outputs. Determining which one contains errors or the usual output would be confusing.

In summary, we can customize a `FlagSet`'s usage message using the `Usage` function field. Passing the result of the `Output` method to `Fprintf` allows us to set the usage and error message output to be printed. We can get the name of a `FlagSet` using the `Name` method.

> **NOTE** Custom usage messages clarify required positional arguments and optional flags, improving usability by explicitly communicating how to use tools correctly.

4.5.3 Setting a positional argument

Let's modify our parser to switch the `url` flag to a positional argument. In the following listing, we set a custom usage message using `Usage`, remove the `url` flag's definition, parse the flags, and then get the URL from the first positional argument using `Arg(0)`.

Listing 4.10 Positional argument (`hit/cmd/hit/config.go`)

```
package main

import (
    "fmt"
```

```
    . . .
)

. . .

func parseArgs(c *config, args []string) error {
    fs := flag.NewFlagSet("hit", flag.ContinueOnError)
    fs.Usage = func() {
        fmt.Fprintf(fs.Output(), "usage: %s [options] url\n", fs.Name())
        fs.PrintDefaults()
    }

    fs.Var(asPositiveIntValue(&c.n), "n",
        "Number of requests")
    fs.Var(asPositiveIntValue(&c.c), "c",
        "Concurrency level")
    fs.Var(asPositiveIntValue(&c.rps), "rps",
        "Requests per second")

    if err := fs.Parse(args); err != nil {
        return err
    }
    c.url = fs.Arg(0)

    return nil
}
```

We have removed the url flag definition.

◄──── **Sets the first positional argument to the url field when parsing finishes**

The final usage message looks like this:

```
$ go run ./hit/cmd/hit -h
usage: hit [options] url
  -c value
        Concurrency level (default 1)
  -n value
        Number of requests (default 100)
  -rps value
        Requests per second
```

Now let's run the command with flags and a positional argument together:

```
$ go run ./hit/cmd/hit -c 2 -n 100 https://github.com/inancgumus
Sending 100 requests to "https://github.com/inancgumus" (concurrency: 2)
```

We've typed the positional argument last and observed it in the output.

> **NOTE** Arg() returns an empty string if there's no positional argument at the provided index. Arg(0) returns "" if there's no positional argument at index 0, for example.

Our tool is getting better with each section. Switching the URL to a positional argument suggests that users always have to provide it, separating it from optional flags.

4.6   *Validation*

Our HIT tool's parser validates flags but misses some edge cases. It doesn't catch when the required URL argument is not provided or check whether the concurrency level is less than the number of requests, for example. In this section, we'll focus on validating these edge cases. This will simplify troubleshooting for our users and make the tool more user-friendly. Because the `FlagSet` doesn't support validating mandatory arguments or interdependent flags, we'll validate them by checking the `config` fields manually when parsing finishes.

4.6.1   *Writing a custom validator*

Listing 4.11 introduces a function that validates the `config` fields. We'll call this function from the `parseArgs` function. We format errors consistently and similarly to the `flag` package's, so the tool's errors remain consistent and won't surprise users.

Listing 4.11   Validator (`hit/cmd/hit/config.go`)

```go
package main

import (
    "net/url"
    . . .
)

func validateArgs(c *config) error {
    u, err := url.Parse(c.url)
    if err != nil {
        return fmt.Errorf("invalid value %q for url: %w", c.url, err)
    }
    if c.url == "" || u.Host == "" || u.Scheme == "" {
        return fmt.Errorf(
            "invalid value %q for url: requires a valid url", c.url,
        )
    }
    if c.n < c.c {
        return fmt.Errorf(
            "invalid value %d for flag -n: should be greater than flag -c:
            %d", c.n, c.c,
        )
    }
    return nil
}
```

The `validateArgs` function is written top to bottom and is straightforward. Writing code top to bottom reflects the execution order at runtime, making the logic flow more explicit. Keeping validation in one function streamlines reading, upkeep, and understanding.

> **TIP**   Write code to be readable from top to bottom to improve understanding.

We shouldn't take this as a hard rule against breaking up a function if it gets too complex, however. It's tough to set a strict rule for when to do this, but generally, begin with a solid, single-piece code, and split it as it grows complex and demands more reuse.

4.6.2   *Validating flags with a custom validator*

It's time to integrate the custom validator function we implemented. The next listing calls `validateArgs` after parsing to validate the fields. Because the `FlagSet` isn't involved in this validation, we force the `FlagSet` to print the usage message if an error occurs.

Listing 4.12   Integrating the validator (`hit/cmd/hit/config.go`)

```go
func parseArgs(c *config, args []string) error {
    fs := flag.NewFlagSet("hit", flag.ContinueOnError)
    fs.Usage = func() {
        fmt.Fprintf(fs.Output(), "usage: %s [options] url\n", fs.Name())
        fs.PrintDefaults()
    }

    fs.Var(asPositiveIntValue(&c.n), "n", "Number of requests")
    fs.Var(asPositiveIntValue(&c.c), "c", "Concurrency level")
    fs.Var(asPositiveIntValue(&c.rps), "rps", "Requests per second")

    if err := fs.Parse(args); err != nil {
        return err
    }
    c.url = fs.Arg(0)

    if err := validateArgs(c); err != nil {
        fmt.Fprintln(fs.Output(), err)
        fs.Usage()
        return err
    }

    return nil
}
```

Validates the parsed flag values

Prints the validation error to the FlagSet's output

Forces the FlagSet to print the usage message

Let's try out the code. We should see validation errors:

```
$ go run ./hit/cmd/hit
invalid value "" for url: requires a valid url
usage: hit [options] url
  -c value
        Concurrency level (default 1)
  -n value
        Number of requests (default 100)
  -rps value
        Requests per second
$ go run ./hit/cmd/hit -n 1 -c 2 "https://github.com/inancgumus"
invalid value "1" for flag -n: should be greater than -c: "2"
. . .
```

These errors will simplify troubleshooting for users when they pass incorrect arguments.

4.7 Exercises

1 Write a program that prints `os.Args` to the console. Run the program with different arguments to see what it prints. Compile it using `go build`, and then rerun it.

2 Call `os.Exit` with different status codes, and run the program.

3 Write a program that defines various flags using the `flag` package.

4 Implement a custom flag type that can validate positive `Duration` values.

5 Add a new flag called `timeout` to the `parseArgs`'s `FlagSet`.

6 Add a flag type that accepts only the following HTTP methods: `GET`, `POST`, and `PUT`.

7 Write a program that prints all the positional arguments. Use the `Args` method at https://pkg.go.dev/flag#Args to determine the number of positional arguments.

8 Set the `Usage` function to another function that prints a different usage message.

9 Write a CLI tool that mimics `git`'s subcommand behavior, such as `git commit -m "initial commit"` and `git push --force`, by defining a separate `FlagSet` for each subcommand so that it parses only that subcommand's flags and arguments.

Summary

- Separate core functionality from interface, such as a CLI program, to provide reusability. The `cmd` directory is a convention to store the code for executable programs.

- Arguments typically represent required program inputs, whereas flags are options. Command-line arguments (`os.Args`) are string values. The `flag` package parses given arguments into the specified type-safe variable that we can use in our programs.

- Explicitly terminate programs using `os.Exit` with nonzero codes upon errors, providing clear signals about the program's execution status.

- Higher-order functions accept or return functions. Using higher-order functions, we can adapt and handle differing behavior uniformly, such as updating various variable types with a common value parser function signature, allowing us to store parsers in a map.

- A closure returned by a function can access that function's surroundings.

- Idiomatic code is left-aligned, which makes exit conditions clear. Avoid deeply right-aligning the code with conditionals; that makes the code harder to grasp.

- Wrap errors with `fmt.Errorf` using `%w` to create error chains with extra context. `errors.Is` detects and returns `true` if an error exists in the given error chain.

- The `flag` package can parse flags, generate usage messages, and more. `flag .FlagSet` ties each `*flag.Flag` to a variable. Access positional arguments using `FlagSet.Arg`. Customize usage messages with `FlagSet.Usage`.
- Implement the `flag.Value` interface to provide custom flag parsers, and register them on a `flag.FlagSet` with `FlagSet.Var`. We can attach methods to any concrete types in our package, which enables even a simple type like an `int` to satisfy interfaces.

Dependency injection 5

This chapter covers

- Exploring challenges to testability
- Improving testability by isolating dependencies
- Using dependency injection techniques for testability

In chapter 4, we developed a user-friendly command-line program called the HIT tool, which provides a command-line interface (CLI) for the HIT client. We learned how to parse command-line arguments and flags using the standard library's `os` and `flag` packages.

This chapter focuses on testing the HIT tool using various dependency injection techniques. First, we'll explore the challenges we might face while testing CLI tools and see how to make our tool testable. Next, we'll add CLI tests to verify the tool's functionality and unit tests for its flag parser to cover edge cases. The combination of these tests will help ensure that our tool works correctly from the user's perspective while handling edge cases effectively.

By the end of this chapter, you'll have a solid understanding of testing CLI tools. Although this chapter explains testing a command-line tool, you can apply the same techniques to any project in which you want to isolate dependencies to have more testable code.

> **NOTE**   This chapter requires basic knowledge of interfaces. Check out appendix D for an introduction to interfaces in Go.

5.1   *Challenges to testability*

Testing a CLI tool should be no different from testing any other code. Still, the `main` function's black-box nature makes testing tricky because it doesn't take explicit inputs or return results.

> **NOTE**   These testability issues aren't specific to the `main` function. Any code that leans on globals, hides side effects, or is difficult to observe poses a challenge to testing.

Although `main` is like a black box, it has side effects because it typically uses global variables, like `os.Stdout`. Figure 5.1 shows that these globals are beyond our direct control.

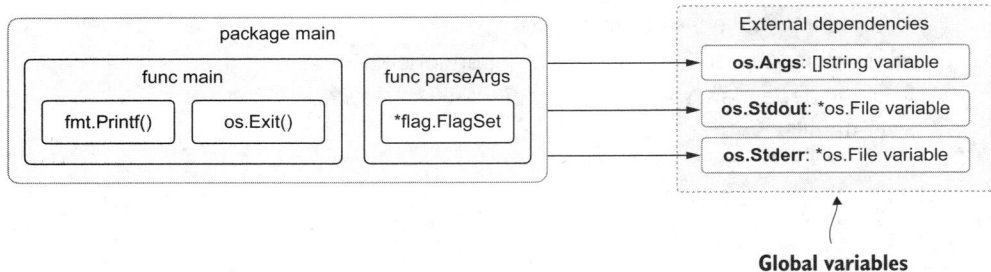

Figure 5.1   The `main` function interacts with global variables that are beyond our direct control.

Our `main` function

- Prints directly to the `os.Stdout` variable with `fmt.Printf`
- Reads command-line arguments from the variable `os.Args`
- Calls `parseArgs`, which prints to the `os.Stderr` variable using `fmt.Fprintf` and `flag.FlagSet`

This list includes examples from our program and is a starting point. There's always more to consider when dealing with different programs. We can run the program, capture its inputs and outputs, and observe it from outside, but this approach would require more code. Alternatively, we could directly assign fake values to these global variables during testing (a technique called monkey patching). Parallel testing code that uses global variables is challenging, however, because other code may also modify these variables. We would need to handle concurrent access, or we might have to avoid parallel testing, which could lead to longer test times.

All these approaches may help, but they won't help us write testable code. It is more effective to isolate global dependencies and use the ones we can control directly during tests; otherwise, we get flaky tests or other issues that are challenging to debug.

TIP A flaky test randomly passes or fails between runs.

5.2 *Testable programs*

Making the `main` function testable may seem daunting because it does not accept input parameters or return values. But there's an effective way out. In this section, we'll explore how to test the business logic of the HIT tool rather than the `main` function directly.

5.2.1 *Overview*

First, we need to understand how to decouple our program logic from its dependencies. As figure 5.2 shows, we delegate the `main` function's responsibilities by extracting

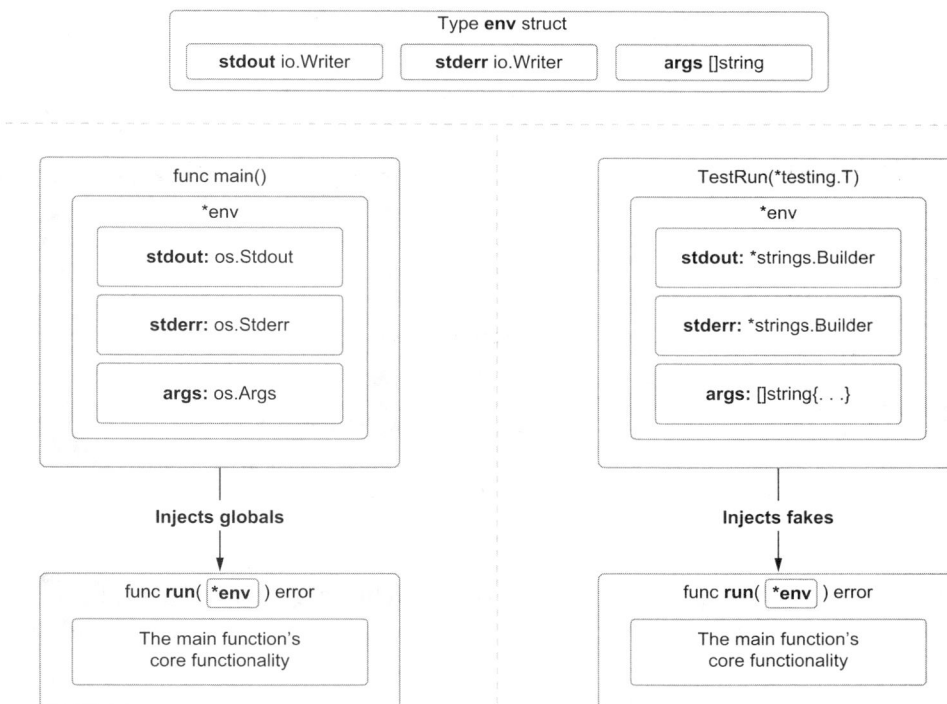

Figure 5.2 Moving `main`'s code into a `run` function that accepts an `*env` struct. The `env` struct has fields for us to inject the global variables, such as the `os.Stdout`. This approach allows `main` to inject real globals to `run`, and tests can inject controlled fakes that we can observe from tests later.

its functionality into a new function, run, which takes a pointer to the env struct. This struct serves as a vessel for dependencies, allowing us to inject real dependencies or simple fake ones, such as in-memory buffers, to capture our program's output during testing. With this approach, we'll transform our tool into a testable one.

Because we cannot change the main function's signature, we'll make the run function testable by delegating the main function's responsibilities to it. We'll test the run function because it is explicitly testable, making tests straightforward and reliable.

In this section, we first declare the env type and learn about the io.Writer interface. Then we'll move on to the main function and extract its functionality to the run function. Finally, we'll update the parser code to adapt to the changes. By the end of this section, we'll have testable code that we can test later in the chapter.

This refactoring will not affect the program's behavior. Injecting fake inputs and outputs from tests into the run function, however, will change the entire scene for testability.

5.2.2 A place to store dependencies

Now that we know how to make the tool more testable, let's start grouping its dependencies in env, such as os.Stdout and os.Args, using the io.Writer interface and a [] string, as shown in the next listing.

> **Listing 5.1 The env type (hit/cmd/hit/hit.go)**

```
package main

import (
    "io"
    . . .
)

type env struct {
    stdout io.Writer
    stderr io.Writer
    args   []string
    dryRun bool
}
```

- Abstracts standard output
- Abstracts standard error
- Command-line arguments
- Enabling the dry run mode prevents actual HTTP requests (needed in later chapters).

We declared the env struct with the interface field, io.Writer, to abstract standard outputs and a string slice to inject command-line arguments. This struct will enable us to pass the run function to the real dependencies, such as os.Stderr, or fake ones for testing the tool.

5.2.3 io.Writer's role

Because we use the Writer interface in the env fields, let's understand its role. We can satisfy the Writer interface by implementing its Write method. This method writes a byte slice to a destination stream and then returns the number of bytes written and an error:

```
type Writer interface {
    Write(p []byte) (n int, err error)
}
```

`Writer` standardizes and abstracts writing to any output stream, such as standard output, a file, or network connection. (Think of it as being like `OutputStream` in Java, `Stream.Write` in C#, or `RawIOBase.write` in Python.) `Writer` is one of the most ubiquitous interfaces in Go's standard library, and countless implementations of the interface are available in the wild. We'll use these `Writer` implementations for running and testing the HIT tool:

- `os.File`, which represents an operating system file handle
- `strings.Builder`, which provides an in-memory byte buffer

To make our tool work the same way as before, while users run it, we will assign `os.Stdout` and `os.Stderr` to the env struct's `stdout` and `stderr` fields; they are an `*os.File`, which is a `Writer` implementation. While testing the tool, we will use the `strings.Builder` type, which is another `Writer`, to record the tool's output.

Deep dive: io.Writer and io.Reader

The `io` package's `Writer` and `Reader` interfaces provide key insights for designing efficient APIs, enabling `Writer` and `Reader` implementations to achieve maximum performance. They follow the same design: delegating the management of memory management to callers. Recall the `Writer` interface:

```
type Writer interface {
    Write(p []byte) (n int, err error)
}
```

The caller provides a byte slice to the `Write` method for the data to be written to the destination `Writer`, such as an `*os.File`. Then the `Writer` writes as many bytes as possible because it can partially write the bytes. To improve efficiency, we might split the bytes and call `Write` repeatedly to send data to the destination. This approach helps us manage memory efficiently, especially when we have extensive data or the stream has size limitations for single writes.

`Writer`'s design allows us to allocate memory once and call `Write` successively without reallocating memory. It delegates the memory management to the caller.

Instead of the `Writer` allocating a new byte slice for each `Write` call, the caller can reuse the same slice across successive `Write` calls, minimizing memory use. This is especially important when dealing with large streams of data. If `Write` returned a slice each time instead, it would lead to unnecessary allocations between successive `Write` calls. Similarly, the `Reader` interface is designed on the same principle:

```
(continued)
type Reader interface {
    Read(p []byte) (n int, err error)
}
```

Instead of returning a newly allocated slice for each read operation, the caller passes a preallocated byte slice to the `Read` method. A `Reader` fills this slice with the incoming data, such as reading bytes from a file. This design eliminates frequent memory allocations, which increases performance, particularly in resource-intensive data transfers.

5.3   Decoupling

Now that we have the `env` type to abstract external dependencies, we can move on to the implementation. Here are our steps in this section and the following sections:

1 Declare the `run` function next to the `main` function.
2 Move the `main` function's core logic to the `run` function.
3 Pass the global dependencies in an `env` struct from `main` to `run`.
4 Update the tool's flag parser to use the injected dependencies.
5 Prepare the integration with the upcoming HIT client.

Making these changes won't change the HIT tool's behavior from the outside. When we finish this refactoring, we'll test the HIT tool manually (until we test it automatically in section 5.4) to see whether it still works as expected.

5.3.1   Decoupling from the environment

So far, we've identified global dependencies and abstracted them through the `env` struct. Now we'll move the `main` function's core logic to a new, testable function called `run`. This refactoring allows us to manage and test the logic independently of global dependencies. We'll review the current `main` function's code and then implement the `run` function.

A FUNCTION THAT IS DIFFICULT TO TEST

Recall the current `main` function to compare the differences:

```
func main() {
  c := config{
    n: 100,
    c: 1,
  }
  if err := parseArgs(&c, os.Args[1:]); err != nil {
    os.Exit(1)
  }
  fmt.Printf(
```

Current global dependencies

```
        "%s\n\nSending %d requests to %q (concurrency: %d)\n",
        logo, c.n, c.url, c.c,
    )
}
```

As we can see, the current `main` function has three external dependencies:

- `parseArgs` reads the command-line arguments from the `os.Args` slice.
- `os.Exit` terminates the program when parsing fails.
- `Printf` prints the HIT tool's messages directly to `os.Stdout`.

As mentioned, `main` can continue to use these global dependencies because we are not trying to make it directly testable. Instead, our goal is making the new `run` function testable. To achieve that goal, we'll transfer `main`'s logic to `run` and pass dependencies explicitly to it. Because `run` will use abstracted dependencies, testing it is straightforward.

A TESTABLE REPLICA

As the following listing shows, we move the `main`'s core logic to the new `run` function. With these changes, `run` has a well-defined set of inputs and outputs, which makes it predictable and straightforward to observe and validate under test conditions.

> **Listing 5.2 Refactoring the `main` function (`hit/cmd/hit.go`)**

```
func main() {
    if err := run(&env{
        stdout: os.Stdout,            Sets an environment for the rest of the
        stderr: os.Stderr,            program with real global dependencies
        args:   os.Args,
    }); err != nil {
        os.Exit(1)            ◄——  Exits with a status code
    }                              of 1 if an error occurs
}

func run(e *env) error {   ◄——  Gets the globals as input to run
    c := config{                 in a controlled environment
        n: 100,
        c: 1,
    }
    if err := parseArgs(       Reads the command-line
        &c,                    arguments from the env.args slice
        e.args[1:],     ◄——  Prints to a Writer instead of
        e.stderr,       ◄——  writing directly to os.Stderr
    ); err != nil {
        return err      ◄——  Returns an error instead of
    }                         terminating the program

    fmt.Fprintf(                 Prints to a Writer instead of writing directly to os.Stdout
        e.stdout,
        "%s\n\nSending %d requests to %q (concurrency: %d)\n",
        logo, c.n, c.url, c.c,
```

```
    )

        return nil
}
```

We've moved the `main` function's logic into the `run` function:

- `parseArgs` reads the command-line arguments from the slice `env.args`, removing the dependency on `os.Args`. It also writes parsing errors and usage messages to `env.stderr`, allowing us to capture and inspect them in tests.
- Instead of using `os.Exit`, `run` returns an explicit error, which lets us test errors without the program's exiting abruptly, making it easier to write reliable tests.
- Rather than printing directly with `Printf` to `os.Stdout`, we use `Fprintf` to write to a `Writer`, such as `os.Stdout` or `strings.Builder`, which enables us to observe and verify printed output without relying on `os.Stdout`.

The `run` function is a testable replica of the earlier `main`. The `main`'s earlier functionality is inside `run`, which no longer depends on globals. When `main` calls `run`, it works with globals. When called by tests, `run` can use fakes, allowing us to observe its input and output.

`main` itself has become extremely simple, and we no longer need to test it. Instead, we can test `run`. Because `run` operates on its input, `env`, instead of globals, it has no side effects. We can test it in parallel without potential race conditions.

5.3.2   *Decoupling the parser's output*

We successfully decoupled the program's core logic from the environment by introducing the `run` function and the `env` struct. Now let's focus on the flag parser. The current parser outputs to `os.Stderr`, tightly coupling it to global dependencies.

Similar to what we did with the `run`, we'll decouple the flag parser's output from globals by adjusting the `parseArgs` function to accept a `Writer` as a parameter so that we can observe its output from tests. As listing 5.3 shows, we add a `Writer` input to `parseArgs` and then redirect its `FlagSet`'s output to that `Writer` using the `SetOutput` method. The `FlagSet`'s `Output` method returns the `Writer` we set using the `SetOutput` method.

Listing 5.3   Setting `FlagSet`'s output (`hit/cmd/hit/env.go`)

```
package main

import (
    "io"
    . . .
)

func parseArgs(
    c *config,
    args []string,
```

```
        stderr io.Writer,                    ┌─── Takes an abstract
) error {                             ◄──────┘    Writer for output
    fs := flag.NewFlagSet("hit", flag.ContinueOnError)
    fs.SetOutput(stderr)              ◄──────┐
                                             │  Sets the FlagSet's output Writer, which
    fs.Usage = func() {                      │  can be retrieved with fs.Output()
        fmt.Fprintf(
            fs.Output(),
            "usage: %s [options] url\n",          Writes to the Writer
            fs.Name(),                            returned by fs.Output()
        )
        fs.PrintDefaults()
    }

    fs.Var(asPositiveIntValue(&c.n), "n", "Number of requests")
    fs.Var(asPositiveIntValue(&c.c), "c", "Concurrency level")
    fs.Var(asPositiveIntValue(&c.rps), "rps", "Requests per second")
    if err := fs.Parse(args); err != nil {
        return err
    }
    c.url = fs.Arg(0)

    if err := validateArgs(c); err != nil {
        fmt.Fprintln(fs.Output(), err)        Writes the usage to the Writer
        fs.Usage()                            returned by fs.Output()
        return err
    }

    return nil
}
```

Earlier, we designed `parseArgs` to write to the same output as `FlagSet`, so we didn't need to make significant changes. We needed to set only the `FlagSet`'s output.

Taking a `Writer` as input makes `parseArgs` flexible because we can pass in any `Writer`. Because we abstract the parser's parameter, we can run it with fake or real dependencies. Although tests can pass a fake that captures the output, `main` can pass in `os.Stderr`.

Although we pass an entire `env` struct to the `run` function, we don't do so for `parseArgs` and pass only `stderr`. The difference is that `run` executes the entire program, and using the `env` makes sense, whereas `parseArgs` needs only the `env`'s `stderr` to write to `os.Stdout`.

Also, taking a `Writer` input directly instead of getting it from an `env` makes `parseArgs` easier to understand and test. If it took an `env`, we would need to create an `env` for each test, put a `Writer` in it, and pass it to `parseArgs`. This would make tests more complicated to read and maintain. We could still make it take an `env` if it needed every field in `env`. We should weigh and decide the options in each situation, as there is always a tradeoff.

NOTE It's also fine to pass individual inputs to `run` instead of via the `env` struct. In our case, we used `env` as the `run`'s only input because `env` clarifies that the `run` function executes the entire program and can access everything about its environment.

5.3.3   *Preparing for the HIT client*

We've decoupled the core logic and flag parser from their dependencies. In this section, we'll prepare the HIT tool to integrate with the upcoming HIT client, which measures and reports an HTTP server's performance. We'll add a `runHit` function within our existing code, allowing us to call it from the `run` function while controlling whether to execute actual HTTP requests.

We add a conditional check using the `dryRun` field from the `env` as follows. This way, we have the option to bypass the HIT client's execution for testing or demonstration purposes.

Listing 5.4 **Preparing for the HIT client** (`hit/cmd/hit.go`)

```go
func run(e *env) error {
    c := config{
        n: 100,
        c: 1,
    }
    if err := parseArgs(&c, e.args[1:], e.stderr); err != nil {
        return err
    }
    fmt.Fprintf(
        e.stdout,
        "%s\n\nSending %d requests to %q (concurrency: %d)\n",
        logo, c.n, c.url, c.c,
    )
    if e.dryRun {                              // Skips sending actual HTTP
        return nil                             // requests when enabled
    }
    if err := runHit(&c, e.stdout); err != nil {
        fmt.Fprintf(
            e.stderr,
            "\nerror occurred: %v\n",
            err,
        )
        return err
    }

    return nil
}

func runHit(c *config, stdout io.Writer) error {    // We will implement this
    return nil                                       // function in chapter 6.
}
```

We want our CLI program tests to focus on testing our tool rather than on the HIT client's internals, so we avoid testing the HIT client, which we will integrate later. To do that, we've added a conditional to skip running runHit when dryRun (which we added earlier to env) is enabled. This way, run won't run runHit. Also, dryRun is useful for users who want to simulate the tool's output without triggering performance tests on a target HTTP server.

> **NOTE** As an exercise, define a new flag that toggles the dryRun field.

We use a simple conditional to avoid running the HIT client from our tool. This approach is pragmatic. We don't always have to use interfaces for testing if we can use a simple conditional. We would need an interface if we wanted to simulate HIT's interactions (or needed to switch between types) to test how our code responds to them.

> **TIP** Go often favors the most straightforward solution that meets the need.

We're prepared for the HIT client and will integrate it in later chapters.

5.3.4 Demonstration

Before we move on to writing tests, let's quickly check whether the HIT tool still works as expected after the refactoring we did to make it testable. Type the following command to run our HIT tool:

```
$ go run ./hit/cmd/hit https://github.com/inancgumus

 __ __      __      _____
/\ \_\ \    /\ \    /\__  _\
\ \  __ \   \ \ \   \/_/\ \/
 \ \_\ \_\   \ \_\     \ \_\
  \/_/\/_/    \/_/      \/_/
Sending 100 requests to "https://github.com/inancgumus" (concurrency: 1)
```

This confirms that our program still launches, prints the logo, and shows the correct request plan. It defaults to sending 100 requests with a concurrency of 1. Let's check whether our tool can still handle incorrect flags:

```
$ go run ./hit/cmd/hit -n HIT
invalid value "HIT" for flag -n: strconv.ParseInt:
  parsing "HIT": invalid syntax
usage: hit [options] url
  -c value
        Concurrency level (default 1)
  -n value
        Number of requests (default 100)
  -rps value
        Requests per second
```

This output shows that our flag parser still works correctly. The n flag expects a number, but we gave it a string. The program prints a helpful error followed by the usage message. If the -n flag were accepted, the tool would have used the provided value instead of the default 100.

We began this section with a functional but not very testable CLI tool. After refactoring to decouple it from the global state, we made the tool testable without altering its behavior. We can now test it with automated tests or run it with real dependencies.

5.4   CLI tests

Previously, we refactored the HIT tool to decouple it from global state, making it ready for automated testing while still allowing it to run normally with real dependencies. In this section, we'll test our tool using automated tests, verifying that it handles arguments, flags, and log messages correctly.

First, we'll capture and inspect the tool's output using Go's built-in strings.Builder type. Then we'll add the testEnv struct, which provides a convenient testing environment for observing the program's inputs and outputs from tests. Additionally, we'll add a testRun function, which will use env and testEnv, to run our tool conveniently from tests. We'll also discuss zero values, the differences between pointer and nonpointer types with differing method sets, and variadic functions to improve our Go knowledge. Last, we'll test our tool.

5.4.1   Observing with a strings.Builder

Before testing our tool, we need to learn how to read its output so we can observe and test what it writes to standard output and error. To do that, we'll briefly explore the strings.Builder type. Recall the env type from section 5.2.2:

```
type env struct {
    stdout io.Writer
    stderr io.Writer
    args   []string
    dryRun bool
}
```

Our program uses the env struct's stdout field to output to standard out and the stderr field to output to standard error. We can use these fields to observe and test the data written by our tool and confirm that it matches the expected values.

We cannot read from these Writer fields directly, however, because a Writer only allows us to write data into it. Instead, we need a type that enables us to read the content written into it. This type should also function as a Writer, allowing us to assign it to one of these env fields as a Writer and then read the written content.

Fortunately, the standard library's strings.Builder type meets these requirements. Builder buffers the data written to it. Because the stdout and stderr fields are a Writer, we can assign a Builder to these fields and then read the buffered content as a string.

You may recall the Builder from chapter 3, in which we used it to optimize the url .String method. Here's how to create a new Builder, write to it, and read from it:

```
var sb strings.Builder
sb.WriteString("hello")
sb.WriteString(" world")
sb.String()
```

◄── **Declares a Builder variable that holds an in-memory bytes buffer**

Appends the string values

◄── **Returns "hello world"**

NOTE See the documentation at https://pkg.go.dev/strings#Builder for more details.

Note that the `sb` variable's type is `Builder`, not `*Builder`. Although the `Builder`'s methods are on a pointer receiver (`*Builder`), Go can pass a `*Builder` to them even when we call them on a `Builder` (e.g. `sb.WriteString`), so we don't need to declare a `*Builder` explicitly. We don't need to do the following to use the pointer receiver methods, for example:

```
sb := new(strings.Builder)
sb.WriteString("hello world")
```

◄── **Declares sb as a *Builder and assigns it a new *Builder**

Instead, we can declare a `Builder`, as we did previously. Moreover, we can use its methods right away after declaring a `Builder` because its zero value is useful. Section 5.4.2 examines this technique and explains why it's useful.

Still, although we can declare a `Builder` and use it right away, because it has an internal buffer, we must pass it as a pointer to other functions; otherwise, it may panic or act unexpectedly. Chapter 3 examines the details of the `Builder`'s internal buffer.

Deep dive: Be careful with unintentional copying

Although using zero values simplifies code by preventing many issues, we should be mindful when working with types that hold internal states, such as `sync.Mutex` and `strings.Builder`. Copying them causes surprises or panics because each copy no longer has the same state. The following `value` struct has a `Mutex` value in the `mu` field, for example:

```
type value struct { mu sync.Mutex }
```

◄── **Mutex is ready to use without us having to initialize it.**

This type has a `do` method on a value receiver that locks and unlocks the mutex:

```
func (v value) do() {
    v.mu.Lock()
    defer v.mu.Unlock()
    // do something
}
```

◄── **The do method is on a value receiver that receives a nonpointer value.**

Whenever the `do` method is called, the `mu` field is copied, which would be incorrect:

(continued)

```
var v value
v.do()                        value.mu is copied.
v.do()
```

To prevent this issue, we must use a pointer receiver method to avoid copying the mutex:

```
func (v *value) do() { . . . }          ◀──  A pointer receiver method
```

Linters are useful for catching this type of `sync.Mutex` misuse. They don't always flag unintentional copying for our custom types, however, so it's important to be cautious. See appendix D for more information about method receiver types and copying.

5.4.2   Streamlining tests

As mentioned, to streamline testing, we'll introduce a `testEnv` type that provides a straightforward way to observe what our tool writes into standard outputs from tests. As the following listing shows, `testEnv` has `Builder` fields to observe the HIT tool's output.

> **Listing 5.5   Test environment** (`hit/cmd/hit_test.go`)

```
package main

import "strings"

type testEnv struct {
    stdout strings.Builder
    stderr strings.Builder
}
```

We would like to create a new `testEnv` from a test, pass an `env` to our tool's `run` method, and observe the tool's output from the `testEnv`'s `stdout` and `stderr` `Builder` fields. One easy way to achieve that goal is to link these fields to the corresponding fields of the `env` type.

NOTE   Recall that the `env` type has `stdout` and `stderr` `io.Writer` fields.

LINKING THE FIELDS

We can link the fields of `env` and `testEnv` similarly to what we did with our custom flag parser in chapter 4, when we linked a variable to a flag value parser using the variable's pointer. In the same vein, for example, we can declare a new `testEnv` variable and then initialize the `env`'s relevant fields to point to the corresponding fields of the `testEnv`:

```
var tenv testEnv
e := &env{
    stdout: &tenv.stdout,                    The env's fields point
    stderr: &tenv.stderr,                    to the testEnv's fields.
    . . .
}
```

We link the env's fields to the testEnv's fields using *strings.Builder pointers. Whenever we write to the env's stdout and stderr fields, we can observe what was written using the testEnv's stdout and stderr fields. The following example writes Go's first release date to env.stdout using Fprintln:

```
fmt.Fprintln(
    e.stdout, "Go 1.0 was released in 2012",    Fprintln can write to a Writer,
)                                                and env.stdout is a Writer.
```

Then we can observe what was written to the env.stdout field through testEnv .stdout:

```
fmt.Println(&tenv.stdout)   ◄────┐  Prints: Go 1.0 was released in 2012
```

Pointer (e.g., *Builder) and value types (e.g., Builder) have different method sets. The *Builder's method set has String and Write methods, for example. We pass a *Builder to Println so that Println can call *Builder.String automatically. We could have called tenv.stdout.String() too, but we achieved the same thing with less code. In a similar vein, we assigned &tenv.stdout to env.stdout because *Builder is an io.Writer. Passing tenv.stdout wouldn't work because Builder lacks the Write method.

NOTE Check out appendix D to learn more about method sets and interfaces.

USING ZERO VALUES

The *Builder type satisfies the Writer interface with a Write method declared on a pointer receiver. But the Builder type (nonpointer) doesn't satisfy Writer. So why do we use nonpointer Builder fields in the testEnv type rather than *Builder?

We declare the testEnv's stdout and stderr fields as a Builder, not as pointers. This way, Go can initialize them automatically so we can use them right away. Otherwise, we would have to initialize each field before using it or face possible nil-pointer issues if we forgot to do so.

Let's declare a testEnv, write to the Builder, and then print it. The following usage is possible because the testEnv fields are initialized automatically with a Builder:

```
var tenv testEnv                                  Usable without initializing the
tenv.stdout.WriteString("hello")   ◄──────┘       stdout Builder field manually
_ = tenv.stdout.String()           ◄──────┐
                                           Returns "hello"
```

This time, as an example, instead of using `Builder`, let's use `*Builder` fields:

```
type testEnv struct {
    stdout *strings.Builder
    stderr *strings.Builder
}
. . .
```
Declares the stdout and stderr fields as *Builder (as a pointer) instead of Builder (as a nonpointer)

Next, we'll type and run the code we wrote earlier. When we use the `testEnv` that uses `*Builder` fields, we see a `nil`-pointer dereference panic:

```
var tenv testEnv
tenv.stdout.WriteString("hello")
runtime error: invalid memory address
            or nil pointer dereference
```
Panics because the stdout field is nil

We have to initialize the `*Builder` fields explicitly, as follows, to prevent the panic:

```
tenv := testEnv{
    stdout: new(strings.Builder),
    stderr: new(strings.Builder),
}
tenv.stdout.WriteString("hello")
```
Explicitly initializes the field with a pointer to a new strings.Builder

Calling stdout.WriteString no longer panics because the stdout field is now a non-nil pointer to a strings.Builder.

Instead of using this kind of ceremony, it's more effective to use a type's zero values if the type supports them. Zero values reduce initialization overhead and potential errors, making the code cleaner and more reliable. That's why we use `Builder` fields in `testEnv`.

5.4.3   *Adding a helper*

Our program's `run` function takes a pointer to the `env` type. The `run` function writes to the env's `stdout` and `stderr` fields rather than using `os.Stdout` and `os.Stderr` directly. We also added `testEnv` to create a convenient testing environment alongside the `env` type.

Like `env`, `testEnv` has `stdout` and `stderr` fields that allow us to observe what was written to the env's corresponding fields, but linking all these fields can be cumbersome. To simplify linking the fields, we'll add a function that prepares a new test environment. As listing 5.6 shows, this function initializes the remaining `env` fields, including `args` for command-line arguments and `dryRun` to stop sending HTTP requests to an HTTP server when enabled. Finally, it runs the HIT tool's `run` function to execute the HIT tool in dry-run mode.

Listing 5.6   Test runner helper (`hit/cmd/hit_test.go`)

```
func testRun(args ...string) (*testEnv, error) {
    var tenv testEnv
```
Automatically initializes the Builder struct fields (stdout and stderr)

Takes an arbitrary number of strings (args ...string)

```
err := run(&env{
    args:   append([]string{"hit"}, args...),
    stdout: &tenv.stdout,
    stderr: &tenv.stderr,
    dryRun: true,
})
return &tenv, err
}
```

Runs the HIT tool

Sets the args field to a slice with "hit" and the elements in args

Links the env and testEnv stdout and stderr fields

Prevents running the HIT client during testing

Returns a prepared testing environment and an error from the run method

The testRun function sets up a test environment to observe the HIT tool's outputs. It runs the tool with command-line arguments using the run function and returns both the test environment and any errors from the run. This approach helps us test the tool conveniently and observe its outputs, as well as any execution errors, during testing. The following sections explain parts of this code.

VARIADIC FUNCTIONS

The testRun function is variadic because it takes a variadic string input:

```
args ...string
```

The ellipsis allows testRun to accept an arbitrary number of string values.

Suppose that we call the function as follows:

```
testRun("-c=2", "-n=1", "https://github.com/inancgumus")
```

Here, the args parameter automatically turns into a []string within the function. That's why we can call testRun without having to declare a string slice beforehand, unlike this example:

```
testRun([]string{
  "-c=2", "-n=1", "https://github.com/inancgumus",
})
```

This won't work with the current testRun because it's a variadic function.

See the nearby sidebar to learn more about variadic functions.

APPENDING A SLICE TO A SLICE

To simulate a realistic testing environment, we insert the HIT tool's name into the first element of args. Recall from listing 5.2 that the run function uses args[:1]. If we hadn't added a first element to the args, the run function would panic after we called it from tests. The append part of listing 5.6 works as follows:

- The built-in append function appends one or more elements to a slice and returns a new slice with the appended elements. See appendix C for details about append.
- The []string{"hit"} part returns a new string slice.
- The args... part returns the elements in the args string slice.

As a result, the `args` field contains `"hit"` plus the elements in the `args` slice. That `args` field contains `"hit"`, `"-c=2"`, `"-n=4"` when we call the `testRun` with `"-c=2"`, `"-n=4"`, for example.

Deep dive: Variadic functions

There are two ways to call a variadic function like the `testRun` function:

```
testRun("-c=2", "-n=1", "https://github.com/inancgumus")
testRun([]string{"-c=2", "-n=1", "https://github.com/inancgumus"}...)
```

In both cases, `testRun` declares a new local `args` slice within the function (listing 5.6):

- For the first way, the local slice has a new backing array.
- For the second way, the local slice shares the backing array with the input slice.

In the first case, modifying the local slice's elements would stay local. In the second case, if `testRun` modifies the elements, the changes would be seen outside the function. Suppose that when it's called, `testRun` internally modifies the first element to `"MODIFIED"`:

```
func testRun(args ...string) (*testEnv, error) {
    args[0] = "MODIFIED"
    . . .
}
```

We call it like this:

```
args := []string{"-c=2", "-n=1", "https://github.com/inancgumus"}
testRun(args...)
```

The original slice becomes `[MODIFIED -n=1 https://github.com/inancgumus]`. If we want to avoid using a function to change the input slice's elements, we should pass the individual elements or pass a copy of the slice before calling the function. Let's pass a copy:

```
args := []string{"-c=2", "-n=1", "https://github.com/inancgumus"}
testRun(append([]string{}, args...)...)    ◄──── Uses args... because append
                                                  is also a variadic function
```

The original slice does not change: `[-c=2 -n=1 https://github.com/inancgumus]`. We create an empty string slice (`[]string{}`) and then copy the original slice's elements to that slice (`args...`). The resulting slice has a new backing array containing the original slice's copied elements. The `testRun` function can no longer modify the original slice's elements because we're copying the elements to a slice with a new backing array. See appendix C for more details about slices and backing arrays.

5.4.4 Writing CLI tests

Now that we have `testEnv` to provide a test environment and `testRun` to run the run function from tests and observe the output, let's write CLI tests in the next listing. The first test tests the tool's behavior with a valid input; the second test does the opposite. We observe the standard output and error to see what's being written to them.

Listing 5.7 Adding CLI tests (`hit/cmd/hit_test.go`)

```go
package main

import (
    "strings"
    "testing"
)

. . .

func TestRunValidInput(t *testing.T) {
    t.Parallel()

    tenv, err := testRun("https://github.com/inancgumus")
    if err != nil {
        t.Fatalf("got %q;\nwant nil err", err)
    }
    if n := tenv.stdout.Len(); n == 0 {
        t.Errorf("stdout = 0 bytes; want >0")
    }
    if n := tenv.stderr.Len(); n != 0 {
        t.Errorf(
            "stderr = %d bytes; want 0; stderr:\n%s",
            n, tenv.stderr.String(),
        )
    }
}

func TestRunInvalidInput(t *testing.T) {
    t.Parallel()

    tenv, err := testRun(
        "-c=2", "-n=1", "invalid-url",
    )
    if err == nil {
        t.Fatalf("got nil; want err")
    }
    if n := tenv.stderr.Len(); n == 0 {
        t.Error("stderr = 0 bytes; want >0")
    }
}
```

Len returns the number of bytes written to the Builder's buffer.

Because testRun takes variadic strings, we can pass an arbitrary number of string arguments.

After running `testRun`, we use the returned `testEnv` to check what our tool writes. Earlier, we linked the `testEnv`'s `stdout` and `stderr` fields directly to the corresponding fields in the tool's environment, `env`. This linking lets us capture output easily during testing.

In the first test, `TestRunValidInput`, we call the tool with a valid URL (`https://github.com/inancgumus`). First, we verify that no error occurs. Then we check whether the tool writes something to `stdout`. If it doesn't, the tool isn't behaving correctly. Finally, we confirm that nothing appears in `stderr` because the input is valid and no errors should be reported.

In `TestRunInvalidInput`, we intentionally pass invalid arguments (`"-c=2"`, `"-n=1"`, and `"invalid-url"`) to test how the tool handles errors. We expect an error and explicitly check that it is not `nil`. We also confirm that it correctly reports this error by verifying that it writes a message to `stderr`. If nothing is written, the tool fails to handle invalid inputs correctly. We can run the tests to see whether they pass:

```
$ go test ./hit/cmd/hit -v
--- PASS: TestRunValidInput
--- PASS: TestRunInvalidInput
```

Using `testEnv`, we captured the tool's output and kept our tests isolated from external factors. We've improved our knowledge of zero values, method sets, and variadic functions, which will be helpful later in the book and in our real-life programs.

5.5 Unit testing

High-level CLI tests are practical for verifying the overall program behavior but may overlook subtle bugs or focus too much on the shape of the program's inputs and outputs. This is where unit tests become essential. They confirm that each component functions correctly in isolation.

Now that we've tested the HIT tool with CLI tests, it's time to test the flag parser code with unit tests. To keep the test code brief, I'll provide enough test cases without covering every single edge case (an excellent opportunity for you to practice).

5.5.1 A helper type

Before diving in, let's revisit the `parseArgs`'s signature:

```
func parseArgs(c *config, args []string, stderr io.Writer) error
```

Recall that `parseArgs` parses command-line flags and arguments for the HIT tool. As shown in the following listing, we start by defining the `parseArgsTest` struct according to this function's signature to pass its inputs to `parseArgs` from tests later.

Listing 5.8   Adding a shared test case type (`hit/cmd/hit/config_test.go`)

```
package main

import "testing"
```

```
type parseArgsTest struct {
    name string
    args []string
    want config
}
```

This struct lets us group test inputs and expected outcomes effectively. We separate test data from the test logic, making the tests more straightforward to understand and maintain.

5.5.2 *Unit-testing the parser*

Now that we have `parseArgsTest`, as listing 5.9 shows, we reuse it from the happy and sad path tests. For the first test, we pass the flags and verify whether we get the correct flag values. For the second test, we pass invalid flags and expect an error from the function.

Because earlier chapters covered unit testing extensively, including subtests and parallel test execution, I won't explain every detail of this test code. If the following code is confusing, revisiting chapters 2 and 3 will refresh your understanding.

Listing 5.9 Testing with valid flags (`hit/cmd/hit/config_test.go`)

```
func TestParseArgsValidInput(t *testing.T) {
    t.Parallel()

    for _, tt := range []parseArgsTest{
        {
            name: "all_flags",
            args: []string{"-n=10", "-c=5", "-rps=5", "http://test"},
            want: config{n: 10, c: 5, rps: 5, url: "http://test"},
        },

        // exercise: test with a mixture of flags
    } {
        t.Run(tt.name, func(t *testing.T) {
            t.Parallel()

            var got config
            if err := parseArgs(&got, tt.args, io.Discard); err != nil {
                t.Fatalf("parseArgs() error = %v, want no error", err)
            }
            if got != tt.want {
                t.Errorf("flags = %+v, want %+v", got, tt.want)
            }
        })
    }
}

func TestParseArgsInvalidInput(t *testing.T) {
    t.Parallel()

    for _, tt := range []parseArgsTest{
        {name: "n_syntax",  args: []string{"-n=ONE", "http://test"}},
        {name: "n_zero",    args: []string{"-n=0",   "http://test"}},
```

```
        {name: "n_negative", args: []string{"-n=-1",  "http://test"}},

        // exercise: test other error conditions
    } {
        t.Run(tt.name, func(t *testing.T) {
            t.Parallel()

            err := parseArgs(&config{}, tt.args, io.Discard)
            if err == nil {
                t.Fatal("parseArgs() = nil, want error")
            }
        })
    }
}
```

We've written two tests demonstrating how to test our parser against valid and invalid scenarios. Feel free to add more test cases and improve coverage. Practicing these techniques is crucial to internalizing them effectively. Practice makes perfect.

In the first test, we iterate through test cases with valid arguments. We call the parser for each case and check whether the updated `config` struct matches our expectations. The second test checks how our parser handles invalid flags. Here, we're specifically verifying that the parser returns errors correctly when encountering incorrect arguments, such as passing a negative number where only positives make sense or passing strings when numbers are expected.

For the `parseArgs`'s `stderr` parameter, we pass `io.Discard`, which is perhaps the most straightforward `Writer` implementation. `Discard` throws away the bytes passed to its `Write` method. We use it to avoid cluttering test logs with usage messages when parsing fails. Let's run these tests to see the results:

```
$ go test ./hit/cmd/hit -run=TestParseArgs -v
--- PASS: TestParseArgsValidInput
  --- PASS: TestParseArgsValidInput/all_flags
--- PASS: TestParseArgsInvalidInput
  --- PASS: TestParseArgsInvalidInput/n_syntax
  --- PASS: TestParseArgsInvalidInput/n_negative
  --- PASS: TestParseArgsInvalidInput/n_zero
```

We've successfully transformed a previously untestable command-line tool into one that's easy to test by systematically decoupling it from environmental dependencies. We moved the `main` function's core functionality to a custom `run` function, which takes dependencies as arguments instead of relying on global ones. We used the `io.Writer` interface to decouple the tool from `os.Stdout` and `os.Stderr`, and we used a string slice to inject command-line arguments to decouple it from the `os.Args` dependency.

> **TIP** For an alternative way to test command-line programs, check out the `script` package. It is extensively used in the standard library to test the `go` tool and is now available for use in other command-line programs. See https://pkg .go.dev/rsc.io/script.

Using build tags

Not every program's tests run as quickly as the HIT tool's. Sometimes, we want to skip long-running tests, especially when they involve operations that take a long time to complete. Here are some common strategies to use in such situations:

- Use the `testing.Short` function.
- Use the `t.SkipNow` method.
- Use a build tag.

Let's look at the first two options before heading to the build tags. We can use `testing.Short` to check whether the `short` flag is provided. If so, we can use `t.SkipNow` to skip the current test function:

```
func TestSomething(t *testing.T) {
   if testing.Short() { t.SkipNow() }
   . . .
}
```

The `TestRun` function is skipped if we run the tests with the `short` flag:

```
$ go test -v -short
--- SKIP: TestSomething
```

Using the combination of `Short` and `SkipNow` can be cumbersome when dealing with many tests. Build tags offer a streamlined alternative. A *build tag* is a compiler directive that includes or excludes files during the build based on specific conditions. For example, we might have an `integration` build tag like the following (the one that starts with a `//`) to mark tests that interact with external systems such as databases:

```
//go:build integration
package mypackage
```
◄— This build tag's name is integration here, but a build tag can have any name.

Warning: avoid adding spaces after the double slashes. It's not `// go:build`. Otherwise, it would be an ordinary comment. Without spaces, it becomes a build tag.

The first line, which looks like a comment, is a build tag that tags the file with the `integration` tag. After tagging, we can run only the test files with that tag. To do so, we should explicitly pass the tag as follows when we want to run the tests in those files:

```
$ go test -tags=integration
```

Build tags are commonly used to distinguish unit tests from integration tests. We can also use build tags for nontest files. They help compile code conditionally for specific platforms, manage different development environments, and turn on or off feature availability. Visit https://pkg.go.dev/cmd/go#hdr-Build_constraints for more information.

Summary

- Testing functions with no explicit input or output parameters may be difficult. Extracting the logic of these functions into another function may lead to more testable code.
- Tests that rely on global variables are challenging to test and can lead to flaky tests. We can make a function (or any other code) testable by decoupling it from its dependencies.
- `io.Writer` standardizes and abstracts writing operations to any byte stream.
- Zero values reduce initialization overhead and potential errors, making the code simpler.
- Providing helpers for testing makes testing the code more convenient and practical.
- Variadic functions can take an arbitrary number of the same type.
- Balancing high-level and low-level tests is the key to writing correctly functioning programs.

Synchronous APIs
for concurrency

This chapter covers

- Designing synchronous APIs that treat concurrency as an implementation detail
- Standardizing the processing of sequences of values using push iterators
- Structuring concurrent processing with the pipeline pattern

Having finished the HIT tool, we can focus on the HIT client within the `hit` package. It allows our tool to send concurrent requests to measure HTTP server performance.

HTTP provides a realistic context for the concurrency patterns we'll discuss in this chapter, helping us see how and where to use them. Because these patterns apply broadly—not only to HTTP—I'll save HTTP-specific details for chapter 7 to keep the focus strictly on concurrency.

As chapter 1 hinted, channels use a message-passing approach that simplifies concurrent programming by making the data flow between goroutines explicit. This chapter dives into the concurrent pipeline pattern to demonstrate this approach in practice.

The `hit` package will show us how to structure a straightforward package API that appears to be synchronous from the outside but runs concurrently inside. We'll begin with a package that works sequentially and refactor it to work concurrently without changing its exported API. By chapter's end, you'll learn how to structure concurrent code effectively in Go.

6.1   Overview

We'll implement the HIT client as the `hit` package, which users can import directly into their programs. The HIT tool will be the first user of this new package. Our goal is a synchronous and straightforward API. We'll start by walking through the package's design, API, and directory structure. In section 6.2, we'll start implementing the `hit` package.

6.1.1   Package hit

As figure 6.1 shows, the `hit` package is an HTTP client that allows users to send requests to an HTTP server, gather results, and summarize them. The following list breaks down the package's exported API. The `Result` and `Summary` are struct types; the rest are functions:

- `Send()` sends a single HTTP request and returns a `Result`.
- `Result` is a performance result, such as how long it takes a target server to respond, how many bytes are returned, and the HTTP status code received.
- `SendN()` sends `N` concurrent HTTP requests using `Send` and returns a `Results` iterator that pushes each `Result` to consumers.
- `Results` is an iterator that allows users to iterate over `Result` values.
- `Summarize()` takes a `Results` iterator and returns a performance `Summary`.
- `Summary` is a summary of `Result` values, including the total number of requests, errors, downloaded bytes, and total duration of all requests.

The key functions in our design are `Send` and `SendN`. `Send` sends a single request, whereas `SendN` sends multiple HTTP requests. Having separate functions isolates concerns. `SendN` uses `Send` to send requests. We'll also have an `Options` struct to allow expert users to fine-tune the client to their needs, such as passing their own function through the `Options` input to customize the request-sending behavior of `SendN`.

Our core data types are `Result` and `Summary`: one for a specific performance result and another for a summary of results. Instead of using a single type, I represent two different concepts with two different types to separate responsibilities.

This approach keeps the API clean without overloading it with unnecessary details. If multiple requests fail, each `Result` includes a specific error. By contrast, `Summary` provides the total number of errors without including individual error details.

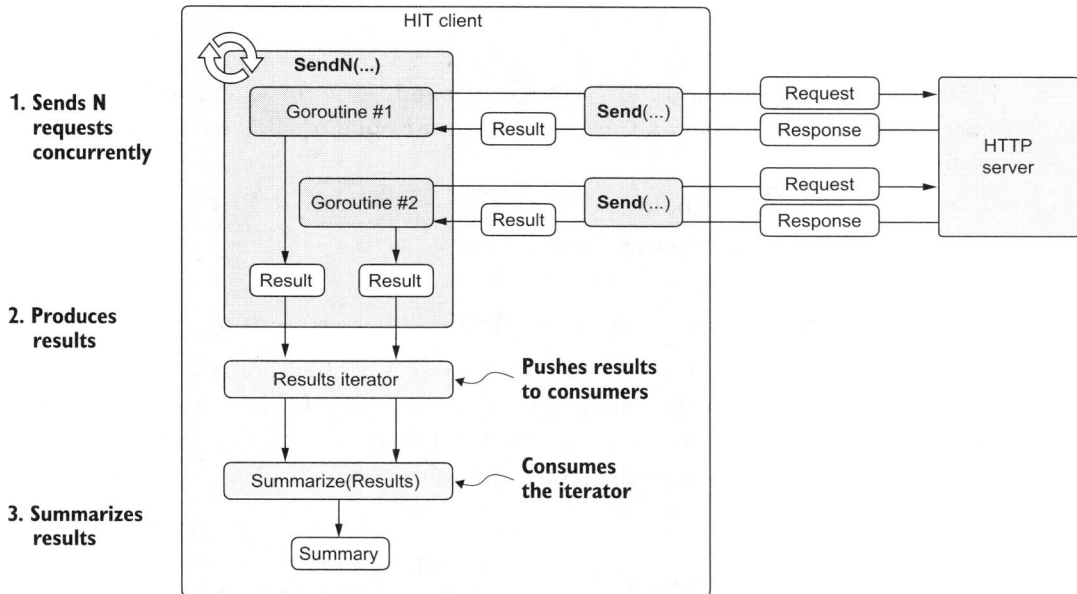

Figure 6.1 **The flow of requests and results.** `SendN` uses `Send` to send concurrent HTTP requests to the server and returns an iterator that pushes each `Result` to `Summarize`, which consumes the iterator to produce a `Summary`. **Although the figure shows two goroutines, the number depends on the concurrency level configured.**

TIP Avoid overloading types with extra responsibility for maintainable code.

Although `Send` returns a single `Result`, because `SendN` sends multiple requests, it returns a `Results` iterator that pushes each `Result` to consumers. Users can consume this iterator, process each `Result`, and produce a `Summary`. For convenience, we provide a `Summarize` function that consumes the `Results` iterator and automatically produces a `Summary`.

NOTE We can also remotely liken the HIT client's functionality to that of a Map Reduce concept. See https://mng.bz/WwV1 for more details.

`SendN` initially provides functionality for sending sequential requests. Instead of starting with concurrency, we'll send requests one after another. Beginning this way keeps the code manageable and straightforward, avoiding unnecessary complexity. When the sequential version is working well, we'll introduce concurrency.

NOTE Turning sequential code into concurrent code is straightforward in Go when structured correctly. This chapter shows how to structure concurrent code.

6.1.2   Package API

When it comes to packages, an API is everything exported from a package, which is crucial because it's what other packages depend on and use. An API is the contract between the package and its users. Here are some guidelines for designing a useful API:

- It should be synchronous by default.
- It should avoid unnecessary abstractions.
- It should be straightforward to use.
- It should be composable, allowing users to use it in creative ways.

Useful package APIs are simple for beginners to use but offer more experienced users enough knobs to twiddle. Beginners can start using the API right away; experts can fine-tune its behavior to meet their needs. We'll follow the preceding guidelines for the `hit` package. Let's explore the package's API by looking at the declaration of the exported items:

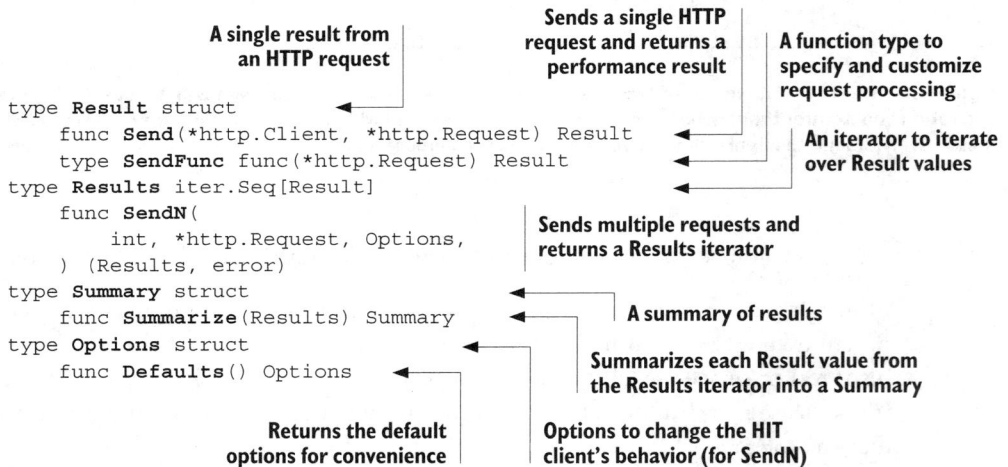

```
                  A single result from            Sends a single HTTP
                    an HTTP request              request and returns a        A function type to
                                                  performance result         specify and customize
                                                                              request processing

type Result struct
    func Send(*http.Client, *http.Request) Result
    type SendFunc func(*http.Request) Result                                An iterator to iterate
type Results iter.Seq[Result]                                                over Result values
    func SendN(
        int, *http.Request, Options,           Sends multiple requests and
    ) (Results, error)                          returns a Results iterator
type Summary struct
    func Summarize(Results) Summary             A summary of results
type Options struct
    func Defaults() Options              Summarizes each Result value from
                                         the Results iterator into a Summary

         Returns the default           Options to change the HIT
         options for convenience       client's behavior (for SendN)
```

As we can see from this API, we treat concurrency as an implementation detail. The `hit` package's exported API does not expose channels. Every part of the API hides concurrency behind well-defined types and functions that work together to provide a synchronous API.

Similarly, most of the standard library is synchronous, even if it's internally concurrent. Recall from chapter 2 that we can run a subtest using the `T.Run` method, for example. Although `T.Run` executes the given function in a new goroutine, it doesn't leak concurrency in its API.

We can easily run synchronous functions concurrently using a `go` statement. Exposing concurrency directly in a package's API forces users to deal with concurrency even if they don't need it.

In section 6.2, we'll implement our package to work sequentially. Starting in section 6.6, we'll make it concurrent by using the concurrent pipeline pattern without changing the package's exported API. We can do this because we hide concurrency behind a synchronous API. From the user's perspective, the package's API will remain the same.

> **TIP** Concurrency is an implementation detail. Design package APIs as synchronous, and leave the decision about using a package's API concurrently to its users.

6.1.3   Directory structure

Before implementing `hit`, let's get familiar with the directory structure:

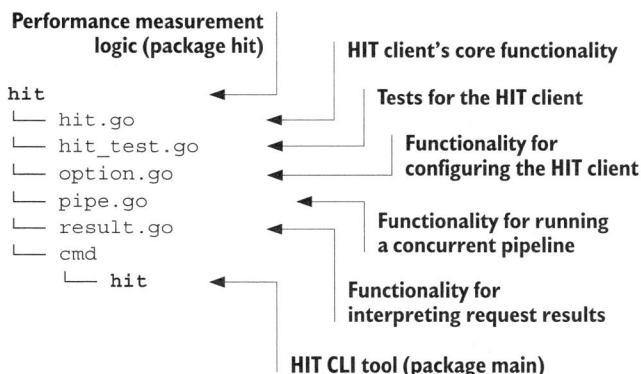

The files in the root directory make up the `hit` package. Each file belongs to the `hit` package and provides different functionalities, such as an HTTP client, the package's public API, functions to run a concurrent pipeline, and performance results. The `cmd/hit` directory contains the HIT command-line interface (CLI) tool that we developed in earlier chapters.

6.2   Foundations

Now that we're familiar with the overall design and structure of the `hit` package, we can start implementing the necessary foundation. First, we declare the `Result` type for storing a single performance result. Then we implement the `Send` function to send a single request and return a `Result`. The `SendN` function will send multiple requests using the `Send` function after we implement the `Results` iterator in section 6.3.

6.2.1   Result

We are starting to implement the sequential version of the `hit` package with the `Result` type. As the following listing shows, `Result` stores the performance metrics of a single request. The `Send` function, which we'll add in section 6.2.2, will send a request and return a `Result` value.

Listing 6.1   Implementing `Result` (`hit/result.go`)

```go
package hit

import "time"

// Result is performance metrics of a single [http.Request].
type Result struct {
    Status   int            // Status is the HTTP status code
    Bytes    int64          // Bytes is the number of bytes transferred
    Duration time.Duration  // Duration is the time to complete a request
    Error    error          // Error received after sending a request
}
```

The `Result` type is at the core of our `hit` package. We'll build the remaining package functionality around it. After sending a request, `Send` will return the request's `Result`, including the HTTP status code, the number of bytes transferred, and the duration. `Result` also has an `Error` field that becomes non-nil if an error occurs while the request is sent.

After sending a request with `Send`, we can observe the performance metrics of that request by looking at the returned `Result`. When we've added the necessary code to send a single request, we'll start sending multiple requests using the `SendN` function.

Generating documentation links automatically

Let's look at the following comment in listing 6.1:

```go
// Result is performance metrics of a single [http.Request].
```

I use square brackets in the comments to generate documentation links. Including `[http.Request]` in the `Result` type's comment generates a link to the `http` package's `Request` type when viewed in text editors or documentation. Users can interact with this link when they go to the package's documentation at https://pkg.go.dev.

6.2.2   *Send*

As mentioned in the chapter introduction, this chapter focuses on concurrent programming rather than dealing with the specifics of HTTP. We'll put off sending HTTP requests until the next chapter. Doing so also helps us create a solid and decoupled structure.

Now that we have the `Result` type, we can move to the `Send` function, which simulates sending a request and returns the `Result` of that request, as the next listing shows. The `http.Client` type is for sending HTTP requests. The `http.Request` type carries information about an HTTP request, such as the URL of the target server.

Listing 6.2 Simulating HTTP requests (`hit/hit.go`)

```
package hit

import (
    "net/http"          ◄——  The http package
    "time"                    implements HTTP.
)

// Send sends an HTTP request and returns a performance [Result].
func Send(_ *http.Client, _ *http.Request) Result {
    const roundTripTime = 100 * time.Millisecond

    time.Sleep(roundTripTime)

    return Result{
        Status:   http.StatusOK,
        Bytes:    10,
        Duration: roundTripTime,
    }
}
```

The underscore signals that the function does not use these inputs.

Simulates sending a request

Assumes that the server response was successful

We've declared `Send` in a new `hit.go` file. Until chapter 7, we won't use the `Send`'s parameters, so we'll ignore them by using an underscore. `Send` blocks the execution for 100 milliseconds (ms) to simulate sending a request. Finally, it returns a successful result.

We started simple and built the foundation to send a simulated request. Earlier, we also declared the `Result` type to store a performance result, which will be helpful in later sections.

6.3 Iterators

Now that we can `Send` a request and get a `Result` back, we're ready to send multiple requests and return a `Results` iterator. We'll work on the following functionality:

- `SendN` returns a `Results` iterator that pushes each `Result` to consumers.
- `Results` is an iterator type that allows consumers to consume `Result` values.
- `Summarize` consumes the `Results` iterator and returns a `Summary` value.
- `Summary` is a summary of multiple `Result` values.

We'll start by adding the `Results` type. Then we'll add the `SendN` function to send multiple requests, returning a `Results` iterator. Finally, we'll consume this iterator from the `Summarize` function to produce a performance `Summary`.

6.3.1 Push iterators

As of Go 1.23, the standard library and compiler support custom iterators, which are similar to generators in Python, sequences in Kotlin, and iterators in JavaScript. *Iterators* are functions that standardize the way we push values from a sequence, such as a slice or a channel, to consumers and let them retrieve each pushed value through the iterator using the core language constructs, such as a `for-range` loop.

Returning an iterator from a function instead of a slice or channel to consumers decouples iteration from the underlying data structure. This approach also allows us to transition from an internal sequential code to a concurrent one without changing the `hit` package's API.

Moreover, iterators may lead to more efficient execution, as consumers have more control over the iteration. They can gather all the values from the iterator or stop short without issues, for example. With a slice, however, the producer first needs to store and return all the produced values to the consumer. See the sidebar "Deep dive: Why do we return an iterator instead of a slice?" in section 6.3.2 for more information.

The compiler has built-in support for iterators. Just as we can use a `for-range` loop to iterate over a slice, we can use it to loop over an iterator. We might use a `for-range` loop to go through each `Result` as the HIT client generates them while sending multiple HTTP requests. For example, we could get each `Result` as it arrives from the iterator and print a progress bar in real time while results are being received.

> **TIP** See https://go.dev/blog/range-functions for more information on iterator types, their uses, history, and reasons for their introduction.

DECLARING A CUSTOM ITERATOR TYPE

Now that we've looked at the benefits of using custom iterators, let's declare one. In our case, `SendN` will return the `Results` iterator type, as shown in the next listing. We'll use the standard `Seq` type to declare the `Results` iterator, which allows iterating over each `Result` sequentially (iterating over the values one at a time).

Listing 6.3   Implementing the `Results` iterator (`hit/result.go`)

```go
package hit

import (
    "iter"          ◀─────┐  The iter package provides basic definitions
    "time"                 │  and usage details for iterators.
)

                                              Declares a push iterator
// Results is an iterator for [Result] values.    type that allows iterating
type Results iter.Seq[Result]     ◀─────────────  over Result values

. . .
```

This function type declares a push iterator that will allow `SendN` to push each `Result` value to consumers. Next, we'll start explaining the `iter.Seq` type. We'll discuss how to return a `Results` iterator from the `SendN` and push values from the iterator to consumers.

USING PUSH ITERATORS

Our custom push iterator is based on the following `iter.Seq` type. Push iterators push values from a sequence of values into a `yield` function that the iterator's consumer provides. The return value of this `yield` function tells the iterator to push more values or stop:

Declared in the standard library's iter package

```
package iter
type Seq[V any] func(yield func(V) bool)
```

Declares a generic function type

DEFINITION `Seq` is short for *sequence* and pronounced "seek."

`Seq` is a generic type representing a push iterator that can push values to consumers. The type parameter, `V`, can be any type. Think of `V` as a placeholder for any type. In our case, we use the `[Result]` type next to `Seq` to instantiate an iterator for `Result` values:

```
type Results iter.Seq[Result]
```

Declares an iterator type that can iterate on Result values

This expression, `iter.Seq[Result]`, is identical to the following type:

```
type Results func(yield func(Result) bool)
```

This function type takes another function named `yield` as input. The `yield` function takes a `Result` value and returns a `bool`. This iterator allows us to push `Result` values to consumers.

NOTE Consumers provide a `yield` function to an iterator to receive values.

PUSHING VALUES TO CONSUMERS

Now that we know what the `Seq` and `Results` types look like, let's go deeper into how to produce and consume values. In our case, `SendN` returns the `Results` iterator, and consumers provide the `yield` function to the iterator. The iterator generates a `Result` for each request and then calls the consumer's `yield` function, pushing that `Result` to the consumer. The iterator continues doing so until it pushes each `Result` or the consumer's `yield` returns `false`. Figure 6.2 shows how to produce and consume `Result` values using the `Results` iterator:

1 Calling `SendN` returns a `Results` iterator as a closure.
2 Consumers pass their `yield` function to this closure.
3 The closure calls `yield` to push the next `Result` to the consumer.
4 Step 3 repeats until all values have been pushed or `yield` returns `false`.

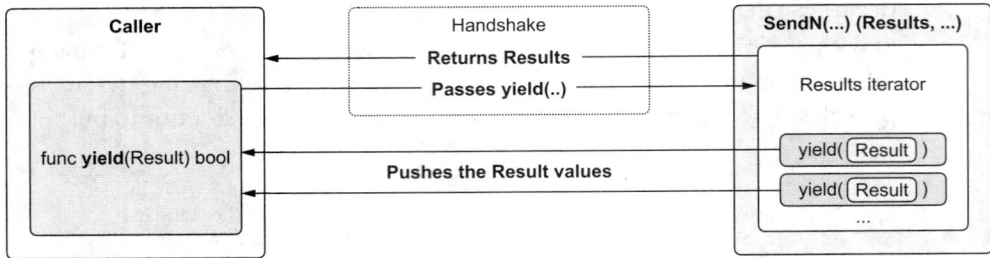

Figure 6.2   The `Results` iterator pushes values by calling the consumer's `yield`.

Consumers can optionally return `false` from their `yield` function to stop iterating over `Result` values. Also, as we'll see in section 6.3.2, the Go compiler has integrated support for iterators and can return `false` automatically from the `yield` function.

6.3.2   *Producing values*

Now that we've implemented the `Results` iterator type and discussed how iterators push values to consumers using a `yield` function, we're ready to implement the `SendN` function. By implementing `SendN`, we'll learn how to push `Result` values through an iterator. In section 6.3.3, we'll add the `Summarize` function to consume these values.

As listing 6.4 shows, `SendN` returns an iterator. This iterator sends HTTP requests using `Send`, pushing each `Result` to the consumer's `yield` function to deliver it to the consumer.

NOTE   Chapter 7 explains why using the `http.DefaultClient` isn't ideal.

Listing 6.4   Returning a push iterator (`hit/hit.go`)

```
package hit

import (
    "fmt"
    . . .
)

. . .

// SendN sends N requests using [Send].
// It returns a single-use [Results] iterator that
// pushes a [Result] for each [http.Request] sent.
func SendN(
    n int, req *http.Request,
) (Results, error) {                          ◄──── Returns a
    if n <= 0 {                                      Results iterator
        return nil, fmt.Errorf("n must be positive: got %d", n)   as a closure
    }
```

```
        // other checks are omitted for brevity

    return func(yield func(Result) bool) {
        for range n {
            result := Send(http.DefaultClient, req)
            if !yield(result) {
                return
            ;
        }
    }, nil
}
```

Sends n requests in a loop

Simulates sending the request using Go's default HTTP client

Pushes the Result to yield

Stops pushing results if the yield function returns false

`Send` returns a `Result`, whereas `SendN` returns a `Results` iterator, which allows consumers to walk over each `Result`. The iterator stops when `yield` returns `false` or the iterator's loop ends.

As we saw in section 6.3.1, the underlying type of `iter.Seq[Result]` is `func(yield func(Result) bool)`. That's why we return a closure with the same signature from the `SendN` function as a `Results` iterator. Because this closure is a higher-order function that takes a `yield` function, consumers can pass a `yield` function to the closure.

We push a `Result` value to the consumer by calling the `yield` function and receive a `bool` value from the consumer indicating whether to produce more values. Because the consumer passes the `yield`, they can stop our iterator by returning `false` from their `yield` function. We'll see this behavior in action after implementing the `Summarize` function as a consumer in section 6.3.3.

For now, `SendN`'s iterator processes requests sequentially, waiting for one to complete before sending the next, until we refactor `SendN` to send requests concurrently. This approach forces us to keep the `SendN`'s API sequential even after we switch to a concurrent pipeline.

Deep dive: Why do we return an iterator instead of a slice?

If we return a slice instead of an iterator, `SendN` has to allocate enough memory to store all the `Result` values. In `SendN`, we declare a slice of `Result` with size `n` and then fill it with `Result` values as each request completes:

```
func SendN(. . .) ([]Result, error) {
    . . .
    results := make([]Result, n)
    for i := range n {
        results[i] = Send(. . ., req)
    }
    return results, nil
}
```

Returns a []Result instead of an iterator

Preallocates a []Result with n elements

Saves the next Result in the results slice

Return the slice with (a possibly large) backing array that contains all the Result values gathered

(continued)

The `make` function is an efficient way to make a slice when we know the size. This returning-a-slice approach comes with some drawbacks:

- *Memory allocation*—The slice's backing array needs to store all `Result` values.
- *No early exit*—With a slice, all results are computed and stored before they are returned. Even if consumers need only a few results, `SendN` generates and stores all of them, which can be inefficient if consumers don't need to process all of them.

By contrast, using iterators (e.g., `iter.Seq[Result]`) prevents the preceding issues:

- *Efficiency*—The iterator pushes each `Result` as needed, reducing memory use.
- *Early exit*—It allows consumers to stop early.
- *Flexibility*—It gives consumers more control over the execution flow.

Returning slices may allocate more memory up front for all values even if consumers need only a few. Iterators yield results lazily, saving memory and allowing early exit.

6.3.3 Consuming values

Now that we've explored how to return iterators, let's learn how to consume them. We'll work on the following to allow users to access an overall performance summary:

- `Summarize` consumes a `Results` iterator and returns a `Summary` value.
- `Summary` is a summary of performance `Result` values, including total requests, errors, downloaded bytes, and duration of all requests.

After implementing the `Summarize` function, we'll understand how to consume iterators.

SUMMARY

After sending multiple requests, users typically need a clear overview of the results. For that purpose, as the next listing shows, we declare the `Summary` type that we'll return from `Summarize` later.

Listing 6.5 `Summary` type (`hit/result.go`)

```go
// Summary is the summary of [Result] values.
type Summary struct {
	Requests int                 // Requests is the total number of requests made
	Errors   int                 // Errors is the total number of failed requests
	Bytes    int64               // Bytes is the total number of bytes transferred
	RPS      float64             // RPS is the number of requests sent per second
	Duration time.Duration       // Duration is the total time taken by requests
	Fastest  time.Duration       // Fastest is the fastest request duration
	Slowest  time.Duration       // Slowest is the slowest request duration
	Success  float64             // Success is the ratio of successful requests
}
```

By looking at a `Summary` value, users can quickly diagnose problems, measure efficiency, and decide whether further optimization or debugging is necessary for their servers.

SUMMARIZING

Now that we've declared the `Summary` type to represent a summary of performance `Result` values, let's next learn how to consume iterators. Recall that `SendN` returns a `Results` iterator that sends multiple requests and allows users to consume each `Result`. Instead of calculating a `Summary` on their own, however, users can use the `Summarize` function.

Users can call `Summarize` with a `Results` iterator to get a `Summary` value. `Summarize` iterates over each `Result` value from the iterator, processes the values, and returns a single `Summary` value that gives users the overall performance results of a target server.

Listing 6.6 Summarizing the results (`hit/result.go`)

```go
package hit

import (
    "net/http"
    . . .
)

. . .

// Summarize returns a [Summary] of [Results].
func Summarize(results Results) Summary {
    var s Summary
    if results == nil {
        return s
    }

    started := time.Now()
    for r := range results {
        s.Requests++
        s.Bytes += r.Bytes

        if r.Error != nil ||
            r.Status != http.StatusOK {
            s.Errors++
        }
        if s.Fastest == 0 {
            s.Fastest = r.Duration
        }
        if r.Duration < s.Fastest {
            s.Fastest = r.Duration
        }
        if r.Duration > s.Slowest {
            s.Slowest = r.Duration
        }
    }
    if s.Requests > 0 {
        s.Success = (float64(s.Requests-s.Errors) /
```

Prevents panic when Summarize is called with a nil Results iterator

Iterates over the Result values until the iterator stops

Considers HTTP status OK a success. (Many other status codes mean success, but I'm keeping the code simple.)

```
            float64(s.Requests)) * 100
    }
    s.Duration = time.Since(started)
    s.RPS = float64(s.Requests) / s.Duration.Seconds()

    return s
}
```

> Sets the time duration between two time.Time values. time.Since is a shortcut for time.Now().Sub(t).

NOTE Iterating with a `nil` iterator results in a panic. `Summarize` prevents this panic by checking for a `nil` iterator. If `results` are `nil`, `Summarize` returns a zero `Summary`.

`Summarize` gets each `Result` from the `Results` iterator and returns a `Summary`. It takes an iterator parameter because it doesn't care where the `Result` values come from. (Iterators standardize the way we consume sequences of values.) Whether those values come from a `[]Result` or a `chan Result`, the `Summarize`'s API remains the same.

We use an ordinary `for-range` loop to iterate over an iterator. Each iteration returns the next `Result` value until the iterator depletes all the values. Alternatively, we could stop the iterator by returning from `Summarize` or use a `break` statement in the loop.

The compiler has built-in support for iterators. Using a `for-range` calls the iterator function automatically (refer to listing 6.4), passing it a `yield` function. Then it calls `yield` with a copy of the next `Result` value. If we terminate the loop before the iterator delivers us all `Result` values, `yield` automatically returns `false`, causing a well-behaved iterator such as `Results` to stop early without pushing the remaining values.

Deep dive: Passing around values instead of pointers

You may wonder why we don't pass around a `*Result` and use `Result` instead:

```
type Result struct
    func Send(. . .) Result
type Results iter.Seq[Result]
```

Objects in many other popular object-oriented languages are typically passed with a reference to a hidden pointer that points to the object's memory location. In Go, however, we can choose whether to pass a pointer to a value (as a `*Result`) or the value itself (as a `Result`). A `Result` value is stored in memory as is, without any hidden pointer (though a struct's memory layout and size may vary slightly due to struct padding and alignment).

We prefer not to use pointers to `Result` values when passing them around. Instead, we copy them. (Go is pass-by-value.) When returning a `Result` from `Send`, passing it to `yield` in `SendN`, or iterating over results in `Summarize`, we pass copies of the `Result` values.

The first reason is that we don't need to mutate `Result` values, so passing them by value is semantically correct. Also, using a value type ensures that each goroutine works with its own copy, preventing shared state and leading to more predictable, consistent behavior.

There is also an efficiency aspect, but it's more nuanced than it seems. Pointers are memory-efficient because they avoid copying the original value they point to while passing them around (such as to functions). Returning pointers (i.e., `Send()` `*Result`), however, often triggers heap allocation. The garbage collector must track these pointers until they and their pointed values go out of scope and are no longer referenced.

Considering that the HIT client may handle millions of `Result` pointers when measuring server performance, this could lead to significant garbage-collector overhead. Returning values is often more efficient because the values are likely to be passed on the stack (more efficient than heap memory in general), reducing or eliminating the need for the garbage collector's involvement. The values are also more likely to be cached by the CPU for faster access, whereas pointers may require slower fetches from main memory (heap memory).

In summary, although performance aspects could be important, our primary reason is semantic correctness. Because we don't need to mutate `Result` values, passing by value ensures clarity and correctness, so it's the most idiomatic, maintainable approach for our program.

6.3.4 Testing

Now that we have `Summarize`, let's test it to see iterators in action. As listing 6.7 shows, `TestSummarizeFastestResult` verifies whether `Summarize` can find the fastest `Result` correctly. `TestSummarizeNilResults` verifies that `Summarize` doesn't panic when given a nil iterator.

Listing 6.7 Testing `Summarize` (`hit/result_test.go`)

```
package hit

import (
    "slices"        ◄────────  Provides helpers that make
    "testing"                  working with slices convenient
    "time"
)

func TestSummarizeFastestResult(t *testing.T) {
    results := []Result{
        {Duration: 2 * time.Second},
        {Duration: 5 * time.Second},
    }
                                    Converts iter.Seq[Result] to Results
    sum := Summarize(               because Summarize expects a Results
        Results(            ◄────
            slices.Values(results),  ◄────  Returns an iterator
        ),                                  from the results slice
    )
```

```
        if sum.Fastest != 2*time.Second {
            t.Errorf("Fastest=%v; want 2s", sum.Fastest)
        }
    }

    func TestSummarizeNilResults(t *testing.T) {
        defer func() {
            if err := recover(); err != nil {          ◄────┐ Turns off the panic
                t.Errorf("should not panic: %v", err)
            }
        }()
        _ = Summarize(nil)
    }
                        ┌ As an exercise, add
    . . .        ◄──────┘ more tests here.
```

Now that the tests are ready, let's run them:

```
$ go test ./hit -v
--- PASS: TestSummarizeFastestResult
--- PASS: TestSummarizeNilResults
```

In the first test, we initialize a []Result in which the duration of the first Result is shorter than the second. Then we turn the []Result into an iterator by calling the standard library's slices.Values function. Next, we convert the iterator to Results so we can pass it to Summarize. Finally, we validate whether we get the correct Result (the fastest one).

NOTE   slices.Values returns an iterator that yields the given slice's elements.

In the second test, we verify whether Summarize panics when it gets a nil iterator. If it panics, we use the built-in recover function in the deferred function, catch the panic, and prevent it from spreading to the test, thereby preventing a crash of the whole test run.

This technique shows us how to test a function that can cause panic. Calling the recover function inside a defer allows us to turn off panics; otherwise, we won't stop the panic. If Summarize panics, we get the error and mark the test failed with that error message.

We can trigger panics manually using the built-in panic function. Using the panic and recover functions is fine in tests. Generally, however, use panic and recover as a last resort in nontest code; they disrupt normal control flow and reduce maintainability. Instead, handle errors explicitly. These functions are intended to handle extremely unexpected situations from which the program cannot recover, such as programmer mistakes.

Deep dive: The generic slices.Values function

The slices package declares the generic Values function as follows:

```
func Values[Slice ~[]E, E any](s Slice) iter.Seq[E]
```

This generic function can convert any type of slice to an iterator:

- `Slice` and `E` are type parameters. Think of them as placeholders.
- `[]E` is the slice type, and `E` is the slice's element type.
- `~[]E` matches any type whose underlying type is `[]E`, such as `type T []E`, not only `[]E` itself. Otherwise, `Values` would accept the exact `[]E` type but not `T`.

For convenience, we use `Values` to convert `[]Result` to an iterator. When we pass a `[]Result` to `Values`, for example, the compiler automatically allows us to use `Values` as follows:

```
func Values(s []Result) iter.Seq[Result]
```

We can pass a `[]Result` into `Values` and get back an `iter.Seq[Result]` that allows us to iterate on `Result` values. Otherwise, we would have to turn the slice into an iterator manually. `Values` is a helper function that makes our lives more convenient.

6.4 Options

Now that we have a strong foundation, we'll add an `Options` input to `SendN` for experts who may want to tweak its behavior. For users who don't want to customize `SendN`'s behavior, we'll add a `Defaults` function that they can pass to `SendN` to run it with default options.

Most users can pass `Defaults` to `SendN` instead of dealing with the hassle of passing custom options. Whether users pass `Defaults` or custom `Options`, `SendN` will take care of providing sensible defaults (e.g., passing 0 as concurrency sets it to 1).

6.4.1 Providing options

As listing 6.8 shows, we declare the `Options` type with the following fields:

- `Concurrency` determines how many goroutines to use while sending requests.
- `RPS` limits the number of requests that can be sent per second.
- `Send` allows users to specify a custom `SendFunc` to use while sending requests. The default request sender remains as the `hit` package's `Send` function. In chapter 7, we'll switch to a custom sender as the default for more efficiency.

Listing 6.8 Providing options (`hit/option.go`)

```
package hit

import "net/http"

// SendFunc is a type of function that sends an
// [http.Request] and returns a [Result].
type SendFunc func(*http.Request) Result

// Options defines the options for sending requests.
```

```
// Uses default options for unset options.
type Options struct {
    // Concurrency is the number of concurrent requests to send.
    // Default: 1
    Concurrency int

    // RPS is the requests to send per second.
    // Default: 0 (no rate limiting)
    RPS int

    // Send processes requests.
    // Default: Uses [Send].
    Send SendFunc
}

// Defaults returns the default [Options].
func Defaults() Options {
    return withDefaults(Options{})
}

func withDefaults(o Options) Options {
    if o.Concurrency == 0 {
        o.Concurrency = 1
    }
    if o.Send == nil {
        o.Send = func(r *http.Request) Result {
            return Send(http.DefaultClient, r)
        }
    }
    return o
}
```

> **Returns a new Options with the defaults**

> **Applies the default options for the missing options**

> **We can compare function values to nil.**

> **Uses the Send function by default while sending requests**

We've introduced `Options` to let expert users customize `SendN`'s behavior when sending multiple requests. `Defaults` returns sensible defaults, and `SendFunc` allows customization of request senders. Because `Send` requires an `http.Client`, we pass it the default HTTP client.

`Options.Send` is set to a function that sends an HTTP request using Go's default HTTP client. We use a closure to set the default request sender because the `Send` function takes a `Client`, but `Options.Send` does not. You can think of this closure as an *adapter* that bridges between `Options.Send` and `Send`, which takes an extra `*http.Client` parameter.

NOTE   Closures are extremely helpful as adaptors between function types.

6.4.2 *Accepting options*

Currently, `SendN` doesn't accept options. Previously, we introduced the `Options` struct, which gives expert users more control when sending multiple requests. As the next listing shows, we update `SendN` to accept an `Options` parameter, letting users customize its behavior.

Listing 6.9 `SendN` **with options** (`hit/option.go`)

```
func SendN(
    n int, req *http.Request, opts Options,
) (Results, error) {
    opts = withDefaults(opts)          ◄──────  Sets the default options
    if n <= 0 {                                  for missing options
        return nil, fmt.Errorf("n must be positive: got %d", n)
    }
    // other checks are omitted for brevity

    return func(yield func(Result) bool) {
        for range n {
            if !yield(opts.Send(req)) {   ◄──────  Uses the Options.Send
                return                             function to send requests
            }
        }
    }, nil
}
```

We've made three changes to the SendN function:

- We added an `opts` parameter of type `Options` to the function.
- `SendN` calls `withDefaults` to fill any unset options with defaults.
- `SendN` sends requests using the `Options.Send` function. `SendN` no longer needs to pass an HTTP client to `Send` because the `Options` takes care of setting it.

By setting default options for the missing ones, we ensure sensible defaults that enable SendN to operate correctly. We perform this detection by checking the zero value of an option. Suppose that we add a `MaxRetries` option to retry the requests, and its default value is 5. It will be hard to tell whether users want to turn `MaxRetries` off by setting it to 0 or leaving it unset; both scenarios can appear the same because an integer's zero value is also 0.

> **TIP** See appendix F for a deep explanation of this issue. The appendix also discusses an alternative pattern for handling options: Rob Pike's self-referential functions.

With `Options` and `Defaults`, SendN becomes more flexible without sacrificing simplicity. Users can customize request-sending behavior or rely on sensible defaults.

6.5 *Integration*

Now that the sequential version of the HIT client is ready, we can integrate it with the HIT tool. Doing so allows us to control the client's behavior with command-line flags and demonstrate its use. We'll modify the tool to call the client and print a summary.

6.5.1   *Printing a summary*

Whereas the HIT client sends requests and gathers results, the HIT tool deals with the user interface. For this reason, as shown in the following listing, we declare a new function in the HIT tool to print the Summary generated by the HIT client to the console.

> **Listing 6.10   Printing a summary (`hit/cmd/hit/hit.go`)**

```go
package main

import (
    "math"
    "time"
    "github.com/inancgumus/gobyexample/hit"
    . . .
)


. . .

func printSummary(sum hit.Summary, stdout io.Writer) {
    fmt.Fprintf(stdout, `
Summary:
    Success:   %.0f%%
    RPS:       %.1f
    Requests:  %d
    Errors:    %d
    Bytes:     %d
    Duration:  %s
    Fastest:   %s
    Slowest:   %s
`,
        sum.Success,
        math.Round(sum.RPS),
        sum.Requests,
        sum.Errors,
        sum.Bytes,
        sum.Duration.Round(time.Millisecond),
        sum.Fastest.Round(time.Millisecond),
        sum.Slowest.Round(time.Millisecond),
    )
}
```

Prints a formatted summary to a Writer (e.g., os.Stdout)

Formats a float number without any decimal places (rounding to the nearest whole number). %% prints a literal % sign.

Formats a float number with one digit after the decimal point

The printSummary function receives a Summary and writes an easy-to-read summary to the Writer. It prints the success percentage of the number of successful requests to the total requests made. Then it prints metrics such as requests per second, request count, errors, data transferred, and various timings. Fprintf helps us format these values neatly, giving users an easy-to-follow overview of the performance results.

6.5.2   *Integration*

Now we'll integrate the HIT client into our HIT tool. As listing 6.11 shows, we update the existing runHit function to call SendN and print the resulting summary.

Recall from chapter 5 that the tool runs `runHit` automatically after parsing the command-line flags.

Listing 6.11 Integrating the HIT client (`hit/cmd/hit/hit.go`)

```go
package main

import (
    "net/http"
    . . .
)

. . .

func runHit(c *config, stdout io.Writer) error {
    req, err := http.NewRequest(
        http.MethodGet, c.url, http.NoBody,
    )
    if err != nil {
        return fmt.Errorf("creating a new request: %w", err)
    }
    results, err := hit.SendN(
        c.n, req, hit.Options{
            Concurrency: c.c,
            RPS:         c.rps,
        },
    )
    if err != nil {
        return fmt.Errorf("sending requests: %w", err)
    }

    printSummary(
        hit.Summarize(results),
        stdout,
    )

    return nil
}
```

Creates a new HTTP GET request without a request body

Returns a Results iterator that sends c.n HTTP GET requests to c.url

Specifies the number of concurrent HTTP requests to send

Limits the number of HTTP requests to send per second

Summarizes the results by iterating over the Results iterator

Prints the summary to a Writer, such as os.Stdout

We update `runHit` to create a new HTTP request with the target URL. Then we send multiple requests to this URL using `SendN`. After receiving the `Results` iterator, we `Summarize` and print a performance `Summary` to the provided `Writer`.

> **NOTE** `NewRequest` takes a `Reader` as the last parameter to set the request's body. This is useful when sending a body, such as in a POST request. Because we don't need a body, we pass `NoBody`, a `Reader` that does nothing but satisfy the `Reader` interface.

With this integration complete, the HIT tool and client work together to send requests and output an easy-to-follow summary. Because the HIT client handles request logic, our tool remains simple, focusing on user interaction and displaying performance summaries.

6.5.3   *Demonstration*

Now that we've integrated the HIT client with the HIT tool, let's simulate sending multiple requests, get the results, print a summary, and see whether everything works together:

```
$ go run ./hit/cmd/hit -n 10                          Sends 10 requests to the
                        https://x.com/inancgumus       target URL one at a time


 /\ \_\ \    /\ \    /\___ _\
 \ \  __ \   \ \ \   \/_/\ \/
  \ \_\ \_\   \ \_\      \ \_\
   \/_/\/_/    \/_/       \/_/

Sending 10 requests to "https://x.com/inancgumus" (concurrency: 1)

Summary:
    Success:  100%
    RPS:      10.0
    Requests: 10
    Errors:   0
    Bytes:    100
    Duration: 1.082s
    Fastest:  100ms
    Slowest:  100ms
```

Each request among 10 requests takes 100 ms because the `Send` function sleeps for 100 ms (recall `Send` from listing 6.2). The total duration is about 1 second. All requests are successful. `RPS` is `10` because HIT sends 10 requests per second.

This concludes the first part of the HIT client. We've designed a sequential package API that hides complexity behind a simple API. Now that we have enough functionality and a strong foundation, we can refactor the HIT client internals to send concurrent requests.

6.6   *Concurrent pipeline pattern*

Sending requests to a server one after the other shows how well the server handles individual requests. When many requests come together, sending them won't reflect how the server performs under load. By using concurrency, we can significantly increase the number of requests sent to the server and give users a better view of the server's performance.

In this section and the following sections, we'll transform the HIT client into a concurrent one by using the pipeline pattern without changing the `hit` package's synchronous API.

6.6.1   *Benefits of concurrent pipelines*

Concurrency involves structuring a program with independent tasks that can run simultaneously or at overlapping times. Go makes concurrency intuitive, easier to grasp, and effective for crafting predictable and scalable concurrent programs. The concurrent pipeline pattern is a good example: it structures concurrent execution into stages that run in a sequence.

Think of a concurrent pipeline like a UNIX pipeline or an assembly line. A concurrent pipeline consists of several stages that work concurrently, connected by channels to transfer messages. The first stage produces a message and sends it to the next stage until the message reaches the last stage. The last stage delivers the final results to consumers.

The concurrent pipeline pattern has the following benefits:

- *Flexibility*—It's easier to add or remove stages without modifying their code.
- *Reusability*—We can reuse parts in different pipelines and programs.
- *Modularity*—Stages are separate and focused, making them easier to maintain.

6.6.2 Designing a concurrent pipeline

Now that we are somewhat familiar with the pipeline pattern, let's apply it to the HIT client to see it in practice and understand what it is and how to create one. We plan to refactor the `SendN` function to support a concurrent pipeline that sends requests concurrently to a server while maintaining the existing design that returns an iterator.

As figure 6.3 shows, calling `SendN` runs a pipeline with the following stages, which run concurrently, are connected through channels, and pass messages to the next:

- *Producer*—Produces and delivers `*Request` messages to the next stage
- *Throttler*—Slows the passage of each `*Request` in the pipeline if activated
- *Dispatcher*—Spawns goroutines that send HTTP requests and collect results

The dispatcher's output, unlike previous stages, is a `Result` channel. The dispatcher goroutines send HTTP requests and pass each `Result` to this channel. `SendN` listens to this channel continuously and pushes each `Result` to the consumer through the `Results` iterator.

Messages flow between pipeline stages through channels. The stages run concurrently and pass messages forward until they reach dispatcher goroutines, which send requests to the target server. After sending a request, dispatcher goroutines forward each `Result` to the dispatcher's output channel. `SendN` listens to this channel and pushes each `Result` through the iterator, letting consumers receive results as the worker goroutines send HTTP requests and produce results.

Even after applying this new design, the `SendN` function's API remains the same except that it sends HTTP requests and delivers results concurrently. In the following sections, we implement these stages one at a time. After we implement each stage, we'll integrate it into the pipeline to run that stage and connect it to the subsequent stages.

> **NOTE** The following sections require basic knowledge of concurrent programming in Go. Check out appendix E for details on goroutines and channels.

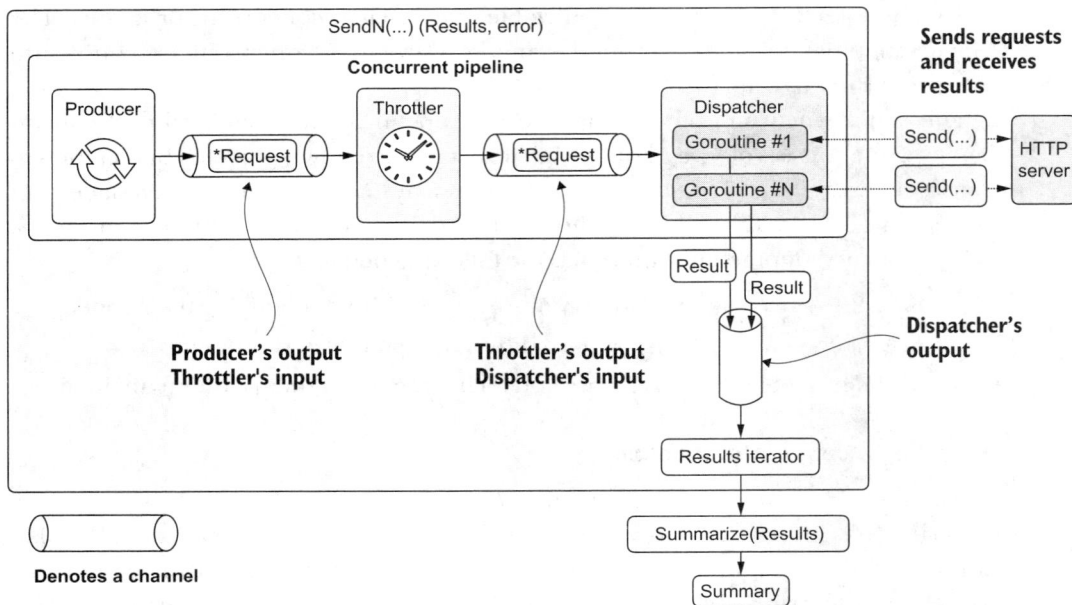

Figure 6.3   `SendN` runs the pipeline and returns a `Results` iterator. Stages run concurrently and are connected through channels. Dispatcher goroutines call the configured `Send` function to send concurrent HTTP requests and return results.

6.7 *Producer stage*

Now that we've learned how the concurrent pipeline lets us structure a concurrent program into separate stages that run concurrently and communicate through channels, we'll start by adding the producer stage. Other stages will receive each `*Request` from the producer, optionally throttle them, send them to the server, and collect results. At the end of this section, we'll integrate the producer stage as the first step in building the pipeline.

As figure 6.4 shows, the producer stage sends each `*Request` to the next stage through its output channel as many times as the number of configured HTTP requests it needs to send.

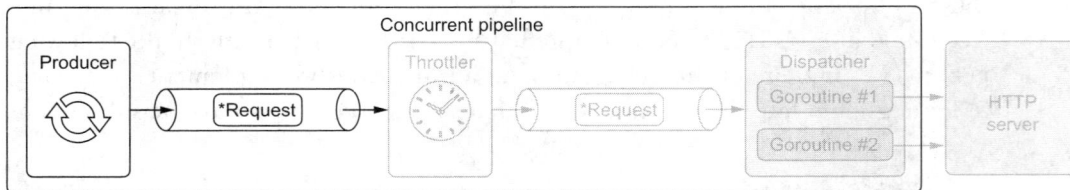

Figure 6.4   The producer sends messages to the next stage.

When the producer closes its output channel, the rest of the stages stop automatically because they are listening to the producer's channel and receive a close signal. This approach allows us to produce the required number of *Requests and stop the remaining stages automatically.

6.7.1 Implementation

In this section, we'll implement the producer stage, as shown in listing 6.12. Because the producer is the pipeline's first stage, it doesn't have an input channel. Instead, it has only an output channel. It initializes the channel, launches a goroutine that relays the provided request to the output channel n times, and returns the output channel without waiting for the goroutine to return. When the goroutine sends all the messages, it closes the channel.

When we connect the producer stage to the next one and run the pipeline, the next stage listens to this output channel even after the `produce` returns. The next stage stops operating automatically because it gets a close signal after the producer goroutine closes this channel.

TIP See appendix E for more on coordinating goroutines by closing channels.

> **Listing 6.12 Implementing the producer stage (`hit/pipe.go`)**

```
package hit

import "net/http"

func produce(
    n int,
    req *http.Request,
) <-chan *http.Request {
    out := make(chan *http.Request)

    go func() {
        defer close(out)
        for range n {
            out <- req
        }
    }()

    return out
}
```

Relays each *Request to the next stage through this output channel

Initializes a new output channel that can relay Request pointers

Launches a new goroutine that runs the closure concurrently

Closes the output channel right before the closure returns

Sends the *Request to the output channel

Returns the output channel

We've implemented the producer stage with the `produce` function. The input n is the number of messages to relay to the next stage. Because the next stage would be the consumer, we return a `<-chan *http.Request`, allowing the next stage to receive but not send.

For now, the producer has exactly one responsibility: relaying *Requests to the next stages. This approach separates *Request generation from HTTP request handling.

Because we've isolated concerns, stages stay focused and straightforward, making them easier to test and maintain.

> **NOTE**   Directional channels (send-only and receive-only) make introducing bugs less likely and clarify our intentions as to what to do (and what we cannot and should not do) with a channel. See appendix E for details.

6.7.2   *Integration*

Let's integrate the producer into our pipeline. As the following listing shows, we integrate the producer into the new `runPipeline` function, which coordinates pipeline stages, such as linking them together and returning the pipeline's results.

> **Listing 6.13   Integrating the producer stage (`hit/pipe.go`)**

```
func runPipeline(n int, req *http.Request, opts Options) <-chan Result {
    requests := produce(n, req)
    _ = requests        ◀─────┐
    return nil                 │ Allows the code to compile
}
```

After adding the remaining stages, we'll integrate `runPipeline` into `SendN`. In section 6.9.2, `SendN` pushes each `Result` to consumers as they arrive from the pipeline:

```
func SendN(. . .) (Results, error) {
    . . .
    results := runPipeline(n, req, opts)    ◀─────  Runs the pipeline and
    return func(yield func(Result) bool) {          saves its output channel
        for result := range results { . . . }   ◀─  Listens to the pipeline's output
    }, nil                                          and pushes each Result to
}                                                   consumers as they arrive
```

We integrated the producer stage as the first stage of the pipeline and saved its output channel to the `requests` variable. Because the other stages don't exist yet, we assigned it to a blank identifier to silence the "variable is unused" compiler error. Next, we'll implement the throttler stage and connect its input directly to this channel.

6.8   *Throttler stage*

We can't reliably measure a server's performance if we overload it; excessive load can lead to unpredictable server behavior and skewed results. To prevent overload, we'll slow the message flow in our pipeline when requested. Slowing the pipeline keeps the target server within its limits, allowing us to gather realistic, accurate measurements.

Let's continue building our pipeline by adding the throttler stage. The throttler will receive these messages from the producer, optionally slow them to prevent server overload, and pass them downstream. At the end of this section, we'll integrate the throttler into our pipeline, bringing us one step closer to a fully functional concurrent pipeline.

As figure 6.5 shows, the throttler stage receives messages from the producer and sends them to the dispatcher stage after a user-defined delay. It controls how quickly messages flow through the pipeline, preventing overload and helping us collect accurate measurements.

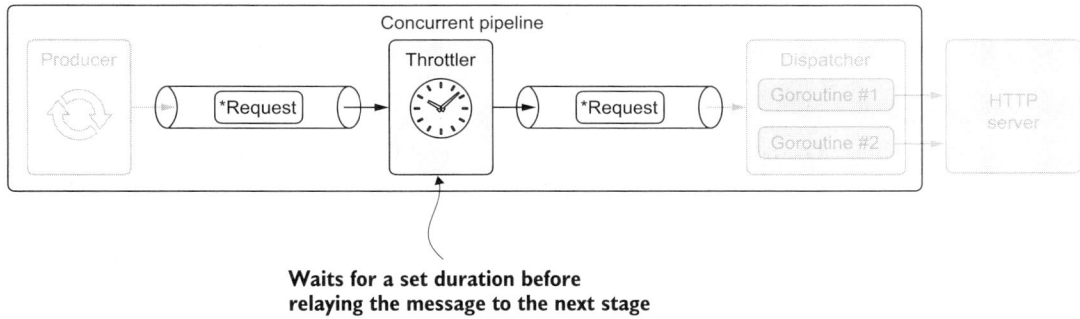

Figure 6.5 **The throttler stage slows the flow of messages in the pipeline.**

The throttler stage sits between the producer and dispatcher stages, controlling the rate of messages flowing through our pipeline. By adding a delay before forwarding each message, we prevent the dispatcher goroutines from overwhelming the target server.

6.8.1 Implementation

Now that we understand the throttler's role, let's implement it as a separate stage. As the next listing shows, we declare the `throttle` function, which takes messages from its input channel, applies a delay, and forwards messages downstream through its output channel.

Listing 6.14 Implementing the throttler stage (`hit/pipe.go`)

```
package hit

import (
    "net/http"
    "time"
)

. . .

func throttle(
    in <-chan *http.Request,           ← Receives messages from this input channel
    delay time.Duration,               ← Determines how long to wait before relaying the next message
) <-chan *http.Request {               ← Relays messages to the next stage through this output channel
    out := make(chan *http.Request)

    go func() {
        defer close(out)
```

```
t := time.NewTicker(delay)    ◄──────  Creates a Ticker that
for r := range in {           ◄───              ticks at intervals set
    <-t.C                     ◄────
    out <- r                  ◄────     Receives the next message
}                                              from the input channel
}()

return out                         Blocks the goroutine until the next tick
}                                  Sends the message to the output channel
```

The throttler takes messages from an input channel and forwards them to an output channel. Between messages, it applies a `delay` using the standard library's `time.Ticker` type, which delivers a tick at fixed intervals. Our throttler waits for these ticks from the `Ticker`'s `C` channel before forwarding a message, spacing messages with the given delay.

NOTE   In early versions of Go, not closing a `Ticker` caused a goroutine leak. As of Go 1.23, closing a `Ticker` is unnecessary because Go can do that for us.

Deep dive: time.Ticker vs. time.Sleep

`time.Sleep` blocks the current goroutine:

```
time.Sleep(10 * time.Second)      ◄───   Blocks the current
                                         goroutine for ten seconds
```

On the other hand, `Ticker` allows us to wait for multiple channels:

```
                                       Allows waiting for multiple
                                       channels simultaneously
t := time.NewTicker(. . .)
select {                          ◄───   Listens to the Ticker's
case <-t.C:                       ◄───          C channel
case <-cancellationSignal:        ◄───
    return                        ◄───   Listens to the cancellationSignal channel
}
                                       Allows us to cancel the operation
                                       when a cancellation signal arrives
```

Compared with `Sleep`, `Ticker` makes our code more responsive. In chapter 7, which explores cancellation, we'll gain a better understanding of why `Ticker` is a better choice. See appendix E for an explanation of the `select` statement.

6.8.2   *Integration*

Now we'll add the throttler to the pipeline, linking it immediately after the producer. When it's integrated, users can optionally activate the throttler to control message flow and measure the server's performance accurately without overloading it. In the next listing, we conditionally add the throttler stage to the existing pipeline based on the configured RPS option. If RPS is greater than 0, we activate the throttler to slow the messages from the producer before forwarding them to the dispatcher stage.

Listing 6.15   Integrating the throttler stage (`hit/pipe.go`)

```
func runPipeline(n int, req *http.Request, opts Options) <-chan Result {
    requests := produce(n, req)
    if opts.RPS > 0 {                          ◄─────────   Activates the throttler only if
        requests = throttle(                                the RPS option is configured
            requests,
            time.Second/time.Duration(opts.RPS),
        )                                       Wraps the original producer
    }                                           channel with the throttler's
    return nil                                       output channel
}
```

We integrated the throttler stage into the concurrent pipeline right after the producer stage. When users set a positive RPS option, the pipeline activates the throttler, wrapping the original channel with a throttled version. If the RPS option isn't set, the throttler remains passive, and messages pass from the producer to the next stage without delay.

Next, we'll implement the dispatcher stage and connect it directly to the output of the throttler or the producer, depending on whether throttling is active.

6.9   *Dispatcher stage*

In this section, we'll implement the dispatcher stage and connect it directly to the output of the throttler or the producer, depending on whether throttling is active. Sending sequential requests doesn't reflect how a server handles concurrent load, however. As figure 6.6 shows, the dispatcher spawns multiple worker goroutines to send HTTP requests to the server concurrently and gather the results, allowing us to measure the server's performance under load accurately.

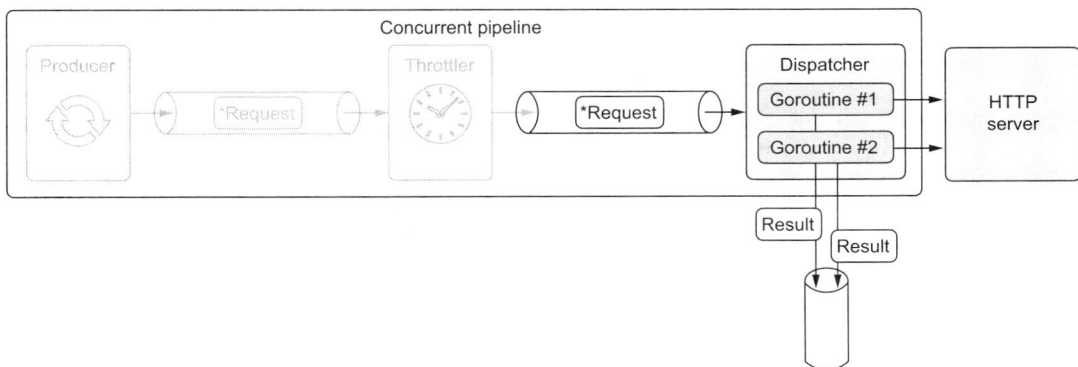

Figure 6.6   The dispatcher goroutines send HTTP requests, process HTTP responses, calculate a `Result`, and deliver `Result`s to the dispatcher's output channel.

Besides these worker goroutines, we have a monitoring goroutine, which monitors active worker goroutines. The monitor closes the dispatcher's output channel after all the workers finish. Otherwise, closing the channel before the workers finish could lead to race conditions. A worker might try to send to the channel after we close it, for example, leading to panics.

Closing the dispatcher's output channel is also critical for its listeners. When the monitoring goroutine closes the channel, it indicates that the channel will no longer transmit `Result` values and signals receivers to stop listening to the pipeline results. As we'll see in section 6.9.2, `SendN`'s iterator stops pushing results to consumers and returns when this channel closes.

NOTE   Closing a channel signals the receivers that no more values will be sent.

6.9.1   *Implementation*

Now that we understand how the dispatcher coordinates goroutines, we're ready to implement it. In listing 6.16, we implement the dispatcher as a pipeline stage that launches worker goroutines. These workers receive messages from the dispatcher's input channel, send them concurrently to the server, and return the results through the dispatcher's output channel.

We also start a monitoring goroutine that watches the number of active workers using the standard library's `WaitGroup` type. The monitoring goroutine closes the output channel when all workers finish.

Listing 6.16   Implementing the dispatcher (`hit/pipe.go`)

```
package hit

import (
    . . .
    "sync"
)

. . .

func dispatch(
    in <-chan *http.Request,       ◀──  Receives messages from
    concurrency int,                    this input channel
    send SendFunc,
) <-chan Result {                  ◀──  Specifies the number of
    out := make(chan Result)            worker goroutines to launch

    var wg sync.WaitGroup          ◀──  Specifies the function to use while
    wg.Add(concurrency)                 sending an HTTP request and returning
                                        a Result value (e.g., hit.Send())
    for range concurrency {
        go func() {                ◀──  Sends Result values to
            defer wg.Done()             this output channel
```

Receives messages from
this input channel

Specifies the number of
worker goroutines to launch

Specifies the function to use while
sending an HTTP request and returning
a Result value (e.g., hit.Send())

Sends Result values to
this output channel

Initializes a new WaitGroup.
(Its zero value is useful.)

Sets the WaitGroup counter to
the number of worker goroutines

Launches as many goroutines
as the number of concurrency

Decrements the WaitGroup counter
when the worker goroutine returns

```
        for req := range in {
            out <- send(req)
        }
    }()
}

go func() {
    wg.Wait()
    close(out)
}()

return out
}
```

Receives the next *http.Request until the input channel is closed

Sends the HTTP request to the server and pushes the Result value to the dispatcher's output channel

Waits until all workers finish and then closes the dispatcher's output channel

Immediately returns after spawning all the goroutines so that the caller can process results concurrently

The dispatcher initializes its output channel and sets up a `WaitGroup` to track active worker goroutines. It immediately launches worker goroutines along with a monitoring goroutine and returns the output channel right away. Returning the channel allows the caller (such as `SendN`) to start receiving results concurrently as soon as they become available.

TIP See appendix E for more information about the `WaitGroup` type.

Workers listen to the dispatcher's input channel and receive `*Requests` from the previous stage (such as the producer or throttler). Then the workers send HTTP requests to the server. When a worker finishes making a request, it sends the `Result` to the dispatcher's output channel, where `SendN` picks it up and pushes it to consumers via the `Results` iterator (we'll implement this behavior in section 6.9.2).

The monitoring goroutine uses the `WaitGroup` to wait until all workers complete their tasks. `WaitGroup` works as a counting semaphore, with each call to `Add` incrementing an internal counter. Workers call `Done` when they finish, decrementing this counter. The monitoring goroutine pauses on the `Wait` call until this counter hits `0`, ensuring that the monitoring goroutine doesn't close the dispatcher's output channel prematurely. Closing this channel signals the receiver that no more results will arrive, causing the `SendN`'s `Results` iterator to stop pushing more values.

Using a `WaitGroup` is helpful because it allows us to track the life cycle of workers and ensure that they finish before we close the dispatcher's output channel. Without it, the monitoring goroutine wouldn't know when all workers were done, potentially leading to race conditions: workers might send results to a closed channel, which could cause runtime panics. Let's highlight two more interesting approaches used here:

- The dispatcher uses the *fan-out pattern* in practice, distributing incoming tasks across multiple goroutines. This pattern helps balance heavy workloads, improving scalability and throughput, such as in data processing.
- By delegating HTTP request logic to the provided `SendFunc`, the dispatcher remains decoupled from request-handling specifics. It gives users complete control of sending HTTP requests without modifying the dispatcher. Users can easily

add authentication, implement retry logic with exponential backoff, or set different timeouts based on various endpoint requirements, and so on.

Now that we've completed the dispatcher stage, our pipeline is capable of sending requests concurrently and gathering results.

> **TIP** See appendix E for an approach that uses buffered channels to limit concurrency.

6.9.2   *Integration*

We've implemented the dispatcher; now let's integrate it into our pipeline. In listing 6.17, the dispatcher stage becomes the final stage of the pipeline. It receives messages—directly from the producer or from the throttler, if it's activated—and spawns worker goroutines to handle these messages concurrently. Each worker calls the `Send` function (from the `Options`) to send an HTTP request, process the response, and get a `Result`. Finally, the workers send these `Result` values to the dispatcher's output channel.

Listing 6.17   Integrating the dispatcher stage (`hit/pipe.go`)

```go
func runPipeline(n int, req *http.Request, opts Options) <-chan Result {
    requests := produce(n, req)
    if opts.RPS > 0 {
        requests = throttle(
            requests,
            time.Second/time.Duration(opts.RPS),
        )
    }
    return dispatch(
        requests, opts.Concurrency, opts.Send,       ◀─┐  Returns the dispatcher's
    )                                                   └─ output channel
}
```

The `runPipeline` function returns the dispatcher's output channel directly. With this integration, we've finished our concurrent pipeline. Next, we'll update the `SendN` function to receive `Result` values from this channel and push them through its iterator to consumers. The next listing updates `SendN` to run the pipeline, saves the returned output channel, and pushes each `Result` from the channel to consumers through the iterator.

Listing 6.18   Updating the iterator to run the pipeline (`hit/hit.go`)

```go
func SendN(n int, req *http.Request, opts Options) (Results, error) {
    opts = withDefaults(opts)
    if n <= 0 {
        return nil, fmt.Errorf("n must be positive: got %d", n)
    }
    // other checks are omitted for brevity
```

```
    results := runPipeline(n, req, opts)

    return func(yield func(Result) bool) {
        for result := range results {
            if !yield(result) {
                return
            }
        }
    }, nil
}
```

◄── **Runs the pipeline and gets the pipeline's output channel**

◄── **Receives Result values from the channel as long as it remains open**

◄── **Pushes each Result to the consumer using the consumer's yield function**

Stops pushing results after the consumer's yield function returns false

Now users can call `SendN` and receive these results right away as they become available through the iterator. We have achieved concurrency transparently without changing the `hit` package's exported API because we treat concurrency as an implementation detail.

Our concurrent pipeline sends requests and collects results, but there is a problem: if users stop consuming results before the iterator pushes them all, the pipeline will still run in the background. In real-world scenarios, we often need to halt ongoing operations, such as when users cancel a long-running request or we reach a certain error threshold. Right now, our pipeline lacks this capability. To address this issue, we'll add cancellation support in chapter 7 by introducing the standard library's `context` package into our pipeline, allowing us to signal all pipeline stages to stop gracefully when necessary.

TIP See appendix E for details on goroutine leaks and how to prevent them.

6.9.3 *Demonstration*

We've integrated all the pipeline stages and updated our `SendN` function to receive results from the pipeline's output channel. Now it's time to see this refactoring in action. We'll run the HIT tool with different concurrency and throttling settings. We'll observe how the new changes affect performance, showing the practical benefits of our concurrent design.

First, we'll send 100 requests without concurrency (with a single worker). This process will take around 10 seconds because the pipeline handles requests sequentially, and the worker calls the `Send` function, which sleeps for 100 ms. It's similar to the behavior before applying concurrency:

```
$ go run ./hit/cmd/hit -n 100 -c 1 https://x.com/inancgumus
. . .
Sending 100 requests to "https://x.com/inancgumus" (concurrency: 1)
Summary:
    Success:  100%
    RPS:      10.0
    Requests: 100
    Errors:   0
    Bytes:    1000
    Duration: 10.116s
    Fastest:  100ms
    Slowest:  100ms
```

Next, we'll send the same number of requests but with 10 workers. This change should speed the process by a factor of 10, completing the run in just over 1 second:

```
$ go run ./hit/cmd/hit -n 100 -c 10 https://x.com/inancgumus
. . .
Sending 100 requests to "https://x.com/inancgumus" (concurrency: 10)

Summary:
    Success:  100%
    RPS:      99.0
    Requests: 100
    Errors:   0
    Bytes:    1000
    Duration: 1.012s
    Fastest:  100ms
    Slowest:  100ms
```

For the final simulation, we'll activate the RPS option, limiting the rate to 25 requests per second. With 10 workers running concurrently, the process should take ~4 seconds:

```
$ go run ./hit/cmd/hit -n 100 -c 10 -rps 25 http://example.com
. . .
Sending 100 requests to "http://example.com" (concurrency: 10)

Summary:
    Success:  100%
    RPS:      25.0
    Requests: 100
    Errors:   0
    Bytes:    1000
    Duration: 4.102s
    Fastest:  100ms
    Slowest:  100ms
```

We've demonstrated how concurrency handles requests under different conditions (sequentially, concurrently, and with throttling enabled). Our new refactoring works as intended, scaling according to the provided concurrency and throttling options.

We've also demonstrated an important detail: concurrency is not parallelism. *A program can run sequentially or concurrently without altering its concurrent structure.* It runs sequentially when the concurrency level is set to 1, behaving as though it weren't concurrent at all. But when we increase the concurrency level, the program scales gracefully. This example shows that concurrency is about structuring a program for concurrent execution, but whether it executes sequentially or in parallel depends on its runtime behavior.

Amdahl's Law reminds us of a crucial reality: as concurrency grows, performance gains may shrink. The unavoidable, nonparallelizable parts of systems become the bottleneck, capping how far we can scale. Concurrency is a tool, not a magic wand that solves all problems. Adding more concurrency beyond available resources has diminishing returns and can backfire. In our case, after some threshold, the target server won't keep up and may crash, or our own system will run out of memory or other resources.

TIP Maximizing concurrency doesn't always mean more speed. See https://mng.bz/8X6w for more information.

6.9.4 *Outro*

Before we wrap up this chapter, let's take one last look at the `SendN` function:

```
func SendN(. . .) (Results, error)
```

`SendN` hides the complexity of concurrency from users so they don't need to worry about managing goroutines and channels themselves. Our `hit` package's API appears to be synchronous even though it runs goroutines and uses channels internally. It doesn't expose or require any concurrency-specific language constructs. What users get when they call `SendN` is `Results`. Now suppose that `SendN` exposed its concurrency details in its API directly:

```
SendN(. . .) (<-chan Result, error)
```

In this case, users would need to manage concurrency themselves, which would complicate their code. By keeping the API synchronous, we maintain flexibility. The internal code can switch between sequential and concurrent behavior without affecting users. We've followed this approach throughout the chapter, designing the package's API to hide concurrency.

We started the section with a program that could only send sequential requests and made it concurrent. Now we have a program that sends and processes concurrent requests. We added concurrency to the `hit` package without changing its API. Because concurrency is an implementation detail, users wouldn't notice that we made the `hit` package concurrent.

To implement the pipeline, we didn't need to modify the existing code except `SendN`. This example shows how easy it is to add new features or do refactoring when the code is decoupled.

In chapter 7, we'll improve the `hit` package by adding cancellation propagation using the `context` package. We'll also send HTTP requests instead of simulating them. Also, our pipeline can leak goroutines if consumers stop early. To fix this problem, chapter 7 uses the `context` package to cancel ongoing operations when necessary.

6.10 *Exercises*

1 Test `Summarize`, `Send`, `SendN`, and other functions to ensure that they work as expected.

2 Calculate the average request duration in `Summary`.

3 Modify `Send` to introduce random status codes and errors. See appendix E for an example of producing random values with the `rand/v2` package.

4 Add the `Errors map[string]int` and `Statuses map[int]int` fields to `Summary`. Then update `printSummary` to print errors and statuses in a histogram.

5 Instead of calling `Summarize` in the HIT client, iterate on the returned `Results` iterator, print each `Result` as it comes, and print a progress bar.

6 Enhance `SendN` to handle a user-defined maximum error threshold. Modify the test cases to validate the threshold, stopping when the error count exceeds it.

7 Add a `NewRequest` field to `Options` that allows users to generate a new request with different URLs dynamically. Use this option in the producer stage.

8 Write an algorithm that automatically calculates the target server's optimal RPS. Enable this algorithm when users provide a new `-rps=auto` flag. Provide a custom flag type that accepts integer and string values by satisfying `flag.Value`.

9 Instead of sending requests using a set number of upfront dispatcher goroutines, use the limiting concurrency with buffered channels approach explained in appendix E. When you finish, write a benchmark for the current and alternative approaches.

10 Write another CLI tool from scratch that can calculate and print the performance of multiple servers. Import and use the `hit` package from the tool to achieve that goal.

Summary

- Ideal package APIs are straightforward for beginners to use and experts to customize.

- Concurrency is a way to structure a program so that it runs concurrently, possibly in parallel. Treating concurrency as an implementation detail simplifies usage and allows transitioning from sequential to concurrent execution without breaking client code.

- Iterators standardize and abstract the consumption of sequences, improving efficiency, flexibility, and control compared with slices while hiding concurrency details like channels.

- A concurrent pipeline is a group of reusable stages that run concurrently and communicate with channels, enabling composition, reusability, and flexibility. The fan-out pattern distributes work across multiple goroutines, which may enhance scalability.

- Directional channels make introducing bugs less likely and clarify intention.

- Avoid using `panic` and `recover` for error handling because they disrupt normal control flow and reduce maintainability. Instead, handle errors explicitly with `error` values.

7

Responsive and efficient programs

This chapter covers

- Propagating cancellation signals using the `context` package
- Efficiently processing HTTP using the `net/http` package
- Efficiently consuming byte streams using the `io` package
- Understanding Go's interface embedding and composition mechanics
- Employing idiomatic testing techniques using the `RoundTripper` interface
- Testing against a test HTTP server using the `httptest` package

Using Go involves more than learning basic language mechanics. The path to fully grasping it also involves effective use and understanding of the patterns and techniques in its standard library. Rather than learn from isolated code snippets that provide a limited view of Go's capabilities, we'll continue to apply Go to projects that closely resemble real-world ones.

7.1 *Revisiting the concurrent pipeline*

Chapter 6 focused on designing a synchronous API for the `hit` package and structuring concurrent code using the concurrent pipeline pattern. Figure 7.1 shows how the pipeline operates. The `SendN` function returns a `Results` iterator that sends concurrent requests using the `Send` function and pushes each `Result` to consumers. The convenience function, `Summarize`, consumes each `Result` from the iterator and produces a `Summary`.

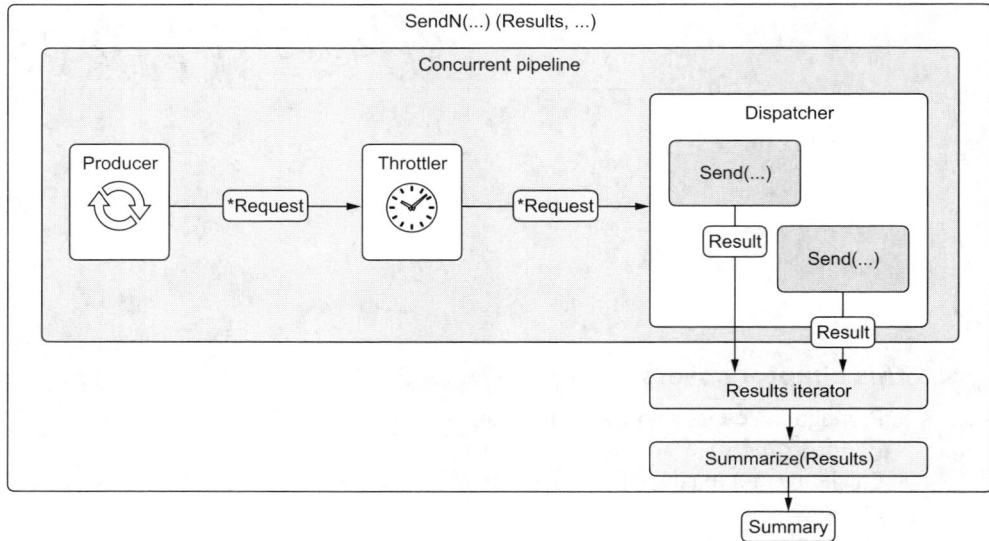

Figure 7.1   `SendN` **runs a concurrent pipeline that simulates sending requests using** `Send`. **It returns a** `Results` **iterator that pushes each** `Result` **from the pipeline to consumers.** `Summarize` **consumes the iterator and produces a** `Summary`.

The current pipeline leaks goroutines if consumers stop before fully consuming the iterator, however. Also, we're simulating sending HTTP requests. This chapter addresses these issues by focusing on cancellation propagation using the `context` package, sending HTTP requests using `http`, processing HTTP responses efficiently with `io`, and testing with `httptest`.

By chapter's end, you'll know how to use cancellation signals for efficient, reliable, and responsive programs. You'll also know how to process I/O streams efficiently, as well as how to test HTTP clients against HTTP servers and intercept requests and responses. We'll dive into many key Go principles and philosophies along the way.

7.2 *Cancellation propagation*

Our current concurrent pipeline may continue running in the background, even after consumers stop receiving results, which may cause goroutine leaks and waste resources.

In real-world programs, we frequently need a way to stop ongoing operations when they're no longer needed, such as when users cancel requests or we reach a timeout.

In this section, we'll dive into the standard library's `context` package and propagate cancellation signals across our project. We'll start by passing a `Context` to the pipeline, allowing us to stop the pipeline when necessary. Finally, we'll use `Context` in the HIT tool, allowing users to stop the HIT client, such as by pressing Ctrl+C to end the program.

> **NOTE** Ctrl+C sends an interruption signal to the running foreground process, such as the HIT tool, telling it to stop immediately. It's often handy for halting unresponsive or long-running tasks. Handling this signal enables a process to shut down gracefully.

7.2.1 *What is Context?*

Suppose that we want to process millions of channel messages and need to cancel this operation or stop processing messages after a specific time. But our current pipeline, once started, continues until it has processed every message. The idiomatic way to cancel such long-running work safely is to use the `context.Context` type.

> **NOTE** `Context` is the idiomatic way to propagate cancellation signals. Before that, gophers used other solutions, leading to code inconsistencies. The `context` package standardized consistent cancellation propagation across projects.

Suppose that our concurrent pipeline takes a `Context` parameter. We could pass a `Context` to the pipeline before starting it. In the following code snippet, the `ctx` variable's type is `Context`, which we pass to the `runPipeline` function:

```
ctx, cancel := context.WithCancel(     ◄──┤ Derives a cancellable Context
    context.Background(),                 │ from the root Context
)                                   ◄──┤ Returns a root Context
results := runPipeline(ctx, . . .)  ◄──┤
                                       Passes the Context to the
                                       pipeline as the first argument
```

I'll explain in detail how this code works in section 7.2.2. As figure 7.2 shows, when we cancel this `Context`, the producer stage detects that the `Context` is done, closes its output channel, and stops, causing a domino effect in the remaining stages, stopping automatically when the stages detect the "channel is closed" signal.

`Context` does not stop the pipeline on its own: the producer stage actively listens to a cancellation signal from the passed `Context` and closes its output channel. Because we designed the next stages to stop when this channel closes, those stages stop right afterward.

> **NOTE** A consumer must actively listen to and catch cancellation signals from a passed `Context` and handle its cancellation themselves after detecting a signal.

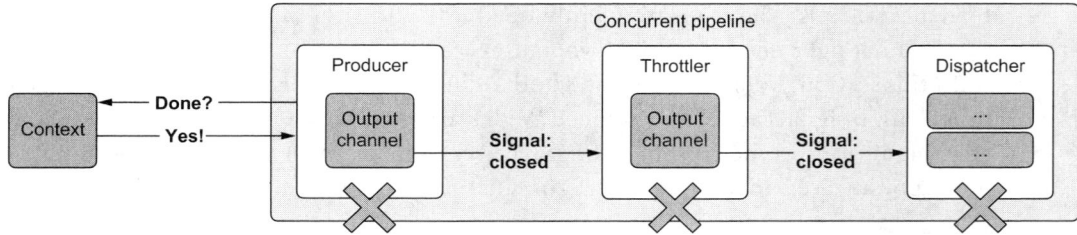

Figure 7.2   **Closing the producer stage's output channel after it detects that the** `Context` **was canceled causes the remaining pipeline stages to detect the channel closure and stop.**

7.2.2   *Context is like a tree*

Think of `Context` as being a tree with roots and leaves, starting from a parent and branching into children, as shown in figure 7.3. Those on the left are the parents of some of those on the right. Cutting a parent branch removes the entire branch. Cutting a child's branch, however, doesn't remove the parents.

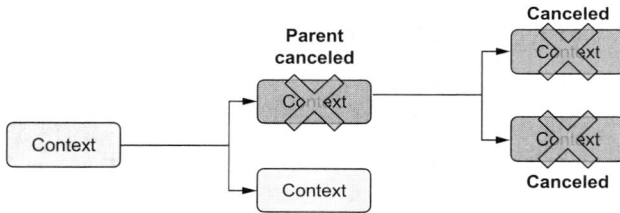

Figure 7.3   **Cancellation signals propagate through the hierarchy. Canceling the parent cancels both the parent and its children. The cross-out indicates the cancellation.**

Because `Context`s are hierarchical, we need a root `Context` to begin with:

```
root := context.Background()          ◄─── Returns a root Context
```

We can't cancel a root `Context` or change it to be cancellable because a `Context` is immutable, but we can derive a new cancellable `Context` from it. The fact that a `Context` is immutable makes it easy to reason about its life cycle and propagate it safely.

`Context` is an interface with various implementations, which allows us to chain these implementations easily. We can derive a timeout `Context` like this:

```
child, cancel := context.WithTimeout(          ◄─── Returns a new Context
    root,                                            and a func() to cancel it
    15*time.Second,   ◄─── Automatically
)                          cancels in 15         Derives the timeout Context
                           seconds               from the root Context
```

This `Context` cancels automatically after 15 seconds; it runs an internal goroutine to track the time. We can cancel it earlier by calling the `cancel()` function. Because a `Context` may have internal goroutines, it's critical to call the returned `cancel()` function eventually.

> **NOTE** Always cancel a `Context` to free resources after you finish using it.

We can chain the previous `Context` further, building a tree:

```
grandChild, cancel := context.WithTimeout(child, 5*time.Second)
```

This `Context` has a lifetime of 5 seconds before it is canceled. Notice that it cannot surpass its parent `Context`'s lifetime, which is 15 seconds. The cancellation in a parent `Context` also cancels its children, but a child cannot affect its parents.

Functions such as `WithTimeout` and `WithCancel` return an explicit `cancel` function for two reasons:

- Not every `Context` can be canceled.
- An explicit result value requires us to receive it (i.e., assign it to a variable), making the function's intent clear. If the cancellation function were a method on `Context`, such as `Context.Cancel`, it would be implicit, and we might forget calling that method.

Now that we understand how `Context` works, let's look at its most important methods. We can check whether a `Context` is canceled by receiving from its `Done` channel:

```
<-grandChild.Done()
```
◄──── **Blocks until the Context is canceled**

This channel blocks until the `Context` is canceled. We listen to this channel and exit when a cancellation occurs. We can marry this receive operation with a `select` statement and listen to another channel at the same time, so we can do other work if the `Context` is not canceled. For example, the producer stage can keep sending messages until the `Context` is canceled.

Finally, `Err()` can tell us the reason for the cancellation or return `nil` if the `Context` was not canceled. Let's assume that 5 seconds have passed and `Context` was canceled:

```
grandChild.Err()
```
◄──── **Returns an error with the message "context deadline exceeded"**

We've seen enough examples and are ready to use `Context` in the HIT client. In the following sections, we'll make several changes to the code until it compiles. We'll add a `Context` parameter to our functions and then pass a `Context` to them.

Deep dive: context.Cause

The `context.WithCancelCause` function allows us to derive a `Context` with a cancellation reason. It also returns a `cancel` function that we can use to pass an `error` value:

```
ctx, cancel := context.WithCancelCause(
    parentContext,
)
. . .
cancel(errors.New("higgs boson doomsday"))
. . .
fmt.Println(context.Cause(ctx))
```

— Derives a Context that allows propagating the cancellation reasons

— Setting the reason for the cancellation

— Prints "higgs boson doomsday"

This is especially useful in programs that require cancellation reasons for debugging or in logs to understand what's happening. See https://pkg.go.dev/context#Cause.

7.2.3   *Context in practice*

As listing 7.1 shows, we update our pipeline runner and the producer stage to accept a `Context`. We pass this `Context` from the runner to the producer. The producer tracks this `Context`. When the `Context` is canceled, the producer closes its output channel and returns. Also, we attach the `Context` to each `*Request` by cloning before sending it to the output channel.

Listing 7.1   Cancellable pipeline (`hit/pipe.go`)

```
package hit

import (
    "context"
    . . .
)

func runPipeline(
    ctx context.Context,
    n int, req *http.Request, opts Options,
) <-chan Result {
    requests := produce(ctx, n, req)
    if opts.RPS > 0 {
        requests = throttle(requests, time.Second/time.Duration(opts.RPS))
    }
    return dispatch(requests, opts.Concurrency, opts.Send)
}

func produce(
    ctx context.Context,
    n int, req *http.Request,
```

— Takes a Context from the caller (e.g., SendN)

— Propagates the Context to the producer stage

```
) <-chan *http.Request {
    out := make(chan *http.Request)

    go func() {
        defer close(out)
        for range n {
            select {
            case out <- req.Clone(ctx):
            case <-ctx.Done():
                return
            }
        }
    }()

    return out
}
```

Closes the output channel right before the closure returns

Blocks until picking one of the channels that is ready to receive or send

Clones the *http.Request to include the Context and then tries to send the *Request to the output channel

Listens to the Context's cancellation signal

Stops the producer after the Context is canceled

We modified the pipeline runner and the producer to accept a `Context`. Then we propagated the `Context` from the runner to the producer and eventually to each `*Request`.

> **TIP** Conventionally, `Context` is passed as the first parameter for consistency. Avoid storing a `Context` in a struct (https://go.dev/blog/context-and -structs).

We used a `select` statement to wait on two channels at the same time. When the `Context` is canceled, the producer stage closes the output channel and stops. Subsequent stages (throttler or dispatcher) detect the channel's close signal, close their output channels, and stop. If the `Context` is not canceled, the producer stage sends the next message to its output channel. The dispatcher listens to this output channel, receives a `*Request`, and uses it to send an HTTP request to the target HTTP server. We clone this `*Request` to include the `Context` using the `Request` type's `Clone` method. This way, we propagate cancellation signals to HTTP requests and stop them automatically even if they are in flight after the `Context` is canceled.

> **NOTE** `Request.Clone` makes a shallow copy of the `Request` with a `Context`. It doesn't clone the `Request.Body`, for example. We'll learn about `Body` in section 7.3.

7.2.4 Deriving a new Context

Now that we can stop the pipeline, let's move on to the `SendN` function. `SendN` returns a `Results` iterator that pushes each `Result` from the pipeline to consumers. Because `SendN` runs the pipeline, we'll modify `SendN` to take a `Context`, as shown in the next listing. We avoid any goroutine leaks by deriving a `Context` from the original and canceling it before the iterator stops.

Listing 7.2   Deriving `Contexts` (`hit/hit.go`)

```go
package hit

import (
    "context"
    . . .
)

func SendN(
    ctx context.Context,
    n int, req *http.Request, opts Options,
) (Results, error) {
    . . .
    ctx, cancel := context.WithCancel(ctx)         ◄──── Derives a new
    results := runPipeline(ctx, n, req, opts)      ◄──── cancellable Context

                                                   Propagates the derived
    return func(yield func(Result) bool) {         Context to the pipeline
        defer cancel()                             ◄────
        for result := range results {              Cancels the derived Context
            if !yield(result) {                    to stop the pipeline right
                return                             before the iterator returns
            }
        }
    }, nil
}
```

Users can stop the `SendN` and the pipeline by canceling the passed `Context`. Recall that `SendN` returns an iterator that receives results from the pipeline's final stage: the dispatcher. Now suppose that users call `SendN`, get a few results from the iterator, and stop consuming the remaining results. If users don't cancel their `Context`, our pipeline may keep running, leaking goroutines. That's why `SendN` derives a new `Context` and cancels it right before the iterator returns, letting the pipeline stop gracefully even if a user's `Context` remains alive.

We may still leak goroutines if the iterator returns while active dispatcher goroutines are waiting to send results to the dispatcher's output channel, because there is no iterator to receive these results. The goroutines can get stuck because unbuffered channels require both sender and receiver to be ready.

We can solve this problem by explicitly responding to `Context` cancellation signals in every pipeline stage, not only the producer stage. Because the iterator eventually cancels the `Context`, remaining stages stop trying to send a message and return when they detect that the `Context` is canceled. As an exercise, solve this problem on your own to deepen your understanding. Hint: as in the producer stage, use a `select` statement. If you get stuck, see the first exercise in section 7.7.

7.2.5   *Is Ctrl+C the end?*

Now that `SendN` takes a `Context`, we must pass it one. Any `Context` will work, but let's improve the user experience. If a user presses Ctrl+C to stop the HIT tool, it shuts down immediately without showing any results. Instead, using `NotifyContext`, we can prevent interrupt signals from terminating the program and gracefully shut it down ourselves. When the `NotifyContext` is canceled, the program continues, but the iterator stops, allowing users to display the accrued results, as the next listing shows.

Listing 7.3 Catching interruption signals (`hit/cmd/hit/hit.go`)

```go
package main

import (
    "context"
    "os/signal"
    . . .
)

func runHit(c *config, stdout io.Writer) error {
    ctx, stop := signal.NotifyContext(
        context.Background(),
        os.Interrupt,
    )
    defer stop()
    . . .
    results, err := hit.SendN(ctx, c.n, req, hit.Options{
        Concurrency: c.c,
        RPS:         c.rps,
    })
    if err != nil {
        return fmt.Errorf("sending requests: %w", err)
    }
    printSummary(hit.Summarize(results), stdout)

    return ctx.Err()
}
```

Derives a notification Context from the root Context — `ctx, stop := signal.NotifyContext(`

Passes os.Interrupt to NotifyContext to capture interrupt signals — `os.Interrupt,`

Stops capturing interrupt signals right before the runHit function returns — `defer stop()`

Prints the results after the iterator and the pipeline stop — `printSummary(hit.Summarize(results), stdout)`

Returns a non-nil error if the Context is canceled — `return ctx.Err()`

We've derived a notification `Context` and passed it to `SendN`. Using the `Err` method, we returned a possible error (e.g., due to cancellation) from the `Context`. The `Notify-Context` function returns a `stop` function. Until we call `stop`, interrupt signals won't stop the program. The first signal will cancel the notification `Context`, however, causing the iterator and the pipeline to detect the `Context` cancellation signal and stop. Let's run the program and press Ctrl+C:

```
$ go run ./hit/cmd/hit -n 1_000_000 -c 100 https://x.com/inancgumus
. . .
Sending 1000000 requests to "https://x.com/inancgumus" (concurrency: 100)
^C
Summary:
    Success:  100%
    RPS:      991.0
    Requests: 2300
    Errors:   0
    Bytes:    23000
```

Pressing Ctrl+C after a while — `^C`

```
        Duration: 2.32s
        Fastest:  100ms
        Slowest:  100ms                    ┌─ Err() returns an error because
error occurred: context canceled   ◄──────┘  the NotifyContext is canceled.
exit status 1
```

When we press Ctrl+C, NotifyContext captures the interrupt signal from the operating system, preventing the program from closing right away. Then the notification Context gets canceled. The HIT client's pipeline detects the Context cancellation and stops, along with the Results iterator, which stops yielding Result values. As planned, even after the program is interrupted, we can see the summary up to the moment of cancellation.

We've learned that the context package helps us build reliable, efficient, and responsive programs. By using Context to propagate cancellation signals, we made the HIT client more reliable and reduced resource leaks. Now the pipeline can handle cancellations properly, stopping extra unnecessary work and shutting down gracefully. We'll dive into implementing and testing HTTP clients for the remainder of this chapter.

7.3   HTTP and efficient I/O operations

In chapter 6, we implemented the Send function to simulate sending an HTTP request. In this section, we'll learn how to use the http package to send HTTP requests using the http.Client type and efficiently process HTTP responses using the io package.

We'll start with an overview of the http package. We'll begin implementing the Send function from scratch to send an HTTP request and receive an HTTP response. By the end of this section, we'll know how to read effectively from any I/O data source, not just HTTP.

7.3.1   *Round-tripping*

The net/http package has two prominent types:

- http.Client to send requests to an HTTP server
- http.Server to serve HTTP requests to clients

We'll dive into the first one in this chapter and leave the second one for later chapters. Let's start by understanding how to send an HTTP request and receive an HTTP response.

> **NOTE**   Sending a request and returning a response is an *HTTP round trip*. In section 7.4, we customize the Client's round-trip behavior to provide a more performant Client.

As figure 7.4 shows, we can send an http.Request to a server using the http.Client and receive an http.Response. We can read the Response.Body as a byte stream. Client uses http.Transport to send a Request and receive a Response. Transport's pool maintains Transmission Control Protocol (TCP) connections to the server for efficiency, as we'll see in section 7.4.

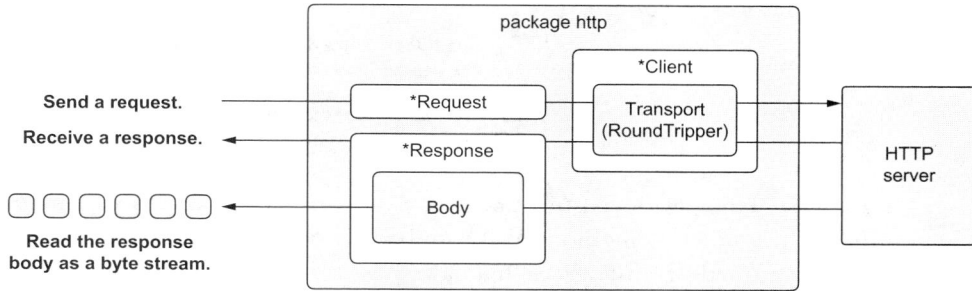

Figure 7.4 Sending a request to a server using an HTTP client and receiving a response. When we receive a response, we can read its body as a byte stream.

We know that we can create a new `Request` using the `http.NewRequest` function:

```
req, err := http.NewRequest(                    Returns a new *http.Request
    http.MethodGet, "http://...", http.NoBody,  and an error if NewRequest fails
)
```

Recall that we used the `Request`'s `Clone` method earlier to attach a `Context` to a `Request`. We can also use `NewRequestWithContext` to get a new `Request` with a `Context` right away:

```
req, err := http.NewRequestWithContext(         Returns a new *http.Request
    context.Background(),                        with a Context attached
    http.MethodGet, "http://...", http.NoBody,
)
```

Now we can call `Client.Do` to send this `Request` to a server and receive a `Response`:

```
res, err := http.DefaultClient.Do(req)          Sends the HTTP request to the server
                                                and returns an *http.Response
```

> **NOTE** `DefaultClient` is a variable with the `http` package's default `Client`.

One way to check whether a request is successful is to look at its HTTP status code:

```
if res.StatusCode == http.StatusOK { . . . }
```

Although we can access information like an HTTP status code, the returned `Response` does not include the server's full response. For that, we need to dig into the `Body` field.

7.3.2 Interface composition

The `Response` type's `Body` field is an `io.ReadCloser`, a composition of two interfaces:

```
type ReadCloser interface {
    Reader
    Closer
}
```

**ReadCloser has a Read method because
the Reader interface has a Read method.**

**ReadCloser has a Close method because
the Closer interface has a Close method.**

`ReadCloser` embeds the existing `io.Reader` and `io.Closer` interfaces. Embedding an interface promotes its methods to the embedder. So `ReadCloser` has `Read` and `Close` because it embeds the interfaces that have these methods. `Reader` looks like this:

```
type Reader interface {
    Read(p []byte) (n int, err error)
}
```

**Specifies the behavior of reading a chunk
of bytes into a []byte from a stream**

`Closer` looks like this:

```
type Closer interface {
    Close() error
}
```

**Specifies the behavior of closing an underlying
resource (e.g., TCP connections or files)**

> **TIP** When we're embedding interfaces, the convention is to name the new interface with an `-er` suffix only once. We use `ReadCloser` instead of `Reader-Closer`, for example, Similarly, `ReadWriteSeeker` embeds `Reader`, `Writer`, and `Seeker` interfaces.

Now that we understand `ReadCloser`, let's consider a hypothetical example to see why `ReadCloser` embeds `Reader` and `Closer` instead of declaring their methods directly:

```
type ReadCloser interface {
    Read(p []byte) (n int, err error)
    Close() error
}
```

Although this code behaves identically to the original `ReadCloser`, Go favors composition, and we often declare larger interfaces by embedding smaller ones. The embedding approach used in the original `ReadCloser` instantly shows that a type must satisfy both `Reader` and `Closer` to qualify as a `ReadCloser`. Because `Reader` and `Closer` are widely used, embedding prevents duplication, clarifies the `ReadCloser`'s intent, and improves readability and understanding.

Standard library interfaces such as `Reader` and `Closer` are central to Go's approach to system programming, prioritizing efficient use of I/O resources. Calling `Client.Do`, for example, returns a `Response` without downloading the response body immediately.

The `Response.Body` field is a `Reader`, allowing us to read the response incrementally in smaller chunks of bytes. This approach avoids loading large responses into memory at the same time, and `Body`, as a `Closer`, lets us release resources when finished.

TIP Closing the `Body` allows the `http.Transport` to reuse HTTP connections.

Composition and efficient stream processing are two key themes in Go. Interfaces like `ReadCloser` are built from smaller standard interfaces to clarify their intent. Interfaces such as `Reader` and `Closer` also establish explicit standard protocols for handling byte streams efficiently. They promote incremental reading of data and explicit release of resources, ultimately leading to improved performance and reliability in programs.

Deep dive: Embedding an interface in a struct

Although the `Response.Body` field is a `ReadCloser`, sometimes we want to assign a plain `Reader` to it, such as during testing. However, a `Reader`, like `bytes.Buffer`, lacks a `Close` method, so we can't assign a `Buffer` directly to a `Response.Body`. In such cases, we can wrap a `Reader` with `io.NopCloser`, turning the `Reader` into a `ReadCloser` with a no-operation `Close` method:

```
var response http.Response
var buf bytes.Buffer
response.Body = io.NopCloser(&buf)     ◄──────┐ Wraps a Reader and
                                              │ returns it as a ReadCloser
```

For teaching purposes, here is how we could implement the `NopCloser` ourselves:

```
type nopCloser struct {        ┌── Embeds and satisfies the Reader interface.
    io.Reader         ◄────────┘   (nopCloser gets a Read method.)
}

func (nopCloser) Close() error {   ◄───┐ Satisfies the Closer interface
    return nil
}

func NopCloser(r io.Reader) io.ReadCloser {   ◄──┐ Wraps a Reader and
    return nopCloser{r}                           │ returns it as a ReadCloser
}
```

`nopCloser` has a `Read` method because it embeds `Reader`. Calling `nopCloser`'s `Read` automatically calls the embedded `Reader`'s `Read`. It also has a `Close` method, satisfying the `ReadCloser` interface. Other than satisfying `Closer`, calling `Close` does nothing else—hence the name no-operation `Closer`.

7.3.3 ReadAll: Eat it all

Returning to the HIT client, `Send` returns a `Result` with a `Bytes` field that tells us the number of bytes downloaded after a request is sent and a response, including the response body, is received. To provide this information, we need to read the `Response.Body` and find the downloaded bytes.

Because the `Body` field is a `Reader`, we can stream it as chunks of bytes. Streaming bytes this way can reduce the memory footprint of our programs because we don't need to store the server's complete response in memory. Unfortunately, many beginners fall into the trap of reading the whole body into memory using io.ReadAll (reads from Reader to []byte) like this:

```
bytes, err := io.ReadAll(response.Body)
```
← Copies every byte received from the Body into memory

Copying bytes into memory this way looks like figure 7.5.

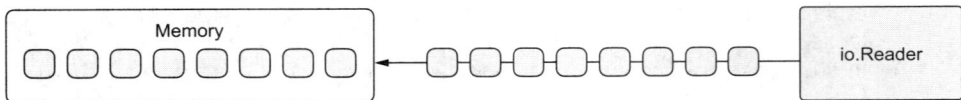

Figure 7.5   Reading and storing everything from the io.Reader in memory

ReadAll initially reads the bytes into a newly allocated 512-byte memory block (in Go 1.24, as the behavior may change in later versions). After that, it calls the append function repeatedly and allocates a new backing array, perhaps multiple times depending on the source stream's number of bytes (e.g., response.Body). So ReadAll not only reads every byte into memory but also likely allocates memory multiple times, which may put pressure on the garbage collector, leading to inefficient memory and CPU use.

Although there are valid use cases for this approach (e.g., if we know the body size), our situation is different: we can't always reliably guess the body size in advance because the HIT client can send HTTP requests to any server. More important, we don't care about the downloaded body content—only its size. Taking a different approach is worthwhile for efficiency purposes.

7.3.4   *Copy: Eat small, be small*

Instead of reading the server's full response content into memory using io.ReadAll, we can use the following io.Copy function to transfer bytes in a more memory-efficient way:

```
func Copy(
    dst io.Writer,
    src io.Reader,
) (written int64, err error)
```
← **Writes to a destination stream**
← **Reads from the source stream**
← **Returns how many bytes it has written and an error**

Copy transfers 32 KB chunks of bytes from a Reader to a Writer, as shown in figure 7.6.

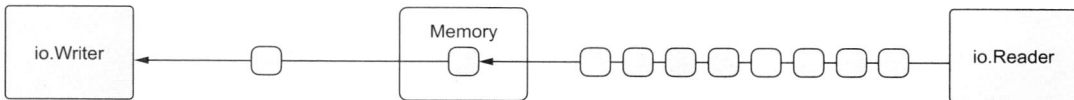

Figure 7.6 Reading from the `io.Reader` by reusing a 32 KB buffer in memory. `Copy` reads a 32 KB data block into its buffer and writes before reading the next one.

`Copy` uses 32 KB of memory while transferring bytes from a `Reader` to a `Writer` even if, as in our case, the server responds with 1 TB of data. Then it returns the number of bytes written and an error if an error occurred while transferring the bytes from the `Reader` to the `Writer`.

Because we want to find only the total number of bytes downloaded, we'll use a `Writer` that discards everything written to it: `io.Discard`. Think of it as `/dev/null`. `Copy` reads the response body and discards the downloaded data without storing it:

```
numberOfBytesDownloaded, err := io.Copy(
    io.Discard, response.Body,          ◄─────  Reads from the response body
)                                               and discards what it reads
```

This way, we use 32 KB of memory while downloading the entire response body.

> **TIP** We can use the same techniques to efficiently read from or write to a file, a network connection, an in-memory buffer, and so on because Go's I/O functionality prioritizes satisfying the `Reader` and `Writer` interfaces.

Deep dive: CopyBuffer

A friend of `Copy` is `CopyBuffer`, which allows us to specify the buffer size, giving us more control of it. We can optimize the copy operation to meet our specific requirements. Larger buffers may result in fewer read and write operations, which reduces system call overhead and improves throughput. When we're working with memory-constrained environments, smaller buffers may help prevent large memory allocations. Learn more at https://pkg.go.dev/io#CopyBuffer.

7.3.5 *Putting it all together*

Now that we know how to use the `http.Client` to send an `http.Request` to a server and receive and process the returned `http.Response` by reading its `Body`, let's update our `Send` function. As the next listing shows, we're implementing it from scratch to process requests and responses.

Listing 7.4 Processing a request and response (`hit/hit.go`)

```
package hit

import (
```

```
    . . .
    "io"
)
. . .
func Send(client *http.Client, req *http.Request) Result {
    started := time.Now()
    var (
        bytes int64
        code  int
    )
    resp, err := client.Do(req)
    if err == nil { // no error
        defer resp.Body.Close()
        code = resp.StatusCode
        bytes, err = io.Copy(
            io.Discard,
            resp.Body,
        )
    }
    return Result{
        Duration: time.Since(started),
        Bytes:    bytes,
        Status:   code,
        Error:    err,
    }
}
```

Annotations:
- Sends the HTTP request to req.URL and returns an *http.Response and an error
- Processing the *http.Response only if successful
- Closes the Response.Body to reuse the HTTP connection
- Returns the number of bytes transferred
- Throws away the data written
- Reads from the HTTP response body
- Calculates the elapsed round-trip time

We've implemented `Send` to send an HTTP request with the provided `Client`. The `Response.Body` field allows us to read the response body content after sending a request. If the request is successful, we count the downloaded bytes by reading the entire `Body`.

`Copy` returns the total number of bytes transferred. We store this resulting number in the `Result.Bytes` field. We use the `Copy` function to learn about the response body size with minimal memory overhead while discarding the downloaded content with `Discard`.

After reading the `Body`, we close it to reuse the TCP connection to the server. If `Do` returns an error, we don't close it because `Body` might be `nil`. As we've seen many times, we check for errors after running a function that returns an error to decide whether to continue. We don't always need to check for errors, however:

```
resp.Body.Close()
```

Annotation: Discards the error returned

By this point, we've processed everything we needed, such as the HTTP status code and the number of bytes downloaded. In this case, if closing the `Body` results in an error, it's unnecessary to check this error because we already have everything we need. Not all close operations work this way, however. After writing to a file, for example, we must always check for errors after closing it. Failing to close the file properly can cause data loss because many operating systems flush buffered data to the file during the close process.

> **Deep dive: io.EOF and io.Copy**
>
> Reading from a `Reader` may return an `io.EOF` error. `EOF` is not an error; it's a signal that tells us we've reached the end of the data stream and can read no more. Still, `io.Copy` never returns an `EOF` because its primary purpose is to read from a `Reader` until `EOF`. It doesn't report `EOF` as an error; instead, it returns a `nil` error.

7.3.6 *Demonstration*

We can send an HTTP request and process the response with the new `Send`. Let's run the HIT tool against an HTTP server:

```
$ go run ./hit/cmd/hit -n 10 -c 10 https://duckduckgo.com
. . .
Sending 100 requests to "https://duckduckgo.com" (concurrency: 10)

Summary:
    Success:   100%
    RPS:       285.0
    Requests:  100
    Errors:    0
    Bytes:     4926500
    Duration:  351ms
    Fastest:   11ms
    Slowest:   88ms
```

We've sent and processed 100 successful HTTP requests with 10 dispatcher workers in around 350 milliseconds. Next, we'll optimize our HIT client and make it even more efficient.

7.4 *Optimization*

When a client establishes a TCP connection, it can send HTTP requests to the server. But establishing the initial TCP connection is quite chatty and expensive. It's similar to the following (although TCP messages have more complex details, such as window sizes):

```
Server: Hello, would you like to hear a TCP joke? [SYN]
Client: Yes, I'd like to hear a TCP joke. [SYN, ACK]
Server: OK, I'll tell you a TCP joke. [ACK]
Client: OK, I'll hear a TCP joke. [ACK]
Server: Are you ready to hear a TCP joke? [DATA, ACK]
Client: Yes, I am ready to hear a TCP joke. [ACK]
Server: OK, I'm about to send the TCP joke.
        It will last 10 seconds. [DATA, ACK]
Client: OK, I'm ready to hear the TCP joke
        that will last 10 seconds. [ACK]
. . .            ◄─────
                       │  HTTP request and response
                       │  happen somewhere here.
```

Fortunately, HTTP allows the server and client to keep previously established connections alive until they time out—a feature called *keep-alive*. Clients can reuse existing TCP connections to send HTTP requests without reconnecting using this feature.

Suppose that the HIT client sends 1 million requests with 10 dispatcher goroutines. Its performance would be subpar because it uses `http.DefaultClient` (the default `http.Client`), which keeps 100 connections open and allows only 2 to be reused for the same host. The HIT client would reconnect each time to send more than two requests to the same host.

Although two goroutines could send requests over these two TCP connections without reconnecting, others need to open new ones to send more. We can't measure a server's performance accurately using the `DefaultClient`; we'll find another way.

In this section, we'll explore the `http.Client` type so we can gain enough knowledge to optimize its performance. Then we'll configure a more performant custom `Client` and use it to send HTTP requests.

7.4.1   *Client and its RoundTripper*

Go favors composition, but composition is not limited to interfaces. Structs can have interface fields for extensibility and reusability. The `Transport` field of the `http.Client` struct, for example, is of the `RoundTripper` interface type, enabling the `Client` to delegate the HTTP request and response handling to various `RoundTripper` implementations.

Figure 7.7 shows that `Client` doesn't establish TCP connections or send HTTP requests by itself. Instead, it delegates this duty to a `RoundTripper`, which can handle TCP connections and HTTP requests and responses, as well as manage a pool for reusing TCP connections for efficiency.

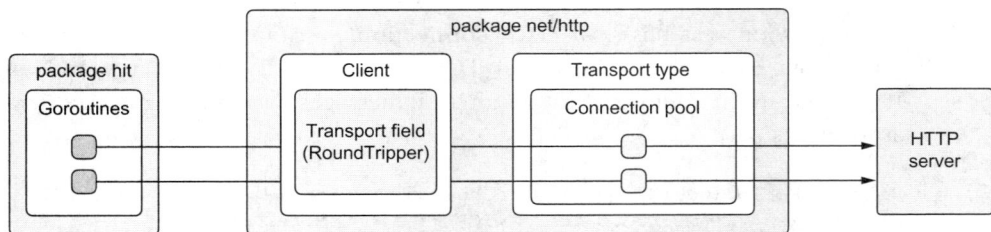

Figure 7.7   The HIT client goroutines send concurrent HTTP requests to the HTTP server via the `http.Client`, with TCP connections in the `http.Transporter`'s pool.

The `http.Client` type and its `Transport` field look like this:

```
type Client struct {
    Transport    RoundTripper          Delegates HTTP request and response
                                        processing to a RoundTripper implementation
```

```
CheckRedirect func(
    req *Request, via []*Request,
) error
Timeout          time.Duration
    . . .
}
```

← **Specifies the HTTP redirect handling behavior**

← **Specifies the maximum time limit for each round trip**

The `http.RoundTripper` interface looks like this:

```
type RoundTripper interface {
    RoundTrip(*http.Request) (*http.Response, error)
}
```

← **Sends the http.Request and returns an http .Response and an error**

The `Client`'s `Transport` field, the `RoundTripper` interface, allows switching between protocol implementations, such as HTTP/1 and HTTP/2. We'll implement this interface in section 7.5, set it to this field, and test the HIT client without running a server.

A `RoundTripper` implementation may establish TCP connections, send HTTP requests, and return HTTP responses. The `http.Transport` type, for example, is a `RoundTripper` with a connection pool. Because it has a connection pool to reuse connections for efficiency, we should reuse the same `Transport` while sending HTTP requests.

> **NOTE** `http.DefaultTransport` is the `http` package's default `RoundTripper`. `http.DefaultClient` uses the `DefaultTransport` for requests and responses.

Let's look briefly at the `Client`'s remaining fields. `CheckRedirect` allows us to handle HTTP redirects; we can assign it a function to prevent redirects. The `Timeout` field allows us to set the maximum timeout for a round trip—the time between establishing a connection, sending an HTTP request, and processing the response. We'll use both.

> **NOTE** Many standard library types are designed with extension points, such as having interface fields and accepting interface parameters. These types are flexible, highly configurable, and inherently testable by their design.

7.4.2 Tweaking the connection pool

Now that we're familiar with how `Client` works, as listing 7.5 shows, we configure a more efficient customized `Client` with a custom `Transport` as the default for the HIT client, and we set it as the default client for the `Send` option. The dispatcher worker goroutines in the concurrent pipeline call this option while sending HTTP requests.

Listing 7.5 Optimizing `http.Client` (hit/option.go)

```
package hit

import (
    . . .
```

```
    "time"
)

func withDefaults(o Options) Options {                    Configures a custom http.Client
    . . .
    if o.Send == nil {                                    Configures a custom http.Transport
        client := &http.Client{
            Transport: &http.Transport{                   Matches the number of idle
                MaxIdleConnsPerHost: o.Concurrency,       connections per host to the
            },                                            concurrency level option
            CheckRedirect: func(
                _ *http.Request, _ []*http.Request,
            ) error {
                return http.ErrUseLastResponse            Disables HTTP redirects
            },
            Timeout: 30 * time.Second,
        }                                                 Cancels HTTP requests
        o.Send = func(r *http.Request) Result {           that take over 30 seconds
            return Send(client, r)
        }
    }                                                     Uses the custom Client
    return o
}
```

We've configured a custom `Client` and `Transport` in our HIT client. We set `Max-IdleConnsPerHost` to match the concurrency level to prevent unnecessary connection churn. This way, each dispatcher goroutine can reuse the same idle connection without constantly reconnecting to the same server while sending many HTTP requests.

We also enabled `CheckRedirect` to prevent HTTP redirects. Otherwise, we might inadvertently measure the combined response times of the initial and redirected URLs, which would lead to misleading data about the performance.

Finally, we set `Timeout` to stop HTTP requests and responses that take more than 30 seconds to keep the HIT client's pipeline moving smoothly. Without this setting, a worker could get stuck waiting for a slow response, blocking the subsequent request from being processed in the pipeline. If other workers hit the same delay, the pipeline could clog, significantly affecting performance. By enforcing a timeout per request, we enable dispatcher workers to skip long-running requests and continue, which helps to prevent bottlenecks in the pipeline and makes it more likely to run smoothly.

> **TIP** `Client` has other options that customize its behavior. You can find them all at https://pkg.go.dev/net/http#Client and https://pkg.go.dev/net/http#Transport.

7.4.3   *Demonstration*

Now that we've tuned the HIT client's `Client` and `Transport`, let's benchmark the previous version of the HIT client that uses `DefaultClient` and then the one with our tuned version. We'll run the following benchmarks against an unloaded local HTTP server. You can find the server code at https://go.dev/play/p/Bf4QuOC1xpg. First, run the previous HIT tool that uses `DefaultClient`:

```
$ go run ./hit/cmd/hit -n 100_000 -c 10 http://localhost:8082
    . . .
    Success:  84%
    RPS:      1552.0
    Errors:   15591
    Duration: 1m4.451s
```

The sheer number of TCP connections cause errors.

Run the new version of the HIT tool:

```
$ go run ./hit/cmd/hit -n 100_000 -c 10 http://localhost:8082
    . . .
    Success:  100%
    RPS:      60425.0
    Errors:   0
    Duration: 1.655s
```

After the optimizations, the HIT client became significantly more performant, and users can measure HTTP server performance more accurately. We reuse the same `Transport` to exploit the connection pool when sending requests and avoid unnecessarily reestablishing TCP connections to the same host. The pool reacquires an idle connection after the request ends and releases that connection for another request, improving performance.

7.5 Testing

We've seen that `Client` separates responsibilities by having a `RoundTripper` interface field called `Transport`. This field allows us to use any `RoundTripper` implementation to process HTTP requests and responses. In this section, we'll implement this interface for testing. Testing with a fake `RoundTripper` shows how easily we can test code that depends on single-method interfaces by implementing these interfaces with simple function types.

7.5.1 Satisfying RoundTripper

`Send` takes a `Client` to send HTTP requests and receive responses. To modify its request and response-handling behavior, we can pass a fake `RoundTripper` to the `Client`'s `Transport` field. First, we'll revisit the `RoundTripper` interface to refresh our memory:

```
type RoundTripper interface {
    RoundTrip(*http.Request) (*http.Response, error)
}
```

Unlike most other languages, Go allows us to satisfy an interface with a function type. We don't always have to use a struct. A function type can satisfy `RoundTripper` and turn a regular function into a `RoundTripper` implementation. Then we can set that function to the `Transport` field as a `RoundTripper`, pass the `Client` to `Send`, and test `Send`'s behavior.

Also, we don't have to state that our function type implements the `RoundTripper` interface explicitly. Go can tell automatically whether a type meets the interface requirements by looking at its methods. Implementing the `RoundTrip` method for this function type is enough. The next listing shows the `roundTripperFunc` function type that satisfies `RoundTripper`.

Listing 7.6 Satisfying `RoundTripper` (`hit/hit_test.go`)

```
package hit

import "net/http"

// roundTripperFunc is an adapter to allow the use of ordinary
// functions as an [http.RoundTripper]. If the receiver f is a
// function with the appropriate signature, roundTripperFunc(f)
// is an [http.RoundTripper] that calls the receiver.
type roundTripperFunc func(         ┐  Declares a function type
    *http.Request,
) (*http.Response, error)

func (f roundTripperFunc) RoundTrip(   ┐  Satisfies the
    r *http.Request,                   ┘  RoundTripper interface
) (*http.Response, error) {
    return f(r)      ◄──  Calls the receiver with the *Request
}                         and returns a *Response
```

We declared a function type matching the signature of the `RoundTrip` method. Then we attached a `RoundTrip` method that calls its receiver: a `roundTripFunc` that takes a `*Request` and returns a `*Response`. Let's look at an example. First, we need a function that matches the signature of the `RoundTrip` method. When we have that function (or a closure), we can convert it to a `roundTripperFunc`:

```
                                    Converts the closure function
                                    to a roundTripperFunc
rt := roundTripperFunc(     ◄──
    func(r *http.Request) (*http.Response, error) {   ◄──  A closure with a
        . . .                                               matching signature
    },       ◄──  We can process the *Request              of roundTripperFunc
)                 and return a *Response here.
```

This `rt` variable's type is `roundTripperFunc`, and its value is a function pointer that points to the closure we use. Calling `RoundTrip` on `rt` (i.e., `rt.RoundTrip(. . .)`) calls that closure. Because the `rt`'s type satisfies `RoundTripper`, we can set it to the `Transport` field:

```
client := &http.Client{
    Transport: rt,     ◄──  Sets rt as the http
}                           .Client's RoundTripper
```

This `Transport` field's type is `RoundTripper`. We can set `rt` to the field because the `roundTripper` type satisfies the `RoundTripper` interface. When we send a request using this `client`, it passes a `*Request` to our `rt.RoundTrip()` and receives a `*Response`.

In short, any concrete type can implicitly implement an interface. `roundTripper-Func` is a function type that does not explicitly specify that it implements `RoundTripper`. Instead, it solely implements a `RoundTrip` method. Unlike most other programming languages, this approach leads to decoupled types and eliminates type hierarchies.

> **NOTE** As we'll learn in chapter 8, this pattern (testing with a function type) is idiomatic and used frequently in Go. `http.HandlerFunc` satisfies the `http.Handler` interface, for example, making it convenient to turn a regular function with a right signature into a `Handler` that can serve HTTP requests.

7.5.2 Testing with a RoundTripper

Testing with a fake `RoundTripper` is especially useful for unit-testing functions that use a `Client` or `RoundTripper` without running an HTTP test server. Because a `Round-Tripper` takes a `*Request` and returns a `*Response`, we can simply return a fake `*Response`.

Now that we have a `roundTripperFunc` type that we can use to convert a function with a right signature to a `RoundTripper`, we can test the `Send` function with a fake `RoundTripper`. As the next listing shows, we test whether `Send` returns the correct HTTP status, as expected.

Listing 7.7 **Testing with a fake** `RoundTripper` (hit/hit_test.go)

```go
package hit

import (
    "net/http"
    "testing"
)
. . .
func TestSendStatusCode(t *testing.T) {
    t.Parallel()

    req, err := http.NewRequest(http.MethodGet, "/", http.NoBody)
    if err != nil {
        t.Fatalf("creating http request: %v", err)
    }

    fake := func(_ *http.Request) (*http.Response, error) {
        return &http.Response{
            StatusCode: http.StatusInternalServerError,
        }, nil
    }
    client := &http.Client{
        Transport: roundTripperFunc(fake),
    }
```

```
      result := Send(client, req)

      if result.Status != http.StatusInternalServerError {
          t.Errorf(
              "got %d, want %d",
               result.Status, http.StatusInternalServerError,
          )
      }
  }
```

We wrote a test that verifies whether `Send` returns correct HTTP status codes. We added a fake closure that returns an internal server error HTTP status code in a `Response` with a `nil` error. We skipped the `Request` parameter, which we don't need for this test. Then we converted this closure to a `RoundTripper` implementation using our `roundTripperFunc`. We set the `RoundTripper` to the `Transport` field, making it the `Client`'s HTTP request and response `RoundTripper`. Finally, we called `Send` with the custom `Client`. `Send` will call our fake `RoundTripper` via the `Client`, get the status code, and save and return it in a `Result`. Now we can run our test:

```
$ go test ./hit -run=TestSendStatusCode
ok      github.com/inancgumus/gobyexample/hit    0.194s
```

The test used a `RoundTripper` to customize the request and response-handling behavior. It didn't require us to launch an HTTP server to test the `Send` function. Satisfying an interface with a function and testing it is one idiomatic method of testing in Go. Using a custom `RoundTripper` in tests allows precise control of HTTP responses.

Deep dive: synctest

The `Send` function internally calls the `time.Now` and `time.Since` functions to calculate the round-trip duration. Using these functions makes it difficult to test the `Send` function, however, because we can't control the current time while testing the function.

Fortunately, Go 1.24 comes with an experimental package called `synctest` that allows us to control time in tests even if we directly use time-related functions like `time.Now` in a function. Note that because it's experimental, its API can change in future Go versions.

Visit https://pkg.go.dev/testing/synctest to learn more about it. As an exercise, test the `Send` function with the `synctest` package to validate whether it calculates durations correctly. Run `Send` with a fake `RoundTripper` that sleeps for 1 hour, for example.

7.6   *HTTP testing*

`RoundTripper` is useful for unit-testing functionality by bypassing TCP and HTTP layers. To ensure that our program works well in production, we should also run HTTP tests involving the HIT client to send HTTP requests over the network and process performance results.

In this section, we'll learn how to run the HIT client against an HTTP test server that we'll launch using the standard library's `httptest` package and its `Server` type. Because this test `Server` runs an HTTP server, we can test the HIT client over the TCP and HTTP networking layers.

7.6.1 *Package httptest*

Before we start testing the HIT client, let's learn how to run a test HTTP server:

- The `httptest.Server` type runs an `http.Server` that is tuned for testing.
- The `Server` type serves HTTP requests with an `http.Handler`.
- The `Handler` is an interface with a `Handle` method.

To test the HIT client against a test HTTP server, we need to pass a `Handler` to the `Server`. Instead of implementing the `Handler` interface, we'll use an adapter function type called `HandlerFunc` to turn our function into a `Handler` that can serve HTTP requests. We can start a test HTTP server using the `httptest.NewServer`:

```
func NewServer(
    handler http.Handler,
) *httptest.Server
```
**Starts and returns an *httptest.Server that
serves HTTP requests with the http.Handler**

This function requires a `Handler` to serve HTTP requests:

```
type Handler interface {
    ServeHTTP(ResponseWriter, *Request)
}
```

We can convert a closure to a `Handler` using `HandlerFunc` and pass it to `NewServer` to start a new HTTP test server:

```
server := httptest.NewServer(
  http.HandlerFunc(
    func(_ http.ResponseWriter, _ *http.Request) {
      . . .
    },
  ),
)
```
**Converts the closure to an
http.Handler implementation**

**Matches the signature of
the http.HandlerFunc type**

Serves the HTTP request here

We've converted a closure to a `Handler` using `HandlerFunc`. `HandlerFunc` works similarly to the `roundTripperFunc` we implemented earlier. The latter converts a function with the right signature to a `RoundTripper`, and `HandlerFunc` converts a function to a `Handler`. When we have a `Handler`, we pass it to the `NewServer`, which launches a new HTTP server for testing purposes. This test server calls our closure to serve every incoming HTTP request. After we launch a test server, we can get its URL using the `URL` method:

```
server.URL()
```
**Returns "http://127.0.0.1:61507"
(automatically chooses the port number)**

When we are done working with the `Server`, we can close it to free resources:

```
server.Close()
```

Now we're ready to test the HIT client.

7.6.2   *Testing the client*

We'll test whether the HIT client can send the specified number of HTTP requests to the test HTTP server, drain the results, and determine whether the number of requests matches. The test is simple, but it allows us to understand testing against an HTTP server. As shown in the following listing, we launch a test HTTP server, incrementing the atomic counter for each incoming HTTP request, and then measure the total number of requests.

> **Listing 7.8   Testing** `SendN` `(hit/hit_test.go)`

```
package hit

import (
    "net/http/httptest"
    "sync/atomic"
    . . .
)

func TestSendN(t *testing.T) {
    t.Parallel()

    var hits atomic.Int64          ◀──┐  Declares an atomic 64-bit integer
                                       │  that we can use concurrently
    srv := httptest.NewServer(http.HandlerFunc(
        func(_ http.ResponseWriter, _ *http.Request) {
            hits.Add(1)        ◀──┐
        },                        │  Increments the atomic counter
    ))                            │  for each incoming HTTP request
    defer srv.Close()

    req, err := http.NewRequest(http.MethodGet, srv.URL, http.NoBody)
    if err != nil {
        t.Fatalf("creating http request: %v", err)
    }
    results, err := SendN(t.Context(), 10, req, Options{
        Concurrency: 5,
    })
    if err != nil {
        t.Fatalf("SendN() err=%v, want nil", err)
    }

    for range results { // just consume the results
    }
    if got := hits.Load(); got != 10 {
```

```
            t.Errorf("got %d hits, want 10", got)
        }
    }
}
```

We've written an HTTP test that runs the HIT client against a test HTTP server. Because `Server` runs a `Handler` in a new goroutine, we use an atomic integer to count the number of requests to prevent race-condition issues. Declaring the atomic integer starts its value at `0`. The `Add` method increments it, and `Load` retrieves its current value.

> **TIP** Visit https://pkg.go.dev/sync/atomic to learn more about `sync/atomic`.

We use `defer` to set the `Server` to close when the test function returns. When we call `Close`, the `Server` stops listening for connections and closes any idle or new connections. Then we call `SendN` to send 10 requests to the test HTTP server over five goroutines. The `*testing.T.Context` method returns a `Context` that is canceled after the test finishes. Finally, we drain the results from the iterator and compare the results. Run the test:

```
$ go test ./hit -run=TestSendN
ok      github.com/inancgumus/gobyexample/hit    0.198s
```

7.7   Exercises

1   As explained in section 7.2.4, some stages may never stop if users don't receive all the pipeline results from the iterator. Pass the `Context` to all stages. Stop each stage when the `Context` is canceled, allowing each stage to stop even if users don't consume all the results. You can find the solution in the book's GitHub repository at https://mng.bz/EwOO.

2   In `runHit`, pass a `Context` from `WithTimeoutContext` to `NotifyContext`.

3   Satisfy the `Reader` interface with a type that reads from a `[]byte`.

4   Satisfy the `Writer` interface by implementing a type that counts the number of bytes written to it. Provide a field to retrieve the number of bytes written.

5   Call `Copy` with the two types you created in the preceding two exercises.

6   Use `io.ReadAll` in `Send` instead of `io.Copy`, and benchmark the difference.

7   Remove `response.Body.Close` from `Send`, and benchmark the difference.

8   Add a `hit.Options.Client` for setting the `http.Client` used by the HIT client.

9   Declare a `LogRoundTripper` type that implements `RoundTripper` and takes another `RoundTripper` (e.g., `http.DefaultTransport`). It should log incoming request URLs and delegate request and response handling to the given `RoundTripper`. Set this new `RoundTripper` through the HIT client's new `hit.Options.Client` to test it.

10 Add more tests and benchmarks for the `hit` package. Verify the edge case conditions for the `SendN` function, for example, such as returning different HTTP status codes.

11 Write a test that turns off the `dryRun` mode and tests the HIT tool by running it against a test HTTP server, passing it flags, and checking the results.

Summary

- `context.Context` is the idiomatic way to propagate cancellation signals across package APIs and goroutines. To respond to cancellation signals from a `Context`, a consumer must actively listen to them.

- Explicitly propagate cancellation signals with `Context`. Canceling a parent `Context` cancels it and its children, allowing us to stop unnecessary work.

- Stream data incrementally from an `io.Reader` rather than reading it entirely into memory to minimize memory usage and improve efficiency and reliability.

- Reuse resources, such as TCP connections from a performance-tuned pool, instead of repeatedly allocating new ones to reduce overhead and significantly boost performance.

- Compose larger interfaces, such as `io.ReadCloser`, from smaller ones, such as `io.Reader` and `io.Closer`, to clarify intent and improve reusability. Embedding existing interfaces adds their methods to the embedder, clarifying the new behavior.

- Interface fields and parameters can help improve reusability and testability.

- Simplify unit-testing by satisfying interfaces (e.g., `RoundTripper`) with simple types, such as functions, for easy substitution of real implementations with test-specific ones.

- Balance precise, fast unit tests using test doubles such as a fake `RoundTripper` with tests against real components to ensure correctness in realistic conditions.

- Use concurrency-safe counters and types, such as those from the `sync/atomic` package, to prevent race conditions when accessing shared data concurrently.

Structuring
packages and services

This chapter covers

- Effectively organizing and structuring packages to avoid import cycles
- Simplifying the use of types by making their zero value useful
- Protecting against unsafe concurrent use of shared state with mutexes
- Implementing and testing HTTP servers with the `http` and `httptest` packages
- Recording HTTP responses with custom test helpers to streamline testing

Representational State Transfer (REST) is an API design approach that enables programs to communicate, typically over HTTP, using methods like GET and POST. This chapter and the next two chapters explain how to structure maintainable packages and avoid import cycles, showcasing a microservice that serves clients over HTTP with a REST API. Our project will touch on many Go philosophies and patterns for writing maintainable code. Each chapter focuses on a specific set of packages and patterns to explain each in depth:

- This chapter dives into our service's core logic and REST API.
- Chapters 9 explores functional composition patterns.
- Chapter 10 dives into persistence, integration testing, and interfaces.

Because structuring and organizing multiple packages is a common hurdle for most gophers, we'll explore how to structure a service after we see an overview of our project. Then we'll work on the core business logic. After that, we'll begin implementing the REST API using the standard library's `http` package. Finally, we'll test the API using the `httptest` package.

8.1   *Organizing and structuring packages*

Bite is a fictional startup that aims to disrupt online link management services. The company's first service is a REST API that shortens long URLs to short keys for easy sharing and redirects clients to the original URLs from short keys. Let's start with a sneak peek. First, we serve our REST API over HTTP that listens for incoming HTTP requests:

```
$ ./linkd
. . .app=linkd addr=localhost:8080
```
Listens for HTTP requests at localhost:8080

Sending a POST request to our server shortens the link and returns a key:

```
$ curl link/shorten -d'url=https://x.com/inancgumus'
OQzXIiL4
```
Sends an HTTP POST request using the -d flag

Shortens the given URL into a eight-character key

Sending a GET request to our server with the key redirects us to the original URL:

```
$ curl link/r/OQzXIiL4
Location: https://x.com/inancgumus
```
Visiting this URL in a browser redirects to the original URL.

As figure 8.1 shows, our service consists of two primary packages:

- The `link` package provides the core logic for link management services.
- The `link/rest` package provides HTTP handlers to shorten and resolve links.

Incoming HTTP requests go to our HTTP handlers (functions or methods that serve HTTP requests), which use the `link.Shortener` service in our core logic to `Shorten` and `Resolve` links. Before we switch to a persistent SQL database in chapter 10, the `Shortener` service will store links in memory to keep things simpler.

The `link` package provides the following types:

- The `link.Link` struct stores the original URL and its shortened `link.Key`.
- The `link.Shortener` service shortens URLs and resolves `link.Keys`.

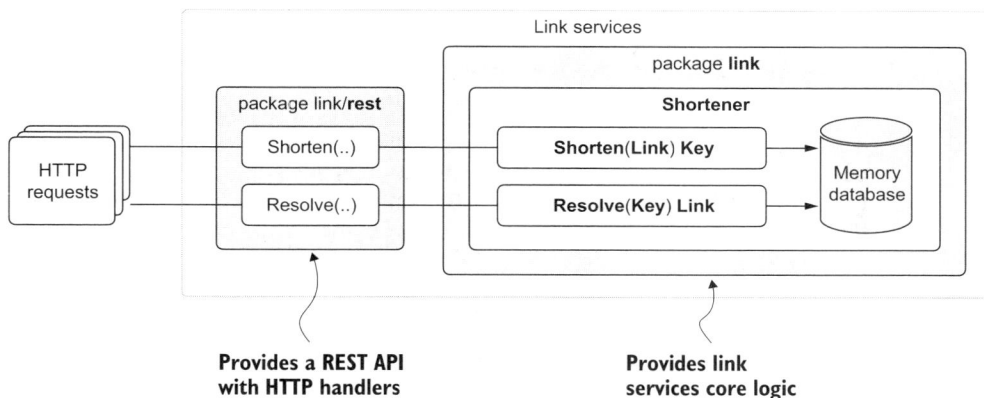

Figure 8.1 The `Shorten` and `Resolve` handlers provide a REST API over HTTP using the `Shortener` service, which is backed by an in-memory database.

The `link/rest` package provides a REST API with these HTTP handlers:

- `rest.Shorten` passes a `Link` to `Shortener.Shorten` to get a shortened `Key`.
- `rest.Resolve` passes a `Key` to `Shortener.Resolve` to get the original `Link`.

TIP Consistent function (and method) names improve the comprehension of the code. The `link/rest` package, for example, has a `Resolve` function that uses `Shortener.Resolve`.

After we add the core logic in section 8.2, we'll add HTTP handlers in section 8.3.

Pick clarity over brevity

> *There are only two hard things in computer science: cache invalidation and naming things.*
>
> —Phil Karlton

Names are critical for a program's clarity and maintainability. Because we read more code than we write, the code should clearly indicate its purpose. Package names and items should be descriptive, have a clear purpose, and be easy to type and remember.

We have a flaw in our naming choices, however. Keen-eyed readers may have noticed the stutter in the `link.Link` type and wondered whether it was idiomatic. (The `link` package declares `Link`, resulting in a stutter when used from external packages.)

The `Link` type stutters because the `link` package name already provides context, making `Link` somewhat redundant. Although renaming `Link` to something like `.Item` would prevent this, it would create confusion within the package code itself because it would be too generic. Retaining `Link` maintains clarity inside the package even if it stutters for external users. This approach also aligns with examples like the standard library's `url.URL`, `time.Time`, and `list.List`.

Instead, we should be careful about repeating the package name unnecessarily. Our current `link.Shortener` type, for example, has a clear, concise name that is easy to understand, type, and remember. By contrast, `link.LinkShortener` doesn't significantly improve our understanding. The documentation can provide extra details if necessary.

In summary, it's acceptable for a package's type to have the same name as the package itself. It's best to avoid stuttering, but it's a guideline for idiomatic code, not a strict rule. As long as the package and its items are clear, it's idiomatic even if they stutter.

8.1.1   *Avoiding import cycles*

Organizing packages can be tricky. Because package organization depends on factors like business domain and team preferences, there are no hard-and-fast rules, only guidelines and tradeoffs. A small project may remain in the same package for a long time until it grows and needs to be split into multiple packages. We'll structure our project with multiple packages from the get-go because we want it to resemble real-world scenarios and serve as an example of how to structure numerous packages.

The first guideline is to follow a layered design, much like the standard library. When this central idea becomes clear, it's easier to see how our project should be structured.

> *. . . import cycles force programmers to think more about their dependencies.*
> —Rob Pike (Go repository, issue 30247)

Go never allows *import cycles*, which is the most important rule to remember. If package A imports package B and B imports A, the result is a compile-time error. As figure 8.2 illustrates, if the standard library's `http` package imports the `net` package, but the `net` package also imports the `http` package, Go will complain about an import cycle.

Figure 8.2   An imaginary import cycle scenario in which packages import each other

Organizing *packages as layers* can prevent such issues, simplify the codebase, and make the code easier to understand. In this approach, the lower-level packages are more general than the higher-level ones. As we move up, packages become more specialized. There is only one import direction: higher layers can import from lower layers, but not vice versa.

In figure 8.3, the standard library's `io` package provides basic input and output functionality and protocols. The `net` package imports the `io` package to provide network protocols and functionality, and the `http` package imports `net` for HTTP. The `http` package implements HTTP on top of the protocols and functionality offered by `net`.

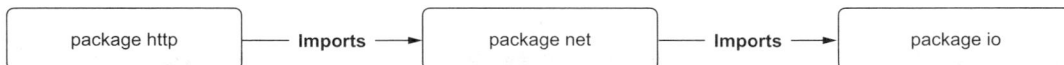

```
┌──────────────────┐              ┌──────────────────┐              ┌──────────────────┐
│   package http   │── Imports ──▶│   package net    │── Imports ──▶│   package io     │
└──────────────────┘              └──────────────────┘              └──────────────────┘
```

Figure 8.3   A layered package organization prevents import cycles. Packages do not have a hierarchy; they are flat, meaning that each package is independent. Still, it might be helpful to think of and organize packages as though they were layered.

Besides layering, another guideline is to view packages as *niche providers* of functionality rather than as generic containers. By contrast, packages like `common`, `util`, `shared`, and `helper` attract unrelated code, leading to maintenance headaches. Packages are not storehouses where we can put unrelated things together. Instead, think of packages as boutiques that provide niche and specialized services via their package API. Good packages are experts in their domain.

Dividing responsibilities doesn't always mean creating multiple packages, however. If we frequently use some packages together, that might be a sign to merge them into a single package. Each package in the standard library typically focuses on a single domain. The `http` package, for example, includes the `Server`, `Client`, `Request`, and `Response` types in one place. Declaring these types in the same package prevents import cycles, and the code stays cohesive and straightforward rather than being scattered across multiple minipackages.

We should be mindful, however, about putting everything into a single package; we want to avoid overloading a package with extra functionality. Although the `http` package is cohesive, for example, it conflates some types with extra duties. It uses the `Request` type for both server and client functionality, leading to a fragile, confusing, hard-to-use API.

Eventually, with the layered approach in mind—and by treating packages as cohesive *domain experts* that provide specialized services—we can prevent import cycles and produce code that's easy to read, maintain, and evolve. This focus on domain clarity, well-chosen names, and functionally distinct packages is at the heart of Go's approach to structuring packages.

8.1.2   *Structuring packages in practice*

Now that we have discussed some guidelines for structuring packages, let's return to our link-services project. We'll explore the package structure and introduce the packages that we'll use throughout this chapter and the following chapters; then we'll review their functionality.

Figure 8.4 shows a layered package structure for our link-services project in which each package imports only from below, never from above. The `link/rest` package can depend on the `link` package, for example, but `link` must not depend on `link/rest`. As we go up the layers, packages become more specialized (except `linkd`, which is not importable). Going down leads to more foundational ones.

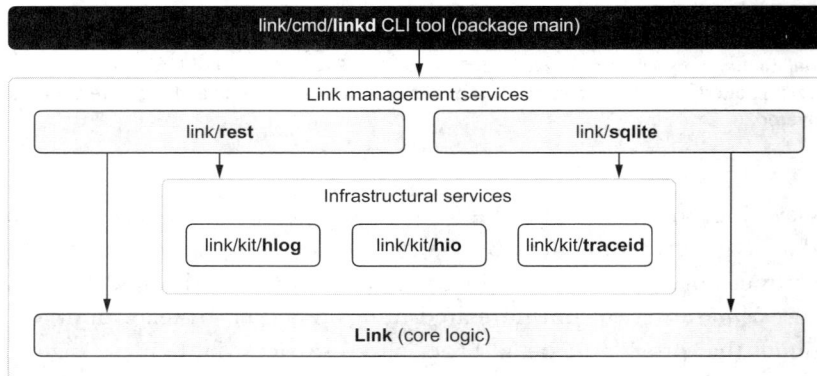

Figure 8.4   A layered approach to organizing packages

Each package is an expert in its area and provides something unique:

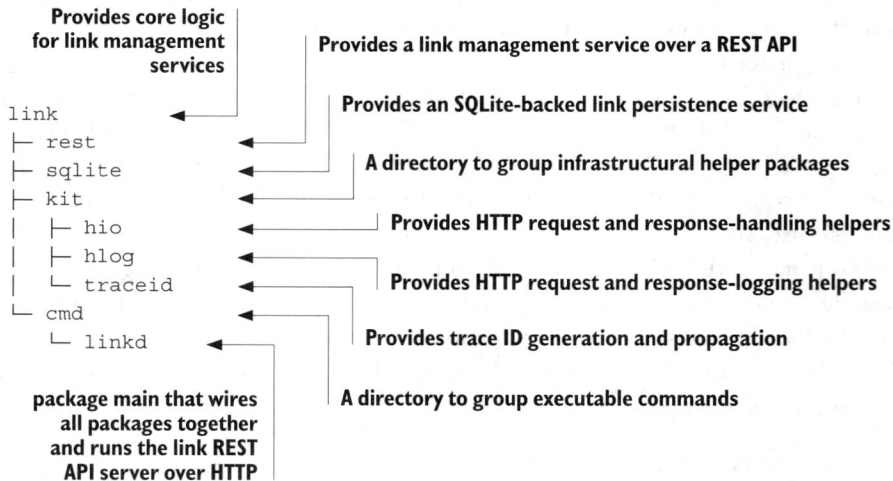

This structure prevents import cycles by maintaining explicit dependencies. The `link` package provides core link management services without depending on our other packages. The `link/rest` package builds on top of the `link` package and provides a

REST API over HTTP. Finally, the `linkd` command (`main` package) wires all packages to run an HTTP server that serves our REST API.

Our structure also provides a flexible way to adapt to Bite's potential offerings. We could add a tool besides `linkd` (e.g., `cmd/link`) to shorten links through a command-line interface (CLI) instead of using the REST API. This tool could use the `link` package directly, skipping `link/rest`. Or we could provide another CLI tool (e.g., `cmd/linkc`) as an HTTP client to talk to our HTTP server.

Organizing packages in a layered structure helps us prevent import cycles. Thinking of packages as providers helps us create expert packages with convenient APIs. Proper naming enhances clarity and use. These approaches often lead to maintainable package structures that prevent import cycles and improve clarity.

When we finish implementing the core logic in `link` in section 8.2, we'll move on to `rest` in section 8.3. We'll leave implementing the remaining packages for chapters 9 and 10.

Deep dive: The internal directory convention

Go has a special directory called `internal` that restricts package imports. Suppose that our directory structure looked like this:

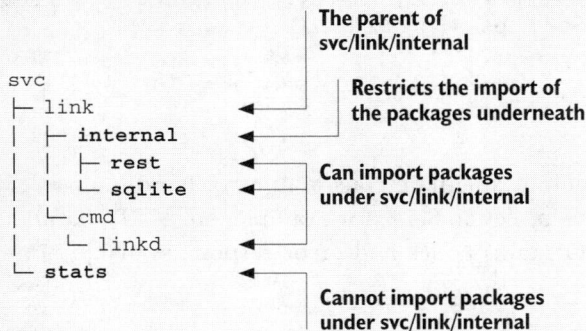

```
                              The parent of
                              svc/link/internal

svc
├── link                       Restricts the import of
│   ├── internal               the packages underneath
│   │   ├── rest
│   │   └── sqlite            Can import packages
│   └── cmd                   under svc/link/internal
│       └── linkd
└── stats

                              Cannot import packages
                              under svc/link/internal
```

The parent directory of `internal` is `link`. Any package below `link` or its subfolders can import packages in `internal` because they share a root directory: `link`. `cmd/linkd` can import `internal/rest`, for example, but `stats` cannot because it sits outside `link`. In this case, `stats` is an external package and doesn't have the same root as our `internal`.

An `internal` directory enforces encapsulation, signaling that certain packages aren't part of a module's API. This reduces the risk of breaking external dependencies with internal changes and allows packages inside to evolve without introducing breaking changes. In our scenario, extra boundaries add little value because our module is for our use. But if we decide to share it, we'll likely use `internal` so that later changes to our code won't break its dependent code. Check out https://go.dev/doc/modules/layout for more information.

8.2   *Core*

Now that we've outlined the structure of our service, we can focus on the service's core logic in the `link` package. We'll start by declaring common errors that we use across our project. Then we'll declare our core types, such as `Link` and `Key`. Each type has specific validation methods to ensure that user-provided inputs are correct. Finally, we'll provide a `Shorten` function to shorten a URL and implement the `Shortener` service to shorten and resolve links.

This section also discusses how to use zero values to make types more usable and reliable. In addition, it dives into classical mutexes, which eliminate race conditions.

The rest of our service project depends on the core logic we implement in this section. Section 8.3 implements HTTP handlers in the `link/rest` package, which uses the core logic and serves HTTP requests. In chapter 10, the `link/sqlite` packages uses the same core functionality to persist and retrieve links from a persistent SQLite database.

Additional services

Although we provide a `link.Shortener` service, extra services we could provide later could also fit into our package structure. Imagine a `link.Analytics` service that provides link statistics. Its core logic could go into the `link` package, the REST API into `rest`, and persistence into `sqlite`. Rather than creating new packages, using the existing structure can help us avoid import cycles and provide a nice structure for expanding the project. See https://mng.bz/dWZO.

8.2.1   *Errors*

The following variables help us maintain consistent error handling between our project's packages. As we'll see in section 8.4.3, for example, our HTTP handlers will translate these errors to HTTP status codes and error responses, making our REST API responses consistent.

Listing 8.1   Standardized errors (`link/error.go`)

```go
// Package link provides link management services.
package link

import "errors"

var (
    ErrConflict   = errors.New("conflict")      ◀── errors.New returns an error
    ErrNotFound   = errors.New("not found")          value that contains an error
    ErrBadRequest = errors.New("bad request")        message as a string.
    ErrInternal   = errors.New("internal error")
)
```

Because we use exported package-level variables, we risk allowing codes from other packages to change their values of these variables (e.g., setting them to different errors), but no reasonable gopher would ever do so. Declaring shared errors in the package scope is a widely used idiomatic practice followed by the standard library. To avoid potential misuse and confusion, prefixing an error variable with `Err` is idiomatic, as in `ErrBadRequest`, which distinguishes the variable's purpose from other no-error variables and clarifies its intent.

Deep dive: Satisfying the error interface

Using error variables (e.g., `ErrNotFound`) is enough for our project because we would map them only to HTTP status codes. If we need extra context, it might be helpful to declare custom error types that satisfy the `error` interface, adding extra behavior and data. The following `NotFoundError` satisfies `error`, letting us store an `ID`. Naming it with an `Error` suffix is idiomatic, clarifying that it implements the `error` interface:

```
type NotFoundError struct{ ID string }
func (e *NotFoundError) Error() string {          ◄————  Satisfies the
    return fmt.Sprintf("%q not found", e.ID)              error interface
}
```

Because the `*NotFoundError` type satisfies the `error` interface with its `Error` method, we can return a `*NotFoundError` from a function as an `error` value:

```
func Resolve() error { return &NotFoundError{ID: "42"} }
```

Then we can match this error using `errors.As` (which we'll explore in chapter 10):

```
var nfe *NotFoundError
if err := Resolve(); errors.As(err, &nfe) {      ◄————  Extracts the custom error
    fmt.Printf("unknown item: %s\n", nfe.ID)             from the error value
}
```

Custom errors are nice, but we must be mindful of a subtle trap. The following code, for example, returns a `nil *NotFoundError` instead of returning `nil` directly for success:

```
func ResolveBad() error {
    var err *NotFoundError          ┐  Returning a nil
    return err              ◄—————— ┘  *NotFoundError for success
}
```

We should have returned `nil` for success directly, not as a `nil` custom error. Otherwise, the returned `error` would never be `nil`. The following use panics, for example:

```
                                                      Detects the error as a non-nil
                                                      error and runs Printf with a
if err := ResolveBad(); errors.As(err, &nfe) {  ◄———  nil *NotFoundError
    fmt.Printf("unknown item: %s\n", nfe.ID)   ◄————
}                                                     Panic: invalid memory address
                                                      or nil-pointer dereference
```

> *(continued)*
>
> An interface value, such as an `error` value, has a type and a value part. The `nfe` variable stores a non-`nil` `*NotFoundError` type and a `nil` value. Because its type part is not `nil`, `nfe` is not `nil`, even though its value part is a `nil` `*NotFoundError` value.
>
> You can try this example at https://go.dev/play/p/Fsb3iiBK1lX to better understand this misuse. You can also read appendix D to learn more about interface values.

8.2.2 Core

With standardized errors in place, our next step is implementing the core functionality for link management services. We'll start with the core types, `Link` and `Key`, and then add validation methods. Finally, we'll add a function to shorten a `Link.URL` to a `Link.Key`.

CORE TYPES

We'll start by declaring the `Link` and `Key` types, as shown in the next listing. `Link` consists of a long `URL` and its shortened `Key`.

Listing 8.2 Core types (`link/link.go`)

```go
package link

import "strings"

// Link represents a link.
type Link struct {
    // URL is the original URL of the link.
    URL string
    // Key is the shortened key of the URL.
    Key Key
    // Additional fields can be added here if needed.
}

// Key is the shortened key of a [Link] URL.
type Key string

// String returns the key without leading or trailing spaces.
func (key Key) String() string { return strings.TrimSpace(string(key)) }

// Empty reports whether the [Key] is empty.
func (key Key) Empty() bool { return key.String() == "" }
```

The `Link` type is the main type of our link services, representing a link concept with the original `Link.URL` and the shortened `Link.Key`. By creating a distinct `Key` type, we avoid the likely misuse of passing a plain string to a function that requires a `Key` type.

It's still possible to use a constant string like a string literal in place of a Key type, however, because in Go, constants are typeless until their context gives them a fixed type. Link{Key: "hello"} is a valid use, for example. Here, "hello" is a string literal that gets converted to a Key type automatically because we assign it to a Key field.

NOTE Learn more about untyped constants at https://go.dev/blog/constants, and see appendix D to learn more about types and underlying types.

VALIDATION

As the next listing shows, we add validation methods to our core types. These methods check the business rules and ensure that we have the correct data to improve our project's reliability.

Listing 8.3 Validation (link/link.go)

```
package link

import (
    "errors"
    "fmt"
    "net/url"
    . . .
)

// Validate validates the [Link].
func (lnk Link) Validate() error {
    if err := lnk.Key.Validate(); err != nil {            ◄── Delegating the validation
        return fmt.Errorf("key: %w", err)                      of the key to itself
    }                                                     ◄── Returns a new error
    u, err := url.ParseRequestURI(lnk.URL)                     that wraps the error
    if err != nil {                                            from Validate with %w,
        return err                                             creating an error chain
    }
    if u.Host == "" {                                     ◄── ParseRequestURI is
        return errors.New("empty host")                        stricter than Parse when
    }                                                          detecting incorrect URLs.
    if u.Scheme != "http" && u.Scheme != "https" {
        return errors.New("scheme must be http or https")
    }
    return nil
}

// Validate validates the [Key].
func (key Key) Validate() error {
    // We use generate (8-hex-character) by default, but allow
    // user-defined keys up to 16 characters for convenience.
    const maxKeyLen = 16
    if len(key.String()) > maxKeyLen {
        return fmt.Errorf("too long (max %d)", maxKeyLen)
    }
    return nil
}
```

These validation methods have the same signature: `Validate()` error. This consistent signature allows us to abstract the validation method using an interface when necessary. In chapter 9, we declare an interface with a single `Validate` method. This interface helps us automatically validate incoming data immediately after parsing, so our downstream code can safely assume the data is valid, improving reliability.

TIP   Keep method signatures aligned to improve reusability.

URL SHORTENER

Next, in listing 8.4, we add the `Shorten` function that shortens a long URL to a short `Key`. It generates a new `Key` if the provided `Link.Key` is empty or uses the given `Key`, validates the `Link`, and returns a `Key`. In section 8.2.3, we'll call `Shorten` from the `Shortener` to shorten URLs.

Listing 8.4   `Shorten (link/link.go)`

```go
package link

import (
    "crypto/sha256"
    "encoding/base64"
    . . .
)

// Shorten shortens the [Link] URL and generates a new [Key]
// if the [Key] is empty. Otherwise, it returns the same [Key].
// It returns an error if the [Link] is invalid.
func Shorten(lnk Link) (Key, error) {
    if lnk.Key.Empty() {
        sum := sha256.Sum256([]byte(lnk.URL))      // Calculates the SHA-256 hash of the URL
        lnk.Key = Key(                              // Converts the string to a Key
            base64.RawURLEncoding.EncodeToString(   // Encodes the hash to a Base64 string to reduce its size and make it URL-safe
                sum[:6],                            // Takes the first 6 bytes of the hash to create a shorter key
            ),
        )
    }
    if err := lnk.Validate(); err != nil {
        return "", fmt.Errorf("validating: %w", err)
    }
    return lnk.Key, nil
}
```

We've written a function that can shorten URLs. Shortening a URL takes a few lines of code thanks to the standard library's support for traditional hash and encoding algorithms.

First, we calculate the URL's SHA-256 hash and encode the first 6 bytes to Base64 to make it shorter. This encoding may produce non–URL-safe characters, so we use `Raw-URLEncoding` to ensure that the key is safe to use in a URL. This approach is imperfect, but it serves nicely as an example. In real-world use, collisions become likely around 16 million keys—or possibly even sooner. See the following sidebar for details.

> ### Deep dive: Avalanche effect and birthday paradox
>
> Using hash functions to generate short keys is never collision-free. In our case, SHA-256 deterministically maps a URL to a 256-bit digest; changing even 1 bit yields an unrelated digest (the avalanche effect). Taking the first 48 bits and encoding them with `RawURLEncoding` packs the bits into eight URL-safe characters (48 ÷ 6). With only 48 bits, the birthday paradox puts a 50% collision chance at about $2^{24} \approx 1.7 \times 10^7$ distinct URLs. It's fine for demonstration but may be risky to use at web scale.

8.2.3 Service

We've finished implementing the core functionality for our link management project. We're keeping the `link` package free from other dependencies to prevent import cycles. Because `link` has no external dependencies and is only logic, testing it would be straightforward.

With the core functionality in place, let's integrate it into the `Shortener` service. The HTTP handlers in the `link/rest` package will use this service to shorten and resolve links. We'll start by discussing the differences between constructors and zero values and then learn why we should make `Shortener` safe for concurrent use by multiple goroutines.

MAKING A TYPE'S ZERO VALUE USEFUL

As listing 8.5 shows, we declare `Shortener`, which stores links in a `links` map field. Next, we add the `Shorten` method to store a link in the map. Because adding an entry to a `nil` map causes panics, we initialize the map one time before we add a link.

Listing 8.5 Shortener service (`link/shortener.go`)

```
package link

import (
    "context"
    "fmt"
)

// Shortener shortens and resolves [Link] values from an in-memory storage.
type Shortener struct {
    links map[Key]Link          ◀──────  A map of pairs of
}                                         Key and Link values

// Shorten shortens the [Link] URL and may update the [Key] if the key
// is empty. If the link is valid, it stores it in an in-memory storage.
func (s *Shortener) Shorten(
    _ context.Context, lnk Link,   ◀──────  We'll use the Context
) (Key, error) {                            parameter in later chapters.
```

```
        var err error
        if lnk.Key, err = Shorten(lnk); err != nil {
            return "", fmt.Errorf("%w: %w", err, ErrBadRequest)
        }

        // Persist the link in the in-memory storage.
        if _, ok := s.links[lnk.Key]; ok {
            return "", fmt.Errorf(
                "saving: %w", ErrConflict,
            )
        }
        if s.links == nil {
            s.links = map[Key]Link{}
        }
        s.links[lnk.Key] = lnk

        return lnk.Key, nil
    }
```

Generates a new key for the link URL if the link's key is empty

Reads the link from the map and returns ErrConflict if the link with the key doesn't exist

Initializes the map using an empty map literal if the map is nil

Adds the link to the map with its key

We've implemented the `Shortener` service and its `Shorten` method to shorten links. Because the `Shortener`'s zero value is useful, we can declare a variable and use it right away:

```
var links Shortener
links.Shorten(. . .)
```

Declares a Shortener variable instead of calling an additional constructor

Automatically initializes the nil map before adding an item to the map

Otherwise, we would have to provide a constructor to initialize the map:

```
func NewShortener() *Shortener {
    return &Shortener{links: map[Key]Link{} }
}
```

Initializes and assigns an empty map to the links field

Making a type's zero value useful simplifies code and enhances flexibility. It removes the need for initialization, reduces boilerplate, and makes types easier to compose into structs or use in tests without additional setup and ceremony, making the codebase cleaner and safer.

TIP   Design the types so that their zero value is useful. If forcing a zero value to be useful adds complexity, however, it might be better to use a constructor.

Different ways of initializing a map

There are two ways to initialize a map:

- *With a map literal*—`map[Key]Link{}`
- *With the built-in* make *function*—`make(map[Key]Link)`

Both approaches are the same. But `make` is helpful if we also want to preallocate a map:

```
links := make(map[Key]Link, 1_000)
```
◄─── **Preallocates and returns a map with 1,000 empty entries**

You can learn more about the basic use of map types in appendix C.

READING FROM A NIL MAP IS SAFE

Now that we can shorten links, our next goal is to resolve links from shortened keys. As the next listing shows, `Resolve` queries for the specified key and returns the corresponding link if that key exists. If the key doesn't exist or if the map is `nil`, it returns `ErrNotFound`.

Listing 8.6 `Shortener.Resolve(link/shortener.go)`

```go
// Resolve resolves the [Key] to its original [Link].
func (s *Shortener) Resolve(_ context.Context, key Key) (Link, error) {
    if key.Empty() {
        return Link{}, fmt.Errorf(
            "validating: empty key: %w", ErrBadRequest,
        )
    }
    if err := key.Validate(); err != nil {
        return Link{}, fmt.Errorf(
            "validating: %w: %w", err, ErrBadRequest,
        )
    }

    // Retrieve the link from the in-memory storage.
    lnk, ok := s.links[key]          ◄───── Reading from a nil map is safe.
    if !ok {
        return Link{}, fmt.Errorf(
            "retrieving: %w", ErrNotFound,
        )
    }

    return lnk, nil
}
```

This time, we don't need to initialize the map because reading from a `nil` map returns the zero value of the map's element type. By knowing how maps work, we make the `Shortener`'s zero value useful and convenient to use without requiring a constructor.

NOTE Reading from a map doesn't require initialization and returns its element type's zero value. `map[string]int`'s element type, for example, is `int`. Reading from it returns `0` if the map is `nil` because the `int` type's zero value is `0`. Also, reading from a `nil` `map[int]bool` returns `false` because the `bool` type's zero value is `false`.

fmt.Errorf and errors.Is

Returning a specific error variable or type lets callers identify it in the error chain. We can use `errors.Is` to check whether the error is `ErrBadRequest` and handle it:

```
err := fmt.Errorf(
    "unexpected issue: %w", ErrBadRequest,
)
if errors.Is(err, ErrBadRequest) { . . . }
```

Returns a new error that wraps ErrBadRequest

Looks for ErrBadRequest in the error chain in err. Here, errors.Is returns true.

Otherwise, we might never find errors we're looking for inside an error chain:

```
if err == ErrBadRequest { .. }
```

This statement returns false.

This comparison returns `false` because `err` is not equal to `ErrBadRequest`; `err` is a chain of errors. Remember to use `errors.Is` for safer, more accurate error handling. Try this example yourself at https://go.dev/play/p/GStjuwZnmaY.

8.2.4   *Mutex*

Now that we have the `Shortener` service that stores links in a map, let's make it safer. We're planning to have our HTTP handlers use the same `Shortener` service. But `Shortener` keeps links in a map. Because handlers serve each HTTP request in a new goroutine for efficiency, concurrent use of this map can cause race conditions, such as crashes or data corruption.

To eliminate these issues, we'll protect the map from concurrent use by using a mutex. This mutex acts as a gatekeeper, letting only one goroutine at a time use the map. This approach might also reduce throughput, so we'll find a more efficient way to let goroutines read from the map but allow only a single goroutine to write into the map, improving efficiency.

> **TIP**   Writing efficient code is idiomatic as long as it doesn't hurt clarity.

Why not use channels instead?

Channels are used primarily to coordinate between goroutines rather than synchronize shared states. Managing shared states through channels would add unnecessary complexity and overhead. Mutexes are simpler and more efficient for protecting shared data directly.

Channels introduce extra synchronization complexity and overhead (memory and processing), making mutexes simpler and more efficient for straightforward state protection. Use mutexes for simple state protection; they're generally more efficient than channels.

PROTECTING ACCESS TO A RESOURCE WITH A MUTEX

Figure 8.5 shows goroutines that read and write to the same map (shared state) concurrently. In our case, retrieving a link is a read operation, whereas saving a link is a write operation.

In the first case (top), the left goroutine writes stale data due to previous updates from the right one. In the second case (bottom), we protect access to the state with a mutex, allowing one goroutine to finish its read and write before the other to prevent stale writes.

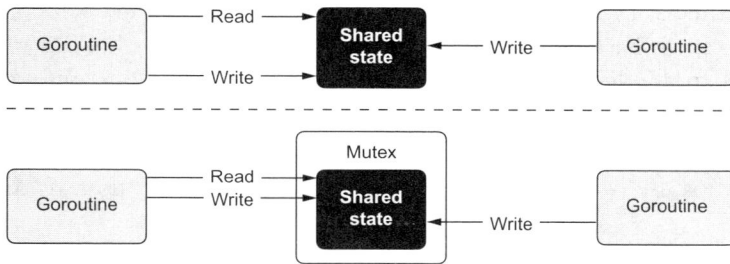

Figure 8.5 Multiple goroutines using the same state may cause race conditions. A mutex gives them safe, orderly access to the shared state.

A mutex has two main operations:

- *Locking*—Grants exclusive access to a goroutine, blocking others waiting to lock
- *Unlocking*—Allows one of the goroutines to lock the mutex

NOTE A mutex is initially in an unlocked state.

A goroutine that locks a mutex blocks others by saying, in essence, "Wait until I finish my work." When it unlocks the mutex, one of the other goroutines can lock it and tell others the same thing. Because locked mutexes block other goroutines, however, read and write throughput may be reduced. To improve efficiency for specific scenarios, Go provides `Mutex` and `RWMutex` types:

- `Mutex` provides exclusive access to a single goroutine at a time.
- `RWMutex` allows multiple goroutines to read, but only one goroutine at a time can write.

Put simply, `RWMutex` allows multiple goroutines to read a shared state concurrently. It blocks others only when a write operation is in progress. Because we expect more reads than writes in our project, we'll go with the `RWMutex` type for efficiency reasons.

Deep dive: Mutex vs. RWMutex

Mutex might be more useful if reads and writes are balanced or if writes are more frequent. If reads are more frequent, however, RWMutex can improve throughput. Its benefits diminish if the write operations are frequent or long-running because readers can starve. Although RWMutex might improve performance in read-heavy cases, it's worth benchmarking both mutex types to see which one provides the best efficiency for a specific case.

MUTEXES IN PRACTICE

We've covered the basics of mutexes for protecting shared states and decided to use an RWMutex to give exclusive access to a single writer while allowing multiple readers. Now we can put this knowledge to work and protect our program from race conditions, as shown in the next listing.

Listing 8.7   RWMutex **protection** (`link/shortener.go`)

```go
package link

import (
    "sync"
    . . .
)

// Shortener shortens and resolves [Link] values from an in-memory storage.
// It's safe for concurrent use from multiple goroutines.
type Shortener struct {
    muLinks sync.RWMutex          ◀── The zero values of Mutex and RWMutex
    links   map[Key]Link               are useful, and we don't need to
}                                       initialize these types manually.

func (s *Shortener) Shorten(_ context.Context, lnk Link) (Key, error) {
    . . .
    s.muLinks.Lock()              ◀── Blocks if the mutex is locked (regardless
    defer s.muLinks.Unlock()      ◀──    of the lock type: write/read)

    if _, ok := s.links[lnk.Key]; ok {    Allows a goroutine to lock the
        return "", fmt.Errorf(. . .)       mutex for writing or reading
    }
    if s.links == nil {
        s.links = map[Key]Link{}
    }
    s.links[lnk.Key] = lnk

    return lnk.Key, nil
}

func (s *Shortener) Resolve(_ context.Context, key Key) (Link, error) {
    . . .
    s.muLinks.RLock()             ◀── Blocks if the mutex
                                         is locked for writing
```

```
    defer s.muLinks.RUnlock()                    Allows goroutines to lock the mutex
                                                  for reading or a goroutine for writing
    lnk, ok := s.links[key]
    if !ok {
        return Link{}, fmt.Errorf(. . .)
    }

    return lnk, nil
}
```

We protect the map from unsafe concurrent use:

- Only one goroutine can write into the map at a time.
- Multiple goroutines can read the map unless there's a writer.

We use the following RWMutex methods for locking and unlocking:

- Lock locks RWMutex for exclusive write access, and RLock locks it for read access.
- For unlocking, we call Unlock after Lock while we call RUnlock after RLock.

If we forget to unlock the mutex, goroutines waiting to lock it will wait forever. Eventually, our program will become unresponsive and use so much memory that it may crash. To eliminate these issues, we use a defer to reduce our chances of forgetting to unlock the mutex.

> **NOTE** It's idiomatic to add a comment if a type or a function is safe for concurrent use, such as "It's safe for concurrent use from multiple goroutines."

Now the in-memory-backed Shortener service is safe for concurrent use, establishing a nice baseline for using and sharing state from our HTTP handlers. Section 8.3 discusses how to integrate our new Shortener service into the HTTP handlers.

What's with the hat?

Conventionally, the mu in muLinks stands for *mutex hat*. To simplify maintenance and reduce unintentional mistakes, it's common to name the mutex after the fields it protects and to position the mutex right above those fields (which is why it is referred to as a *hat*.)

8.3   HTTP

Unlike most other languages, Go makes us productive from Day 1. Instead of searching for and learning an endless number of frameworks and libraries, Go's comprehensive standard library lets us get started crafting reliable, scalable HTTP servers and clients.

Now that we have a core functionality, let's start implementing the link/rest handlers. We'll explore how to implement them using the http package, which allows us to run an http.Server, listen for client connections, and handle http.Requests with http.Handler implementations.

Adding a `ServeHTTP` method to a type satisfies the `Handler` interface. Then, as figure 8.6 shows, we can register a `Handler` implementation on the `Server` to serve requests.

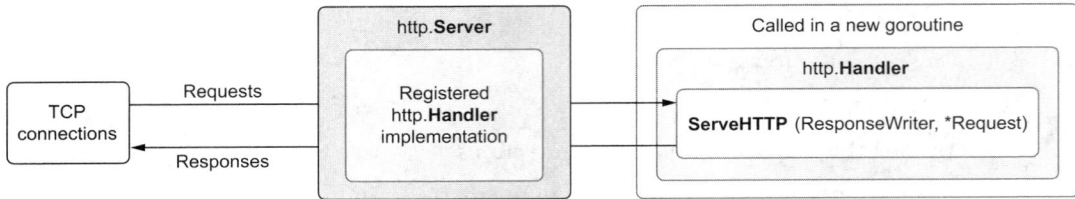

Figure 8.6   The `http.Server` routes incoming HTTP requests to its `http.Handler` by calling the `Handler`'s `ServeHTTP` method, passing an `http.ResponseWriter` and `http.Request`. Then the `Handler` can use the `ResponseWriter` to respond to clients via the `Server`.

To handle HTTP requests concurrently, `Server` runs the registered `Handler`'s `ServeHTTP` method in a separate goroutine. Unlike most other languages, in which launching a single thread for each request could be overkill, Go handles this process effortlessly because goroutines are lightweight, and Go's scheduler multiplexes them onto operating system threads. It's not surprising to see that a simple HTTP server can handle ~100,000 requests per second.

NOTE   See the Go scheduler discussion in chapter 1 for more information.

The `ServeHTTP` method takes `http.ResponseWriter` and `*http.Request` parameters. `Request` contains HTTP request details, such as URL and query parameters. `ResponseWriter` is an interface with the following methods that we can use to send HTTP responses to clients:

- `Header()`—Sets HTTP response headers
- `WriteHeader(code int)`—Sets the HTTP status code (default is `200` if not called)
- `Write([]byte)`—Writes the response body to the client

We must call these methods in the proper order for them to work correctly. (We'll see their use in section 8.3.1 and beyond.) We should set headers and status before writing the body, for example. We don't have to use any of these methods if we don't want to respond to clients.

8.3.1   *Health check*

Having glimpsed the `http` package, in this section, we'll create the `link/rest` package's first handler: a health check handler. This handler responds with a simple `"OK"` message to confirm that the link server is functioning. Health checks are vital in production environments for load balancers and orchestrators like Kubernetes; they enable us to monitor service availability and remove or restart unhealthy service instances as necessary for improved system reliability.

Now that we know what to do, let's implement the handler as shown in listing 8.8. `Health` takes a `ResponseWriter` to respond to clients and a `Request` to read the request. It responds `"OK"` by implicitly calling `ResponseWriter.Write` via Fprintln, which takes a `Writer`. Because `ResponseWriter` is a `Writer`, Fprintln can call its `Write` method.

Listing 8.8   A health check handler (`link/rest/health.go`)

```
// Package rest provides link services with a REST API over HTTP.
package rest

import (
    "fmt"
    "net/http"
)

// Health serves the health check requests.
func Health(w http.ResponseWriter, r *http.Request) {      ◀── Responds "OK" to clients
    fmt.Fprintln(w, "OK")                                       using ResponseWriter.Write
}
```

We've implemented our first handler, which writes `"OK"` to clients. By default, handlers write a status code `200`, meaning success. Handlers do that automatically if we don't specify a status code using `WriteHeader` before calling `Write`. This is useful because we don't have to return a `200` status code manually. Our handler doesn't write an HTTP status code using `WriteHeader`, for example, but it still responds with an HTTP status code of `200`.

8.3.2   Serving HTTP

Now that we have the `Health` function, we're almost ready to serve HTTP requests. We can use the `http.ListenAndServe` function to start an HTTP server as follows:

```
http.ListenAndServe(
    "localhost:8080", /* http.Handler here */,      ◀── An http.Handler implementation
)                                                       serves all incoming HTTP
                                                        requests at localhost:8080.
```

Behind the scenes, `ListenAndServe` configures and starts a `Server` that routes incoming requests to the registered `Handler` that we set. We can use `Health` to serve HTTP requests after we convert it to a `Handler` using the `HandlerFunc` type:

```
http.ListenAndServe(
    "localhost:8080", http.HandlerFunc(Health),      ◀── http.HandlerFunc converts
)                                                        the Health function to a
                                                         Handler implementation.
```

HandlerFunc converts `Health` to a `Handler` on the fly. `HandlerFunc` is like an adapter that converts a function to one that satisfies the `Handler` interface (and you may remember `HandlerFunc` from chapter 7's testing section):

```
type HandlerFunc func(ResponseWriter, *Request)  ◀┐
```
> **HandlerFunc can convert only a function with this signature (which Health's signature matches).**

```
func (f HandlerFunc) ServeHTTP(
    w ResponseWriter, r *Request,
) {
```
> **HandlerFunc implements the Handler interface with the ServeHTTP method.**

```
    f(w, r)  ◀─
}
```
> **Calls the converted function (e.g., Health), passing it the ResponseWriter and Request**

Calling the `ServeHTTP` method calls the converted function—in this case, `Health`—so the `Server` started by `ListenAndServe` will call `Health` for every incoming HTTP request.

8.3.3 *HTTP server*

Having crafted a health check handler, let's write a program to run an HTTP server. This step marks the beginning of our `linkd` program, which runs our link HTTP server. As listing 8.9 shows, we add a `config` type to define the configuration of our server program. Next, we add a `main` function, parse the flags, set a logger, and call the `run` function. The `run` function launches an HTTP server to serve HTTP requests using the `Health` handler. We'll add more handlers in section 8.4.

> **Listing 8.9 Running an HTTP server (`link/cmd/linkd/linkd.go`)**

```
package main

import (
    "context"
    "errors"
    "flag"
    "fmt"
    "log/slog"
    "net/http"
    "os"
    "github.com/inancgumus/gobyexample/link/rest"
)

type config struct {
    http struct {
        addr string
    }
    lg *slog.Logger
}
```
> **Groups our program's configuration under a single config type**

```
func main() {
    var cfg config
    flag.StringVar(
```

```
        &cfg.http.addr, "http.addr",
        "localhost:8080", "http address to listen on",
    )
    flag.Parse()

    cfg.lg = slog.New(                                    Creates a logger that always
        slog.NewTextHandler(os.Stderr, nil),              logs to os.Stderr with the
    ).With("app", "linkd")                                app=linkd key-value pair
    cfg.lg.Info("starting", "addr", cfg.http.addr)

    if err := run(context.Background(), cfg); err != nil {
        cfg.lg.Error("failed to start server", "error", err)
        os.Exit(1)
    }
}

func run(_ context.Context, cfg config) error {
    err := http.ListenAndServe(                           Launches an HTTP server that
        cfg.http.addr,                                    serves HTTP requests with the
        http.HandlerFunc(rest.Health),                    Health HTTP handler
    )
    if !errors.Is(err, http.ErrServerClosed) {
        return fmt.Errorf(                                Returns an error other than
            "server closed unexpectedly: %w", err,        http.ErrServerClosed if the
        )                                                 server stops unexpectedly
    }
    return nil
}
```

We created a program that runs an HTTP server, routing all HTTP requests to `Health`. The server's default listening address is `localhost:8080`. We also set up a logger to announce that the server is starting. We'll use this logger in our other handlers. Now let's run this program to launch the server and start serving HTTP requests:

```
$ go run ./link/cmd/linkd              We'll omit the time prefix in the log
time=2061/07/29 23:58:00               message from now on for brevity.
  level=INFO msg=starting app=linkd addr=localhost:8080
```

Because the server waits for incoming connections, we can send a request to the server from another terminal using our favorite HTTP client (or a browser):

```
                            Sends an HTTP GET request to the HTTP server
$ curl -i localhost:8080
HTTP/1.1 200 OK             Automatically writes a 200 OK HTTP status code
OK
                           Written to ResponseWriter.Write by fmt.Fprintln
```

We've implemented and run an HTTP server program that handles health check requests. Now we're ready to add the link-shortener HTTP handlers to this program.

TIP   Visit https://pkg.go.dev/net/http for more information on the `http` package.

The slog package

Go 1.21 introduced `slog` for structured logging, making it easier to format logs as key–value pairs and integrate seamlessly into larger systems. It standardizes logging with Go's standard library without third-party modules. We can instantiate a new `Logger` with the built-in `slog` handlers, such as `TextHandler` and `JSONHandler`, or craft our own. `TextHandler`, for example, formats logs in human- and machine-readable form:

```
lg := slog.New(slog.NewTextHandler(os.Stderr, nil))
lg.Info("server started", "address", "localhost:8080", "version",
➡"1.0.0")
```

Output:

```
time=2009-11-10T23:00:00.000Z level=INFO
➡msg="server started" address=localhost:8080 version=1.0.0
```

Here's another with `JSONHandler`:

```
lg := slog.New(slog.NewJSONHandler(os.Stderr, nil))
lg.Info("server started", "address", "localhost:8080", "version",
➡"1.0.0")
```

Output:

```
{"time":"2009-11-10T23:00:00Z","level":"INFO",
➡ "msg":"server started",
➡ "address":"localhost:8080","version":"1.0.0"}
```

These examples show how `slog` adapts to different needs, making logging simple, efficient, and versatile. Visit https://go.dev/blog/slog for more information.

8.4 HTTP handlers

We have an HTTP server running, capable of receiving HTTP requests and responding with a health check handler. It's time to expand its functionality by adding more handlers in the `link/rest` package. We'll start with the `Shorten` and `Resolve` functions, which return handlers that manage links using the `Shortener` service.

8.4.1 Handler closures

`Shorten` is a higher-order function that returns a closure as a `Handler`, as shown in listing 8.10. The closure extracts the key and the URL from the request's POST body and shortens the URL using the `Shortener` service. If successful, it responds with the shortened key and the `Created` HTTP status code. Otherwise, it calls the `httpError` function to respond with an error status. (In section 8.4.3, we'll add `httpError` to map errors to status codes.)

Listing 8.10 Shorten handler (`link/rest/shortener.go`)

```
package rest

import (
    "fmt"
    "log/slog"
    "net/http"
    "github.com/inancgumus/gobyexample/link"
)

// Shorten returns an [http.Handler] that shortens URLs.     ← Takes a Logger
func Shorten(                                                     and Shortener
    lg *slog.Logger, links *link.Shortener,            ←
) http.Handler {                                        ←      Returns a Handler
    return http.HandlerFunc(func(
        w http.ResponseWriter, r *http.Request,                Converts and returns the
    ) {                                                        closure to a HandlerFunc
        key, err := links.Shorten(r.Context(), link.Link{
            Key: link.Key(
                r.PostFormValue("key"),                    Extracts the key and URL
            ),                                             from the request's POST body
            URL: r.PostFormValue("url"),
        })
        if err != nil {
            httpError(w, r, lg, fmt.Errorf(                Responds with an
                "shortening: %w", err,                     HTTP error on failure
            ))
            return                 ←        Stops processing the request
        }

        w.WriteHeader(http.StatusCreated)             Responds with the Created HTTP
        fmt.Fprint(w, key)                            status code and the shortened key
    })
}
```

`Shorten` takes its dependencies directly and returns a `Handler`. `Shorten` takes a logger, for example. This approach makes testing straightforward because we can replace it with a no-op logger to suppress or capture logs for inspection. By contrast, using a global logger would make correct use and testing harder and more likely lead to unexpected issues if another part of the code uses and modifies the same logger.

TIP Explicitly specifying what a function requires to work improves clarity.

`Shorten` uses `PostFormValue` to extract the key and URL from the request body. If the body is parsed and the link is shortened, the closure responds with `StatusCreated`.

If an error occurs, the handler stops processing the request after responding with a status code.

> **NOTE**   Always return from a handler after an error to stop further processing. Otherwise, we risk unintended side effects, such as security issues, duplicate operations, or inconsistent responses.

Before wrapping up, let's see how we might register `Shorten` on a `Server`:

```
http.ListenAndServe(
    "localhost:8080",
    Shorten(. . .),           Registers the returned closure from
)                             Shorten as the http.Server's Handler
```

Because `Shorten` returns a `Handler` and `HandlerFunc` implements the `Handler`, Go allows directly returning the closure (a `HandlerFunc`) as a `Handler`. `Server` remains unaware of the closure's underlying type (`HandlerFunc`), calling it for each incoming HTTP request.

Deep dive: Use value-receiver methods for map types

`Request.PostFormValue` parses the request body and populates the `Request` `.PostForm` field, which is a `map[string][]string` allowing multiple values per key. If the request body had multiple values for the tag key, they would be stored as

```
map[string][]string{ "tags": {"idiomatic", "go"} }
```

The standard library's `url` package declares the `Values` type like this:

```
package url
type Values map[string][]string
```

`Values` is a map type with the following methods for convenience and consistency:

```
func (v Values) Add(key, value string) { v[key] = append(v[key], value) }
func (v Values) Del(key string)        { delete(v, key) }
```

With the `Values` type, instead of exposing the raw map type, the standard library provides a consistent API for handling query parameters and form data. It also prevents accidental misuse of the underlying map, keeping the API reliable and extensible. Moreover, because a map value is already a pointer, the methods of `Values` are on a value receiver instead of a pointer receiver.

8.4.2   Redirecting

Now that we have the `Shorten` handler for shortening links, the next step is adding the `Resolve` handler to resolve shortened keys and redirect users to the original URLs.

Listing 8.11 Resolve handler (`link/rest/shortener.go`)

> **Passes the Request's Context to let Shortener.Resolve stop if the client cancels the request (or another reason)**

```go
// Resolve returns an [http.Handler] that resolves shortened link URLs.
// It extracts a {key} from [http.Request] using [http.Request.PathValue].
func Resolve(lg *slog.Logger, links *link.Shortener) http.Handler {
    return http.HandlerFunc(func(w http.ResponseWriter, r *http.Request) {
        lnk, err := links.Resolve(
            r.Context(),
            link.Key(r.PathValue("key")),      // Extracts the requested
        )                                      // key from the URL path
        if err != nil {
            httpError(w, r, lg, fmt.Errorf(    // Responds with an HTTP
                "resolving: %w", err,          // error if the resolve
            ))                                 // operation fails and returns
            return
        }

        http.Redirect(
            w, r, lnk.URL, http.StatusFound,   // Redirects the client
        )                                      // to the original URL
    })
}
```

The `Resolve` function's signature is similar to that of the `Shorten` function. When `Resolve` gets a `Link` from the `Shortener`, it calls `http.Redirect` to send a `302` HTTP status code and a `Location` header with the `Link`'s original URL. If the key is `"go"` and the URL is `"https://go.dev"`, the request and response will look like this:

```
$ curl -i localhost:8080/r/go
HTTP/1.1 302 Found
Location: https://go.dev
```

NOTE Wildcard segments allow us to define dynamic URL routes.

This request won't work until we route HTTP requests to `Resolve`, however. The `PathValue` method can extract wildcard segments from a `Request`, but only if they've been preloaded. With a URL pattern like `"/r/{key}"`, calling `PathValue("key")` on a request for `"/r/go"` returns `"go"`. Without preloading, it returns an empty string. We'll use a router from the standard library to preload these details into the `Request` automatically.

If you're familiar with routers like Express (Node.js) and Flask (Python), this approach should make sense. A router extracts segments from URL paths. In section 8.5, we'll set up a router to handle this preloading so that our handler can access the wildcard segments.

8.4.3 *HTTP status codes*

Now that we've added all the handlers for the link-shortening REST API, as listing 8.12 shows, we declare the `httpError` function to map our standard errors to their corresponding HTTP status codes so that our handler functions can respond with correct HTTP status codes. We respond with an error message and the HTTP status code. We shouldn't expose our system internals to clients, however, so if an internal error occurs, we mask it but log it, letting us diagnose and fix potential issues by reviewing the logs.

Listing 8.12 Errors to HTTP status codes (`link/rest/shortener.go`)

```
package rest

import (
    "errors"
    . . .
)


. . .

func httpError(
    w http.ResponseWriter,
    r *http.Request,
    lg *slog.Logger,
    err error,
) {
    code := http.StatusInternalServerError        ◀── Sets the HTTP status code
    switch {                                           to internal server error by
    case errors.Is(err, link.ErrBadRequest):          default if no errors match
        code = http.StatusBadRequest
    case errors.Is(err, link.ErrConflict):
        code = http.StatusConflict                 Maps the domain errors
    case errors.Is(err, link.ErrNotFound):         to HTTP status codes
        code = http.StatusNotFound
    }
    if code == http.StatusInternalServerError {
        lg.ErrorContext(
            r.Context(),
            "internal", "error", err,              Masks the internal error
        )                                          content from the client but
        err = link.ErrInternal                     logs it for administrators
    }
    http.Error(w, err.Error(), code)        ◀── Responds with the error
}                                               message and HTTP status code
```

NOTE Calling `Error` on an `error` returns the error message as a string.

We've mapped our errors into HTTP status codes using a `switch`. Unlike in C or Java, we don't use `break` after a `case` because Go's `switch` breaks automatically after each match. After running the `switch`, we call `http.Error` to respond with the status code and message.

8.5 Routing

Now that we have HTTP handlers, we need to route incoming HTTP requests. We'll discuss the purpose of an HTTP router and explore the standard library's router implementation, `ServeMux`. Then we'll configure a `ServeMux` in our `linkd` program to route requests to the `link/rest` API handlers, such as `Shorten` and `Resolve`.

8.5.1 ServeMux

The `http.Server` allows us to register only a single `Handler`. That's not a limitation; it's part of the simple design. As figure 8.7 shows, a `Handler` can also be a router (or a muxer) that forwards HTTP requests to others based on URL paths, such as `/shorten`, `/r/`.

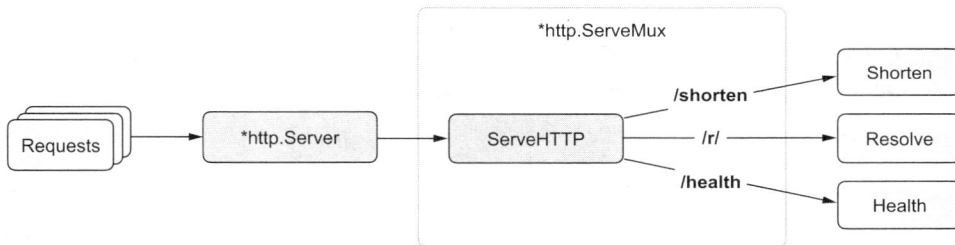

Figure 8.7 `ServeMux` **is a** `Handler` **that routes requests to other** `Handlers`.

When a client requests the route

- `/shorten`—Server calls `ServeMux.ServeHTTP`, which calls `Shorten`.
- `/r/go`—Server calls `ServeMux.ServeHTTP`, which calls `Resolve`.

> **NOTE** I keep it simple by saying " . . . calls `Shorten`." A technically correct way of putting it is " . . . calls the `http.Handler` returned by the `Shorten` method."

We'll see how dynamic routes like `/r/` work after we learn how to register routes:

- `ServeMux.Handle()` registers a `Handler` directly.
- `ServeMux.HandleFunc()` converts a function to a `Handler` before registering it.

We can register our handlers like so:

```
mux := http.NewServeMux()
mux.Handle("POST /shorten", Shorten(. . .))
mux.HandleFunc("GET /health", Health)
```

Registers the Handler returned by Shorten to handle incoming POST requests to the /shorten route

Converts the Health function to a Handler and registers it for GET requests to the /health route

We use `Handle` to register `Shorten` because calling it returns a `Handler`. But we use `HandleFunc` to convert and register `Health` because `Health` is a function, not a `Handler`.

For the `Resolve` handler's route, we need to use a wildcard segment, such as `/r/{key}`:

```
mux.HandleFunc("GET /r/{key}", Resolve(. . .))
```
◄— Registers the Resolve handler for any route matching /r/{key}

When a request like `/r/go` comes, `ServeMux` loads `"go"` into the `Request` and sends it to `Resolve`, which retrieves the `"go"` after calling the `Request.PathValue` with `"key"`:

```
func(w http.ResponseWriter, r *http.Request) {
    . . .r.PathValue("key"). . .
}
```
◄— Returns "go"

`ServeMux` parses `"/r/go"` and calls the `Request.SetPathValue` method to set `"go"`. Otherwise, `PathValue` returns an empty string. `SetPathValue` is also helpful for testing a handler because we may not always use `ServeMux` to set segments automatically.

8.5.2   Routes

Now that we know how to register handlers, let's register all our handlers, as follows.

Listing 8.13   **Routing with** `ServeMux` (link/cmd/linkd/linkd.go)

```
package main

import (
    "github.com/inancgumus/gobyexample/link"
    . . .
)

func run(_ context.Context, cfg config) error {
    shortener := new(link.Shortener)

    mux := http.NewServeMux()
    mux.Handle(
        "POST /shorten",
        rest.Shorten(cfg.lg, shortener),
    )
    mux.Handle(
        "GET /r/{key}",
        rest.Resolve(cfg.lg, shortener),
    )
    mux.HandleFunc("/health", rest.Health)

    err := http.ListenAndServe(
        cfg.http.addr,
        mux,
    )
    if !errors.Is(err, http.ErrServerClosed) {
        return fmt.Errorf("server closed unexpectedly: %w", err)
```

- Returns a new *link.Shortener
- Registers the returned Handler closures on the new ServeMux
- Converts Health to a Handler and then registers it on the ServeMux
- Registers the ServeMux on the Server to route all incoming requests

```
    }
    return nil
}
```

We have registered the `link/rest` API handlers on the `ServeMux` and registered the `ServeMux` as the `Server`'s handler. All incoming requests go first to the `ServeMux`:

```
http.Server -> ServeMux.ServeHTTP -> Handler.ServeHTTP (e.g., Shorten())
```

Incoming requests go through a chain of handlers until one of our handlers, such as the `Shorten` handler, receives the requests.

8.5.3   Demonstration

Now that we have a router and handlers, let's give it a try:

```
$ curl -i localhost:8080/shorten -d 'url=https://github.com/inancgumus'
HTTP/1.1 201 Created
OQzXIiL4
$ curl -i localhost:8080/shorten -d 'url=https://github.com/inancgumus'
HTTP/1.1 409 Conflict
shortening: saving: conflict                    Shorten calls Shortener
$ curl -i localhost:8080/r/OQzXIiL4       ◄     .Shorten, gets link.ErrConflict,
HTTP/1.1 302 Found                                and calls httpError().
Location: https://github.com/inancgumus
$ curl -i localhost:8080/r/inanc                Sends an HTTP GET request
HTTP/1.1 404 Not Found
resolving: retrieving: not found
$ curl -i localhost:8080/shorten -XGET    ◄     Intentionally making a GET
HTTP/1.1 405 Method Not Allowed                 request to a POST route
$ curl -i localhost:8080/shorten
        -d 'url=http://'
shortening: validating: empty host: bad request   Intentionally sending an
                                                   invalid URL and getting an
                                                   error from rest.Shorten
```

WARNING   Relaunch the server after modifications to avoid running stale code.

Now we can route requests to specific handlers based on route patterns. This approach simplifies route handling and prepares our server for more complex scenarios.

TIP   Visit https://pkg.go.dev/net/http#ServeMux for more details on routing.

8.6   *Timeouts*

Now that our HTTP server is running, let's think ahead and ensure that it can handle real-world traffic reliably. Handling client requests presents some challenges. Imagine that our server is handling numerous client requests that take too long to read. If these requests pile up, they can overwhelm the server, making it unresponsive or causing it to crash. To prevent this, we can set timeouts that define how long the server should wait before giving up. Figure 8.8 shows the timeouts and time intervals we can set.

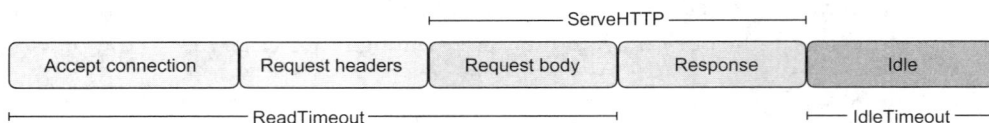

Figure 8.8   Request and response life cycle and timeout intervals

We have two critical server timeout settings: `ReadTimeout` and `IdleTimeout`. These settings protect the server from potential issues caused by slow or unresponsive clients:

- `ReadTimeout` starts a timer when the server accepts a connection and stops when it receives the request, ensuring that the server doesn't waste time on slow requests.
- `IdleTimeout` sets the total time the server keeps a connection open while waiting for a new request. If no request comes, the server closes the connection.

Although `ListenAndServe` provides a simple way to start a server, it doesn't allow us to configure timeouts. To enable these protections, we should configure a `Server` as follows.

Listing 8.14   Setting server timeouts (`link/cmd/linkd/linkd.go`)

```
package main

import (
    "time"
    . . .
)

type config struct {
    http struct {
        addr      string
        timeouts struct{ read, idle time.Duration }      ◀─┐ Declares a timeouts struct
    }                                                       │ field with two time.Duration
    lg *slog.Logger                                         │ fields (read and idle)
}

func main() {
    var cfg config
    . . .
    flag.DurationVar(
        &cfg.http.timeouts.read, "http.timeouts.read",
        20*time.Second, "read timeout",
    )
    flag.DurationVar(
        &cfg.http.timeouts.idle, "http.timeouts.idle",
        40*time.Second, "idle timeout",
```

```
    )
    flag.Parse()
    . . .
}

func run(_ context.Context, cfg config) error {
    shortener := new(link.Shortener)
    . . .
    srv := &http.Server{
        Handler:     mux,
        Addr:        cfg.http.addr,
        ReadTimeout: cfg.http.timeouts.read,
        IdleTimeout: cfg.http.timeouts.idle,
    }
    if err := srv.ListenAndServe(); !errors.Is(
        err, http.ErrServerClosed,
    ) {
        return fmt.Errorf("server closed unexpectedly: %w", err)
    }
    return nil
}
```

The ServeMux routing configuration from earlier

ServeMux serves all incoming requests.

Configures the address the server listens on

Timeout for reading request data

Timeout for keeping connections alive

Starts listening for incoming requests

Setting these timeout values makes the server more resilient. Without them, slow clients could tie up server resources indefinitely, leading to performance degradation or server failure under heavy load. By configuring timeouts, we control how long the server waits at various stages of handling a request, improving its ability to manage resources effectively.

We should configure these timeout settings carefully based on our programs' needs and behavior. A server handling large file uploads, for example, may need a longer `ReadTimeout` than one processing very quick API calls. Similarly, `IdleTimeout` should be balanced to allow the client to stay connected without holding on to connections longer than necessary.

> **NOTE** We protect the server from unresponsive or malicious clients. We can also use the standard library's `http.TimeoutHandler` to protect the server from long-running handlers. See https://pkg.go.dev/net/http#TimeoutHandler for more information.

Using HTTPS

To protect against menace-in-the-middle attacks, we can launch the server using the `ListenAndServeTLS` method (similar to `ListenAndServe`) to listen and respond over HTTPS connections. Visit https://mng.bz/QwZG to learn more.

Still, it is common to run a server over HTTP and use a reverse proxy to handle HTTPS. A reverse proxy can manage Transport Layer Security (TLS) termination, decrypt HTTPS requests, and pass them as HTTP to the server listening to HTTP This can simplify both development and HTTPS setup.

8.7   Testing

Testing a handler involves providing it a `Request` and a `ResponseWriter` and observing its response. We'll start by using `httptest.ResponseRecorder` to capture and inspect a handler's response. Then we'll dive into using test helpers.

8.7.1   Response recording

Because `ResponseRecorder` is a `ResponseWriter`, we can pass it to a handler to observe the responses it generates. The following example shows passing test-only values to `Health`:

```
                                                    ResponseRecorder records
                                                    what the handler responds.
w := httptest.NewRecorder()         ◄───┐
r := httptest.NewRequest(http.MethodGet, "/", nil)  ◄───┐
Health(w, r)                                     Instead of returning an
                                                 error, this method panics
                                                 if the inputs (e.g., HTTP
                                                 method) are incorrect.
```

We can inspect the handler's response through `w`. We could log the handler's response status code and response body using `*testing.T.Log` like this:

```
t.Log(w.Status)         // logs 200
t.Log(w.Body.String())  // logs OK  ◄───  Body is a *bytes.Buffer. Calling String returns
                                          the buffer's accumulated bytes as a string.
```

To recap, we can pass a `Request` and a `ResponseWriter`, like `ResponseRecorder`, to a handler, observe, and verify that its response matches what we expect.

8.7.2   Testing a handler

Now that we know how to observe handler responses from tests, let's test a handler. As the following listing shows, we pass a `ResponseRecorder` and a `Request` to `Health`; then we check the HTTP response status code and body to confirm that the handler's response is correct.

Listing 8.15   Testing a handler (`link/rest/health_test.go`)

```
package rest

import (
    "net/http"
    "net/http/httptest"
    "strings"
    "testing"
)

func TestHealth(t *testing.T) {
    t.Parallel()

    rec := httptest.NewRecorder()
```

```
Health(rec, httptest.NewRequest(
    http.MethodGet, "/", nil,
))
```
> The URL path we type here isn't important because we're calling the handler directly.

```
    if rec.Code != http.StatusOK {
        t.Errorf("got status code = %d, want %d", rec.Code, http.StatusOK)
    }
    if got := rec.Body.String(); !strings.Contains(got, "OK") {
        t.Errorf("\ngot body = %s\nwant contains %s", got, "OK")
    }
}
```

We created a `ResponseRecorder` to capture the `Health` handler's response. Then we called `Health` and checked whether its status code was `StatusOK` and the response body contained `"OK"`. Any mismatch will output an error with the actual and expected values. Let's run the test:

```
$ go test ./link/rest -v
--- PASS: TestHealth
```

8.7.3 Test helpers

Using `httptest.NewRequest` in tests is more convenient than using `http.NewRequest` because `httptest.NewRequest` panics instead of returning an error. So we don't need to check for an error after creating a request with `httptest.NewRequest`, but it would be more convenient if it were a test helper that makes tests fail, producing nice error output instead of stopping the whole test run with a panic.

IMPLEMENTING A TEST HELPER

Test helpers simplify tests and reduce repetitive code. The following `newRequest` is a test helper that internally calls `NewRequest` to create a new `*Request`.

Listing 8.16 Adding a test helper (`link/rest/shortener_test.go`)

```
package rest

import (
    "io"
    . . .
)

// newRequest creates a new [http.Request] for testing.
// It fails the calling test if it cannot create the request.
func newRequest(
    tb testing.TB,
    method string, target string, body io.Reader,
) *http.Request {
    tb.Helper()

    r, err := http.NewRequest(method, target, body)
    if err != nil {
```
> newRequest takes testing.TB, so it works in both tests and benchmarks.

> The tb.Helper() call marks newRequest as a test helper, improving error reporting.

```
        tb.Fatalf(
            "newRequest() err = %v, want nil",
            err,
        )
    }
    return r
}
```

Fails the calling test, e.g.,
TestHealth, if an error occurs

Now that we have a test helper, let's use it in our test, as shown in the following listing. This helper stops only `TestHealth`, not the whole test run, after an error. Other tests can continue to run.

> **TIP** Using `testing.TB` allows us to use `newRequest` in both regular tests and benchmarks. `testing.TB` is an interface that `*testing.T` and `*testing.B` satisfy.

Listing 8.17   Testing with a test helper (`link/rest/health_test.go`)

```
func TestHealth(t *testing.T) {
    . . .
    Health(rec, newRequest(
        t, http.MethodGet, "/", http.NoBody,
    ))
    . . .
}
```

Using newRequest to create
a new *Request instead of
calling httptest.NewRequest

We've implemented a test-helper function and used it in our test. By calling `Helper()`, we mark `newRequest` as a test-helper function. When an error occurs, `newRequest` reports it from the line in the calling test (e.g., `TestHealth`) rather than inside `new-Request`, making it easier to locate the exact line where the test failed, making debugging easier.

TESTING WITH A TEST HELPER

Next, we'll force our test helper to fail to see how test helpers can be useful in practice. We do so by passing an emoji as an HTTP method while calling `newRequest`. Suppose that `TestHealth` calls `newRequest`, and `newRequest` encounters the following error:

```
$ go test ./link/rest -v
. . .
=== CONT  TestHealth
    health_test.go:15: newRequest() err =
    net/http: invalid method "💣", want nil
```

The log shows a line in `TestHealth` rather than a line in `newRequest`:

```
func TestHealth(t *testing.T) {
    . . .Health(w, newRequest(. . .)). . .
}
```

Line 15

Instead of showing a line in `newRequest`, where it fails while creating the request, the log shows line 15, which is the line where `TestHealth` called `newRequest` to create a new request. Getting an error report on the exact line of the test that calls the helper makes fixing issues easier and faster. Otherwise, we wouldn't get the failure's origin easily.

NOTE Test helpers make tests clearer and reduce duplicated test setup code.

As a final piece of advice, avoid returning errors from test helpers; not doing so goes against their purpose of reducing repetition. If errors are returned, each test that uses the helper will have to handle them. It's more effective to use the methods from `testing.TB` (e.g., `Error` and `Fatal`) to handle errors and fail the test within the helper.

In this section, we learned effective techniques for testing HTTP handlers. We used a `ResponseRecorder` to capture handler responses. Then we implemented a test helper to create a new `Request` without panic and obtain accurate line information in case of failures.

8.8 Simplicity

This chapter highlighted important Go philosophies, including simplicity and clarity, guiding us in writing maintainable code by using the powerful standard library and minimal abstractions. We kept the code simple, avoided unnecessary abstractions, and let actual needs drive design decisions. We can always add more when the benefits are clear.

Before wrapping up this chapter, let's discuss Go's approach to upfront abstractions and indirections. We'll also discuss how to design testable types.

8.8.1 Up-front abstractions and indirections

Most programming ecosystems rely on popular architectural styles (e.g., Clean Code), which can add extra abstraction and indirections and may not fit well with Go. This doesn't mean we should avoid using beneficial principles from these styles to write maintainable and testable code. The difference is that our approach is often much leaner.

In Go, it's often more effective to start with small, cohesive packages (perhaps a single one), keeping domain concepts in mind, and introduce multiple packages or indirections only when necessary. This approach respects Go's philosophy of simplicity, eliminating unnecessary abstractions and package sprawl. If our application or team grows, we can branch out to more packages across domain boundaries without getting caught in import cycles.

Rather than trying to predict and implement a complicated, abstracted design up front, we branch out to multiple packages when the project genuinely requires it. Go is built so that large teams can collaborate effectively; it eases late refactoring and code evolution.

We often write simple code without up-front abstractions if there's no immediate and genuine need. Thanks to Go's implicit interfaces, turning a concrete type use into an interface is often straightforward. Until chapter 9, we won't see any interface declarations.

We embrace simplicity, designing types to achieve sufficient decoupling without declaring abstractions up front or introducing indirections upon indirections. Speaking of designing types properly, the next section discusses how to design inherently testable types.

8.8.2   *Inherently testable types*

The `http` and `httptest` packages embody Go's philosophy of creating types that are inherently flexible and testable. This section explores how these types, even without being explicitly designed for testing, enable us to build tests that closely mimic real-world scenarios. `httptest`, for example, depends on `http` and provides the following:

- `NewRequest` returns a `*Request` that we can pass to a `Handler`.
- `NewServer` runs a `Server` configured for testing.
- `NewRecorder` is a `ResponseWriter` to capture responses.

These types don't just mimic behavior with mocks; they use actual `http` package types like `Request`, `Server`, and `ResponseWriter` on the surface or under the hood. This approach lets us test with real types and code instead of mock types created solely for testing, preventing inconsistencies between test and production behavior. This approach is possible because these types aren't designed just for testing; they aim to be helpful and flexible in production code as well. This adaptability makes them *inherently testable.*

We can use the same types in both production and test code. `Server`, for example, can listen on any address and port. This capability allows `httptest` to run isolated servers in a controlled environment that mirrors production. Also, `Server`'s `Handler` field (the `http.Handler` interface) makes it easy to swap handlers and test specific routes.

We can learn from these types. Crafting versatile types makes our code easier to extend, adapt, and test. This approach eliminates the need for extra indirections or wrappers, resulting in practical package APIs that support development and testing seamlessly.

> **NOTE**   This philosophy applies to other programming languages but is often less apparent in those languages, especially in popular programming cultures that prioritize testability over usability and rely more on heavy frameworks. By contrast, Go's philosophy and tendency are to craft simple, lean, useful types that are naturally testable.

In chapter 9, we'll put this philosophy into practice by developing a highly configurable middleware type. We'll learn how to design composable types with the power of functional programming. We'll cover composition patterns, middleware, `Context` values, and handler chaining patterns.

Using Go's http package

Go encourages minimizing dependencies. Doing so helps us avoid inflating the final binary and bugs caused by third-party dependencies or their misuse due to a lack of documentation. All these issues prevent teams from shipping faster.

Many languages encourage frameworks for building HTTP servers, but Go's standard library provides all the essentials out of the box. The `http` package embraces Go's minimal abstraction, keeping code maintainable and aligning with its "less is more" philosophy.

Using the `http` package means that our server stays consistent with Go's ecosystem and integrates easily with third-party tools when necessary. Many external libraries build on top of this package, ensuring compatibility without significant changes to existing code.

The reliability and centrality of Go's standard library make it the preferred starting point for programs of all sizes. It reduces the need to search for and learn multiple frameworks.

Although Go's standard library is powerful, the Go community provides many useful, idiomatic modules that we can easily integrate into our programs. One standout is the `chi` module (https://github.com/go-chi/chi). This module simplifies enhancing our HTTP server programs, supporting features like HTTP authentication, routing based on headers, health checks, and request throttling. What sets it apart is its complete compatibility with Go's `http` package. Using `chi`, we can enhance the `http` handlers we create, blending the simplicity of Go's standard library with the added power of community-driven functionality.

The real benefit is that although we can start with idiomatic `http` handlers, modules like `chi` let us enrich our code without rewriting or making significant structural changes. We keep our code clean and idiomatic while adding advanced features as needed. Third-party modules can enhance our applications with extra features that go beyond the standard library while maintaining the simplicity and composition that Go encourages.

8.9 Exercises

Here are some exercises to hone your skills, from easy ones to difficult ones:

1 Remove the mutex from the `link.Shortener`. Inspect what happens if you share a `Shortener` between handlers. Run the server with the `-race` flag, and send requests to the handlers repeatedly to hit a race condition. Hint: to do that, use the `hit` tool we developed in previous chapters.

2 Test the remaining code in the `link` and `link/rest` packages.

3 Add support for updating the destination URL of an existing shortened URL.

4 Add an integer field to `link.Link`, incrementing with each `Resolve` call. Hint: be careful about race conditions. Use a mutex or an atomic integer (`sync/atomic`).

5 Find a way to prevent potential infinite redirects while resolving links.

6 Make `main` (`linkd`) testable by externalizing dependencies, as in chapter 5.

7 Develop a client API for the `link/rest`. See the next exercise for details.

8 Write a CLI tool that uses the client library. See `cmd/linkc` at https://mng.bz/ rZ1D for details.

9 Improve `Shorten` to remove old links from the map. Otherwise, the map could grow so large that it crashes the machine due to out-of-memory errors. Feel free to resurrect your old computer science books to add better validation logic.

10 Write and test a REST API for the HIT client from chapter 7. For a starting point, see https://mng.bz/V920.

Summary

- Go favors directness and clarity over cleverness and excess indirections. Avoid premature abstractions, introducing them only when genuine needs arise.
- Structure packages in layers to prevent import cycles. Packages should be experts.
- Use shared errors across packages for consistent error handling.
- Make zero values useful, reducing the need for extra initialization.
- Protect shared state with mutexes. Prefer mutexes for simpler state protection.
- `http.Handler` is an interface defining HTTP handling behavior. `http.Handler-Func` is an adapter allowing any function with the correct signature to become a `Handler`, promoting simplicity and composability. `http.ServeMux` itself implements `Handler`, enabling uniformity and composability for routing requests.
- Explicitly specifying what a function requires improves clarity.
- Use `defer` to reliably release resources and prevent leaks.
- Design inherently usable and configurable types that favor reusability, naturally leading to testability without extra complexity or dedicated test constructs.

Composition patterns

9

This chapter covers

- Effectively using composition patterns and functional programming techniques
- Using field embedding and method forwarding to reuse functionality
- Understanding optional interfaces, method-hiding issues, and type assertions
- Propagating request-scoped values across package APIs using Context
- Implementing custom slog.Handlers to log extra attributes automatically
- Wrapping interfaces to modify, extend, and intercept existing behavior
- Extracting implicit behavior using anonymous interfaces

In chapter 8, we implemented a link service, discussed structuring packages, and developed a REST API over HTTP. In this chapter, we'll extend our project, focusing on composition.

In his "Less is exponentially more" article (https://mng.bz/JwN0), Rob Pike says, "If C++ and Java are about type hierarchies and the taxonomy of types, Go is about composition." We may be used to inheritance-based designs, large frameworks, or large manager types when we come from other languages. By contrast, Go's philosophy is similar to UNIX's: *do one thing well*. Our packages provide simple, reusable pieces that allow users to compose them together on top of what we provide.

We'll discuss functional compositional patterns to demonstrate how to design packages that offer reusable and composable functionality, showcasing HTTP middleware. Then we'll dive into propagating trace IDs using `Context` and see how to write custom log handlers by satisfying the `slog.Handler` interface. Finally, we'll discover a handler-chaining pattern for writing robust, convenient HTTP handlers. Along the way, we'll discover the upsides and downsides of Go's implicit interfaces, examining type assertions, field embedding, and optional interfaces.

This chapter shows us how to use interfaces and functions effectively. By the end of this chapter, we'll understand how to structure composable, maintainable code the Go way, focusing on simplicity, modularity, and reusability.

9.1 *Middleware pattern*

In Go, functions are first-class citizens. We can pass them to functions or return them from functions. In chapter 4, we learned that we call such functions *higher-order functions*. As we'll soon discover, middleware is similar, but it takes an interface and returns another. Still, we take advantage of both higher-order functions and interfaces.

As the first version, we'll start with middleware that logs requests but skips logging responses. This version will focus on the core idea of wrapping a handler to add extra functionality. The next section adds support for capturing and logging responses.

9.1.1 *What is HTTP middleware?*

Middleware wraps handlers to add functionality such as logging and tracing without altering the original handler code. Middleware can preprocess requests and postprocess responses. The middleware A in figure 9.1 wraps B, which wraps a handler. Incoming requests pass through them to the handler, and the responses travel back through them before reaching the client.

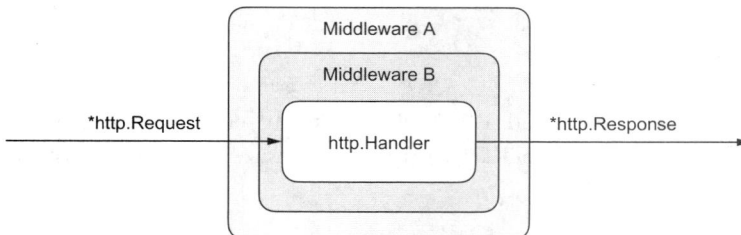

Figure 9.1   Middleware layers process both incoming HTTP requests and outgoing HTTP responses, enhancing functionality without altering the handler code.

Let's look at a code snippet that shows what middleware looks like:

```
func(next http.Handler) http.Handler
```
◄—— **Returns the middleware's Handler that wraps the given Handler**

The middleware takes a handler and returns another. The returned handler can serve requests using the original handler while performing extra tasks: logging, tracing, and so on. This signature also allows us to chain multiple middleware:

```
handler := MiddlewareA(MiddlewareB(Handler))
```
◄—— **The resulting variable's type is http.Handler.**

9.1.2 Example

Suppose that we want to log every incoming request to our HTTP handlers in the `link/rest` package (from chapter 8), such as URL paths (e.g., `/shorten`). Instead of adding logging in each handler, we can use middleware to wrap our `ServeMux` once and log all requests (figure 9.2).

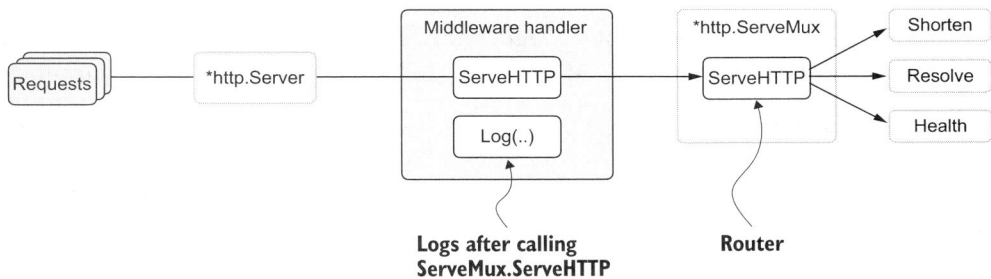

Figure 9.2 The middleware's handler forwards requests to `ServeMux` and then logs.

Our middleware returns a handler that sits between incoming requests and our handlers. The requests go to our middleware first; the middleware forwards them until they reach one of our handlers, such as `Shorten`. After the handler serves the request, middleware logs it.

INTERFACES IN, INTERFACES OUT

Suppose that our middleware function looks like this:

```
func Middleware(next http.Handler) http.Handler {
    return http.HandlerFunc(
        func(w http.ResponseWriter, r *http.Request) {
```
◄—— **Returns a handler that wraps the given handler**

◄—— **Returns the closure as an http.HandlerFunc, which implements http.Handler**

```
        next.ServeHTTP(w, r)
        ...
    },
  )
}
```

The wrapped handler (next) serves the incoming request.

Logs the request details here

This function returns a handler that runs the next handler and then logs the request. To make sure that every incoming request goes through our middleware, we register it:

```
http.ListenAndServe(. . ., Middleware(mux))
```

Registers the middleware's handler that logs requests by wrapping the ServeMux

All incoming requests go through middleware and eventually to handlers. Middleware logs requests when a handler finishes serving a request.

GLOBAL LOGGERS

Our middleware logs with a global logger because we don't pass a logger to it.

> **TIP**   Avoid global loggers. Instead, inject loggers explicitly into middleware or handlers because direct injection simplifies testing and enhances flexibility.

We prefer not to use a global logger because it makes testing harder. (See chapter 5 for the reasons.) Instead, we can configure and pass a specific logger to our function:

```
func Middleware(lg *slog.Logger) func(next http.Handler) http.Handler
```

This function is similar to the previous one but returns middleware. Its usage is more complicated, but the benefits outweigh the costs (allowing us to use a specific logger):

```
wrap := Middleware(/* pass the logger here */)
http.ListenAndServe(. . ., wrap(mux))
```

This time, we pass a specific logger to `Middleware`, get a middleware function, and finally wrap our `ServeMux`. This setup operates as before but without a global logger.

Our new function returns the `func(Handler) Handler` middleware signature. That way, we can chain multiple middleware and use third-party ones without adding extra code to be compatible. Doing so also teaches us a valuable lesson that we've seen many times: keeping function signatures is extremely important for maintainable, reusable, and composable code.

> **TIP**   Be consistent in your function (methods are functions too) signatures.

9.1.3   *Practice*

Now that we're familiar with middleware, we'll implement one (see listing 9.1) that logs request details, such as paths. Our `hlog` package provides HTTP-specific logging to minimize boilerplate and ensure consistent logging. Expert packages like `hlog` improve maintainability. By contrast, generic packages may introduce unnecessary dependencies.

```
// Package hlog provides HTTP logging functionality.
package hlog

import (
    "log/slog"
    "net/http"
)

// MiddlewareFunc is a function that wraps an [http.Handler].
type MiddlewareFunc func(http.Handler) http.Handler

// Middleware returns a middleware that logs requests and responses.
func Middleware(lg *slog.Logger) MiddlewareFunc {
  return func(next http.Handler) http.Handler {
    return http.HandlerFunc(
      func(w http.ResponseWriter, r *http.Request) {
        next.ServeHTTP(w, r)
        lg.LogAttrs(
          r.Context(),
          slog.LevelInfo, "request",
          slog.Any("path", r.URL),
          slog.String("method", r.Method),
        )
      },
    )
  }
}
```

Returns a new middleware function that wraps a handler and returns another

Groups middleware functions under a single type for better documentation

Returns a new handler that runs the next handler and logs

Runs the next handler to serve the request

Emits a log record

Propagates the Request .Context to the logger (which we'll use in section 9.5)

Turns into a key-value pair, like "method=GET"

Emits an information-level log message with the "request" message

Turns into a key-value pair, like "path=/shorten"

We wrote a middleware function that logs request details, such as the URL path. Before seeing this middleware in action in section 9.1.4, let's walk through the code:

1 We use nested closures to provide access to the variables `lg`, `next`.
2 Middleware takes a logger and returns a middleware function.
3 That function returns the middleware's handler, which is its main logic.
4 The middleware's handler runs `next` to serve requests and then logs the requests.
5 The handler repeats the preceding step for every incoming request.

We also declared `MiddlewareFunc` to maintain consistent function signatures and group middleware functions in the documentation to better understand the package's use.

9.1.4 *Learning more about the slog package and the any interface*

For structured logging, we use the standard library's `slog` package. The `slog.String` function returns a `slog.Attr` struct value (a log attribute), which turns into a key-value pair, such as `"method=GET"`, when we pass the result of the `String` function to the `Logger`'s `LogAttrs` method to log. Although we use a `String` attribute, there are many others, such as `Int` for integers. We use our `lg` variable, which is a `*slog.Logger`, to call methods such as `LogAttrs` for logging.

> **NOTE** `slog.Attr` is a log attribute with a string key and a value that can store any type. See the `slog` documentation at https://pkg.go.dev/log/slog for more information.

Because we log every incoming request, efficiency is crucial for optimal performance; because we can pass `LogAttrs` type-safe values, it won't have to guess their types. By contrast, the `Logger.Log` method takes variadic `any` arguments and has to guess the underlying types of these arguments at runtime:

```
lg.Log(. . ., "status", 404)
```
◄— Accepts any types of arguments:
func Log(. . ., args ...any)

> **TIP** Prefer `slog.LogAttrs` for efficient and type-safe logging.

The `any` type is an interface type without methods, also known as an *empty interface*:

```
type any interface {

}
```
◄— Does not declare methods

Because `any` has no methods, every other type satisfies it. This flexibility allows methods like `Log` to accept various types of arguments. There is a cost, however: the compiler can't know the underlying type an empty interface value wraps inside beforehand. As a result, `Log` needs to inspect the underlying type at runtime. Languages like Python, Ruby, and JavaScript don't complain until runtime if we pass the wrong type to a function. Go catches these mistakes much earlier, during compilation—unless we start using `any`. Excessive use of `any` may create surprises in our code's runtime behavior, undermining Go's strong typing advantages.

As we discussed, using `any` may introduce runtime overhead and weaken Go's type safety guarantees. In our logger middleware, however, using the `slog.Any` function, which takes an `any` value argument, provides an advantage over `slog.String`. We log `Request.URL` using `slog.Any` to be more efficient. `slog.Logger` detects and internally calls `URL.String` when the `Logger` is enabled. If we used `slog.String`, we would need to call `URL.String` ourselves even when the logger is off, causing unnecessary overhead:

```
slog.String("path", r.URL.String())
```
◄— r.URL.String() runs even
if the logger won't log.

Sometimes, deferring a value's resolution to runtime, despite the usual compile-time advantages, leads to better efficiency, as demonstrated by `slog.Any` in this example.

9.1.5 Integration

Now that we have middleware, let's wrap the `ServeMux` from chapter 8. As shown in the next listing, we set middleware on the `Server` as its `Handler` after wrapping the `Serve-Mux`. Every incoming HTTP request goes to our middleware before reaching our `link/rest` handlers.

Listing 9.2 Activating the middleware (`link/cmd/linkd/linkd.go`)

```go
package main

import (
    . . .
    "github.com/inancgumus/gobyexample/link/kit/hlog"
)
. . .
func run(_ context.Context, cfg config) error {
    shortener := new(link.Shortener)

    mux := http.NewServeMux()
    mux.Handle("POST /shorten", rest.Shorten(cfg.lg, shortener))
    mux.Handle("GET /r/{key}", rest.Resolve(cfg.lg, shortener))
    mux.HandleFunc("/health", rest.Health)

    loggerMiddleware := hlog.Middleware(cfg.lg)   ◀── Creates a new logger
                                                        middleware with the logger
    srv := &http.Server{
        Handler: loggerMiddleware(mux),   ◀── Wraps the ServeMux with
        . . .                                  the middleware's handler
    }
    if err := srv.ListenAndServe(); . . . {
        . . .
    }
    . . .
}
```

This integration was straightforward. We added logging to the `link/rest` API without changing any handler code, reducing bugs and improving maintainability. Next, let's send an example HTTP request to see the logs:

```
$ curl -i localhost:8080/health
```

Here are the server logs:

Logs using slog.Any("path", r.URL)
and slog.String("method", r.Method)

```
. . .level=INFO msg=request path=/health method=GET   ◀──
```

The flow of the incoming request looks like this:

```
Request -> Server -> Middleware -> ServeMux -> Health
```

When the request arrives, the `Server` forwards it to the middleware's handler by calling its `ServeHTTP` method. The handler forwards the request to the `ServeMux` and then to our health handler. The middleware's handler logs request details after the request is served.

In this section, we combined first-class functions with interfaces. Our middleware can easily be composed with others because it uses a consistent middleware signature. Idiomatic code values efficiency, so we optimized our code to eliminate unnecessary work. Next, we'll improve our middleware by capturing additional response metrics.

> **Configurable and testable types**
>
> `Middleware` uses the concrete `slog.Logger` type to log incoming requests, so we keep our logger middleware flexible by leaving the `Logger`'s configuration to the caller. Many programmers overcomplicate by hiding loggers behind interfaces up front, assuming that this approach makes testing or later replacing the logger straightforward. Despite being a concrete type, however, `Logger` is configurable and designed to integrate with other logger solutions when necessary. Using `Logger` directly simplifies implementations.

9.2   *Logging responses*

Suppose that we want to log handler-response durations to see whether the handlers respond slowly. Unlike request details, such as URL paths and HTTP methods, response details, such as durations, aren't readily available, so we must calculate them, as shown in figure 9.3.

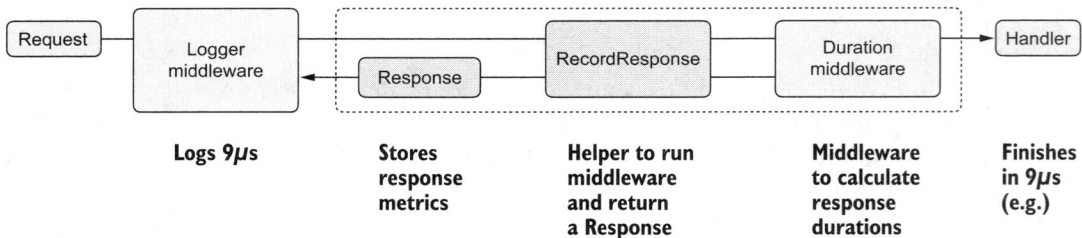

Figure 9.3   `RecordResponse` uses the `Duration` middleware to calculate handler durations.

Our `Middleware` calls `RecordResponse`, which wraps the handler using the `Duration` middleware. `Duration` measures how long the handler takes to respond. After the handler finishes serving the request, `Duration` saves the response duration in a `Response` value. Then `RecordResponse` returns this `Response` to `Middleware`, which logs the duration.

We separate concerns by giving each piece one duty. `Middleware` handles logging, `RecordResponse` orchestrates middleware that measures response metrics, `Duration` measures durations, and `Response` stores response metrics. Keeping each piece independent allows us to add or remove the pieces easily, composing new functionality without complicating the setup. In section 9.3.2, we'll add new middleware to capture HTTP status codes.

9.2.1 Measuring durations

As listing 9.3 shows, we start with the `Duration` middleware, which measures how long it takes a handler to serve a request. The middleware wraps a handler, records the start time, and updates the provided duration variable when the handler finishes serving the request.

Listing 9.3 Duration middleware (`link/kit/hlog/hlog.go`)

```
package hlog

import (
    "time"
    . . .
)

// Duration measures how long a request takes to process by recording the
// time before and after the handler executes. It uses a pointer parameter
// to store the result, allowing it to be used as a building block.
// Not safe for concurrent use. Use it only to process a single request.
func Duration(d *time.Duration) MiddlewareFunc {
  return func(next http.Handler) http.Handler {
    return http.HandlerFunc(func(w http.ResponseWriter, r *http.Request) {
      start := time.Now()
      defer func() { *d = time.Since(start) }()
      next.ServeHTTP(w, r)
    })
  }
}
```

Stores the start time before the handler serves the request

Calculates and stores the handler's serving duration in the linked variable

Instructs the wrapped handler to serve the request

The `Duration` middleware is a building block. It measures durations without assuming where we store its result. Instead of saving the measured duration directly in a `Response`, for example, `Duration` saves the duration via a pointer. This approach makes `Duration` reusable. The returned closure captures this pointer, however, so it's critical that the provided pointer points to a new variable for each request. Otherwise, we may introduce race conditions. Section 9.2.2 shows how to pass new variables to `Duration` safely using `RecordResponse`.

> **TIP** Avoid unnecessary coupling between types to improve composability.

Using `defer` here is idiomatic because it ties the end measurement directly to the handler's completion. The deferred function updates the duration right before returning, ensuring that the measured result is always accurate. Using a `defer` statement is a typical, concise Go pattern for cleanup and finalization tasks.

9.2.2 *Response recording*

We added the `Duration` middleware to measure how long handlers take to process requests, but that's not enough. Next, we plan to capture HTTP status codes, so we want a structured way to store multiple response metrics together and extend later without many code changes.

Listing 9.4 introduces the `Response` struct for holding response details and a helper, `RecordResponse`. This helper chains multiple pieces of middleware, including `Duration` and `StatusCode` (section 9.3.2), runs the wrapped handler, and returns the collected metrics.

> **Listing 9.4 Response recording** (`link/kit/hlog/hlog.go`)

```
package hlog

import (
    "slices"
    . . .
)


// Response holds response related details such as duration.
type Response struct {
    Duration time.Duration
    // More fields are coming soon.
}

// RecordResponse wraps an HTTP handler and captures its response details.
func RecordResponse(
  h http.Handler,
  w http.ResponseWriter, r *http.Request,
) Response {
    var rr Response
    mws := []MiddlewareFunc{
        Duration(&rr.Duration),
        // More middleware is coming soon...
    }
    for _, wrap := range slices.Backward(mws) {
        h = wrap(h)
    }
    h.ServeHTTP(w, r)
    return rr
}
```

The handler to wrap for capturing response details

Used by the final handler to serve requests

Shares the Duration field with the Duration middleware

Iterates over middleware in reverse order (last to first)

Wraps each piece of middleware around the handler

Returns the measured response metrics

Executes the wrapped middleware chain, ending with the original handler

We implemented `Response` and `RecordResponse` to capture and store response metrics. We also demonstrated the middleware chaining pattern:

- Each middleware takes a handler, wraps it, and returns a new handler.

- Each middleware runs sequentially around the wrapped handler, allowing each middleware to store its metrics in a `Response` before and after the handler.

Here's how the process works. `RecordResponse` creates a shared `Response` and passes its fields (by pointer) to response-handling middleware, like `Duration`, which updates the fields via the fields' pointers. (We currently have only one piece of middleware but will add more.)

These pieces of middleware must wrap around the provided handler, `h`, so they execute before the wrapped handler to measure response details accurately. So we wrap the handler starting from the last middleware in the slice. This way, the first middleware serves the incoming request first, followed by subsequent middleware and finally the wrapped handler itself. When processing finishes, `RecordResponse` returns the populated `Response`.

> **TIP** `slices.Backward` returns an iterator that iterates over a slice in reverse.

`RecordResponse` is a helper that encapsulates middleware chaining, providing a `Response` with a single function call. Meanwhile, middleware like `Duration` is a building block that callers can compose individually, allowing fine-grained control of metrics collection.

`Duration` is decoupled and chainable with other middleware that handles response metrics. There's no perfect approach; however—only a tradeoff. The tradeoff is that `Duration` updates a variable through a pointer, which may lead to race conditions if multiple concurrent requests share a variable. Users must ensure that they pass a separate variable to `Duration` for each request, exactly as our `RecordResponse` does. That's what we documented in listing 9.3, reminding users of this important consideration.

9.2.3 Integration

Our logger middleware logs only request details, like paths and methods. As the next listing shows, we're improving our middleware using `RecordResponse` to log response details.

Listing 9.5 Integrating response recording (`link/kit/hlog/hlog.go`)

```go
func Middleware(lg *slog.Logger) MiddlewareFunc {
  return func(next http.Handler) http.Handler {
    return http.HandlerFunc(func(w http.ResponseWriter, r *http.Request) {
      rr := RecordResponse(next, w, r)          // Captures response metrics
      lg.LogAttrs(                               //   by wrapping the handler
        r.Context(),
        slog.LevelInfo, "request",
        slog.Any("path", r.URL),
        slog.String("method", r.Method),
        slog.Duration("duration", rr.Duration),  // Logs the captured
      )                                          //   response duration
    })
  }
}
```

We've integrated `RecordResponse` to capture, store, and log durations. We've improved our middleware without complicating the logging, keeping each piece composable and simple.

`RecordResponse` wraps the `next` handler with our `Duration` middleware, measures how long it takes the handler to process each request, and returns this metric within a `Response`. The logger middleware uses the `slog.Duration` function to log the captured response duration. When the following HTTP request comes

```
$ curl -i localhost:8080/health
```

we see the following server logs:

```
level=INFO msg=request app=linkd path=/health method=GET duration=6.208µs
```

The flow of this incoming requests looks like this:

```
Request -> . . . -> Middleware -> Duration -> ServeMux -> Health Handler
```

In this section, we've progressively improved our middleware to capture and log response metrics. We started by creating small functions, like `Duration`, that handle a single task independently. Then we added composable building blocks, such as `Response` and `RecordResponse`, providing easy extendibility without tightly coupling the parts. Finally, our integration unified these separate pieces. This approach embodies the philosophy of composition: preferring simple, independent parts over complex, coupled ones, enabling users to extend or adapt functionality as needed. Next, we'll apply another compositional pattern to capture HTTP status codes by embedding `ResponseWriter` into another type.

9.3   *Interceptor pattern*

We logged response durations by wrapping handlers using the `Duration` middleware. Now suppose that we want to track HTTP status codes to spot errors or monitor successful responses. Unlike response durations, status codes aren't easily accessible to middleware because handlers send them directly to clients by calling `ResponseWriter.WriteHeader`. We must find a way to intercept the `WriteHeader` method calls to capture status codes.

> **NOTE** Section 8.3 explains that `ResponseWriter` is an interface with a `WriteHeader` method that takes an integer and writes an HTTP status code to clients, such as `200` (OK).

As figure 9.4 shows, we'll introduce an `Interceptor` type that wraps the handler's original `ResponseWriter`. It intercepts the handler's `WriteHeader` calls to capture status codes.

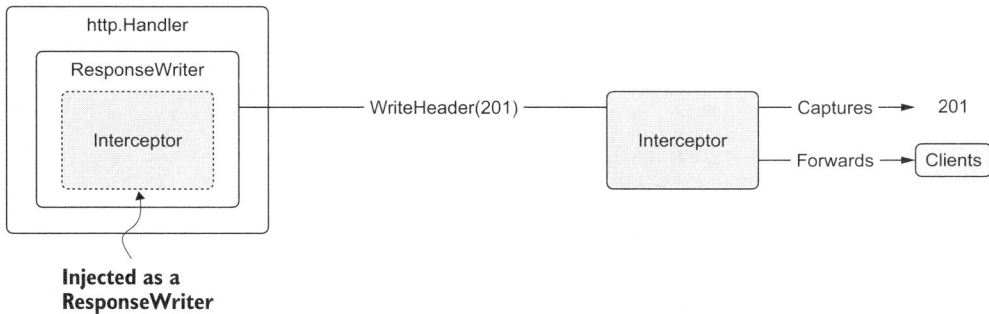

Figure 9.4 `Interceptor` **captures HTTP status codes by intercepting** `WriteHeader`. **Then** `Interceptor` **forwards the call to the underlying** `ResponseWriter`.

We have three requirements for our `Interceptor` type:

- It must be a `ResponseWriter` so we can pass it to handlers.
- It must intercept `WriteHeader` calls so we can capture status codes.
- After capturing the status code, it must forward the `WriteHeader` calls to the original `ResponseWriter` so handlers can respond status codes to clients normally.

We'll meet these requirements by embedding `ResponseWriter` in our `Interceptor` and wrapping it around a handler's original `ResponseWriter`. Embedding automatically forwards all `ResponseWriter` method calls to the embedded `ResponseWriter`, allowing handlers to respond as before. Because our `Interceptor` declares its own `WriteHeader` method, it can capture HTTP status codes transparently, without handlers being aware or needing modification.

First, we'll declare the `Interceptor` and embed the `ResponseWriter` using an anonymous field. Then we'll add `StatusCode` middleware to inject the `Interceptor` into handlers. Finally, we'll update our `RecordResponse` with `StatusCode` and logger middleware to log status codes.

> **TIP** Embedding is useful syntactic sugar. It doesn't override methods but prioritizes the embedding type's methods with the same name. In our case, the `Interceptor`'s `WriteHeader` takes precedence, letting us capture status codes.

9.3.1 Field embedding

Let's start with the `Interceptor` type to capture HTTP status codes. We've learned that embedding forwards all method calls to the embedded type except those we add.

As listing 9.6 shows, we're embedding `ResponseWriter` (anonymously, without a field name) in the `Interceptor` and adding a `WriteHeader` method to capture status codes and notify consumers by calling `OnWriteHeader`. Our `Interceptor` type is flexible and composable. Its only duty is to capture HTTP status codes and notify consumers.

Listing 9.6   Intercepting method calls (`link/kit/hlog/hlog.go`)

**Embeds ResponseWriter to satisfy the interface
and forward its methods automatically**

```
// Interceptor provides hooks to intercept response writes.
type Interceptor struct {
    http.ResponseWriter
    OnWriteHeader func(code int)
}
```

**A callback to notify consumers
when a handler calls WriteHeader**

```
// WriteHeader calls [Interceptor.OnWriteHeader] if provided and
// then calls the embedded [http.ResponseWriter.WriteHeader].
func (ic *Interceptor) WriteHeader(code int) {
    if ic.OnWriteHeader != nil {
        ic.OnWriteHeader(code)
    }
    ic.ResponseWriter.WriteHeader(code)
}
```

**Calls the provided callback
to capture status codes and
deliver them to consumers**

**Forwards the WriteHeader call
to the original ResponseWriter**

`Interceptor` satisfies the `ResponseWriter` interface by embedding it because the compiler automatically *promotes* all of that interface's methods to the `Interceptor` type. Satisfying `ResponseWriter` allows us to pass an `Interceptor` to handlers as a `ResponseWriter`.

When we inject an `Interceptor` into a handler, whenever the handler calls `WriteHeader`, that `Interceptor` captures the HTTP status code and calls `OnWriteHeader` before calling the original `ResponseWriter`. Go automatically forwards the rest of the `ResponseWriter` method calls from the handler to the handler's original `ResponseWriter`.

> **TIP**   Although useful, field embedding can also be dangerous. Embedding a type that implements the `json.Marshaler` interface, for example, can change how our type gets serialized to JSON. Visit https://go.dev/play/p/RvISoxRjFBz for an example.

9.3.2   *Capturing and saving*

Now that we can intercept `WriteHeader` calls, we'll declare the `StatusCode` middleware to capture HTTP status codes into the provided integer variable, as shown in the following listing.

Listing 9.7   `StatusCode` middleware (`link/kit/hlog/hlog.go`)

```
// StatusCode records the HTTP status code into the provided variable.
// Not safe for concurrent use. Use it only to process a single request.
func StatusCode(n *int) MiddlewareFunc {
    return func(next http.Handler) http.Handler {
        return http.HandlerFunc(func(w http.ResponseWriter, r *http.Request) {
```

```
                            Sets the default HTTP status code in
                            case the handler doesn't call WriteHeader
    *n = http.StatusOK   ◀
    w = &Interceptor{          Wraps the original ResponseWriter
      ResponseWriter: w,       to intercept WriteHeader calls
      OnWriteHeader:  func(code int) {   ◀
        *n = code   ◀              Captures the HTTP status code
      },                           whenever WriteHeader is called
    }
    next.ServeHTTP(w, r)   ◀      Assigns the captured code
  })                             to the provided variable
  }
}                       Calls the provided handler
                        to serve the request
```

We've added middleware similar to the previous `Duration` middleware. When a request comes in, `StatusCode` wraps the original `ResponseWriter` with an `Interceptor` to track the handler's `WriteHeader` call and capture the status code without the handler's knowledge.

Because `Server` responds with `http.StatusOK` if the handler never calls `Write-Header`, we initially set the status code ourselves. Otherwise, it would be too late to capture the code. If the handler calls `WriteHeader` with a different code, `OnWriteHeader` updates the provided variable. In any case, we ensure that that variable is updated with a valid status code.

9.3.3 Integration

Now that we've implemented `StatusCode` to capture HTTP status codes, we can integrate it into our response recorder chain and the logger middleware to log HTTP status codes. In listing 9.8, we update `Response` to include a new `StatusCode` field and add our `StatusCode` middleware to the `RecordResponse` helper. Finally, we modify our logger middleware to log the captured HTTP status codes along with response durations.

Listing 9.8 Integrating `StatusCode (link/kit/hlog/hlog.go)`

```
type Response struct {
    Duration    time.Duration
    StatusCode int
}

func RecordResponse(. . .) Response {
    var rr Response
    mws := []MiddlewareFunc{
        Duration(&rr.Duration),
        StatusCode(&rr.StatusCode),   ◀     Shares the StatusCode field with
    }                                       the StatusCode middleware
    for _, wrap := range slices.Backward(mws) {
        h = wrap(h)
    }                               Runs the middleware chain
    h.ServeHTTP(w, r)   ◀           that records response details
    return rr
```

```
}

func Middleware(lg *slog.Logger) MiddlewareFunc {
  . . .
  rr := RecordResponse(next, w, r)
  lg.LogAttrs(. . .
    slog.Duration("duration", rr.Duration),
    slog.Int("status", rr.StatusCode),          ◄─── Logs the captured
  )                                                    HTTP status code
  . . .
}
```

We've updated the `Response` to include a new `StatusCode` field and integrated our `StatusCode` middleware into the `RecordResponse` helper. We've also updated the logger middleware to log the captured HTTP status codes alongside response durations.

When a request arrives, our logger middleware calls `RecordResponse`, which wraps the handler with both the `Duration` and `StatusCode` middleware. The handler serves the request, and each piece of middleware independently captures its respective metric, storing these metrics in a new `Response` struct. When the handler finishes, `Record-Response` returns the populated `Response` to our logger middleware, which logs both the status code and duration.

9.3.4   *Demonstration*

When the following HTTP requests come

```
$ curl -i localhost:8080/health
$ curl -i localhost:8080/nobody
```

we see the following server logs:

```
. . .path=/health method=GET duration=14.083µs status=200
. . .path=/nobody method=GET duration=11.012µs status=404
```

The flow of these incoming requests looks like this:

```
Request -> . . . -> Duration -> StatusCode -> . . . -> Handler
```

This section showed how to use field embedding to satisfy interfaces and intercept methods—practical techniques for programs of all sizes. We offered small and composable functionality that users can mix and match to create their own middleware. Alternatively, users can use helper functions like `Middleware` directly for out-of-the-box functionality.

> **TIP**   Composable building blocks empower a package's users to customize its functionality to their specific needs. This approach encourages reusability and reduces the need for package authors to make frequent modifications.

9.4 Optional interface pattern

We implemented the `Interceptor` type to embed `ResponseWriter` and capture status codes. In this section, we'll learn more about field embedding and discover type assertions. We'll also see how dangerous field embedding interfaces can be in real-world usage if we're not careful. Finally, we'll look at modern solutions for these issues specific to our case.

9.4.1 Type asserting for optional functionality

Because the Go standard library cannot extend existing interfaces like `Response-Writer` without breaking Go 1 backward compatibility, the `http` package introduced *optional interfaces* over time. These interfaces allow a `ResponseWriter`'s underlying types to provide extra features that the `ResponseWriter` does not. Here are a few common examples:

- `http.Flusher` enables sending buffered response data to clients immediately.
- `http.Pusher` enables HTTP/2 server push functionality.
- `http.Hijacker` takes over the underlying TCP connection.

> **NOTE** Concrete types behind interfaces may have additional methods.

Suppose that a `ResponseWriter`'s underlying type implements some or all of these interfaces. In that case, handlers can detect their existence using type assertion and do sophisticated things like stream downloads or hijack the TCP connection for a WebSocket. Here's how the `http` package declares the `Flusher` interface, for example:

```
type Flusher interface {
  // Flush sends any buffered data to the client.
  Flush()
}
```

Handlers can detect the `Flush` method in the underlying type using a *type assertion*:

```
func MyHandler(w http.ResponseWriter, r *http.Request) {    ◄─── Returns true if the
  if flusher, ok := w.(http.Flusher); ok {                        underlying type of w
    flusher.Flush()         ◄───                                  has a Flush method
  }                              The flusher variable's type is
}                                http.Flusher, and it has a Flush method.
```

We call `Flush` after detecting that the underlying `ResponseWriter` has a `Flush` method. Otherwise, the `ok` variable would be `false`, and our handler wouldn't call the method.

Now that we've seen type assertions, let's return to our program to discuss embedding issues.

Go promotes the `ResponseWriter`'s methods to our `Interceptor` because we embed it. But methods like `Flush`, from the original underlying type we can assign at runtime, do not exist in our `Interceptor`. When we pass the `Interceptor` as a `ResponseWriter` to handlers, they won't have access to the `Flush` method because it's not part of our `Interceptor` type (nor the `ResponseWriter` interface), but rather the underlying type's method.

As a result, handlers that want to use the `Flush` method revert to other behavior, thinking that flushing isn't supported even if the original underlying type has the `Flush` method. We can solve this problem by adding an `Unwrap` method to the `Interceptor` that handlers can call to expose the original underlying type.

9.4.2   *Unwrapping all the way down*

We know that field embedding an interface can hide the underlying type's methods. This issue is more complicated than it seems. The underlying type of a `Response-Writer` can be another `ResponseWriter`, and it can go like that—turtles all the way down. Eventually, there may be an underlying type with `Flush`, but it may be buried in this `ResponseWriter` chain.

We may have to look for the `Flush` method recursively, perhaps from the outermost `ResponseWriter` in the `ResponseWriter` chain to the innermost `ResponseWriter` that wraps the original one. Another issue, however, is that the `ResponseWriter` interface doesn't support recursive searching of what wraps it. But we can introduce another optional interface with an `Unwrap` method and use type assertions to access that method. That interface looks as follows:

```
type Unwrapper interface {                    ◀──────  An interface we can use to extract the
    Unwrap() http.ResponseWriter                       underlying ResponseWriter from another
}
```

Introducing another optional interface would make everything more complicated, so Go 1.20 introduced a concrete type to look for optional methods like `Flush` recursively. This type is `ResponseController`, and it can search for optional interfaces recursively in a `ResponseWriter` chain:

```
func MyHandler(w http.ResponseWriter, r *http.Request) {
    err := http.NewResponseController(w).Flush()   ◀──┐
    if errors.Is(err, http.ErrNotSupported) {    ◀──┐ │   Calls Flush if it detects that
        . . .                                       │ │   this ResponseWriter or its
    }                     Returns ErrNotSupported if neither   wrappers support(s) flushing
}                            this ResponseWriter nor its
                             wrappers has a Flush method
```

The `NewResponseController` function returns a new `ResponseController`. Calling `Flush` recursively searches for a `Flush` method in the `ResponseWriter` chain. If none of the `ResponseWriter` wrappers has the `Flush`, that call returns `ErrNotSupported`; otherwise, it calls the original `Flush` method on the first `ResponseWriter` that supports it.

Unlike `ResponseWriter`, `ResponseController` is a concrete type that can evolve with new methods without breaking existing implementations. It eliminates the obscurity of optional interfaces, makes new functionality discoverable in the documentation, and allows checking for optional functionality through `ResponseWriter` with standard error handling. See https://pkg.go.dev/net/http#ResponseController for details.

This approach shows how to extend an interface without changing the interface itself and breaking existing code or relying on fragile type assertions. By wrapping the original interface with a concrete type like `ResponseController`, we isolate type assertions inside that type. This type can provide new methods and internally handle underlying optional behaviors. Such a pattern keeps existing code intact while supporting new functionality. We'll dive into a similar pattern, the *driver pattern*, in chapter 10.

9.4.3 *Unwrap*

Because our `Interceptor` type doesn't have an `Unwrap` method and calling the `ResponseController.Flush` method would return an error, in the next listing, we add the `Unwrap` method to allow `ResponseController` to access the underlying `ResponseWriter`.

Listing 9.9 `Unwrap (link/kit/hlog/hlog.go)`

```
// Unwrap returns the embedded [http.ResponseWriter] to allow
// handlers to access the original when needed to preserve
// [http] optional interfaces like [http.Flusher], etc.
func (ic *Interceptor) Unwrap() http.ResponseWriter {
    return ic.ResponseWriter            ◄── Exposes the underlying
}                                            ResponseWriter
```

Adding `Unwrap` ensures that the `Interceptor` doesn't block access to optional interfaces like `Flusher` and avoids breaking handlers that depend on them. A handler that streams data to a client might call `Flush` to send buffered chunks, for example. Without implementing `Unwrap`, such handlers would fail if we pass them the `Interceptor`.

> **TIP** Wrapping a `ResponseWriter` multiple times is common in middleware. `Unwrap` lets us unearth the underlying ones to access potential optional behavior through them.

Supporting `Unwrap` is helpful but doesn't guarantee that we won't break existing code. Older code may rely directly on type assertions to check whether optional interfaces are supported. Such code can break unless it uses a type assertion to call `Unwrap` and access the underlying wrappers.

We discovered that embedding `ResponseWriter` can hide optional interfaces like `Flusher`. We also adopted the modern approach of implementing an `Unwrap` method to allow modern handlers to unearth and use optional functionality when it exists. In section 9.8, we'll use this `Unwrap` method to stop malicious clients from overwhelming our HTTP service.

9.5   *Context value propagation pattern*

Besides our logger middleware, the handlers and downstream code can log. But matching log entries to their originating requests is difficult without a shared identifier, making troubleshooting guesswork. We can solve this issue by adding a trace ID to log entries:

```
. . .error="unreachable database instance: . . ." trace_id=42
. . .path=/r/go status=500. . .trace_id=42
```

We can simplify troubleshooting by linking critical log entries when issues arise. Without an ID, we could face scattered logs that are frustrating to piece together. As figure 9.5 shows, we'll add new middleware in the new `traceid` package to relay these IDs with `Context`. This middleware wraps downstream handlers, including other middleware, to relay trace IDs, allowing each to access trace IDs when needed.

NOTE   `Context` can carry any type of value across package APIs.

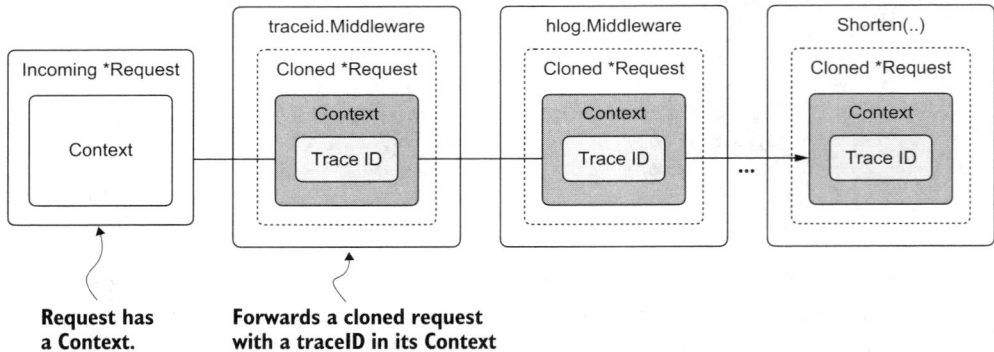

Figure 9.5   Injecting and propagating trace IDs through `Request.Context`

In the figure, `traceid.Middleware` receives and clones a `*Request`, attaching a unique trace ID to the cloned `*Request`'s `Context`. Then it relays this `*Request` downstream. As long as we pass the same `Context`, every part of our program can access the same trace ID.

In the following sections, we'll learn to add values to `Context` and set up middleware for trace IDs. These skills are key for real-world projects and also improve our grasp of Go's type system. Finally, we'll implement a custom `slog.Handler` to automatically extract and log trace IDs from a provided `Context`.

9.5.1   *Generating, storing, and retrieving*

Now that we know how to relay trace IDs, let's see how to store them inside a `Context`. A `Context` can store a single key-value pair. To add a value to a `Context`, we use

```
context.WithValue(parent Context, key any, value any) Context
```

To retrieve a value, we use the `Value` method:

```
Context.Value(key any) (value any)
```

Because `Context` is like a tree, adding a value returns a new `Context`, preserving values from its parents. `Value` searches for the key in the chain, not only in the specified `Context`, allowing us to access values in that one and its parents.

As the next listing shows, the `traceid` package generates trace IDs and attaches and retrieves them from a `Context`. With `traceid`, we consistently handle trace IDs.

Listing 9.10 Package `traceid` (`link/kit/traceid/traceid.go`)

```
// Package traceid provides trace ID related functionality.
package traceid

import (
    "context"
    "fmt"
    "time"
)

// New returns a naively unique trace ID.
func New() string {
  return fmt.Sprintf("%d", time.Now().UnixNano())
}

type traceIDContextKey struct{}        ◄── Prevents collisions with the
                                           Context keys of other packages

// WithContext returns a new [context.Context] with the trace ID.
func WithContext(ctx context.Context, id string) context.Context {
  return context.WithValue(
    ctx, traceIDContextKey{}, id,        Returns a new Context with
  )                                      the trace ID attached
}

// FromContext returns the trace ID from the [context.Context].
func FromContext(ctx context.Context) (string, bool) {
  id, ok := ctx.Value(traceIDContextKey{}).(string)
  return id, ok
}
```

Extracts the trace ID as an any interface value from the Context by the key and uses a type assertion to see whether it's a string

In this code, `New` returns a naive trace ID using timestamps for demonstration. To achieve stronger uniqueness, consider using universally unique identifiers (UUIDs). We skip this step to avoid downloading a package now, but you can do so if you like. See https://go.dev/play/p/8yxDxIvU7iG for example code for generating UUIDs using the https://pkg.go.dev/github.com/google/uuid package.

`WithContext` stores the trace ID in the `Context`, and `FromContext` retrieves it using a type assertion (`.(string)`) because `Context.Value` returns an any type. This assertion returns the trace ID as a string value and a `true` for success, allowing us to extract safely.

The names of our functions are idiomatic. Because the `traceid` package already has the name, we omit the `TraceID` prefix from our functions. If our package had a different name, we would use the `TraceIDWithContext` and `TraceIDFromContext` function names for clarity.

Both functions use the same unexported key type, `traceIDContextKey`, to store and retrieve values from a `Context`. We keep the key unexported so other packages can't access it, eliminating key collisions between packages. Even if another package declares a key with the same `traceIDContextKey` name, these keys never conflict because each key type is scoped to its own package. Ours, for example, is scoped as `traceid .traceIDContextKey`.

> **DEFINITION** A *key collision* occurs when multiple packages use the same key type in a shared `Context` to write/read values, unintentionally overwriting or reading one another's values.

Both our functions use empty structs (`traceIDContextKey{}`) as keys each time they store or retrieve a trace ID from a `Context`. Empty structs never allocate memory, and every new empty struct of the same type (i.e., `traceIDContextKey`) is always equal. This equality ensures both functions consistently access the same trace ID values from the `Context`.

9.5.2   *Middleware*

As listing 9.11 shows, now that we can save and retrieve trace IDs from `Context`, we'll implement the trace ID middleware. This middleware clones the `Request` with a new `Context` with a unique trace ID and passes this cloned `Request` along the downstream handler chain, allowing them to extract the same `Context` when needed.

> **Listing 9.11** `traceid` **middleware** (`link/kit/traceid/http.go`)

```
package traceid

import "net/http"

// Middleware adds a new trace ID to [http.Request.Context].
func Middleware(next http.Handler) http.Handler {
  return http.HandlerFunc(func(w http.ResponseWriter, r *http.Request) {
    if _, ok := FromContext(r.Context()); !ok {
      ctx := WithContext(r.Context(), New())
      r = r.WithContext(ctx)
    }
    next.ServeHTTP(w, r)
  })
}
```

Annotations:
- Checks whether a trace ID exists within the Request.Context
- Derives a new Context with a new trace ID value
- Clones the Request with the new Context containing a new trace ID
- Relays the Context downstream handlers

We call `FromContext` to check whether a trace ID exists in the `Context`. If it does, we skip adding one; other middleware may have already provided it. If not, we use `New` to get a trace ID and store it in a `Context` using `WithContext`. Then we clone the `Request` with this `Context`. Finally, we pass that `Request` to the handler, ensuring that the trace ID is available downstream.

In this section, we learned how to store and propagate request-scoped values using `Context`. Although useful, `Context` stores values as the type-unsafe empty interface (`any`), hiding the underlying types of these values. Misusing `Context` can lead to subtle bugs that are hard to debug. We use `Context` here for trace IDs because these values are peripheral: *they inform but don't dictate how our program works if they're missing.* Avoid relying on `Context` values to control your program logic and flow for maintainable, reliable programs.

9.5.3 *Wrapping slog handlers*

Our `traceid.Middleware` can inject trace IDs into `Request.Context` for each incoming request. As figure 9.6 shows, we'll now implement a `slog.Handler` to add them to the logs automatically on every logging method call, such as `LogAttrs`. Otherwise, we would have to extract these trace IDs from `Context` and pass them every time we call logging methods.

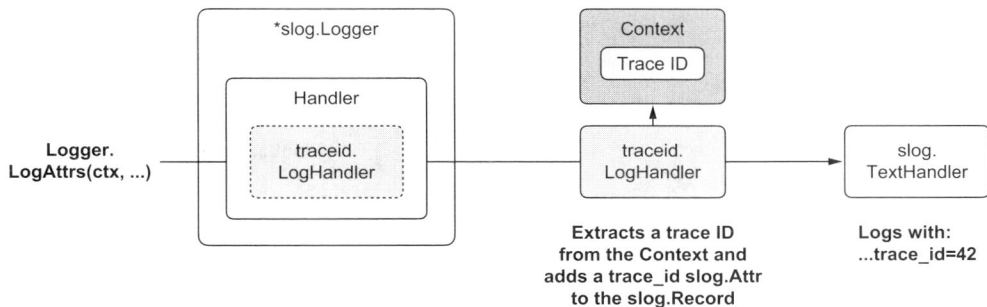

Figure 9.6 Automatically adding attributes to log records by wrapping the original log handler with a custom one that extracts trace IDs from the `Context` **we pass to logging methods, such as** `LogAttrs`

`slog.Logger` provides an API for logging but delegates the actual work, such as formatting log records, to a type such as `slog.TextHandler`, which satisfies the `slog.Handler` interface. This `Logger`, for example, uses a `slog.TextHandler` as a `Handler`:

```
lg := slog.New(slog.NewTextHandler(os.Stderr, nil))
```

NewTextHandler returns *slog.TextHandler,
a Handler implementation.

This one uses our `LogHandler` that wraps the previous `TextHandler`:

```
lg = slog.New(traceid.NewLogHandler(lg.Handler()))   ◄──
lg.LogAttrs(ctx, . . .)   ◄──
```

lg is a *slog.Logger that uses our LogHandler as a Handler.

Calls the LogHandler.Handle method, which adds a trace_id to the log record before forwarding it to TextHandler.Handle

Calling `lg.LogAttrs` automatically outputs a trace ID if the `ctx` has a trace ID:

```
. . .error="unreachable database instance: . . ." trace_id=42
```

`LogHandler` attaches a trace ID `slog.Attr` to a `slog.Record` and calls the `TextHandler`
`.Handle` method, which renders a log output with the trace ID.

9.5.4   *Implementing a slog.Handler*

Now that we know we can output extra log attributes by wrapping `slog.Handlers`, let's
add our own. As listing 9.12 shows, we'll add a `Handler` that wraps an existing one. It
extracts a trace ID from the provided `Context` and injects the trace ID into the `slog`
`.Record`. This way, extra log attributes, such as a trace ID, will appear alongside existing ones during logging.

> **Listing 9.12** `LogHandler (link/kit/traceid/slog.go)`

```go
package traceid

import (
    "context"
    "log/slog"
)
```

Embeds a slog.Handler to satisfy the slog.Handler interface

```go
// LogKey is the key used to store the trace ID in the log record.
const LogKey = "trace_id"

// LogHandler adds trace IDs from [context.Context] to [slog.Record].
type LogHandler struct {
    slog.Handler
    LogKey string // LogKey for the trace ID (Default: [LogKey])   ◄──
}

// NewLogHandler returns a new [LogHandler].
func NewLogHandler(next slog.Handler) *LogHandler {
    return &LogHandler{
        Handler: next,      ◄──
        LogKey:  LogKey,
    }
}

// Handle may add a [slog.Attr] to a [slog.Record].
func (h *LogHandler) Handle(
```

Wraps an existing slog.Handler (e.g., slog.TextHandler), creating a slog.Handler chain

Is called by slog.Logger methods, such as Log and LogAttrs

```
        ctx context.Context, r slog.Record,
) error {
    if id, ok := FromContext(ctx); ok {
        r = r.Clone()
        r.AddAttrs(slog.String(h.LogKey, id))
    }
    return h.Handler.Handle(ctx, r)
}
```

Extracts trace ID from the provided Context

Clones the slog.Record to avoid modifying the original

Adds a trace ID log attribute (e.g., trace_id=42) to the cloned slog.Record

Delegates the handling of the slog.Record to the wrapped slog.Handler

Our `LogHandler` type wraps an existing `Handler`. The `Handle` method extracts the trace ID from the provided `Context`. If a trace ID exists, it clones the `Record` and adds the trace ID as a new `slog.Attr` using the configured log key (e.g., "`trace_id`"), as in this example:

```
lg.LogAttrs(ctx, . . .)
```

Assumes that this Context carries a trace ID value

Output:

```
. . .trace_id=2889906900
```

Calling `LogAttrs` eventually calls `LogHandler.Handle`, passing it a `Context` (assuming that the `lg` is a `Logger` that uses `LogHandler` as its `Handler` and `Context` has a trace ID).

9.5.5 *Implementing WithAttrs and WithGroup*

We can add trace IDs to log records automatically, but we have one remaining issue to fix. `slog.Logger` provides methods to add permanently or group log attributes for convenience, such as `WithAttrs` and `WithGroup`. Using these methods return a new `Logger` with the original `Handler` we wrapped, not our `LogHandler`. As a result, calling `LogAttrs` logs without trace IDs looks like the following:

```
lg = lg.With("ver", "1.0.0").WithGroup("request")
lg.LogAttrs(. . .)
```

Derives a Logger without LogHandler, although the original Handler was LogHandler

Output:

```
. . .ver=1.0.0 request.error="something failed"
```

Loses the trace ID log attribute

As the next listing shows, we'll implement two more `Handler` interface methods: `WithAttrs` and `WithGroup`. They return a new `LogHandler`, preserving our trace ID log attribute.

Listing 9.13 `WithAttrs` **and** `WithGroup` (`link/kit/traceid/slog.go`)

```go
// WithAttrs returns a new [LogHandler] with the provided attributes.
func (h *LogHandler) WithAttrs(attrs []slog.Attr) slog.Handler {
  return NewLogHandler(h.Handler.WithAttrs(attrs))    ◄─────┐
}

// WithGroup returns a new [LogHandler] with the provided group name.
func (h *LogHandler) WithGroup(name string) slog.Handler {
  return NewLogHandler(h.Handler.WithGroup(name))     ◄─────┤
}
```
Returns a new LogHandler wrapping
the original slog.Handler

We've returned a new `LogHandler` from each method, wrapping the original `Handler` to preserve the `LogHandler` behavior. Each returned `Handler` will log with trace IDs.

`LogHandler` integrates with existing `slog` handlers without altering their core logic. It's like middleware for log handlers. Combining it with the trace ID middleware allows us to generate, propagate, and log trace IDs consistently throughout our program.

Deep dive: Performance concerns

Our `LogHandler.Handle` clones the `slog.Record` on each `slog.Logger` method call, allocating a new slice underneath. This extra allocation usually doesn't affect most servers (like ours) because I/O tends to dominate, but it can slow down others. For more details on performance, see the `slog` documentation at https://pkg .go.dev/log/slog and https://mng.bz/X71v.

9.5.6　*Integration*

Now that we have a `traceid` package, middleware to inject trace IDs into a `Request`'s `Context`, and a `LogHandler` to enrich logs with trace IDs, let's see how everything fits into our server. We'll create a new logger and wrap our previous logger middleware as follows.

Listing 9.14　Integrating trace IDs (`link/cmd/linkd/linkd.go`)

```go
package main

import (
    "github.com/inancgumus/gobyexample/link/kit/traceid"
    . . .
)

func main() {
  . . .
  cfg.lg = slog.New(
    slog.NewTextHandler(os.Stderr, nil),
  ).With("app", "linkd")
  . . .
```

```
}

func run(ctx context.Context, cfg config) error {
  . . .
  lg := slog.New(
    traceid.NewLogHandler(cfg.lg.Handler()),
  )

  mux := http.NewServeMux()
  mux.Handle("POST /shorten", rest.Shorten(lg, shortener))
  mux.Handle("GET /r/{key}", rest.Resolve(lg, shortener))
  mux.HandleFunc("/health", rest.Health)

  loggerMiddleware := hlog.Middleware(lg)

  srv := &http.Server{
    Handler: traceid.Middleware(
      loggerMiddleware(mux),
    ),
    . . .
  }
  . . .
}
```

> **Returns a slog.Logger that adds trace ID slog.Attrs to slog.Records**

> **Wraps the existing logger middleware with the traceid middleware to inject trace IDs**

We wrap the existing `Logger`'s `Handler` with our `LogHandler` to add trace IDs to logs. We ensure that the new `Logger` is passed to the rest of our code so that each can automatically log with trace IDs. Then we wrap the existing logger middleware with the trace ID middleware to inject trace IDs into each `Request.Context`. Now the downstream handlers automatically log with trace IDs as they use `LogHandler`.

When the following HTTP requests come, for example

```
$ curl -i localhost:8080/health
```

we see

```
. . .path=/health method=GET. . .trace_id=1747066003015604000
```

We wrapped the `slog.Handler` interface with our `LogHandler` type to add trace ID log attributes from `Context` values. Our code is reusable and self-contained, and we can test and replace it independently, which improves maintainability. Our approach reduces complexity and is consistent with Go's principles of composition with simple independent parts.

9.6 *Handler-chaining pattern*

We've explored middleware patterns, using them to log HTTP requests and responses, capture metrics, and propagate trace IDs. Starting in this section, we'll shift focus from middleware to HTTP handlers. We'll introduce a handler-chaining pattern to eliminate common mistakes like forgetting to return after responding and simplify writing consistent handler responses.

As figure 9.7 shows, the `Shorten` handler (from chapter 8) now delegates response handling by explicitly returning either a `Text` handler (to respond with text) or an `Error` handler (to handle errors). This explicit return forms a handler chain. `Shorten` receives the request, and these subsequent handlers write the response to the clients.

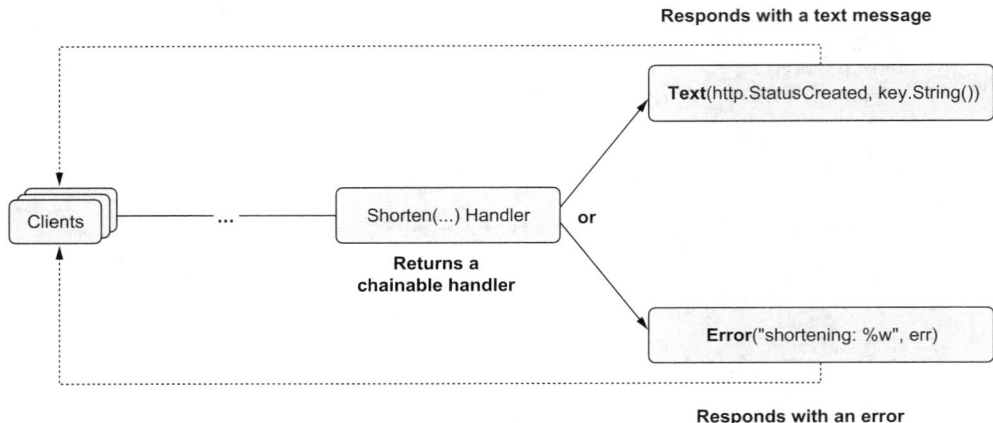

Figure 9.7   `Shorten` delegates response processing to other handlers in the chain.

We'll introduce a chainable handler type that enforces explicit returns from handlers. This type helps prevent subtle bugs such as unintentionally sending unnecessary responses or incorrect headers. Responding with errors, redirects, or JSON will become simpler, clearer, and safer.

In later sections, we'll revisit language mechanics, such as detecting behaviors through interfaces using type assertions. We'll demonstrate how these techniques help us handle practical concerns such as performing validation automatically and protecting our server from malicious clients. We'll also see how these techniques align with Go's philosophy of extending behavior without tight coupling or inheritance, keeping our code simple, composable, and reusable.

9.6.1   Chainable handlers

Consider the following handler code.

```
func redirect(w http.ResponseWriter, r *http.Request) {
  uri, err := . . .
  if err != nil {
    http.Error(w, err.Error(), http.StatusBadRequest)
  }
  http.Redirect(w, r, uri, http.StatusFound)
}
```

Did you spot the issue? If an error occurs, the handler should immediately return after calling `http.Error`. Missing this return means that the handler continues, unintentionally redirecting the client and potentially causing confusion or security issues. Remembering to return after each error response can be tedious and error-prone, however, particularly in large codebases. To prevent such problems, we'll declare a custom handler type, as shown in listing 9.15. Unlike the `http.Handler`, this type requires returning a handler (`hio.Handler`), making it impossible to forget to return. Returning a handler ensures that handlers never unintentionally continue processing after responding, preventing subtle logic errors and unintended responses.

> **Listing 9.15   A chainable custom handler type (`link/kit/hio/hio.go`)**

```
// Package hio (HTTP I/O) offers helpers for HTTP input and output handling.
package hio

import "net/http"

// Handler is a chainable [http.Handler] implementation.
type Handler func(http.ResponseWriter, *http.Request) Handler

// ServeHTTP runs the [Handler] chain until one returns nil.
func (h Handler) ServeHTTP(w http.ResponseWriter, r *http.Request) {
    next := h(w, r)
    if next != nil {
        next.ServeHTTP(w, r)
    }
}
```

Runs the current hio.Handler function

Checks whether the returned hio.Handler function is not nil

Runs the next hio.Handler function in the chain

The hio.Handler chain terminates here (i.e., when an hio.Handler returns a nil hio.Handler).

An `hio.Handler` returns the next `hio.Handler` to enable chaining and guarantee explicit returns. Its `ServeHTTP` method implements the `http.Handler` interface. This method calls the current `Handler` function and, if that function returns a non-nil `Handler`, `ServeHTTP` runs the returned `Handler`. This process continues until the last `Handler` returns `nil`, terminating the chain and immediately ending further request and response handling. Because `hio.Handler` implements `http.Handler` with the `ServeHTTP` method, we can use it as an `http.Handler`.

9.6.2   *Response handlers*

We've introduced a chainable handler type (`hio.Handler`) that requires explicit handler returns, helping to eliminate subtle bugs. Next, we'll add convenient response helpers on top of this type (and use them in the `link/rest` handlers in section 9.6.4):

- `Responder` groups response-helper methods.
- `Error` returns a `Handler` that calls an error handler to handle errors.

- Redirect returns a Handler that redirects clients to another URL.
- Text returns a Handler that responds with a text message.

NOTE   The Handler type here is our hio.Handler, not Go's http.Handler.

RESPONDER

Let's start by adding the Responder type to group response helpers in the next listing.

Listing 9.16 Responder **type (**link/kit/hio/response.go**)**

```
package hio

// Responder provides helpers to write HTTP responses.
type Responder struct {
  err func(error) Handler                          ◀───────┐   Delegates error
}                                                           │   handling to the
                                                            │   consumer
// NewResponder returns a new [Responder].                  │
// err is called when an error occurs during response writing.
func NewResponder(err func(error) Handler) Responder {      │
  return Responder{err: err}                       ◀───────┘
}
```

We declared the Responder type to group helpers. Its err field allows consumers to specify a custom error handler we can call if errors occur during the response. Later, we'll use the httpError function from chapter 8 as an error handler for Responder in section 9.6.3.

With err, consumers can handle errors themselves, such as using slog to log errors. If the Responder used a specific error-handling mechanism directly, such as using slog to log errors, that would reduce its reusability and cause unnecessary slog dependency on the hio package. Reducing direct dependencies improves code modularity and flexibility.

ERROR HANDLER

Next, we'll add our first response helper for writing formatted error responses.

Listing 9.17 Error response helper (link/kit/hio/response.go)

```
package hio

import "fmt"

// Error responds with a formatted error message.
func (rs Responder) Error(format string, args ...any) Handler {
  return rs.err(fmt.Errorf(format, args...))    ◀─────  Passes the error value to the
}                                                       consumer-provided error
                                                        handler function
```

We've added `Error`, which formats an error message and calls and returns the result of the `err` function field to delegate error handling. We can declare a new `Responder` variable and then call the `Error` method to get a `Handler` we can use to respond to clients:

```
rs := NewResponder(func(err error) Handler {
    . . .                                              ◀─────────── Handles the error
    return nil    ◀────┐ Terminates the chain
})
h := rs.Error("bad input: %d", 42)
```

We set the `Responder`'s `err` field to a function that returns a `nil` `Handler` after handling the error, terminating the chain. We can run the returned `Handler` using `ServeHTTP`:

```
h.ServeHTTP(w, r)
```

This method runs the `Handler` that the `err` field returns. Whether a chain runs the next `Handler` depends on the returned `Handler`. The chain stops if consumers have configured `err` to return `nil`; otherwise, the chain continues running the next `Handler` until one returns `nil`. Because we set `err` to return `nil`, the chain terminates.

REDIRECT HANDLER

Next, we'll add another response helper to simplify HTTP redirects. This helper is similar to `Error`, except that this helper returns a closure.

Listing 9.18 Redirect response helper (`link/kit/hio/response.go`)

```
package hio

import (
  "net/http"
  . . .
)

// Redirect redirects the request to the URL with the status code.
func (rs Responder) Redirect(code int, url string) Handler {
  return func(w http.ResponseWriter, r *http.Request) Handler {
    http.Redirect(w, r, url, code)    ◀─────── Redirects the client
    return nil    ◀────┐                         to the provided URL
  }                    └ Terminates the chain
}
```

`Redirect` returns a `Handler` closure that redirects clients to the specified URL and status code when called. Returning `Redirect` from a `Handler` automatically calls this closure when a request comes (when we register that `Handler` on a `Server`, for example). When run, this closure, immediately redirects clients and returns `nil`, terminating the handler chain, and preventing accidental continuation.

TEXT HANDLER

Finally, we'll simplify writing plain-text responses by adding one more response
`Handler`.

Listing 9.19 Text response helper (`link/kit/hio/response.go`)

```
// Text writes a text response with the status code.
func (rs Responder) Text(code int, message string) Handler {
    return func(w http.ResponseWriter, r *http.Request) Handler {
        w.Header().Set("Content-Type", "text/plain; charset=utf-8")
        w.WriteHeader(code)
        fmt.Fprint(w, message)
        return nil                    ◄─── Terminates the chain after setting the response
    }                                      content type and writing a text message
}
```

`Text` returns a `Handler` closure, which sets the response content type, writes the specified status code, and writes a text message to clients. After responding, it returns `nil`,
terminating the chain to prevent another `Handler` from setting the HTTP headers
again. (Because HTTP headers come before response bodies, returning headers after
responding the body indicates logic issues in our code.)

We've added reusable response helpers using our `Handler` type. They reduce code
duplication, improve readability, and eliminate subtle bugs due to forgotten returns.
Next, let's apply the handler-chaining pattern with these helpers to our handlers.

9.6.3   *Responder*

Before moving to the handlers, let's add a helper function to configure a `Responder`
with an error handler in the next listing. We'll reuse this helper within our handlers in
section 9.6.4.

Listing 9.20 Responder helper (`link/rest/shortener.go`)

```
package rest

import (
    "github.com/inancgumus/gobyexample/link/kit/hio"
    . . .
)
                                                      Returns an hio.Handler
                                                      that handles errors
// newResponder returns a new HTTP responder with an error handler
// that maps the errors to the appropriate HTTP status codes.
func newResponder(lg *slog.Logger) hio.Responder {
  err := func(err error) hio.Handler {
    return func(w http.ResponseWriter, r *http.Request) hio.Handler {
      httpError(w, r, lg, err)          ◄─── Handles errors using
      return nil    ◄─── Terminates the chain    the httpError function
    }
  }
}
```

```
    return hio.NewResponder(err)     ◄───┐  Configures and returns a new Responder
}                                        │  that handles errors using the err closure
```

The `newResponder` helper takes a logger and returns a new `Responder`. We set the `Responder`'s error handler to a closure (`err`) that returns a `Handler`. This closure calls `httpError` (chapter 8) and then terminates the handler chain. `httpError` maps common errors of our program, such as `ErrBadRequest`, to corresponding HTTP status codes and calls `http.Error` to respond to clients with those status codes and error messages.

9.6.4 *Integration*

As listing 9.21 shows, we'll update our handlers and include them in the handler chain. In each handler, we create a `Responder` using `newResponder`. The `Shorten` handler outputs a text message by returning a `Text` handler, and `Resolve` redirects to a URL using `Redirect`. We return `Error` to write an error message to clients, terminating the chain.

Listing 9.21 Chainable handlers (`link/rest/shortener.go`)

```go
package rest

import (
    "github.com/inancgumus/gobyexample/link/kit/hio"
    . . .
)

func Shorten(. . .) http.Handler {         ◄──────────┐
    with := newResponder(lg)

    return hio.Handler(func(. . .) hio.Handler {   ◄──┤
        key, err := links.Shorten(. . .)
        if err != nil {
            return with.Error("shortening: %w", err)         Returns the closure as
        }                                                    an hio.Handler, which Go
                                                             automatically converts
        return with.Text(http.StatusCreated, key.String())  to an http.Handler
    })
}

func Resolve(. . .) http.Handler {         ◄──────────┤
    with := newResponder(lg)

    return hio.Handler(func(. . .) hio.Handler {   ◄──┘
        lnk, err := links.Resolve(. . .)
        if err != nil {
            return with.Error("resolving: %w", err)
        }

        return with.Redirect(http.StatusFound, lnk.URL)
    })
}
```

Let's discuss this change step by step to see what happened:

1 `Responder` helps with responding and handling errors.
2 Handlers return an `hio.Handler` to respond, such as `Redirect` or `Text`.
3 Handlers return an `Error` if the processing should stop with an error.

Returning an `hio.Handler` explicitly makes each handler a step in the handler chain. Suppose an HTTP request comes in to shorten a URL. The returned `Handler` from `Shorten` runs and then returns another `Handler`, such as `Text`, to respond with text and status code. The request processing continues until the `Text` handler returns `nil`, stopping the handler chain.

From the outside, nothing has changed: `hio.Handler` is an `http.Handler`, so integration with the `http.Server` remains the same. But internally, we've significantly reduced potential risks such as forgetting to return after responding, improving correctness.

9.7   *Encoding and decoding*

We built chainable HTTP handlers and response helpers earlier, but our handlers responded only with plain text. Real-world services often exchange structured data formats such as JSON, making parsing and validation straightforward, which is especially important for clients and servers.

In this section, we'll learn practical and reliable techniques to decode client requests and encode responses in JSON. We'll use the standard library's `encoding/json` package and introduce reusable helpers to simplify serialization tasks, error handling, and input validation. We'll also dive deeper into anonymous interfaces and type assertions to extract and use behaviors like validation, keeping our handlers concise and composable.

> **NOTE** Visit https://go.dev/blog/json for more details about `json`. Go will soon have a more performant `json/v2` package. Visit https://pkg.go.dev/encoding/json/v2 for details (which is fully compatible with the current `json` package).

9.7.1   *Encoding JSON*

The standard library's `encoding/json` package allows us to do the following:

- Encode a value in JSON using the `json.Marshal` function
- Decode JSON in a value using the `json.Unmarshal` function

In this section, we'll use these functions to implement a `JSON` handler to write JSON responses to clients. In section 9.7.2, we'll use a `DecodeJSON` helper to the JSON payloads from clients.

As listing 9.22 shows, we add a `JSON` response helper similar to the earlier ones, like `Text`. This helper simplifies responding with JSON payloads. We'll implement it like other response helpers, terminating the chain at the end and handling encoding errors with `Error`.

```go
package hio

import (
  "encoding/json"
  . . .
)
. . .
// JSON writes a JSON response with the status code.
func (rs Responder) JSON(code int, from any) Handler {
  data, err := json.Marshal(from)
  if err != nil {
    return rs.Error("encoding json: %w", err)
  }
  return func(w http.ResponseWriter, r *http.Request) Handler {
    w.Header().Set(
      "Content-Type", "application/json",
    )
    w.WriteHeader(code)
    w.Write(data)
    return nil
  }
}
```

Serializes from the value into JSON as a []byte, saved in the data variable

Returns the Error handler if the serialization fails

Writes an HTTP header that allows clients to detect that the output is JSON

Writes an HTTP status code

Writes the JSON payload

Terminates the chain

We've added a JSON helper method to our Responder type, which encodes the provided value into JSON in the []byte variable, data. If encoding fails, it delegates response handling to our Error handler; otherwise, it returns a closure that writes the JSON payload to the client.

As with every response helper, such as Text, returning nil afterward terminates the handler chain and prevents handling the rest of the response, eliminating unintentional mistakes. We call Marshal directly outside the returned Handler closure because we want to fail fast on errors, and that block of code does not require using a ResponseWriter or a *Request.

9.7.2   Decoding JSON

Besides sending JSON payloads to clients, handlers receive JSON payloads. As listing 9.23 shows, we add a helper function to decode JSON payloads from incoming requests bodies (or any Reader). We also validate the decoded data automatically if the underlying type of the to variable has a Validate method; in section 9.7.3, we'll use it to verify inputs in handlers.

```go
package hio

import (
  "encoding/json"
  "fmt"
```

```
    "io"
)

// DecodeJSON reads and decodes JSON.
func DecodeJSON(from io.Reader, to any) error {        Reads the full JSON payload
  data, err := io.ReadAll(from)              ◄───────┘ from the provided Reader
  if err != nil {
    return fmt.Errorf("reading: %w", err)
  }                                                    Decodes JSON payload
  if err := json.Unmarshal(data, to); err != nil {  ◄─┘ into the provided variable
    return fmt.Errorf("unmarshaling json: %w", err)
  }
  v, ok := to.(interface{ Validate() error })         Calls the Validate method
  if ok {                                              of the underlying type
    if err := v.Validate(); err != nil {       ◄───── (e.g., link.Link.Validate())
      return fmt.Errorf("validating: %w", err)
    }
  }
  return nil
}
```

We've declared `DecodeJSON` to decode JSON requests. This helper does the following:

- Reads the entire JSON payload into memory and decodes it into the provided variable.
- Checks the underlying type of `to` using an anonymous interface. If the underlying type has a `Validate` method, we call `Validate` to validate the decoded data.

With `DecodeJSON`, we avoid repeating decoding and validation in our handlers. But `DecodeJSON` can overwhelm our server as it reads the entire JSON payload into memory without limit. Before fixing this problem, let's integrate our new helpers into `Shorten`.

> **TIP** Using anonymous interfaces for type assertions minimizes dependencies on external types or packages, improves maintainability, and reduces coupling.

9.7.3   *Speaking JSON*

We added helpers to respond to JSON and decode incoming JSON data. These helpers simplify handling JSON and prevent repetitive encoding and decoding logic in handlers. Next, we'll integrate these helpers into our existing `Shorten` handler. As the following listing shows, we update `Shorten` to decode the incoming JSON payload from `Request.Body` using `DecodeJSON` and respond using our new JSON response helper.

Listing 9.24   Speaking JSON (`link/rest/shortener.go`)

```
func Shorten(lg *slog.Logger, links *link.Shortener) http.Handler {
  with := newResponder(lg)

  return hio.Handler(. . .) hio.Handler {
    var lnk link.Link
```

```
    err := hio.DecodeJSON(r.Body, &lnk)
    if err != nil {
      return with.Error("decoding: %w: %w", err, link.ErrBadRequest)
    }
    key, err := links.Shorten(r.Context(), lnk)
    if err != nil {
      return with.Error("shortening: %w", err)
    }

    return with.JSON(http.StatusCreated, map[string]link.Key{
      "key": key,
    })
  })
}
```

We've updated `Shorten` to decode and respond with JSON; now it uses our new help-ers (`DecodeJSON` and `JSON`) to simplify handling structured JSON data. Suppose that the `Shorten` handler receives the following JSON payload:

```
{"url": "https://go.dev", "key": "go"}
```

Because we export the `Link`'s fields, `Shorten` can decode incoming data into a `Link`:

```
type Link struct {          ◄─────  This field is exported and will be
    URL string                      mapped to the JSON data's url field.
    Key Key          ◄────
}                                  This field is exported and will be
                                   mapped to the JSON data's key field.
```

Otherwise, the `json.Unmarshal` function wouldn't decode JSON into a `Link`. In this case, `Link`'s `URL` field will hold `"https://go.dev"`, and the `Key` field will store `"go"`. As an example, let's post a JSON payload and receive a JSON response:

```
$ curl -i localhost:8080/shorten                    Sends JSON data
      -d '{"url": "https://go.dev", "key": "go"}'    to the handler
HTTP/1.1 201 Created
{"key":"go"}          ◄─────  Receives JSON data
                             from the handler
```

Let's also check whether `DecodeJSON` calls the `Link`'s `Validate` method automatically:

```
$ curl localhost:8080/shorten -i -d '{"url":"not a URL"}'
HTTP/1.1 400 Bad Request
decoding: validating: parse "not a URL":          ◄─────  DecodeJSON detects and calls
        invalid URI for request: bad request             the Validate method because
                                                         we pass a Link variable.
```

We explored how to implement small helpers to encode and decode JSON, integrating them into our `Shorten` handler to make it speak JSON. But as noted earlier,

DecodeJSON uses io.ReadAll to read the Request.Body without limit. Fortunately, it takes an io.Reader, which means we can wrap the Reader with another one that limits how many bytes it can read to improve server reliability and security. We'll explore this approach in section 9.8.

TIP   json considers only exported fields while encoding and decoding.

9.8   *Wrapping and unwrapping*

We implemented JSON encoding and decoding helpers, integrating them into the Shorten handler. Although these helpers simplified our handler code, our DecodeJSON helper currently reads the entire request payload into memory without any size restrictions, potentially leaving our HTTP service vulnerable to malicious requests or excessive resource use.

This section addresses these issues. We'll wrap the Request.Body with another Reader to enforce a limit on the number of bytes we can read. To handle cases in which the limit is exceeded, we'll use type assertions and the Interceptor's Unwrap method (section 9.4) to recover the original ResponseWriter and disconnect malicious or overly demanding clients.

By the end of this section, we'll improve our service's robustness and understand practical techniques for decoupling the code. We'll also know how to extend behavior by composing interfaces, such as changing the behavior of existing code without modifying it directly.

9.8.1   *Safeguarding against denial-of-service attacks*

Earlier, we learned that DecodeJSON reads the entire request payload without limit. We can use the standard library's http.MaxBytesReader function to prevent large payloads. MaxBytesReader wraps an io.ReadCloser (e.g., Request.Body) and limits the number of bytes we can read. It also takes a ResponseWriter to disconnect clients when necessary:

```
func MaxBytesReader(ResponseWriter, io.ReadCloser, int64) io.ReadCloser
```

Instead of using this function directly, we'll add a helper function, as shown in the following listing. Although our function is trivial for now, we'll improve it to recover the original ResponseWriter and have http.Server disconnect clients when they reach the limit.

> **Listing 9.25**   MaxBytesReader helper (link/kit/hio/request.go)

```
package hio

import (
    "net/http"
    . . .
```

```
)

// MaxBytesReader is like [http.MaxBytesReader].
func MaxBytesReader(
  w http.ResponseWriter, rc io.ReadCloser, max int64,
) io.ReadCloser {
    return http.MaxBytesReader(w, rc, max)
}
```

We added a `MaxBytesReader` helper to our `hio` package. Next, as listing 9.26 shows, we'll wrap the `Request.Body` with this function to limit the number of bytes the `Shorten` handler can read from the incoming `Request.Body`. When we read more than 4 KB (we set it as follows), our `MaxBytesReader` function will return an error, and we'll stop reading.

Listing 9.26 Integrating `MaxBytesReader` (`link/rest/shortener.go`)

```
func Shorten(. . .) http.Handler {
  . . .
  return hio.Handler(func(. . .) hio.Handler {
    var lnk link.Link

    err := hio.DecodeJSON(                    ◄─── Reads from the MaxBytesReader's
      hio.MaxBytesReader(w, r.Body, 4_096),        Reader, which in turn reads from
      &lnk,                                   ◄─┐  the Request.Body
    )                                           │
    . . .                                       └─ Returns a ReadCloser that
  })                                               wraps the Request.Body
}                                                  that limits reads
```

We integrated our `MaxBytesReader` helper into the `Shorten` handler. `DecodeJSON` reads from the limited `ReadCloser` instead of directly from `Request.Body`. If a client exceeds our 4 KB limit, decoding will fail, but the server may not disconnect the client. (We'll discover the reason in section 9.8.2.) To test whether our limit works, we can use `curl` to send a request that exceeds the 4 KB limit:

```
$ curl localhost:8080/shorten
   -d "{\"key\":\"$(printf 'a%.0s' {1..5000})\"}"   ◄─┐ We send 5,000 bytes plus a
HTTP/1.1 400 Bad Request                                │ 10-byte JSON part {"key":""}.
Content-Type: text/plain; charset=utf-8
X-Content-Type-Options: nosniff
. . .

decoding: reading: http: request body too large: bad request
```

Now our handler effectively rejects oversize payloads. There's another issue, however: clients can keep sending data even after the handler stops reading. To handle this situation properly, we need to recover the original `ResponseWriter` and disconnect these clients automatically.

9.8.2   *Unwrapping the original*

When clients exceed the limit, `MaxBytesReader` signals the `Server` through the original `ResponseWriter` to disconnect them. But our earlier `Interceptor` wraps the original `ResponseWriter`. Due to this wrapping, the disconnection mechanism no longer
works.

We previously faced a similar issue and added an `Unwrap` method to our `Interceptor`.
Now we'll use that `Unwrap` method to retrieve the original `ResponseWriter` and restore
the disconnection mechanism. We can't control future middleware that could add more
wrappers around the original `ResponseWriter`, however. To peel off these potential
wrappings, we'll modify our `MaxBytesReader` helper to unwrap `ResponseWriters`, as
the next listing shows.

Listing 9.27   Unwrapping `ResponseWriters` (`link/kit/hio/request.go`)

```go
// MaxBytesReader is like [http.MaxBytesReader], but unwraps the
// original [http.ResponseWriter] if it's wrapped.
func MaxBytesReader(
    w http.ResponseWriter, rc io.ReadCloser, max int64,
) io.ReadCloser {
    type unwrapper interface {              // To detect the presence of
        Unwrap() http.ResponseWriter        // the optional Unwrap method
    }
    for {                                   // Loops until no more
        v, ok := w.(unwrapper)              // wrappers are left
        if !ok {
            break                           // Checks whether the current
        }                                   // ResponseWriter has an Unwrap method
        w = v.Unwrap()
    }                                       // Breaks the loop to return the last
    return http.MaxBytesReader(w, rc, max)  // unwrapped ResponseWriter (if any)
}                                           // Unwraps the underlying ResponseWriter
```

We've declared an interface to extract the `Unwrap` method from the underlying type of
the next `ResponseWriter`. Our helper removes any middleware layers and tries to leave
us with the original `ResponseWriter`. Passing the original to `MaxBytesReader` instructs
the `Server` to disconnect clients when they reach our limit. If the body size exceeds
4,096 bytes, the `Server` stops reading the body and closes the connection, which protects the service from excessive resource use caused by oversize requests, improving
server reliability:

```
$ curl localhost:8080/shorten
  -d "{\"key\":\"$(printf 'a%.0s' {1..5000})\"}"
HTTP/1.1 400 Bad Request
Connection: close
Content-Type: text/plain; charset=utf-8
. . .

decoding: reading: http: request body too large: bad request
```

Now we get a `Connection: close` message. Also, `http.Server` disconnects the client, preventing the client from using the same connection. This disconnection mechanism works similarly to the unwrapping technique we used earlier. Visit https://mng.bz/wZ5q and https://mng.bz/mZRr for details if you're curious.

9.9 Outro

In this chapter, we explored core language mechanics for designing composable and reusable functionality. We used higher-order functions and implicit interfaces, demonstrating composition without inheritance or large frameworks. And we emphasized consistent function signatures and direct dependency injection, avoiding globals for explicit, more testable code.

Next, we used interface embedding to intercept method calls, adding behavior without modifying existing code. Embedding, however, can hide methods unintentionally. Using type assertions allowed us to reveal optional interfaces.

We propagated request-scoped data across boundaries using `Context`. Although useful, `Context` sacrifices type safety by hiding types behind empty interfaces and makes data flow implicit. So `Context` should remain informational, never controlling logic or flow.

We introduced chainable handlers requiring explicit returns, emphasizing explicit control flow to prevent subtle bugs. Anonymous interfaces helped us detect optional methods, simplifying decoding and validation without named interfaces.

Finally, type assertions let us unwrap underlying types, restoring or extending functionality without modifying the original code.

Middleware and handlers are practical examples of fundamental Go mechanics: higher-order functions, implicit interfaces, embedding, anonymous interfaces, type assertions, and careful wrapping and unwrapping. These mechanics embody Go's philosophy: simplicity, modularity, and explicit composition of small reusable parts, leading to maintainable, reusable, and testable code.

9.10 Exercises

1 Write middleware from scratch that logs HTTP requests and responses.
2 Write middleware that adds an HTTP header to every HTTP response.
3 Write middleware that limits the incoming JSON request body to 1 KB.
4 Write `BodySize` middleware that records the `Request.Body` size. Update `Response` and `RecordResponse` functions accordingly. Test this middleware function.
5 Write middleware that propagates user IDs using `Context` values.
6 Write a `slog.Handler` that always logs with the injected user IDs.
7 Improve `traceid.Middleware` to generate trace IDs from the request header's `X-Trace-ID` header (use: `r.Header.Get(..)`). Otherwise, use `New()`.
8 Use `ResponseController` to call the `http.Flusher.Flush` in a handler.
9 Add an `XML` handler in the `hio` package that responds with XML. In your function, use the standard library's https://pkg.go.dev/encoding/xml package.

Summary

- Go favors composition over type hierarchies; less coupling improves reuse. Prefer combining focused pieces of functionality to relying on tightly coupled code.

- Add new behavior by wrapping rather than modifying the existing code. Middleware illustrates this pattern—wrapping handlers without touching their code.

- Embedding a type in a struct anonymously promotes the type's fields and methods to the embedder, forwarding method calls to the embedded one.

- Embedding can hide behaviors and change how the embedder works.

- Use type assertions to detect underlying types and methods from an interface.

- Pass request-scoped values using `Context`. Keep keys unique, using values only for informational purposes, and avoid using `Context` to drive the control flow.

- When composing with wrappers or embedded interfaces, offer a path to the underlying behavior so callers can access optional capabilities. Preferably, provide concrete functionality (e.g., `ResponseController`) to enable behavior.

- Add extra features by wrapping and passing interface values—such as putting a read-limit with an `io.Reader`—to existing code without modifying it.

Polymorphic storage

10

This chapter covers

- Interacting with SQL databases
- Understanding the driver pattern
- Integration-testing external services
- Using the consumer-driven interface approach

In earlier chapters, we built a link service for Bite. Now another team needs persistent storage so that links survive HTTP server restarts. We asked them to implement it and offered help with integration. This chapter shows how the team added persistence to the project.

We'll start with the standard library's `sql` package and use SQLite because it's lightweight and needs no separate installation. The concepts apply equally to other SQL databases, such as PostgreSQL, because the `sql` package abstracts database interactions.

We'll add a new `Shortener` service backed by SQLite and verify it using a test database. Finally, we'll decouple HTTP handlers from this service using consumer-driven interfaces, an approach that requires a different mindset than traditional object-oriented languages. By the end of the chapter, we'll know how to work with SQL databases using the `sql` package and use interfaces effectively to decouple implementations from the code that uses them.

This chapter also shows how to safely add optional behaviors using interfaces and concrete types to prevent breaking existing code, write integration tests for external services, embed files in binaries for simpler deployments, and extract specific errors from error chains. By the end of this chapter, we'll have learned practical techniques we can apply broadly, finishing our journey to writing robust, efficient, reliable, testable, and idiomatic Go code.

10.1 *Interacting with SQL databases*

Go provides two packages to interact with a specific SQL (or row-oriented) database:

- `database/sql` provides a uniform API to interact with various SQL databases.
- `database/sql/driver` defines behaviors that database drivers must implement.

> **NOTE** Unless we implement a driver, we use the `sql` package.

The `sql` package relies on community-provided and open source driver packages to interact with a specific SQL database. As figure 10.1 shows, after we download a driver and register it in the `sql` package, we can start interacting with the database using the `sql` package's API, such as the `Open` function. It returns a `*sql.DB` handle to interact with the database, such as executing SQL queries and returning results.

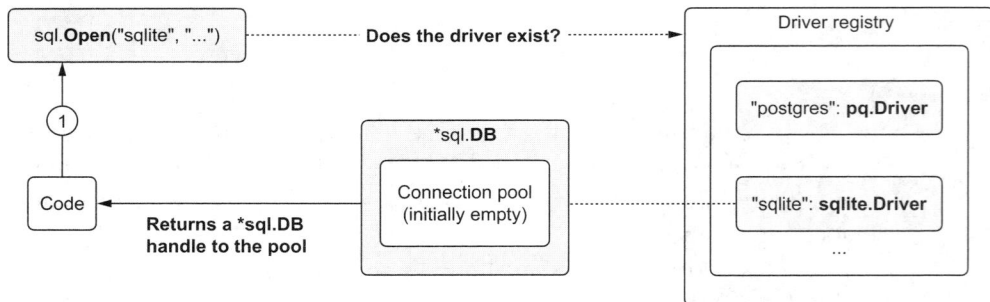

Figure 10.1   The `sql` package abstracts underlying databases with drivers. The `sql` package's registry stores registered drivers, and `*DB` manages a connection pool.

The `Open` function looks like this:

```
func Open(
    driverName string, dataSourceName string,
) (*sql.DB, error)
```

Returns an *sql.DB handle for the specified driver name

It queries the registry and returns a *DB if the driver is registered. The first argument to Open is the driver's name (e.g., sqlite). The second one is the driver-specific connection string (e.g., file:links.db). The following returns a *DB for interacting with an SQLite database:

```
db, err := sql.Open("sqlite", "file:links.db")
```

Or this one for PostgreSQL:

```
db, err := sql.Open("postgres", "dbname=links sslmode=disable")
```

The returned *DB manages a connection pool that simplifies database operations because we don't need to manage each connection (e.g., connect, disconnect, or reuse it) ourselves. The pool initially contains no active connections. We work directly with *DB to run a query; it figures out which connection to use from the pool, establishing or closing connections as needed. *DB also handles features like autoretries on failures, making our code more robust.

DB is a concrete type offering polymorphism through the driver interfaces without being an interface type itself. This approach allows the DB type to provide new features without breaking existing code. See the following sidebar for details on the driver pattern.

Deep dive: The driver design pattern

The sql package has an approach that uses drivers to abstract databases. Let's explore how this approach works by examining the driver pattern, illustrated in the following figure. DB interacts with databases indirectly through the sql/driver interfaces. Drivers communicate directly with their specific database technologies to carry out our SQL queries.

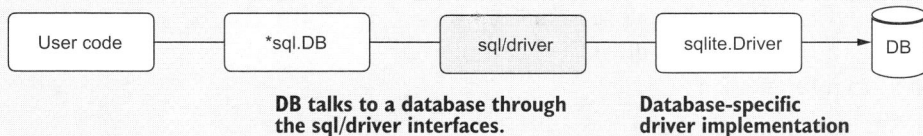

DB talks to a database through the sql/driver interfaces.   **Database-specific driver implementation**

The driver pattern abstracts SQL database communication.

Neither our code nor DB interacts directly with database-specific details. Although the DB type is unaware of driver-specific implementations, it provides common functionality shared by drivers, such as connection pooling and automatic retries, preventing duplication. It also offers many methods (20 methods as of Go 1.24) to carry on database tasks, such as allowing us to execute a query on a database.

(continued)

Because DB is a concrete type, it can evolve independently, adding new methods without breaking existing code. Consider what would happen if DB were a large interface:

- Drivers would have to implement all the DB methods, making driver development difficult.
- Adding new methods to the DB interface later would break all existing code.
- We would use fragile type assertions to detect new and optional DB features (similar to chapter 9's discussion of ResponseWriter's optional interfaces).

DB prevents these issues because it's a concrete type instead of a large interface. The sql/driver package can introduce optional interfaces safely over time without forcing every driver or all user code to adopt them. After Go introduced the context package, for example, driver added the Pinger interface, and DB added a Ping-Context method. Internally, DB uses type assertions to detect optional interfaces, so neither user code nor drivers had to change because the Pinger interface was small and optional.

The Go Cloud Development Kit (Go CDK) follows a similar pattern. It defines common protocols for providers such as Amazon Web Services (AWS), allowing us to use the providers through a uniform, concrete API. See https://gocloud.dev/concepts to learn more about Go CDK's design and its usage of the driver pattern.

By exploring the driver pattern, we've learned that the standard library effectively uses concrete types and small optional interfaces to maintain stable APIs while adding new and optional functionality. This approach shows us how to design maintainable packages that can evolve independently without breaking compatibility with the existing code.

10.1.1 Registering a driver

The sql package provides an abstraction layer with drivers and gives us a uniform way to interact with various SQL databases. But the standard library does not bundle an SQL driver, so calling Open fails if we don't have the necessary driver. Because we want to use SQLite, let's download and register an SQLite driver so we can get a *DB handle to interact with SQLite.

DOWNLOADING A DRIVER

We'll use the go get command to download an SQLite driver module (version 1.38.0 was the latest version when this chapter was written) and add it to our Go module:

```
$ go get modernc.org/sqlite@v1.38.0
```

Although we've downloaded an SQLite driver, we'll write our SQL queries to be fully compatible with the PostgreSQL database. Because the sql package abstracts SQL databases, we could also download a PostgreSQL driver (e.g., pq) and run our program with PostgreSQL.

TIP   For a list of SQL drivers, visit https://go.dev/wiki/SQLDrivers.

We'll keep things simple with SQLite, however. We use a pure-Go SQLite driver, `modernc.org/sqlite`. We could have used another one, `mattn/go-sqlite3`:

```
$ go get github.com/mattn/go-sqlite3
```

This driver is more performant and feature-rich than what we're using, but it uses C bindings and requires us to enable CGO if we want to cross-compile our program:

```
$ CGO_ENABLED=1 go build
```

Enabling CGO complicates cross-compilation, slows builds, and introduces external dependencies. It's best to use CGO when we don't have any other choice or when its advantages significantly outweigh its overhead and complexity. Pick your poison carefully.

NOTE   CGO enables Go code to call C code. You can learn more about CGO at https://go.dev/blog/cgo.

IMPORTING A DRIVER

Now that we've downloaded the driver, we must register it in the `sql` package before connecting to SQLite, as shown in the following listing. We can register the driver by importing it from our package.

Listing 10.1   Registering an SQLite driver (`link/sqlite/sqlite.go`)

```
package sqlite          ◄────┐
                             │ This is our new package: link/sqlite.
import (
    _ "modernc.org/sqlite"   ◄────┐ The blank identifier (underscore) imports the
)                                 │ modernc.org/sqlite package without a name.
```

Our `sqlite` package has the same name as the `sqlite` driver package but is separate, and sharing names doesn't lead to conflicts because the import paths are different. Naming our package `sqlite` lets us use it as an entry point and isolation layer for the rest of our packages, providing SQLite interaction through a single package without scattering SQL-specifics to the rest of our code, improving maintainability. It also helps later to have nice-to-read services such as `sqlite.Shortener`, a `Shortener` backed by SQLite.

The underscore in the `import` tells the compiler we won't use the driver package name `sqlite` in this `sqlite.go` file, but it still allows us to register the driver. This importing use is known as a *blank* or *side-effect import*. If we skip the blank import, we see an "imported and not used" error, or our text editor removes the import, skipping driver registration.

Deep dive: Blank imports and init()

When we import a package, it executes any `init` functions declared in the package once. (Importing a package multiple times, for example, calls its `init` functions only once.) Drivers contain at least one `init` function, enabling them to register themselves automatically within the `sql` package's registry. Here's the SQLite driver's `init` function:

```
                                    The modernc.org/sqlite package

package sqlite
func init() {                       Runs after the package-level
                                    variables are initialized
    sql.Register("sqlite", newDriver())
}                                   Registers the driver
                                    in the sql package
```

This function registers the SQLite driver in this package-level map of the `sql` package:

```
package sql // database/sql
var drivers = make(map[string]driver.Driver)       Package-level variable
```

We often avoid `init` functions because Go calls them implicitly. They can lead to code that is extremely challenging to wrap our heads around and maintain. But these functions can still be useful for implementing global registries as the `sql` package does. Check out https://go.dev/ref/spec#Package_initialization for more information on `init` functions.

KEEPING MODULE GRAPHS TIDIER

After we download the driver, our module file (`go.mod`) looks like this:

```
module github.com/inancgumus/gobyexample

go 1.24.2

require (
  github.com/dustin/go-humanize v1.0.1 // indirect
  . . .
  modernc.org/sqlite v1.38.0 // indirect
)
```

The `require` directives list all our module's dependencies along with their minimum required versions. Go marks some dependencies with the `// indirect` comment. Our module's dependencies require these modules, but our code doesn't depend on them directly. The `sqlite` driver appears as an indirect dependency, even though our code depends on it. Mismarking it as indirect doesn't affect functionality but may confuse us later. We don't want to edit a `go.mod` file directly to prevent mistakes, however. Instead, we can run the following command to tidy our module's dependency graph:

```
$ go mod tidy
```

Now the dependency graph includes the `sqlite` module as a *direct dependency*:

```
module github.com/inancgumus/gobyexample

go 1.24.2

require modernc.org/sqlite v1.38.0

require (
 github.com/dustin/go-humanize v1.0.1 // indirect
 . . .
)
```

`go mod tidy` scans our source code and synchronizes our module's dependencies, preventing potential confusion. Visit https://go.dev/ref/mod for more details on modules.

10.1.2 *Opening a connection pool*

Figure 10.2 shows how to connect to SQLite. We use the following functionality:

- `sql.Open` checks whether the driver exists and returns a `*DB` with an empty pool.
- `DB.PingContext` connects to the database, adding the pool's first connection.

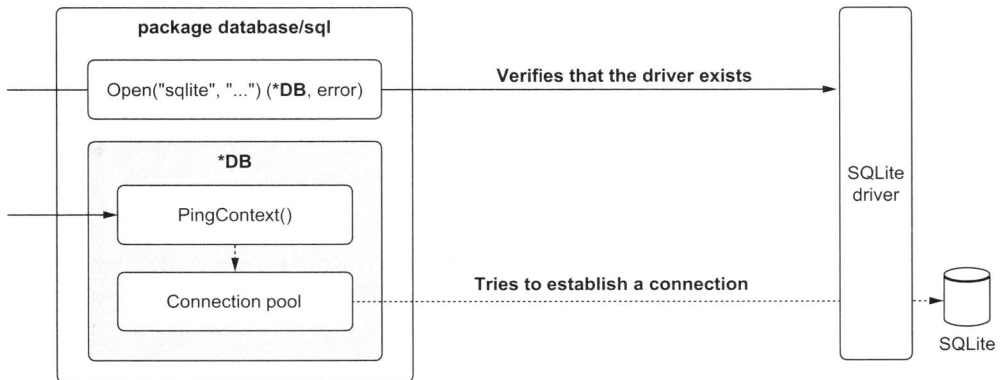

Figure 10.2 **Connecting to the SQLite database using** `Open` **and** `PingContext`

Although `Open` may return an empty pool, `PingContext` adds the first connection if successful. Behind the scenes, `Open` starts a goroutine that listens for new connection requests. `PingContext` tells this goroutine to connect to the database and put the connection in the pool for reuse. Because `*DB` has a connection pool, we must maintain `*DB` throughout our program's life cycle to avoid reconnecting to the same database for every query we send.

TIP   Calling `DB.Close` closes the connection pool. We rarely need to call it, however, because reusing connections from the connection pool eliminates the overhead of establishing new database connections, which involves network latency and handshakes.

Now that we know how to open a connection pool and establish a connection, we'll add the following `Dial` function to verify the driver and connect to SQLite. `Dial` takes a data source name (DSN) that specifies how to connect to SQLite. `Open` verifies the driver's existence in the `sql` package's registry, and `DB.PingContext` checks whether we can connect to SQLite.

Listing 10.2   Dialing the database (`link/sqlite/sqlite.go`)

```
package sqlite

import (
    "context"
    "database/sql"
    "fmt"
    _ "modernc.org/sqlite"
)

// Dial connects to SQLite and applies the schema for convenience.
func Dial(ctx context.Context, dsn string) (*sql.DB, error) {
    db, err := sql.Open("sqlite", dsn)
    if err != nil {
        return nil, fmt.Errorf("opening: %w", err)
    }
    if err := db.PingContext(ctx); err != nil {
        return nil, fmt.Errorf("pinging: %w", err)
    }
    return db, nil
}
```

> Verifies the driver name, opens an empty connection pool, and returns it as *sql.DB

> Adds the first connection to the pool if it can connect to the database successfully

Now we can connect to SQLite using `Dial`, but we can't insert a record into the database or query records from it. For those tasks, we need to define an SQL schema by running a query on the database that will create a table for storing links in the database.

Deep dive: Optimizing the connection pool

`DB` allows us to fine-tune its connection pool's behavior for optimal performance. The pool contains idle and in-use connections and uses an idle connection when executing a database task. If no idle connection is available, it establishes a new connection to the database and use that connection to carry on that task.

The `SetMaxOpenConns` and `SetMaxIdleConns` methods determine the maximum number of active and idle connections allowed in the pool. `SetConnMaxLifetime` and `SetConnMaxIdleTime` determine how long a connection remains reusable and idle.

Setting these values too high (or low) can lead to performance issues and inefficiencies: too many idle connections consume memory and waste resources, and too few can cause excessive connection churn. Instead of guessing these settings, optimize the pool by thoroughly testing and benchmarking, depending on your program's usage patterns. For more details on tuning, visit https://go.dev/doc/database/manage-connections.

10.1.3 File embedding

Now that we can connect to the database, our next goal is defining an SQL schema before persisting links. As listing 10.3 shows, we'll implement a schema file. When we run this schema on the database, it creates a `links` table with `short_key` and `uri` (original URL) columns. One column accepts only unique 16-character keys; the other allows URLs of any length. Uniqueness prevents key conflicts and ensures that each key maps to one URL.

Listing 10.3 Defining the SQL schema (`link/sqlite/schema.sql`)

```
CREATE TABLE IF NOT EXISTS links (          ← Creates the links table if it
    short_key VARCHAR(16) PRIMARY KEY,          doesn't exist in the database
    uri       TEXT NOT NULL               ← Defines a 16-character
);                                              unique keys column
```

Defines a text column
that cannot be null

We could include this schema in a constant in the code, but keeping it in an SQL file is more practical so our text editor can highlight and even lint the SQL syntax. Because our SQL schema is ready, we can run it to create the `links` table in the database. The question is how to execute this schema file. Instead of reading from this file, we can use a nice Go feature called *file embedding* to include the file's content in a variable and the final compiled binary.

Figure 10.3 shows that the compiler can read the entire `schema.sql` file and embed it in the final binary. Then we can retrieve the file's contents from a variable, such as `schema`. Its name doesn't have to be the same as the file's, but we'll name it that way for consistency.

Because the SQL schema file's content is in the binary, we can distribute our program with the schema included, so we can deploy the final binary without additional SQL files.

Listing 10.4 shows how to embed our SQL schema file in a string variable. We import the `embed` package and add a `go:embed` directive to embed the schema in the variable.

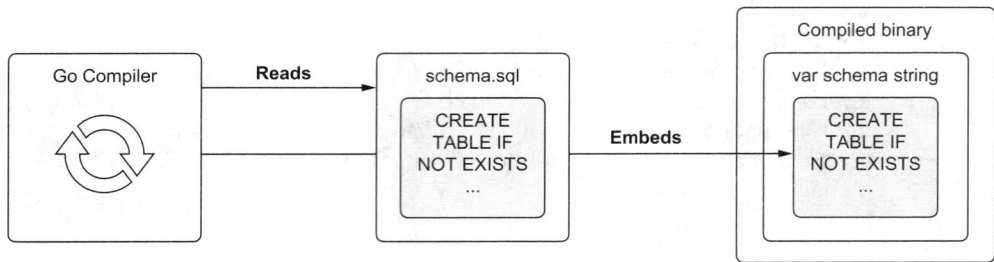

Figure 10.3   The compiler embeds the file in the compiled binary.

Listing 10.4   Applying the schema (`link/sqlite/sqlite.go`)

```
package sqlite

import (
    _ "embed"            ◀──────┐ Activates the file-embedding feature
    . . .
)

//go:embed schema.sql        │ Saves the file's content
var schema string            │ in the schema variable

func Dial(ctx context.Context, dsn string) (*sql.DB, error) {
    db, err := sql.Open("sqlite", dsn)
    if err != nil {
        return nil, fmt.Errorf("opening: %w", err)
    }
    if err := db.PingContext(ctx); err != nil {
        return nil, fmt.Errorf("pinging: %w", err)
    }
    if _, err := db.ExecContext(    ◀──────┐ Skips the first result value
        ctx, schema,                        │ because we don't need it
    ); err != nil {
        return nil, fmt.Errorf("applying schema: %w", err)
    }
    return db, nil
}
```

Before embedding the file, we must import the `embed` package to activate the compiler's file-embedding feature so that it knows we'll embed files. We use a blank import to import `embed` for its side effects. We wouldn't do that if we used something from the `embed` package.

Next, we add an embed directive (`//go:embed`) to tell the compiler to embed the `schema.sql` file. The compiler reads the file's entire content into the `schema` variable. Finally, we create the schema on the database using the `DB.ExecContext` method:

```
ExecContext(ctx context.Context, query string, args ...any) (Result, error)
```

`ExecContext` grabs a connection from the pool, executes the query, and returns the connection to the pool. As we see from its signature, we can pass an arbitrary number of arguments of `any` type to the method. Because we don't need to provide parameters to the database while running the schema, we don't need to pass parameters now.

NOTE Learn more about file embedding at https://pkg.go.dev/embed.

Deep dive: Migrations

Although it's fine in our case, running the schema while connecting to a database can be wasteful if we have a large number of SQL queries in the schema to execute. In such a case, we can use a tool crafted explicitly for this purpose, such as the golang-migrate tool. Instead of running it each time we connect to the database, we can migrate the schema only once.

Another way is to use the `embed.FS` type to build our schema migration solution. The compiler can embed the SQL files from the `schema` directory in the final binary with the following directive, after which we can access each via the `schemaFiles` variable:

```go
//go:embed *.sql
var schemaFiles embed.FS
. . .
files, err := schemaFiles.ReadDir(".")
. . .
for _, schema := range files {
    . . .
}
```

Embeds all .sql files in the schema directory

Provides a filesystem abstraction to access embedded files

Reads all the files in the directory

Loops over the files

Applies the schema file similar to the approach in listing 10.4

Migration tools often support `embed.FS` so we can embed the files and then deliver them to these tools to do the migration. `FS` stands for *filesystem*, providing an abstraction and uniform interface over different filesystems such as UNIX filesystems, zip archives, HTTP-served files, and embedded files. Visit https://mng.bz/yNoB for an example. Also visit https://pkg.go.dev/embed and https://pkg.go.dev/io/fs for more information about the `embed.FS` and `fs.FS` types.

10.2 *Database-backed service*

Now that we can use `Dial` to connect to SQLite, we'll use it in our link service. First, though, let's revisit the `link.Shortener` service type from chapter 8. The HTTP handlers in our `link/rest` package use it to save and retrieve links from its `map` field:

```
package link
type Shortener struct { . . .links map[Key]Link }
func (*Shortener) Shorten(context.Context, Link) (Key, error) {. . .}
func (*Shortener) Resolve(context.Context, Key) (Link, error) {. . .}
```

Our next goal is to persist links with an SQLite-backed `Shortener` service. Figure 10.4 shows the new service. It's similar to `link.Shortener` but can interact with SQLite.

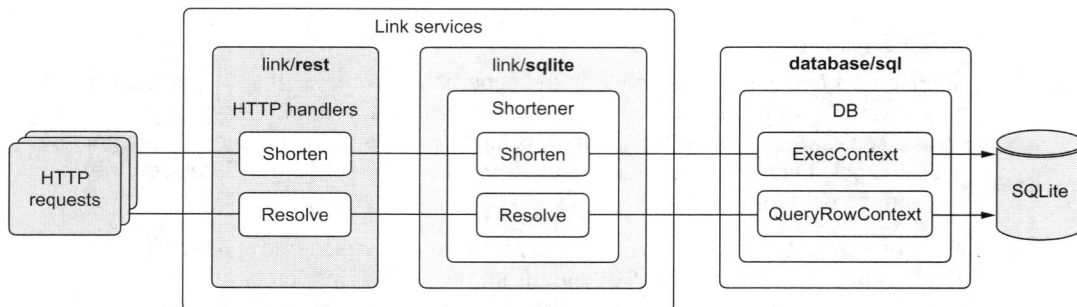

Figure 10.4   Handlers use `Shortener` to shorten and resolve links from SQLite; internally, `Shortener` uses a `*DB` handle to execute queries on the database.

The new `Shortener` lives in the `link/sqlite` package. Similar to `link.Shortener`, `sqlite.Shortener` has the following methods to shorten and resolve links:

- `Shorten` shortens and inserts a link into the database using `DB.ExecContext`.
- `Resolve` uses `DB.QueryRowContext` to resolve a link from the database.

After we implement the new `Shortener` service, we'll modify the `link/rest` package's handlers to support the `link.Shortener` and `sqlite.Shortener` services.

10.2.1 *Insertion*

The `link.Shortener` type didn't require a constructor because its zero value was useful. As the following listing shows, however, we'll add a constructor and a `*DB` field to the `sqlite.Shortener` type because it uses a `*DB` to interact with SQLite. After it shortens a link, it uses its `*DB` field to insert the link into the database using `DB.ExecContext`.

Listing 10.5   Shortening links (`link/sqlite/shortener.go`)

```
package sqlite

import (
    "context"
    "database/sql"
    "fmt"
    "github.com/inancgumus/gobyexample/link"
```

```
)

// Shortener is a link shortener service that is backed by SQLite.
type Shortener struct{
    db *sql.DB
}

// NewShortener returns a new [Shortener] service.
func NewShortener(db *sql.DB) *Shortener {
    return &Shortener{db: db}
}

// Shorten shortens the URL of the [link.Link] and returns a [link.Key].
func (s *Shortener) Shorten(
    ctx context.Context, lnk link.Link,
) (link.Key, error) {
    var err error
    if lnk.Key, err = link.Shorten(lnk); err != nil {
        return "", fmt.Errorf("%w: %w", err, link.ErrBadRequest)
    }

    // Persist the link in the database.
    _, err = s.db.ExecContext(
        ctx,
        `INSERT INTO links (short_key, uri) VALUES ($1, $2)`,
        lnk.Key, lnk.URL,
    )
    if err != nil {
        return "", fmt.Errorf("saving: %w: %w", err, link.ErrInternal)
    }

    return lnk.Key, nil
}
```

Executes the query on the database

Cancels the operation if the Context is canceled

The placeholders in the query will be replaced by these.

Our `Shortener` type has a `DB` field that we can initialize using the `NewShortener` function. The `Shorten` method takes a `Context`. `ExecContext` will cancel the database operation after that `Context` is canceled, which might happen if, say, an HTTP client disconnects.

TIP Pass `Context` downstream to allow the cancellation of ongoing operations.

After shortening the link, we execute the SQL query on the database using `Exec-Context`. The dollar signs in the query are placeholders, allowing us to substitute the `Key` and `URL`. This way, we avoid handcrafted SQL parameters, making SQL injection attacks less likely. Although we use standard SQL, the placeholder syntax is specific to a database. Still, our SQL query is PostgreSQL-compatible, but it may be incompatible with others (e.g., MySQL).

TIP The community-provided `sqlx` package can generate placeholders that work across SQL dialects. Visit https://github.com/jmoiron/sqlx to learn more.

10.2.2 *Test database*

Now that we can persist links in SQLite, let's test our new `sqlite.Shortener` service. First, we'll add a test helper to get a unique in-memory SQLite database for convenience, as shown in listing 10.6. We'll also call `testing.TB.Cleanup` to close the connection pool after the caller test ends. As discussed earlier, we generally don't need to close a connection pool. We may not need to take advantage of a pool in tests, however, because we might run many isolated tests that don't share a pool.

> **Listing 10.6 Adding a test database helper** (`link/sqlite/sqlite.go`)

```go
package sqlite

import (
    "testing"
    . . .
)

// DialTestDB connects to a unique in-memory SQLite database.
func DialTestDB(tb testing.TB) *sql.DB {
    tb.Helper()

    dsn := fmt.Sprintf(
        "file:%s?mode=memory&cache=shared",
        tb.Name(),                            ◄──┐  Returns the caller test name
    )
    db, err := Dial(tb.Context(), dsn)
    if err != nil {
        tb.Fatalf("DialTestDB: %v", err)
    }                                            ┌─ Closes the connection pool
    tb.Cleanup(func() {                   ◄──────┘  when the caller test finishes
        if err := db.Close(); err != nil {
            tb.Logf("DialTestDB: closing: %v", err)
        }
    })

    return db
}
```

Our `DialTestDB` helper gives the caller test a unique in-memory database (`mode=memory`) that is shared (`cache=shared`) by all database connections in the same test. The `TB.Name` method returns the caller test's name (e.g., `"TestFoo"` if `TestFoo` calls `DialTestDB`). This way, we can run future tests concurrently. Each database operation in the same test uses the same database as long as the test calls `DialTestDB` once. We could have set the database name with a random identifier, but using the test name is good enough for our current purposes.

> **TIP** See chapter 8 for more information about test helpers.

Calling `Cleanup` is useful for after-test cleanup. It's similar to the `defer` statement, but there is a difference: a function that we register with `Cleanup` is called when the parent test (the one that calls the test helper) finishes rather than when the test helper, such as `DialTestDB`, returns. Otherwise, if we used a `defer` statement, the database connection would close prematurely before the test ends.

10.2.3 *Integration testing*

Now that we can create unique test databases for each test, we can test the `Shortener`.`Shorten` method using our new `sqlite.DialTestDB` test helper. As the next listing shows, we test whether `Shorten` can shorten a link and return the correct key. Near the end, we verify that `Shorten` disallows shortening links with duplicate keys.

Listing 10.7 Testing `Shortener.Shorten` (`link/sqlite/shortener_test.go`)

```
package sqlite

import (
    "errors"
    "testing"
    "github.com/inancgumus/gobyexample/link"
)

func TestShortenerShorten(t *testing.T) {
    t.Parallel()

    lnk := link.Link{
        Key: "foo",
        URL: "https://new.link",
    }

    shortener := NewShortener(DialTestDB(t))

    // Shortens a link.
    key, err := shortener.Shorten(t.Context(), lnk)
    if err != nil {
        t.Fatalf("got err = %v, want nil", err)
    }
    if key != "foo" {
        t.Errorf(`got key %q, want "foo"`, key)
    }

    // Disallows shortening a link with a duplicate key.
    _, err = shortener.Shorten(t.Context(), lnk)
    if !errors.Is(err, link.ErrConflict) {
        t.Fatalf("\ngot err = %v\nwant ErrConflict for duplicate key", err)
    }
}
```

We've added a test for the `Shorten` method to test it against a new in-memory database.

> **NOTE** For simplicity, we use multiple assertions in the test, but it can be more effective to run subtests for each assertion. See chapter 2 for more information.

We connect to a unique database and pass the `*DB` handle to `NewShortener` to save the handle in the `Shortener.DB` field. Then we call the `Shorten` method. `Shorten` requires us to pass it a `Context`. Instead of creating a new one, we use `Context`, which is canceled automatically when the test finishes (but before any `T.Cleanup` functions run). Using `T.Context` ties everything to the test's lifetime and eliminates manual `Context` management. Finally, we verify that `Shorten` can shorten a link and disallow duplicate links. Let's run the test to see whether `Shorten` works correctly:

```
$ go test ./link/sqlite -run=TestShortenerShorten -v
got err = saving: constraint failed: UNIQUE constraint failed:
                                    links.short_key (1555)
want ErrConflict for duplicate key
```

The test fails because `Shorten` cannot detect duplicate link keys. SQLite returns a constraint error because the `short_key` column is a primary key, and we try to add a duplicate key. Even worse, `Shorten` exposes sensitive database-specific details in the error message. We'll fix these issues by returning our application-specific `link.ErrConflict` from `Shorten` instead of the driver's error. But first, we need to detect the driver's error using the `errors.As` function and return `ErrConflict` on duplicate keys.

10.2.4   errors.As

We can use the standard library's `errors.As` function to detect whether the returned error is an SQLite driver error and then check whether the error code is `1555`—a unique-key violation. Detecting specific driver errors allows us to return more meaningful application-level errors and prevents accidental leaks of sensitive internal database details when errors occur.

> **TIP**   `As` extracts a specific `error` from an error chain and assigns it to a variable.

We'll add a new convenience function for isolating SQLite-specific error-detection code before detecting duplicate keys using the `Shorten` method. As the following listing shows, we use `errors.As` to extract the driver error from the error chain. Then we query for the error code and return `true` if the code is `1555`.

Listing 10.8   Detecting constraint errors (`link/sqlite/sqlite.go`)

```
package sqlite

import (
    // _ "modernc.org/sqlite"        ◀──────┐  We can remove this blank import.
    . . .
    "errors"
    "modernc.org/sqlite"          ◀────┐  Brings the sqlite package name
)                                      │  to the file's scope, allowing us
                                       │  to use the sqlite.Error type
. . .
```

```
func isPrimaryKeyViolation(err error) bool {          We're looking for a *sqlite.Error.
    var serr *sqlite.Error
    if errors.As(err, &serr) {
        return serr.Code() == 1555                              Assigns
        // See: sqlite.org/rescode.html#constraint_primarykey   *sqlite.Error
    }                                                           to serr if
    return false          Returns true if the driver error code is  found
}                         a primary-key-constraint error code
```

We change the side-effect import to a regular import, which enables us to use the `sqlite` package name in the `sqlite.go` file. Now that we can find primary-key errors, let's update `Shorten` to identify duplicate keys. If we find any, we'll return our `Err-Conflict` error. Let's check the primary-key violation error to prevent `Shorten` from returning an internal error.

Listing 10.9 Detecting duplicate keys (`link/sqlite/shortener.go`)

```
func (s *Shortener) Shorten(. . .) (link.Key, error) {
    . . .
    _, err = s.db.ExecContext(. . .)
    if isPrimaryKeyViolation(err) {
        return "", fmt.Errorf("saving: %w", link.ErrConflict)
    }
    if err != nil {
        return "", fmt.Errorf("saving: %w: %w", err, link.ErrInternal)
    }
    return lnk.Key, nil
}
```

Let's test whether `Shorten` can detect duplicate keys now:

```
$ go test ./link/sqlite -run=TestShortenerShorten -v
--- PASS: TestShortenerShorten. . .
```

`Shorten` successfully detected the key conflicts and returned `ErrConflict`. Later, our HTTP handlers will forward `ErrConflict` to clients instead of an SQLite-specific internal error that clutters our logs and can be confusing. Now we return an informative `ErrConflict` message, telling them that the key already exists so they can retry with another key.

Deep dive: Passing a pointer to a pointer (**T of *T)

The `As` function searches for a specific error type in the provided error chain. If it finds that error, it assigns the found error to the variable we provide. This variable must always be a pointer to the type we're looking for, and that type must implement the `error` interface. We can implement the `error` interface by implementing the following `Error` method:

(continued)

```
type error interface {
    Error() string
}
```

The `sqlite` driver's `Error` type, for example, implements the `error` interface with a pointer receiver `Error` method. So `*Error` is an `error`, but `Error` is not:

```
package sqlite // SQLite driver package
type Error struct { . . . }
func (e *Error) Error() string { . . . }
```
→ **The *sqlite.Error type implements the error interface with a pointer-receiver Error method.**

To better understand how `As` works, let's revisit our earlier example:

```
var serr *sqlite.Error
ok := errors.As(err, &serr)
```
→ **&serr's type is **sqlite.Error (a pointer to a pointer to an sqlite.Error).**

Here, we want `As` to find an `error` value of the `*Error` type inside the error chain. Because `As` needs a pointer to the type we want, we pass a pointer to `serr`. So the type we pass is `**Error`; it's a pointer to a pointer to an `Error` value: `**Error -> *Error -> Error`. If we mistakenly passed the `*Error` type instead, the code wouldn't work:

```
var serr sqlite.Error
ok := errors.As(err, &serr)
```
→ **&serr's type is *sqlite.Error (a pointer to an sqlite.Error).**

And the output would be (simplified)

```
panic: sqlite.Error doesn't implement the error interface
```

This is incorrect because `Error` does not implement the `error` interface; only `*Error` does. Because we want to find an `*Error` in the chain, we must pass an `**Error` to `As`.

10.2.5 *Retrieval*

Having looked at inserting links into the database, let's explore retrieving a single row from SQLite using our new `Shortener`'s `Resolve` method. When we want to pull a single row from the database, we use the `DB.QueryRowContext` method.

As figure 10.5 shows

- `Resolve` calls `QueryRowContext` to query the database.
- `QueryRowContext` queries the database through a connection (existing or new).
- `Scan` injects the URL into the `uri` variable and returns the connection to the pool.

TIP If we didn't call `Scan`, we would risk leaking connections. `Scan` reduces resource use by allowing other queries to reuse the same connection from the pool.

In short, `Resolve` calls `QueryRowContext` and then `Scan` to assign the URL to `uri`.

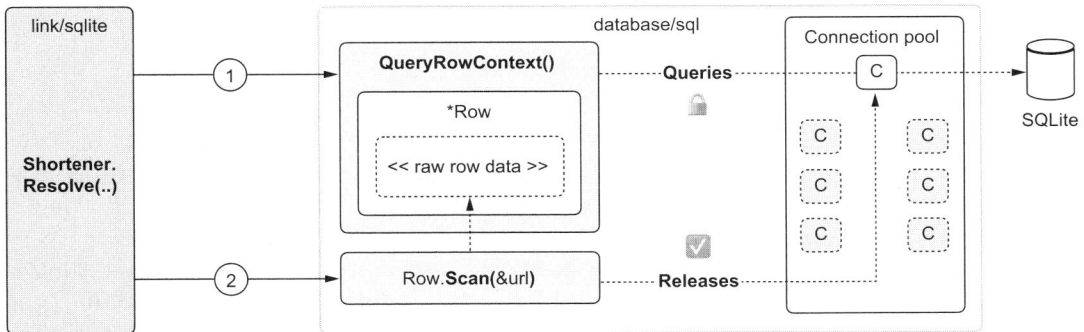

Figure 10.5 `Resolve` **calls** `QueryRowContext` **to retrieve the URL from the database. The connection is reserved until** `Scan` **is called. Calling** `Scan` **copies the previously loaded raw row data into the** `uri` **variable and returns the connection to the pool, allowing other database tasks to reuse the connection.**

Now that we understand how `DB.QueryRowContext` works, let's use it. The following listing adds a new `Resolve` method to the `Shortener` type.

Listing 10.10   Resolving links (`link/sqlite/shortener.go`)

```go
// Resolve resolves a [link.Link] by its [link.Key] from the database.
func (s *Shortener) Resolve(
    ctx context.Context, key link.Key,
) (link.Link, error) {
    if key.Empty() {
        return link.Link{}, fmt.Errorf(. . .)
    }
    if err := key.Validate(); err != nil {
        return link.Link{}, fmt.Errorf(
            "validating: %w: %w",
            err, link.ErrBadRequest,
        )
    }

    // Retrieve the link from the database.
    var uri string                                    // Sends the query to the database
    err := s.db.QueryRowContext(                      // and loads the raw data
        ctx,
        `SELECT uri FROM links WHERE short_key = $1`,
        key,
    ).Scan(&uri)              // Parses and injects the row
                             // data into the uri variable
```

```
        if errors.Is(err, sql.ErrNoRows) {
            return link.Link{}, link.ErrNotFound
        }
        if err != nil {
            return link.Link{}, fmt.Errorf(
                "retrieving: %w: %w",
                err, link.ErrInternal,
            )
        }

        return link.Link{Key: key, URL: uri}, nil
}
```

sql.ErrNoRows indicates that the query didn't return any rows.

Resolve checks whether the shortened key is valid and then queries the links table for a key to get the link's original URL. Next, it scans the URL into the uri variable by passing that variable's pointer to Scan, releasing the connection for later reuse. Finally, it returns a Link.

Scan returns ErrNoRows if the short key doesn't exist in the database. Finally, we return this error as our ErrNotFound. This approach prevents our code from depending on sql.ErrNoRows because not every Shortener (e.g., link.Shortener) is SQL-dependent. Instead, all Shortener implementations return consistent errors, enabling consumer code (such as our HTTP handlers) to handle different Shorteners uniformly without code changes. This approach will also help us to unlock consumer-driven interfaces, as explained in section 10.4.

We've added a new Shortener service that works with SQLite:

- Shorten uses ExecContext to insert a link into the database.
- Resolve uses QueryRowContext and Scan to fetch a URL from the database.

Both are protected against SQL injection attacks using placeholders.

Opinion: Errors tell a short story

Resolve errors tell a story: validating and retrieving. The present continuous-tense usage isn't accidental; it may help us figure out when and how errors occurred.

The error message

```
error: resolving: retrieving: sql: database is closed
```

tells a concise story and is less noisy than this one:

```
error occurred while resolving: cannot retrieve a link:
  failed to connect to the database:
  sql: database is closed
```

Do we have to repeat failed, cannot, error, and so on in error messages, or would it be enough to add an error: prefix once when logging errors? If we pick the second route and stop stuttering words in error messages, we can often surprisingly improve debugging.

10.3 *Valuer and Scanner*

We used `ExecContext` to insert links and `QueryRowContext` to retrieve them from SQLite. Because `sql` abstracts database communication, we can use PostgreSQL or another SQL database without many changes, but this abstraction has limits. Sometimes, we need extra features specific to an SQL database that the `sql` package doesn't directly support. To bridge this gap, the `sql` and `driver` packages have the following `Valuer` and `Scanner` interfaces.

A `driver.Valuer` implementation can transform values before sending them to a database:

```
type Valuer interface {
    Value() (driver.Value, error)    ◄─── Returns a database-compatible value
}
```

An `sql.Scanner` implementation can transform values retrieved from a database:

```
type Scanner interface {
    Scan(src any) error    ◄─── Converts database values to Go types
}
```

These interfaces help us use special database types or custom behaviors.

10.3.1 *Supporting custom database types*

Suppose that we use PostgreSQL, which supports array types and stores their elements packed as binary data in a single database column. The `sql` package doesn't natively support PostgreSQL arrays, but the `pq` driver provides the `pq.Array` type, which implements `Valuer` and `Scanner`. This type converts slices to PostgreSQL arrays and vice versa:

```
var scores []int          ◄─── Will contain [42, 84]
db.QueryRowContext(. . .,
    `SELECT ARRAY[42, 84]`,
).Scan(pq.Array(&scores))  ◄─── Retrieves, converts, and injects
                                 PostgreSQL's array data into scores
```

We retrieve a PostgreSQL array into the `scores` slice:

- `QueryRowContext` retrieves the PostgreSQL array.
- `pq.Array(&scores)` decodes the array into the `scores` slice.

We can also insert this slice as a PostgreSQL array using `ExecContext`:

```
_, err := db.ExecContext(. . .,
    `INSERT INTO results(scores) VALUES($1)`,
    pq.Array(scores))
```

In this example

- `pq.Array(scores)` converts `scores` to a PostgreSQL array.
- `ExecContext` inserts that array into the `results` table.

These examples show how `Valuer` and `Scanner` enable database-specific features without forgoing the abstraction provided by the `sql` package. We'll apply these interfaces ourselves in section 10.3.2 to better understand how they work.

> **NOTE**   See https://pkg.go.dev/github.com/lib/pq#Array for more information.

10.3.2   *Satisfying Valuer and Scanner*

Suppose that we want to automatically encode URLs in Base64 before saving and decode them after retrieving. To do that, we can declare a new type that satisfies the `Valuer` and `Scanner`. As listing 10.11 shows, we declare the `base64String` type, which uses the standard library's `base64.StdEncoding` type for encoding and decoding. We use `EncodeToString` to encode a byte slice into a string and `DecodeString` to decode from a string to a byte slice.

Listing 10.11   `Valuer` and `Scanner` (`link/sqlite/shortener.go`)

```go
package sqlite

import (
    "database/sql/driver"
    "encoding/base64"
    . . .
)


type base64String string

// Value implements the driver.Valuer interface.
func (bs base64String) Value() (driver.Value, error) {
    return base64.StdEncoding.EncodeToString([]byte(bs)), nil
}

// Scan implements the sql.Scanner interface.
func (bs *base64String) Scan(src any) error {
    ss, ok := src.(string)
    if !ok {                                          ◀── Ensures that src is a string
        return fmt.Errorf("decoding: %q is %T, not string", ss, src)
    }
    dst, err := base64.StdEncoding.DecodeString(ss)
    if err != nil {
        return fmt.Errorf("decoding %q: %w", ss, err)
    }
    *bs = base64String(dst)    ◀── Saves the decoded value to
    return nil                     the original base64String
}                                  value pointed by the receiver

// String implements the fmt.Stringer interface.
func (bs base64String) String() string {
    return string(bs)
}
```

We've implemented a type that satisfies the `Scanner` and `Valuer` interfaces:

- The `Scan` method implements the `Scanner` interface.
- The `Value` method implements the `Valuer` interface.

We declared `Value` using a value receiver and `Scan` using a pointer receiver. Although it's best to avoid mixing receiver types, it's necessary sometimes. Using a pointer receiver for `Scan` allows us to inject the decoded string into the original `base64String` via the receiver, `bs`. Finally, because a database column can be of different types, `Scan` takes any type. Using a runtime type assertion (`src.(string)`), we make sure that what we receive is a string.

NOTE See appendix D for reasons to avoid mixing receiver types.

10.3.3 *Encoding and decoding*

Now that our type satisfies `Valuer` and `Scanner`, let's use it in `Shortener`. In listing 10.12, we integrate `base64String` into `Shorten` to encode a URL before sending it to the database and `Resolve` to decode the encoded URL after retrieving it from the database. We use a `base64String` instead of a plain string to encode and decode URLs automatically.

Listing 10.12 Using `base64String` (`link/sqlite/shortener.go`)

```go
func (s *Shortener) Shorten(. . .) (link.Key, error) {
    . . .
    _, err = s.db.ExecContext(
        ctx,
        `INSERT INTO links (short_key, uri) VALUES ($1, $2)`,
        lnk.Key, base64String(lnk.URL),          ◀─────────┐
    )                                                       │
    . . .                                                   │
}                                                           │
                                                            │ Passes a base64String
func (s *Shortener) Resolve(. . .) (link.Link, error) {     │ to encode and decode
    . . .                                                   │ the URL automatically
    var uri base64String                        ◀───────────┤
    err := s.db.QueryRowContext(                            │
        ctx,                                                │
        `SELECT uri FROM links WHERE short_key = $1`,       │
        key,                                                │
    ).Scan(&uri)                                ◀───────────┘
    . . .
    return link.Link{
        Key: key,
        URL: uri.String(),
    }, nil
}
```

Now we can create and retrieve URLs in Base64-encoded and decoded formats. `Shorten` passes the `URL` as a `base64String` to `ExecContext` to encode the `URL` automatically before saving it in the database. Similarly, `Resolve` passes the `uri` as `*base64String` to `Scan` to decode the Base64-encoded URL and inject the decoded URL into the `uri`.

By using `Valuer` and `Scanner`, we extend the capabilities of `sql`. Check out the `uuid` package at https://go.dev/play/p/cDF3Zoiyq5o to see how it uses `Valuer` and `Scanner` to store and retrieve universally unique identifiers (UUIDs) as binary data from the database. Storing them as 16-byte binary data can reduce storage size and might improve performance.

10.4 *Implicit interfaces*

> *Don't design with interfaces; discover them.*
>
> —Rob Pike

Now that the SQLite-backed `Shortener` service is ready, our team will help integrate the other team's new `Shortener` into our REST API, as promised. We'll explore how Go's implicit interfaces can ease this integration with a few code changes.

Interfaces are extremely useful, but misusing them adds unnecessary complexity. Declaring an interface unnecessarily can complicate code and reduce clarity because interfaces add indirection and require additional maintenance. By focusing on concrete types first, we can recognize genuine needs and create meaningful interfaces.

So far, I've deliberately avoided introducing interfaces, but it's time now because we have two different concrete types: `link.Shortener` and `sqlite.Shortener`. Let's explore how and where to declare interfaces and the benefits of following idiomatic practices.

TIP   Every interface should earn its place in the codebase.

10.4.1 *Consumers-first approach*

In Go, it's idiomatic to declare interfaces in the package that consumes them, not in the package that implements them. Instead of providing an interface in the `sqlite` package, consumers like the `rest` package can declare an interface with the methods they need.

Figure 10.6 illustrates this consumers-first approach, in which consumers define the interfaces they need rather than providers. The `rest` package (consumer) owns the `Shortener` interface, allowing us to pass any type with a `Shorten` method to the `rest.Shorten` function, such as our `sqlite` package's (provider) `Shortener` type.

The `rest` package specifies what methods a `Shortener` should have (i.e., `Shorten`). We can use any type that fulfills those methods, such as `sqlite.Shortener`, with the `rest` package. The `sqlite` package doesn't have to explicitly declare that it implements the `rest.Shortener` interface, which is possible due to Go's implicit interfaces.

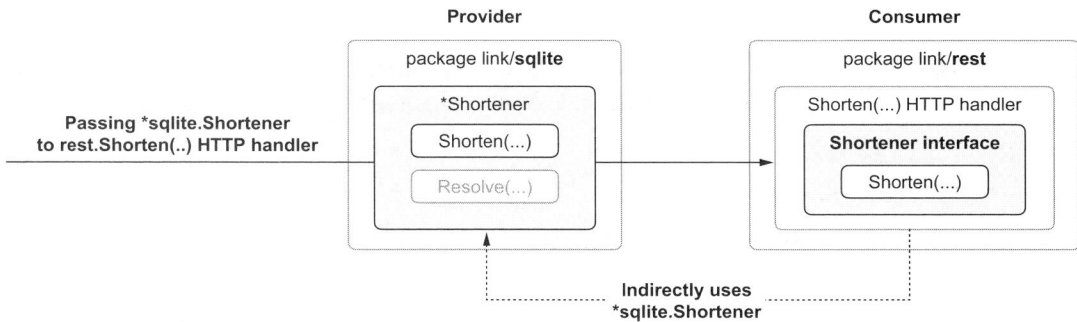

Figure 10.6 The consumer (`rest`) owns the interface rather than the provider (`sqlite`).

By focusing on consumer needs, we avoid bloated interfaces that are difficult to satisfy. Consumer-driven interfaces naturally remain smaller and laser-focused because they include only methods that consumers genuinely require today, rather than methods we think they might need later. Small interfaces clearly communicate their purpose, making them easier to understand and simpler to satisfy because implementations must fulfill fewer methods. Such minimal interfaces are easily embedded in larger ones, improving composability.

Also, by declaring only essential methods, these small interfaces reduce complexity and encourage loose coupling. If a provider later adds more methods to its concrete type, the consumer code remains unaffected because it depends only on methods declared in its local interface (e.g., `rest.Shortener`). Small interfaces help to reduce cascading breaking changes throughout our codebase, significantly improving maintainability.

The consumer-driven interface approach aligns well with Go's core principles, emphasizing simplicity. This approach promotes decoupling, better testability, and ease of maintenance.

Deep dive: Centralizing widely used behaviors

Declaring interfaces on the consumer side helps prevent unnecessary speculation. Consumers define only the behaviors they need, keeping interfaces minimal and relevant. Sometimes, however, multiple consumers need the same behavior. `json`, `xml`, and similar packages have functions to convert arbitrary types to text, for example. Rather than having each consumer package declare its own interface, we may find it more effective to centralize such common behaviors in a single package after they've emerged. The `encoding` package, for example, has a widely used `TextMarshaler` interface:

```
package encoding
type TextMarshaler interface {
    MarshalText() (text []byte, err error)
}
```

(continued)

Types like `net.IP` and `slog.Level` implement this interface without knowing how their encoded form will be used. They simply support encoding themselves as text:

```
package net
type IP []byte
. . .
func (ip IP) MarshalText() ([]byte, error) { . . . }
```

Functions like `json.Marshal` recognize this interface. When we encode an `IP` value using `Marshal`, it delegates text encoding to the `IP`'s `MarshalText` method:

```
type Server struct { Addr net.IP `json:"addr"` }
data, err := json.Marshal(Server{
    Addr: net.IPv4(192, 168, 1, 1),          ┐  Encodes the IP value to JSON
})                                           ┘  by calling IP.MarshalText()
. . .
fmt.Println(string(data))
```

The result of this program is

```
{"addr":"192.168.1.1"}
```

Centralizing widely used interfaces prevents repetition and ensures consistency. But we shouldn't rush to centralize interfaces (e.g., put them in a single package) before discovering common behaviors through concrete uses. When we have multiple uses, we may realize that they share behavior and can see how to centralize it. Discover behaviors first through concrete implementations; then centralize these behaviors with shared interfaces. This practice prevents premature abstractions and unnecessary complexity.

10.4.2 *Providing an interface*

Let's put the consumer-driven interfaces approach into practice. We'll provide two interfaces in the `rest` package for its current requirements: a `Shortener` interface with a `Shorten` method to shorten links and a `Resolver` interface with a `Resolve` method to resolve links.

> **TIP** Adding an `-er` prefix to a single-method interface is a convention. Not all interfaces require this prefix, especially if they don't embed other interfaces.

Our HTTP handlers need these methods only to shorten and resolve links. The `Shorten` handler, for example, requires only a `Shorten` method, so it expects the `Shortener` interface rather than a bloated one with many methods. As the following listing shows, we maintain a clear separation of concerns and avoid bloating the interfaces with unnecessary methods.

Listing 10.13 Declaring interfaces (`link/rest/shortener.go`)

```
package rest            ◄────
                             ┐   We declare the required interfaces
import (                     │   in this consumer package.
    "context"
    . . .
)

// Shortener is a link shortener service that shortens URLs.
type Shortener interface {                        ◄──────
    // Shorten shortens a link and returns its key.      │   Declares an interface with
    Shorten(                                      ◄──────┤   the only method the
        context.Context, link.Link,               ◄──────┤   Shorten handler requires
    ) (link.Key, error)                           ◄──────
}

func Shorten(
    lg *slog.Logger, links Shortener,        ◄────┐  Expects any type with
) http.Handler {                                  │  a Shorten method
    . . .
    key, err := links.Shorten(. . .)
    . . .
}

// Resolver is a link resolver service that resolves shortened URLs.
type Resolver interface {                         ◄──────
    // Resolve retrieves a link by its key.             │   Declares an interface with
    Resolve(                                      ◄──────┤   the only method the
        context.Context, link.Key,                ◄──────┤   Resolve handler requires
    ) (link.Link, error)                          ◄──────
}

func Resolve(
    lg *slog.Logger, links Resolver,         ◄────┐  Expects any type with
) http.Handler {                                  │  a Resolve method
    . . .
    lnk, err := links.Resolve(. . .)
    . . .
}
```

With these one-method interfaces in place, the Shorten handler can accept any type that implements the Shorten method (e.g., sqlite.Shortener) without modifying the rest of the handler code, or the Resolve handler can accept any type with a Resolve method. We replaced the HTTP handler input parameters with interfaces, but the rest of our code remained the same and still compiles. That's one reason why we've avoided declaring interfaces so far. In Go, it's straightforward to declare new interfaces when necessary rather than up front.

We decoupled the rest package from concrete Shortener implementations by declaring these interfaces. Both link.Shortener and sqlite.Shortener satisfy our interfaces, allowing us to pass either to our handlers. (Currently, we pass link.Shortener.) Now other teams can improve the link service's storage backend with any new features they want, such as adding Redis as a cache or using an Amazon Web Services database to store links in the cloud. We don't need to make any other changes to our handlers to support these features.

10.4.3 *Activating the new implementation*

Now that we have declared interfaces, we can activate the sqlite.Shortener service in our program. Recall that our linkd program sets up and runs the link HTTP server. Now we need only add a dsn flag and connect to SQLite, as follows. No other changes are necessary.

We connect to SQLite using Dial. We store the links in the links.db file. The rwc mode opens the file for reading and writing and creates the file if it doesn't exist.

> **Listing 10.14   Integrating sqlite.Shortener (link/cmd/linkd/linkd.go)**

```
package main

import (
    . . .
    "github.com/inancgumus/gobyexample/link/sqlite"
)

type config struct {
    . . .
    db struct{ dsn string }
}

func main() {
    var cfg config
    . . .
    flag.StringVar(
        &cfg.db.dsn, "db.dsn",
        "file:links.db?mode=rwc","database DSN",     ◀── The link.db file will be opened
    )                                                     in read-write-create mode
    . . .                                                 and will store links.
}

func run(ctx context.Context, cfg config) error {
    db, err := sqlite.Dial(ctx, cfg.db.dsn)       ◀── Connects to the
    if err != nil {                                   SQLite database
        return fmt.Errorf("dialing database: %w", err)
    }
    shortener := sqlite.NewShortener(db)          ◀── Returns a new SQLite-backed
                                                      shortener service
    lg := . . .

    mux := http.NewServeMux()
    mux.Handle("POST /shorten",rest.Shorten(lg, shortener))
    mux.Handle("GET /r/{key}", rest.Resolve(lg, shortener))
    mux.HandleFunc("/health", rest.Health)
    . . .
}
```

We've updated the link server to use SQLite with minimal changes. The handlers will shorten and resolve links using the new `sqlite.Shortener`. Let's try this new change by running the server:

```
$ go run ./link/cmd/linkd
level=INFO msg=starting app=linkd addr=localhost:8080
```

In another terminal session, type

```
$ curl -i localhost:8080/shorten -d '{"url": "https://x.com/inancgumus"}'
HTTP/1.1 201 Created
{"key":"gXyMWIga"}
```

Now we can restart the server. Because we use a persistent database, our program will preserve the links. We can resolve the preceding link after a restart:

```
$ curl -i localhost:8080/r/gXyMWIga
HTTP/1.1 302 Found
Location: https://x.com/inancgumus
```

In this book, we've explored many practical Go patterns and idioms through realistic examples, consistently choosing the path toward Mount Simplicity—the realm of idiomatic Go programming. (See the figure on the inside front cover of this book.) Although complexity isn't always preventable or inherently harmful, maintainable code emerges when we handle complexity carefully behind simple and straightforward code. By recognizing pitfalls on Mount Complexity, we've aimed to write effective, testable code. Thank you for reading this far. I hope you found the journey enlightening. One final piece of advice: always keep it simple.

10.5 Exercises

1. Add a separate subtest to shorten a link and another for a duplicate key.
2. Write an integration test for the `Shortener`'s `Resolve` method.
3. Test the `link/rest` handlers using the function adapter technique from chapter 7 (i.e., `roundTripperFunc`). Satisfy the `Shortener` and `Resolver` interfaces with function types. Then pass fake functions to the handlers to unit-test them.
4. Experiment with different SQL drivers (e.g., for PostgreSQL), and modify the code accordingly. Research available SQL drivers, and adjust the connection setup.
5. Implement data compression for links using `Valuer` and `Scanner` interfaces.
6. Create a separate timeout context (using `context.WithTimeout`) in `linkd` while connecting to the database. This ensures that the operation won't wait forever.
7. Add a command-line interface (CLI) flag to switch between different `Shortener`s.
8. Add a new `CachedShortener` type in the `link/rest` package. This type returns a link from the cache if it was resolved before and wraps the `Resolver` interface.

Summary

- Concrete types, such as `sql.DB`, can achieve polymorphism without explicitly exporting large interfaces for complex behavior. Internally, `DB` uses type assertions to detect and use optional driver features. This approach lets `DB` safely introduce new features while keeping the API uniform and stable and without breaking existing code.
- Defining `init` functions can complicate maintenance due to their implicit execution. Prefer explicit initialization for better maintainability, reserving `init` use for rare cases.
- CGO allows us to interact with code written in C, but doing so complicates builds, cross-compilation, and deployment. Prefer Go implementations unless the benefits are clear.
- Embedding files in a binary with file embedding ensures that these resources are accessible at runtime without the need for separate files, simplifying deployment and distribution.
- Using integration tests that resemble real-world use helps us catch issues early by verifying how our code behaves with external systems, preventing surprises later.
- `T.Cleanup` (or `TB.Cleanup`) ensures that cleanup tasks added by tests and test helpers run right before a test finishes, guaranteeing that resources will be released after the test ends.
- Using `errors.As` lets us extract specific errors from an error chain. By extracting and inspecting errors, we can transform low-level errors into meaningful application-level ones without depending on third-party ones.
- Write error messages to tell a concise story, showing what happened without excessive words or details. Straightforward errors help us understand and fix problems quickly.
- Abstraction hides implementation-specific details, as in the `sql` package. Leaving these specifics to consumers, as with the `Valuer` interface, helps them bridge the gap between abstraction and concrete behavior without sacrificing abstraction.
- Defining interfaces after observing shared behaviors ensures that they remain relevant. Letting consumers define these interfaces ensures that they reflect actual requirements, preventing premature abstraction.
- Prioritizing simplicity in code leads to maintainable, readable, and effective code, eliminating unnecessary complexity and overengineering.

index